The Deleuze and Guattari Dictionary

BLOOMSBURY PHILOSOPHY DICTIONARIES

The *Bloomsbury Philosophy Dictionaries* offer clear and accessible guides to the work of some of the more challenging thinkers in the history of philosophy. A–Z entries provide clear definitions of key terminology, synopses of key works, and details of each thinker's major themes, ideas and philosophical influences. The *Dictionaries* are the ideal resource for anyone reading or studying these key philosophers.

Titles available in the series:

The Derrida Dictionary, Simon Morgan Wortham
The Gadamer Dictionary, Chris Lawn and Niall Keane
The Hegel Dictionary, Glenn Alexander Magee
The Heidegger Dictionary, Daniel O. Dahlstrom
The Husserl Dictionary, Dermot Moran and Joseph Cohen
The Marx Dictionary, Ian Fraser and Lawrence Wilde
The Merleau-Ponty Dictionary, Donald A. Landes
The Sartre Dictionary, Gary Cox

BLOOMSBURY PHILOSOPHY DICTIONARIES

The Deleuze and Guattari Dictionary

EUGENE B. YOUNG

WITH GARY GENOSKO AND

JANELL WATSON

BLOOMSBURY
LONDON • NEW DELHI • NEW YORK • SYDNEY

Bloomsbury Academic
An imprint of Bloomsbury Publishing Plc

50 Bedford Square
London
WC1B 3DP
UK

1385 Broadway
New York
NY 10018
USA

www.bloomsbury.com

Bloomsbury is a registered trade mark of Bloomsbury Publishing Plc

First published 2013

Introduction and further reading © Eugene B Young, Deleuze entries © Eugene B. Young and Gregg Lambert (authorship indicated by initials after individual entries), Guattari entries © Gary Genosko and Janell Watson, 2013

Bloomsbury Publishing PLC would like to acknowledge Gregg Lambert who acted as an editorial advisor for this project.

All rights reserved. No part of this publication may be reproduced or transmitted in any form or by any means, electronic or mechanical, including photocopying, recording, or any information storage or retrieval system, without prior permission in writing from the publishers.

Eugene B. Young has asserted his right under the Copyright, Designs and Patents Act, 1988, to be identified as Author of this work.

No responsibility for loss caused to any individual or organization acting on or refraining from action as a result of the material in this publication can be accepted by Bloomsbury Academic or the author.

British Library Cataloguing-in-Publication Data
A catalogue record for this book is available from the British Library.

ISBN: HB: 978-0-8264-4281-9
PB: 978-0-8264-4276-5
ePDF: 978-1-4411-4824-7
ePub: 978-1-4411-0439-7

Library of Congress Cataloging-in-Publication Data
Young, Eugene B.
The Deleuze and Guattari dictionary / Eugene B. Young, with Gary Genosko and Janell Watson.
   pages cm.– (Bloomsbury philosophy dictionaries)
   Includes bibliographical references and index.
ISBN 978-0-8264-4276-5 (pbk. : alk. paper)– ISBN 978-0-8264-4281-9 (hardcover : alk. paper)– ISBN 978-1-4411-0439-7 (ebook (epub)– ISBN 978-1-4411-4824-7 (ebook (pdf)
   1. Deleuze, Gilles, 1925-1995–Dictionaries. 2. Guattari, F?lix, 1930-1992--Dictionaries. I. Title.
B2430.D454Y68 2013
194--dc23
2013015415

Typeset by Fakenham Prepress Solutions, Fakenham, Norfolk NR21 8NN

CONTENTS

Preface vi
Acknowledgments ix
Abbreviations x

Introduction 1
A–Z dictionary 17

Bibliography 339
Index 347

PREFACE

How to use this dictionary

This dictionary on Deleuze and Guattari is meant for those simply with a curiosity or an enthusiasm for their work, and as a reference for scholars, especially if they are utilized in the classroom.

The dictionary contains three different categories of entries: the first involves Deleuze's and/or Guattari's *Works* (*Difference and Repetition*, *Anti-Oedipus*, *Chaosophy*, etc.), another involves their *Influences* (Nietzsche, Freud, etc.), and the largest category involves their *Key Terms* ('Intensity', 'Smooth Space', etc.).

- The *Key Terms* entries utilize a classical dictionary format with definitions and citations. This format is meant to 1) enable readers to make distinctions and connections between the variations or varieties of each term, in order to draw their own conclusions about the relationships between mutations of the same term (and links between specific senses of *different* terms), and 2) illustrate the given usages of terms with examples from the texts, which also serve as a springboard for readers to explore more details. Citations are listed in italics following the definitions.
    - The substantial *Key Terms* entries contain introductory material which provide an opening context for the term, and dissociate it from common presumptions or stereotypes; the introductions also analyze the major transformations that the term undergoes (especially as it appears in different works by Deleuze and Guattari), which are reflected in the different groups of the definitions that follow.

– With regard to the organization of definitions, whenever a term has a distinct source from a thinker other than Deleuze or Guattari (e.g. 'eternal return' from Nietzsche), the original usage of the term from that thinker is listed first (with a citation from their work). Usually this etymological definition is followed by Deleuze's (or Deleuze & Guattari's) interpretation of that specific definition, which may or may not be the most common usage of the term (this may be listed next). From there, the definitions are organized from most to least common usages, though the special combinations or special types of a term are often listed later (e.g. 'territorial assemblage' or 'deterritorialization' for 'territory' may also be common). It is also useful to note that sometimes terms are peculiar to Deleuze or Guattari's lexicon, even if originating with another thinker (e.g. 'Body without Organs' from Artaud), while in other cases they take an idea or well-known concept and transform it (like 'ethics' or 'desire').

- The *Influences* entries discuss why the thinker is important to Deleuze and/or Guattari, what stereotypes about the thinker they complicate or correct, and, related to this, which of the thinker's ideas are relevant to their individual or collaborative project(s). The entries also discuss the major works by D&G in which the thinker appears, and maps the connections between those themes and issues that are explored.

- The *Works* entries prepare the uninitiated reader for the challenges he or she will face when first tackling the work (in terms of style and approach), map out the major concepts presented, discuss the stages of Deleuze's or Guattari's intellectual development or collaboration, and/ or provide information on discursive climates in which particular publications arose.

The best way to use this book is to grasp how the terms, influences, and works *connect* to one another; it is especially important to note that in some cases, an entry may be substantially related to one or two other entries (e.g. assemblage to milieu, nomadism to smooth space, or Spinoza, to Attributes and Modes). Terms in **bold type** are cross-references (in italicized citations of 'key terms' entries, the term being defined is also in bold type throughout); in the index, the pages listed for entries are embolded. Also note that in 'Key Terms' entries, the given definitions apply to the texts cited; however, there are cases where the definitions refer to more than one text (some of which may not be cited; in this case, the texts themselves are listed in brackets following the definition).

Many citations from the texts list two paginations; in these cases, the first refers to the Continuum editions listed in the bibliography, and the second refers to the other editions.

The author of each entry is indicated by initials, which are abbreviated as follows:

- E. B. Y. for Eugene B. Young
- G. G. for Gary Genokso
- J. W. for Janell Watson
- G. L. for Gregg Lambert

Note also that 'D&G' is used throughout the text as an abbreviation for 'Deleuze and Guattari'.

ACKNOWLEDGMENTS

This project represents a considerable effort to more accurately appreciate the relevance, interrelationship, and applicability of Deleuze's concepts, as well as to demystify his work so that it is more accessible to enthusiasts and experts alike. However, approaching the task and seeing it through was complex, and there are many people to whom I owe a debt of gratitude for their invaluable assistance and guidance during the various stages of the project. I would first like to thank the publishers at Continuum, especially Sarah Campbell and Camilla Erskine, for their patience, understanding, and professionalism as the approach to the work was negotiated and refined. Thanks also to Continuum for the generous permission to use multiple citations from their editions of Deleuze's works to exemplify definitions for 'key terms'. I would also like to thank the scholars that they recruited to review an earlier version of the manuscript; special thanks also to Joe Hughes for his thoughtful and detailed feedback and criticism on the final draft. Additionally, I would like to thank Gregg Lambert for recommending this project to me, for acting as an editorial advisor during the proposal stage, and for contributing a number of entries on Deleuze's 'works'. I would also like to thank Gary Genosko and Janell Watson for contributing all of the entries on Félix Guattari's works, key terms, and influences, as well as for their patience and cooperation as the formatting and approach were refined. Special thanks also to James Williams for suggesting the classic definition and citation format for 'Key Terms' entries; thanks also Ian Buchanan and Ronald Bogue for their general advice during the early stages of the project. Thanks especially to my friends and family for their encouragement as I completed the project, to my students who took an interest in Deleuze, and particularly to my father for his unwavering support.

Eugene B. Young
December 2012

ABBREVIATIONS

AO	Anti-Oedipus
AOP	Anti-Oedipus Papers
B	Bergsonism
C1	Cinema I: The Movement Image
C2	Cinema II: The Time Image
CC	Coldness and Cruelty
CM	Chaosmosis
CY	Chaosophy (1995)
D	Dialogues II
DR	Difference and Repetition
ECC	Essays Critical and Clinical
ES	Empiricism and Subjectivity
F	Foucault
FB	Francis Bacon: The Logic of Sensation
FLB	The Fold: Leibniz and the Baroque
GR	Guattari Reader
K	Kafka, Toward a Minor Literature
KCP	Kant's Critical Philosophy
LS	The Logic of Sense
MR	Molecular Revolution

MRB	Molecular Revolution in Brazil
MU	The Machinic Unconscious
N	Nietzsche and Philosophy
NG	Negotiations
PI	Pure Immanence
PS	Proust and Signs
PT	Psychanalyse et transversalité
SC	Schizoanalytic Cartographies
SEP	Expressionism in Philosophy: Spinoza
SPP	Spinoza: Practical Philosophy
SS	Soft Subversions
TE	The Three Ecologies
TP	A Thousand Plateaus
WP	What is Philosophy?

INTRODUCTION

Thought and the Unthinkable:

Repetition and Sensation as the Dynamics of Difference

Eugene B. Young

What is thought?

We assume that we know what it means to think, and tend to use abstract ideas that explain what we observe, imagine, or remember. A journalist may use an idea like 'political partisanship' to assess whether the government is more (or less) functional than it was years ago. Friends may distinguish between men and women based on physical, emotional, or cognitive features. A psychologist or parent might grasp 'well-being' in terms of behavior, health, or discipline. However, in all of these cases, a concept that is *not* given seeks to explain what is given: partisanship explains governmental dysfunction, a dualism between men and women seeks to label and separate what can be observed, and a judgment is placed upon a person's attributes. The issue with such approaches is that the ideas themselves do not truly account for the *dynamics* of what they seek to explain, which are not actually given, because changes and differences are not something that can be observed or recognized; rather, they are always *disguised* by familiar forms and contexts. Change, in other words, is *not* abstract, nor can it be accounted for by abstract ideas, though it is paradoxically also not strictly observable either. If thinking involves locating change, novelty, or *difference* that is never given, then it requires attention towards the (only apparently) recognizable and similar aspects of systems, circumstances, attributes, and relationships (that is, anything subject to change). This attention utilizes the given only as a springboard to determine its hidden dynamics.

While the philosopher Gilles Deleuze does offer a dynamic approach to thinking, his ideas are often confounded by their apparently jargonistic nature ('deterritorialization' and 'body without organs'), and are further distorted by their conflation with those of other 'French Theorists' such as Jacques Derrida and Michel Foucault (who are important in their own right, but make distinctive contributions). In the first case, however, his outlandish utilization of concepts is arguably meant provocatively to draw our attention toward that which we are naturally inclined to neglect (since 'metaphysical' difference is itself never given), and in the second case, while he shares many concerns with Derrida surrounding the oppressive nature of dualisms, and with Foucault surrounding the normalizing effects of knowledge (and 'power'), we will see how he is ultimately a thinker of difference *by virtue of* the apparent *sameness* of sensible forms (rather than by virtue of oppositional constructs), and a thinker of 'power' in terms of our capacity to 'contract' sensible forms (rather than in terms of strategy or possibility). In Deleuze's view, this is because ideas do not explain the given (i.e. what we can observe, remember, and imagine); rather, it is the sensible (which is not given, but occurs within the given), that initiates, develops, and 'explains' ideas. This introductory essay will explore how these sensible forms, which develop ideas, may seem recognizable but are in fact unthinkable because they are always 'serial'—that is, they present themselves as cases of repetition which are conflated or 'contracted' in the mind (rather than reflected upon, recognized, and remembered). We will see that thought is dynamic because it concerns the *difference* between these forms; that is, the act of thinking is caught up or implicated in a movement of difference which displaces and disguises its focus.[1]

Problems reading Deleuze: Jargon and 'French Theory'

Many feel overwhelmed by what appears to be obscure jargon in Deleuze and Guattari's work and are suspicious of the trendiness of their ideas. Pick up any book by Deleuze and/or Guattari and begin reading it out loud to a colleague or friend who has not read their work, and you will probably sound either unbelievably pretentious, or just crazy, as their sentences can be strikingly, almost offensively obtuse; take this example from Deleuze: 'A whole flow of exchange occurs between intensity and Ideas [...]. Ideas are problematic or "perplexed" virtual multiplicities, made up of relations between differential elements. Intensities are implicated multiplicities, "implexes", made up of relations between asymmetrical elements' (DR 305, 244). Or, take this example from Deleuze and Guattari: 'The desiring-machines take form and train their sights along a tangent of deterritorialization that traverses the representative spheres, and that runs along the body without organs' (AO 346, 315). Consulting the French versions will provide little relief, as the terms will appear equally obtuse; while some of their texts were best-sellers when released, they are not written in the style of today's English-speaking public intellectuals. Added to this, due to their emphasis on experimentation, improvisation, chaos, and 'nomadism' that may seem to promote a sort of reckless arrogance, combined with the captivation we might feel by such provocative concepts, you could end up seeing sentences like: 'the becoming of multiplicities are problematized by the territorialization of the assemblages of desire, but the pre-individual field of singularities is actualized by desiring-machines'. It could seem that Deleuze's legacy has been to reinforce an elite culture that feels self-gratified and self-important by demonstrating that they can use a complex language that you can't. The issue is only exacerbated when publications about Deleuze's work claim that the majority of his influence comes from one major thinker (that he is 'Nietzschean' or 'Leibnizian'), or that his work pivots around one concept (that he is ultimately a thinker of the 'virtual' or of 'multiplicity'); the effect that this has is to distort the unique constellation of sources he draws from around a false center, and to explain his concepts by virtue of other obscure concepts.

This issue of the alienating effect of Deleuze's language becomes even more complicated when his terminology is conflated with other 'French Theorists' such as Derrida and Foucault, which would make it appear as if they have the same method; however, this is not entirely unreasonable, since they do share many of the same concerns. Aside from sharing a cultural context and inheriting a similar intellectual history, for example, both Deleuze and Derrida prioritize *difference* as a critical concept, which they distinguish from the oppressive form of *opposition* (in philosophical terms, they both value an anti-dialectical approach to difference and share an affinity for Nietzsche). Also in both cases, they offer models of repetition and displacement as alternatives. In their view, dualisms are perhaps the most pernicious form of static, abstract thinking, in which we find comfort because of the clarity they afford: heroes are opposed to villains, poor are opposed to rich, men are opposed to women. As Deleuze states, however, 'Dualism is what prevents thought. Dualism always wants to deny the essence of thought, namely, that thought is a *process*' (webdeleuze 26/03/1973). Dualism, he claims, is a 'reduction' and a 'flattening of all statements of thought'. Likewise, Derrida, for his part, notes that 'in a classical philosophical opposition we are not dealing with the peaceful coexistence of a *vis-à-vis*, but rather with a violent hierarchy. One of the two terms governs the other (axiologically, logically, etc.)' (Derrida, 1981, 42). This underlines the rationale for an overturning of such hierarchies by 'deconstructing' the oppositions.

In Deleuze's and Derrida's work, *repetition* is characterized as a means of extending difference such that difference cannot be subordinated to opposition or contradiction. In Derrida's terms, this concerns 'tracing' a structural opposition such that it is *displaced* or dislocated onto another field that has no presence (and is effaced). In this sense, 'the trace is the intimate relation of the living present with its outside, the openness upon exteriority in general' (Derrida, 1973, 86); that is, repetition or displacement may make presence 'return', but only by virtue of the effacement of binary oppositions within a general field of difference. Thus it may seem that Deleuze is talking about something similar when he claims that the living present in time, constituted by repetition or contraction, is the first synthesis that is ultimately implicated by syntheses of difference which cannot be reduced to contradiction because of their displacement and disguise in that field.

Another important thinker with whom Deleuze (or D&G) might be conflated at times is Michel Foucault. While Deleuze and Derrida may share a suspicion of oppressive, dualistic modes of thinking, Foucault (also a reader of Nietzsche) is suspicious of the formation of 'knowledge' as a mode of subtle and perhaps 'metaphysical' violence. In this regard, he suggests that there is a hidden violence when knowledge is formed by virtue of a correspondence between what we can 'see' (or observe) to what we can 'say' (or articulate and classify) because it involves one domain 'capturing' the other using 'enterprises of subversion and destruction' (Foucault, 1983, 26). For example, a psychiatrist observes behavior, and creates 'madness'. Such capturing is not a neutral act but involves a *power* relation; as he states, 'the exercise of power perpetually creates knowledge, and, conversely, knowledge constantly induces effects of power' (Foucault, 1980, 51). Interestingly, such power is not 'negative' *per se*, since 'it incites, it induces, it seduces, it makes easier or more difficult' (Foucault, 1982, 789); we want something *from* power and are continually provoked or seduced into increasing the quality and extent of our lives. In this sense, we willfully subject ourselves to the knowledge it produces and strive to regulate and discipline ourselves and others (which often results in conforming to standards of normalcy). And yet, power is also not something that can be *represented*, since it is not *itself* an object of knowledge (it is 'invisible' and 'inarticulable'); but because we want something from it, it is what *makes* us 'see and speak'. Hence the ubiquity of power that underlies all of our actions. 'Thought', for Foucault, would thus either involve the '*strategy*' of power, or the resistance *to* power (but he and Deleuze would agree that it is *not* something that can be *represented*).

It may seem that Deleuze and Foucault share similar concerns about the oppressive nature of knowledge; in Deleuze's reading of Nietzsche, for example, 'knowledge' is that which reacts to and sets limits to life by judging and legislating it. Much like the normalizing or subjectifying effect of knowledge in Foucault's work, Deleuze claims that 'representation and knowledge are modeled entirely upon propositions of consciousness' which preclude unconscious learning and questioning, subordinating ideas to 'common sense' (models of recollection and recognition) which reinforce the identity of the subject (DR 241, 192). These apparently Foucauldian themes are extended in Deleuze's work with Guattari where statements of a 'mental' or 'dominant' reality refer back to subjects that 'enuncitate' themselves in conformity with that reality (TP 143, 129–30): these 'expressions' link up with Foucauldian 'visibilities' or 'contents' that further enmesh or 'territorialize' the subject within institutions or 'assemblages' of power.

Deleuze's foundation: The 'Unthinkable'

Before addressing the deceptively alienating nature of Deleuze's terminology, it is important to clarify some of his own terms and define what thinking means for him, as distinct from his French contemporaries. While Deleuze has an affinity with Derrida surrounding their suspicion of dualisms, they in fact have fundamentally distinct characterizations of sameness and presence (and, by consequence, of 'difference'). On the one hand, deconstruction would involve interrogating and exposing the hierarchy behind oppositions within structural systems (for example, the simple opposition of 'man' and 'woman'); that is, it shows that whenever things are opposed, one is always valued at the expense of another (men and women are often treated unequally), whereas in reality—that is, throughout time—their value is not opposable at all (their aptitude, desire, etc.). Deleuze, on the other hand, arguably takes the perspective that 'dualisms' are *already* alike ('man' and 'woman' may be opposites but they are only opposites because they are *not* mutually exclusive: they are both human beings; in philosophical terms, it was the dialectical reflection of the one in the other that made them opposable in the first place). In this sense, dualisms are actually *repetitions* of each other (if they are already 'alike' then it would be inappropriate to describe them in Derridian terms as undecidable differences which defer onto one another). Deleuze's starting point is thus not difference that is encountered in a structure or (non)linguistic construct; rather, the starting point is the *likenesses* and *similarities* of all things (as apprehended by the senses).[2] In this scenario, difference is never given or ready-made in the form of opposition: it is likeness given in the form of repetition that *displaces* and *disguises* difference. In distinction from Derrida, difference (in contrast to opposition) is also not ascertained in terms of 'alterity' or 'otherness' in general;[3] rather than opposites being displaced or 'repeated' onto, to use Derrida's words, an alterity 'that is not yet—or is no longer—absence, negativity, non-Being, lack, silence' (Derrida, 1987, 173), such that an opposite can be neither one nor the other, it is the *cases of repetition* which, by virtue of thought, move gradually from resemblance to *dissemblance*, such that actual cases express the *displacements* and *disguises* of local (or 'virtual') differences. This shifting, divergence, or movement is precisely the dynamic moment of thinking; Deleuze sometimes refers to such difference as a 'paradoxical object' that is never given but always diverging from any center within the series it displaces. The question remains, however: how are actual differences ascertained, if they are never given?

Deleuze's starting point and foundation for thinking involves what he and Derrida both call the 'living present'; in Deleuze's case, presence is characterized in terms of contraction (repetition), and the unconscious. While Derrida's version of the living present emphasizes the manner in which it is a *trace* that opens self-presence onto the externality of space, Deleuze emphasizes that our physical existence as well as our experience of time is constituted by 'contraction'; as he states, 'Time is constituted only in the originary synthesis which [...] contracts the successive independent instants into one another, thereby constituting the lived, or living, present' (DR 91, 70). As he explains it, organisms are 'made of elements and cases of repetition, of contemplated and contracted' chemicals, and we likewise contract—in a psychic sense—that which we are *capable* of 'contemplating' or synthesizing (ibid). Our tendency to 'contract' is not only the way we experience time, then, but it is an ability or power—before consciousness, reflection, knowledge, or oppositional thinking intervenes—to conflate things together, form associations, and to perceive through resemblances. In other words, if presence in Derrida is impossible because it can only be recognized or perceived by virtue of a trace (as a 'text', whether linguistic or not), in this case, presence as repetition is a 'constantly aborted moment of birth' that cannot be recognized or conceived because it does not occur at the level of consciousness: it concerns *sensation* rather than cognition (ibid). All things, in this sense, are repeated through one another, by virtue of their resemblance or proximity; however, rather than engendering habitual expectations or predictions based on this repetition (expecting the differences 'contracted' by that repetition to simply continue in a general sense), *it is ultimately the role of thought* to conceive of real differences within those systems of repetition or *series*.[4] On the one hand, then, this living present may be the foundation (*fondation*), but on the other hand, that which cannot be lived, and was never and will never be encountered in reality—an 'immemorial memory' (in distinction from a memory that was experienced, such as a childhood trauma)—is the 'more profound' *ground* (*fondement*) which causes those repetitions or contractions to take place, and enables us to conceive of the *difference* that animates them; this difference may be 'symbolic' but it is also not a representation of what is repeated and experienced by our consciousness or understanding. So, sensation forces us to go outside of 'living time' and remember, which in turn forces us to think; in Deleuze's terms, 'the violence of that which forces thought develops from the *sentiendum* [that which can only be sensed] to the *cogitandum* [that which can only be thought]' (DR 177, 141). Thus it is the lived presence of the given (what we can observe, remember, or imagine) that enables us to think, even if that presence is also 'unthinkable' and not completely given because it has to be sensed (to confuse the two regions is to, once again, explain the given by means of that which is not given).

From Deleuze's perspective, 'difference' cannot be thought in general terms but it also cannot be thought in terms that are too specific; in other words, just because difference cannot be given or represented (that is, observed, imagined, or remembered) does not mean that we should be overwhelmed into believing that everything is just connected to everything—whether on a large scale, where each thing is mediated by each other thing as part of global process, or on a small scale, where each specific thing 'implicates' or contains the essence of everything. If thought is the thought of difference, then on the one hand, it is not difference, alterity, or otherness *in general* (that is, differences are not 'infinitely large'), and on the other hand, differences are also not *inessential* (that is, they are not 'infinitely small').[5] To think in terms of change, or novelty, in this sense, involves conceiving of that which is paradoxically both 'local' and 'nonspecific', but this always concerns what we are actually *capable* of 'contemplating' and 'contracting' in terms of our *senses* or 'viscera', *which would preclude infinity*—whether the large or small—since infinity it is *not* something we can experience in 'lived time'. The goal of thinking is to ascertain a variety of series (in whatever domain(s)—aesthetic, natural, social, etc.) whose animation or dynamics can be grasped in terms of variations, resonances, fluctuations, permutations, or transformations that are *between* the repetitions themselves (in technical terms, the question may be: how can the forces which animate systems, or the intensities that resonate within systems, be characterized?). These differences are not thinkable, but also not infinitely small or large, for the same reason: they are developed and localized only by the series (though not *specific* to any one instance in a series) that are apprehended by the senses (and can later be recalled or recognized in a given form).

This issue of the relation of thought with the 'unthinkable', or sensible, brings us to Deleuze's association with Foucault, where power, like thought, is 'invisible' and 'inarticulable'. Now, thought is 'unthinkable' for Foucault only insofar as the human sciences have taken man as the object of analysis and we have become 'double' to ourselves; thus we have attained a new critical distance for fields like sociology and medicine, but at the price of becoming alien or unthinkable (hence his famous claim that 'man is only a recent invention'). Since Foucault's focus is the manner in which power is exercised through and engendered by knowledge, *thought* would, in these terms, perhaps be *conditioned or enclosed* by the institutional frameworks or 'dispositifs' of knowledge/power, whether as 'strategy' or as 'resistance'. In Deleuze's terms, however, if our habits and behaviors are intimately entangled within the institutions of knowledge/power, where all of our 'unthinkable' sensations and experiences are 'diagrammed' (that is, influenced and guided) by what we see and say, then those sensations are, at the same time (and despite that), composed within a domain that is *outside* of knowledge and also outside of the domain of possibility where we are incited or provoked to act in response to power. This domain, like power, involves that which can neither be seen nor said, but unlike power, would not be 'strategic' (even and especially, as we will see, in its resistance to power).

Since Deleuze portrays power in terms of a capacity (*puissance*) to 'contract', this can be distinguished from Foucault's relations of power (*pouvoir*) that are entangled within social and political possibilities (where we are incited or seduced to act). In this sense, if the 'contractile power' of our bodies and our imagination is the impetus that ultimately leads to thought, it is perhaps for this reason that, in Deleuze's work on Foucault, he notes that 'resistances necessarily operate in a direct relation with the outside from which the diagrams emerge. This means that a social field offers more resistance than strategies, and the thought of the outside is a thought of resistance' (F 74, 89–90). What this means is that if thinking is a mode of 'resistance', it does not place itself in an *antagonistic* relationship with knowledge or the institutions engendered by power, since this would *itself* be strategic, and would, in its own right, be a manner of wielding power. Resistance, in other words, is not resistance *to* knowledge or power; rather, it opens up the space of 'non-relation' where 'thinking addresses itself to an outside that has no form'; it is a capacity to think within the sensible, but it is not addressed to anyone or anything; what thought 'resists' is precisely the recollection and recognition that makes us 'know' and makes us into 'subjects'. It is perhaps for this reason that Deleuze claims that resistance is not a 'phenomenon' (Deleuze, 1997): in Deleuzo-Guattarian terms, what motivates us to think is not power, but *desire*, which takes place within 'assemblages' (that is, arrangements of individuals within social and productive structures) and functions whether or not it is enmeshed within 'power relations'.[6]

While Deleuze's approach to thinking may deviate from Derrida and Foucault surrounding the unthinkable origins of thought, an objection may arise: is he still not thinking in dualisms *between* the thinkable and unthinkable, or between thought and sensation? Between difference and repetition? These are in fact misleading questions. Difference, in Deleuze's view, cannot be *opposed* to anything: it is not contradictory because it paradoxically both exceeds and is contained within a series of things. *Difference is not contradictory, nor can it contradict anything, because it is ascertained only through repetition, resemblance, and sameness;* series that constitute systems likewise do not contradict one another because their nature is to repeat; this presence may be paradoxical, but, as Deleuze states, 'the force of paradoxes is that they *are not contradictory*; they rather allow us to be present at the genesis of the contradiction' (LS 86, 74, my emphasis). Thought could not, in other words, 'contradict' the repetitions which *express* it, and be opposed to another thought.

To return to a previous example, a Deleuzian approach to the commonplace difference or 'opposition' between men and women would begin with the presumption that they are both the same, 'vegetative' (or 'univocal') form of life[7] (physical differences aside), and would ask what the differences are within that form (which would include, but would not be limited to, sexual difference). Difference, in short, would be the product of an encounter. How do we encounter men and women? We often encounter them in groups: professionals, families, friends, laborers, audiences, or pedestrians. We then deduce that, despite the apparent homogeny which makes them appear as a group or a series, a different kind of desire animates the interactions and dynamics within each group (such that they are not homogenous at all). Such desire may be characterized by ideas involving industry, consumerism, sympathy, violence, gregariousness, or sexuality, to name a few. In distinction from groups, we also encounter *individuals* and perceive, or are affected by, their expressions, gestures, actions, and explications. In this case, we would ask what the difference is between the familiar world that we inhabit and the unknown world that they inhabit (the two worlds coinciding to form a series); these dynamics are developed only by the different emphases between their world and mine.[8] Such differences can likewise be characterized by ideas involving sexuality (which may or may not be gendered; there are certainly a multitude of sexual dispositions), but also involving disposition, attention, or comprehension (what I am affected by, or what I perceive or conceive, in the *same situation*, may be different than you, thus illuminating many dispositions). In every case, it is the similarities within the encounters that ultimately generate the thought of differences.

Reading Deleuze: Conceptual terms, aesthetic terms

Here we can arrive at a distinction between two basic types of terms in Deleuze's (and D&G's) work, that appeal either to our cognitive processes (involving our ability to differentiate), or to our senses which are 'affective' and 'perceptive' but not 'thinkable' (and involve our ability to synthesize). The second type are easily explained, since they explain themselves and explain the first type:

they are 'extensive'—meaning that they extend the 'unthinkable' or *aesthetic* domains where the first type are developed. They may involve what we can observe, imagine, or even remember (all forms of association), but they do not involve *thought*. The first type, however, cannot be 'explained': they are *paradoxes* that are not meant to be 'understood', solved, or seen as frivolous puzzles that are 'uselessly complicated'; as Deleuze states, 'One would have to be too "simple" to believe that thought is a simple act, clear unto itself' (LS 86, 74). Rather, paradoxes involve 'discovering what can only be thought, what can only be spoken, despite the fact that it is both ineffable and unthinkable—a mental Void' (ibid).

We can now return to the issue of the apparently jargonistic language in Deleuze's work, where 'conceptual creation' may appear flamboyant, pretentious, and excessive. There is no doubt that Deleuze and Guattari use concepts *provocatively*: their concepts grab our attention precisely because of their outlandishness: 'Deterritorialization', 'Desiring-Machines', 'disjunctive syntheses', 'chaosmos', etc. Cultural and historical contexts notwithstanding, it is perhaps the case that outlandish terms are meant to draw our attention *to* the very 'unthinkable' nature *of* difference (we are indifferent to it precisely because it appears *as* indifference). If it is the case that paradox is 'a mental Void', and it is our natural inclination *not to consider* it, that is, to forget it as soon as we encounter it (since it cannot be observed, imagined, or recalled), then it is perhaps a stylistic choice to illustrate the very dynamic between that which we notice but cannot grasp (the given), and that which we can grasp but do not notice (thought).

Deleuze's work consists of, on the one hand, terms which do not explain the given because they lack the form and content which could do so, and instead, encapsulate or instigate the *thought* of differences. On the other hand, it also consists of terms which can be considered 'aesthetic', and may be recalled, recognized, or 'given', but are not thinkable. This distinction between conceptual terms and aesthetic terms is not meant to trivialize the complexity of his work, but to point towards an essential dynamic: if thought is *not* opposed to the unthinkable or non-contradictory fields that develop it (because they can 'only be sensed'), then perhaps Deleuze's and Guattari's idiosyncratic terms, even and *especially* when they seem to be dualisms, are either the one *expressing* the other, or the one *implicating* the other.[9] In other words, thought is developed and explained by unthinkable, aesthetic domains, but at the same time, thought *implies* those domains without explaining them: the 'actual' is the expression or development of the 'virtual'; 'becoming' is the expression or development of 'being'; 'repetition' is the expression of 'difference', and at the same time, the 'virtual' implies the 'actual'; 'being' implies 'becoming'; and 'difference' implies 'repetition'. Of course, it is not as simple as this; for example, 'chaos' would *complicate* 'milieus', which themselves explain the 'assemblages' that are implied by 'de/territorialization'. But for the most part, we can distinguish between terms which function philosophically, and terms which function to extend the terms *aesthetically*.

What does it mean that some of Deleuze's (and D&G's) terms may be 'aesthetic'? It does *not* mean that they use 'figurative' language in the conventional sense, where figures stand in for something else (inside or outside of the text) in a conventionally metaphorical or metonymic fashion. They may do so initially, if we limit ourselves to observation, imagination, recollection, and recognition. However, if aesthetic terms are *implicated* by ideas, then they are synthesized in a new way; rather than being similar or the same, they *displace* and *disguise* those ideas. The ideas themselves may be in a state of perpetual variation due to their dependence on, or determination by, figures; however, the figures that 'explain' them do so only by being unthinkable, only by referring sensation itself to another instance, another movement, variety, or moment of 'contraction' or repetition. Deleuze and Guattari support the notion that philosophy may use the devices of art or literature, without actually *being* art or literature, when they state that the planes of art and philosophy 'can slip into each other to the degree that parts of one may be occupied by entities of the other' (WP 66). What this indicates is that aesthetic devices that are used to create descriptions and imagery may not always form an artistic or literary 'composition', but may *appear* as concepts in a philosophical plane or context (for example, it may be what they call an 'affect of the concept' rather than a 'concept of the affect').

Reading Deleuze can be a rewarding experience, provided that the ideas which are differential do not get swallowed up by including all the other ideas (even 'difference' does not include terms such as the virtual, being, or the assemblage), nor do the differences become too small by being explained by one aesthetic variety, such as 'repetition' or 'serialization'. They all have singular uses, contexts and inflections. It is in this sense that it is always a misleading distortion to claim that there are *central* concepts in Deleuze's work, or that he is fundamentally influenced by one thinker such as Nietzsche or Leibniz. Of course, it is useful to make connections, such as reading one concept through another (e.g. how difference can be read into the virtual), or locating a Spinozist inflection when Deleuze reads Nietzsche. But to consider one group of concepts essential or to consider one thinker to be a pivot point would always be a mistake. Grasping the way that the terms interact, especially the basic dynamic between the conceptual and aesthetic, means to grasp what thinking is for Deleuze. This is why reading *The Deleuze and Guattari Dictionary* ought to be most useful to see *how* his concepts *work*, what their interrelationships are, and not what they 'mean'. The terms themselves are not, in other words, important. To memorize his concepts and internalize the lexicon would only establish a new orthodoxy that betrays the fundamental exigency in Deleuze's work, which is thinking outside of representation.

The given—what we can observe, remember, and imagine—is always a platitude, a cliché. The world is full of them—in fact, that's all the world essentially is. We don't think, or have real ideas, without first encountering what 'everybody knows'. We may have an unmediated encounter with the sensual world, but the moment we try to grasp or 'think' this encounter, it is already being expressed in clichés or abstractions that nullify its true dynamics.[10] Using phrases like 'political partisanship' to explain governmental dysfunction only reinforces a cliché, unless it accounts for the differences that are implied by partisanship across a spectrum of similarities; speaking generally about the differences between men and women accomplishes nothing without first presuming that there is no difference, and allowing differences to be explained only by virtue of sensible forms; speaking about 'well-being' without apprehending the *varieties* and changes in health or behavior would just fixate health onto an abstract criteria. To reinforce what everybody knows is not to think: to think is to dissociate the cliché from the world as it is given, from all the everyday associations that we make and apprehend without thinking, in order to demonstrate what animates those systems of resemblance. In other words, it is unavoidable that we encounter the world without thinking, but that is not how we must remember and express it. By virtue of thought, the world becomes a series of displacements and disguises. It might seem arrogant to believe this should be undertaken, but it arguably more arrogant to presume that clichés or abstract ideas can really account for difference or change. Taking action *without* thinking makes us no better than brute animals or automated machines; as human beings we may encapsulate features of both animals and machines (in terms of our power to contract or repeat), but thinking within those systems is our humanistic, 'spiritual' attribute. Ideas can only explained through the unthinkable systems that develop them, and to think is to account for what is unknown, which is located in the dynamics of the only apparently familiar world.

Notes

1. The final section of this essay will emphasize that serial forms themselves have aesthetic varieties, and suggest that some terms in Deleuze's work have an aesthetic role and others have a conceptual role.
2. See entry on Hegel for Deleuze's explanation of dialectical contradiction and identity (sublation).
3. This is not to create an 'opposition' between Derrida's approach and Deleuze's approach in that one would be a more legitimate approach than the other; it is arguably only by virtue of the similarities of their concerns and their focuses that their different methods can be ascertained. If the exigency or goal of deconstruction is to expose the hierarchical prejudices of other texts, structures, or discourses, then it makes sense that difference or alterity could be considered in general terms (there is no specific, anticipated 'goal', while the critical encounter that exposes oppositions to difference is the exigency). In this manner, the critical and humanitarian values of deconstruction can be differentiated from the interpretive and creative values of a Deleuzian approach, where difference or 'alterity' is conceived as local or circumscribed to actual series within varieties of systems.
4. In *Between Deleuze and Derrida*, Leonard Lawlor frames this difference between Deleuze and Derrida in terms of the simulacra.
5. See entries on Hegel and Leibniz.

6 See entry on *Kafka: Toward a Minor Literature*, which explains D&G's claim that desire 'really functions' when it is not 'territorialized' by power (when social machines lose their abstract function in relation to concrete assemblages and become truly 'abstract').
7 See entry on Proust.
8 See entry on Leibniz and the Other.
9 For further discussion of 'implication' and 'explication' in Deleuze's work, see the entry on *The Fold*.
10 For Deleuze's discussion of breaking with the cliché, see the end of *Cinema* 1 and the opening of *Cinema* 2, and also *The Logic of Sensation* (also discussed in this dictionary).

A–Z dictionary

Abstract machine

Unlike everyday technical machines, Deleuze and Guattari suggest that 'abstract' machines involve the manner in which human beings (or other '**matters**') are caught up within, or are a part of, '*mechanical*' processes. When machines function in a technical sense, they are abstracted, or separate from, their **milieu** (that is, the domain in which they have an effect), and are thus 'self-destructive', or cannot truly maintain themselves; this is in fact the initial sense of the term provided in their text on **Kafka** (which also appears indirectly in *Anti-Oedipus* in terms of the distinction between technology and **assemblages**). However, the term shifts to signify the manner in which 'machines' can be considered in an ontological sense rather than an everyday technical sense in the conclusion to the Kafka text (the term retains this sense in *A Thousand Plateaus*), such that they function to actually *disrupt* rather than *maintain* their separation from actual assemblages. In this manner, human beings are not part technical-machine (à la cyborgs), but part abstract-machine; that is, we *are* machines in the sense that our **desire** is inextricably bound up with machines (it is '*machinic*'), and machines must be connected (or **immanent**) to non-technical processes of desire in order to truly function (see **desiring-machines**).

> 1.a. In D&G's reading of **Kafka** and analysis of social constructs of **desire**, in an initial sense, a technical and physical construct that operates *on* bodies and social or concrete **assemblages** according to symbolic and transcendent imperatives (producing *mechanical* effects); that which **territorializes** and captures desire by limiting it to concrete forms.

> The **abstract machine** *is that of the [penal] colony, or of Odradek or Blumfeld's ping-pong balls. Transcendent and reified, seized by symbolical or allegorical exegeses, it opposes the real* **assemblages** *[...].* [K 86]

b. In an ultimate sense, an immaterial element that disassembles any transcendent or symbolic function of technical, concrete, or social **assemblages** (producing *machinic* effects). [K, TP]

> *In another sense of* **abstract** *(a sense that is nonfigurative, non-signifying, nonsegmental), it is the* **abstract machine** *that operates in the field of unlimited* **immanence** *[...]: the* **concrete assemblages** *are no longer that which gives a real existence to the* **abstract machine** *[...]—it's the* **abstract machine** *that measures the* **mode** *of existence and the reality of the* **assemblages** *[...].* [K 86–7]

2. A set of breaks, interruptions, or cuts that are effectuated in concrete **assemblages**, but are themselves indifferent to and independent of those assemblages because they have neither a predetermined function nor deal with formed substances, but establish **becomings** and engender **intensities** (which are singular).

> **Abstract machines** *consist of unformed* **matters** *and nonformal functions. Every* **abstract machine** *is a consolidated aggregate of matters-functions* (**phylum** *and* **diagram**)*. This is evident on a technological 'plane': such a plane is not made up simply of formed substances (aluminum, plastic, electric wire, etc.) or organizing forms (program, prototypes, etc.), but of a composite of unformed* **matters** *exhibiting only degrees of* **intensity** *(resistance, conductivity, heating, stretching, speed or delay, induction, transduction...) and* **diagrammatic** *functions exhibiting only differential equations or, more generally, 'tensors.'* [TP 562, 511]

3.a. In D&G's cosmology, that which either unifies the composition of **strata** (Ecumenon) or **diagrams** the **plane of consistency** within strata (Planomenon).

> *Either the* **abstract machines** *remain prisoner to* **stratifications***, [...] Or, on the contrary, the* **abstract machine** *cuts across all stratifications, develops alone and in its own right on the* **plane of consistency** *whose* **diagram** *it constitutes [...]* [TP 62, 56]

b. That which is responsible for both conflating and organizing the relationship between **forms of content** and **forms of expression,** and for **deterritorializing** the flow of desire by allowing it to trace an abstract and unlimited line which is **immanent** to concrete **assemblages.**

> *the* abstract machine *[...] constitutes and conjugates all of the* assemblage's *cutting edges of* deterritorialization.*[...] A true* abstract machine *has no way of making a distinction within itself between a plane of* expression *and a plane of content because it draws a single* plane of consistency, *which in turn formalizes contents and expressions according to* strata *and* reterritorializations. [TP 156, 141]

> *a* machine *is like a set of cutting edges that insert themselves into the* assemblage *undergoing* deterritorialization, *and draw variations and mutations of it. For there are no mechanical effects; effects are always machinic, in other words, depend on a machine that is plugged into an assemblage and has been freed through deterritorialization.* [TP 367, 333]

- E. B. Y.

Action-image

The action-image, along with **perception-images** and **affection-images**, is one of the three major types of **movement-images** in Deleuze's taxonomy of the cinema. This image is most responsible for engendering a large or global sense of *realism*, namely, by situating our perception of **affects** (embodied in behaviors of characters) within a **milieu** (or environment), which then compete with other **forces** that change the situation and instigate action (forming a 'set'). Deleuze also shows, however, that there are smaller forms of the action-image which *begin* with inferences of situations that create *anticipation* or *tension* to arrive at an actual situation; a straightforward contrast is between the crime genre, which moves from a situation towards an action or duel, and back to a situation—SAS, and the detective genre, which moves from 'blind actions' to 'obscure situations', and back to actions—ASA (C1 168, 164). Deleuze also explores more complex sequences that navigate between these small and large forms.

1. That which, in the sensory-motor interval of the **movement-image**, organizes possible responses to **perception**.

*The more the re*action *ceases to be immediate and becomes truly possible* action, *the more the* perception *becomes distant and anticipatory and extracts the* virtual action *of things.* [...] *This is therefore the second avatar of the* movement-image: *it becomes* action-image. [C1 67, 65]

2.a. On the one hand, the **perception** of **actualized affects** within a **milieu**; in Deleuze's cinematic schema, the *synsign*. On the other hand, the image of competing **forces** which compose the **actual** situation; in Deleuze's cinematic schema, the *binomial*.

Already, in the milieu, *we distinguish the power-qualities and the state of things which* actualizes *them. The situation, and the character or the* action, *are like two terms which are simultaneously correlative and antagonistic. The* action *in itself is a duel of* forces, *a series of duels: duel with the milieu, with the others, with itself. Finally, the new situation which emerges from the* action *forms a couple with the initial situation. This is the set [ensemble] of the* action-image, *or at least its first form.* [C1 146, 142]

b. Images that function as symbols for possible behaviors or actions in potential situations; in Deleuze's cinematic schema, the *impression*.

It is nevertheless true that the emotional handling of an object, an act of emotion in relation to the object, can have more effect than a close-up in the action-image. [...] *In its most general definition, the* impression *is the inner, but visible, link between the permeating situation and the explosive* action. [C1 163, 159]

3.a. The inference of situations or circumstances that are not immediately apparent based on actions that are apparent, generating general anticipation; in Deleuze's cinematic schema, the *index of lack*.

This action-image *seems to have become particularly self-conscious* [...]. *The situation is thus deduced from the* action, *by immediate inference, or by relatively complex reasoning.* [...] [T]*he index here is an* index of lack; *it implies a gap in the narrative* [...] [C1 164, 160]

b. The inference of two contradictory situations or expectations based on what is given, generating a sense of tension; in Deleuze's cinematic schema, the *index of equivocity*.

> There is a second, more complex type of index, an **index of equivocity**, which corresponds to the second (geometrical) sense of the word 'ellipse' [...] It is as if an **action**, a **mode** of behaviour, concealed a slight difference, which was nevertheless sufficient to relate it simultaneously to two quite distant situations, situations which are worlds apart. [C1 166, 161]

4. The sequence of images which engenders the sense of all possible situations and thus a sense of fragmentation of space, despite the continuance of a linear orientation of time (which adapts to or mutates based on that space); in Deleuze's cinematic schema, the *vector*.

> It is not merely a case of hesitation between two situations which are distant or opposed, but simultaneous. The successive situations, each of which is already equivocal in itself, will form in turn with one another [...] It is no longer an ambient space, but a vectoral space, a **vector**-space, with temporal distances. [...] It is the genetic **sign** of the new **action image**, whilst the index was the sign of its composition. [C1 172, 168]

- E. B. Y.

Active synthesis

Deleuze is critical of **Kant** for his depiction of the empirical **faculties** as purely receptive, without any power of synthesis; his use of 'active' synthesis is therefore a somewhat pejorative term that demonstrates how the 'transcendental' powers of recognition form an illusion of 'global integrations and the supposition of identical totalizable objects', which may eclipse the real changes taking place at the level of **passive synthesis** (DR 125, 101).

1.a. In Deleuze's explanation of the experience of time, the synthesis of the mind that both produces generic principles based on the associations between a past instance and a present instance (**repetition** or **passive synthesis** of **habit**), and produces a generic reflection based on a projection of the **differences** of the past itself, or the pure past (the **differences** or passive syntheses of memory), into the present.

> the **active syntheses** *of memory and understanding are superimposed upon and supported by the* **passive synthesis** *of the* **imagination** *[...]. Furthermore, by combining with the perceptual syntheses built upon them, these organic syntheses are redeployed in the* **active syntheses** *of a psycho-organic memory and intelligence (instinct and learning).* [DR 92, 71]

b. The operation of the mind which is responsible for a fitting together or binding (*emboîtement*) of presents (such that it is no longer transparent to itself as it was when **contracted** in a **passive synthesis**), but is reflected upon and in that sense *re-presented* to the mind that apprehends it; such **perceptions** or occurrences obtain a formal identity through their recognition.

> Active synthesis, *therefore, has two correlative—albeit non-symmetrical—aspects: reproduction and reflection, remembrance and recognition, memory and understanding [...]. As a result, the* active synthesis *of memory may be regarded as the principle of representation* [DR 102, 81]

- E. B. Y.

Actual; Actualization

1. The process whereby the **virtual** is made present in time (in distinction from the realization of a possibility), while preserving the **singularity** and atemporality of the virtual; the incarnation of ideas, their **differenciation**.

> *The* actual *is the complement or the product, the object of* actualization, *which has nothing but the* virtual *as its subject.* [D 149]

> *For Ideas, to be* actualized *is to be* differenciated. *[...] something which exists only in the Idea may be completely determined* (**differentiated**) *and yet lack those determinations which constitute* actual *existence (it is undifferenciated, not yet even individuated).* [DR 350, 280]

- E. B. Y.

Aesthetic paradigm

1. In Guattari's work, as opposed to scientific paradigms, paradigms that are **schizoanalytic, rhizomatic**, and chaosmic, involving processes rather than structures.

> *psychoanalysis, which claimed to affirm itself as scientific, [...] has everything to gain from putting itself under the aegis of this new type of* **aesthetic** *processual* **paradigm**. [CM 106]

2. A **schizoanalytic** approach to clinical treatment which, instead of describing the psyche in terms of structures or stages, views the production of **subjectivity** as a creative process.

> *Grafts of transference [...] [issue] from a creation which itself indicates a kind of* **aesthetic paradigm**. *One creates new modalities of* **subjectivity** *in the same way that an artist creates new forms from the palette.* [CM 7]

3. The creative capacity of **chaosmosis**, the emergence of order from **chaos**, engendering new **autopoietic** entities; this ontological process is exemplified by but not limited to artistic creation.

> *art [...] engenders unprecedented, unforeseen and unthinkable qualities of being. The decisive threshold constituting this new* **aesthetic paradigm** *lies in the aptitude of these processes of creation to auto-affirm themselves as existential nuclei,* **autopoietic** *machines.* [CM 106; see also 112]

- J. W.

Affect

While affect is often used as a synonym for 'emotion', **Spinoza's** philosophical use of the term distinguished between affects of which we are actively the cause, and 'affections' which have some **imaginary** correlate (that is, which are feelings *about* something or someone). Thus we can have affections or 'emotions'—love and hate, hope and fear—when we are in a passive relationship to the world, or we can experience joyful affects as a result of comprehending and **desiring** that which would, in his terms, extend our existence and increase our power.

Deleuze's interest in **Spinoza**'s portrayal of affect has to do with the manner in which adequate ideas are not representative 'images of thought', but conceptions of dynamic and kinetic relations between bodies (often phrased as 'speeds and slownesses'); however, the emphasis changes when he applies the idea to the **Nietzschean** notion of **becoming**, which arguably focuses less on extending existence, and more on a capacity for action and novelty (that is, an affirmation of the necessity *of* chance, rather than a comprehension of necessary relations). In his later work with Guattari, affect is also framed in relation to **percept** and **concept**, and drawn on to distinguish, and show connections between, art and philosophy. The term again appears in Deleuze's cinema books, where affects are part of '**affection-images**', 'action-images', 'qualisigns', and 'icons'.

1. **Spinoza's** term for both the actual effects of external bodies (or **modes**) which cause the body to feel pleasure or pain, and the subjective ideas of the effects that external things produce in our body; these ideas both lead to inadequate ideas and a *passive* relation to the external world (passions) and form the basis for adequate ideas and an *active* relation to the external world (actions).

> By **affect** [*affectum*] I understand the affections [*affectiones*] of the body by which the body's power of acting is increased or diminished, helped or hindered, and at the same time the ideas of those affections [*affectionum*]. If, therefore, we can be the adequate cause of one of these affections, then I understand by the **affect** *an action*; otherwise, I understand it to be a passion. [Spinoza (*The Ethics* I, def. 5) 2000, 75]

2.a. In Deleuze's reading of **Spinoza**, the source of the **expression** of power, degrees of perfection (joy or sadness, love or hate), and of **modes** of existence (good or bad), and of the corresponding ideas which can ultimately (in the shift from inadequate ideas to adequate) cause affects in (or 'self-affect') the body by replacing them with new affects; that which has a **duration** as long as its trace in the mind lasts (until it is replaced by a new affect); an unfavorable bodily disposition caused by chance encounters; or, a favorable bodily disposition that is caused by **reason** (that is, whose cause is intentional and understood) thereby increasing the capacity for action of the body and mind.

> A **mode**'s *essence is a power; to it corresponds a certain capacity of the mode to be* **affected**. *But because the mode is a part of Nature this capacity is always exercised, either in* **affections** *produced by external things (those* **affections** *called passive), or in* **affections** *explained by its own essence (called active).* [SEP 93]

> *The passage to a greater perfection, or the increase of the power of acting, is called an* **affect**, *or feeling, of joy; the passage to a lesser perfection or the diminution of the power of acting is called sadness.* [SPP 50]

b. In Deleuze's and D&G's reading of Nietzsche and Spinoza, a **becoming** which involves a modification in a characteristic relations of **forces** (a capacity of the will to power) or of speed and slowness, which in turn increases or decreases the capacity for action.

> *will to power is manifested as a capacity for being* **affected**. *[...] The* **affects** *of* **force** *are active insofar as the force appropriates anything that resists it and compels the obedience of inferior forces.* [N 57, 63]

> *To every relation of movement and rest, speed and slowness grouping together an infinity of parts, there corresponds a degree of power. To the relations composing, decomposing, or modifying an individual there correspond intensities that* **affect** *it, augmenting or diminishing its power to act; these intensities come from external parts or from the individual's own parts.* **Affects** *are* **becomings**. [TP 283, 256]

3.a. In D&G's conceptualization of Art, that which cannot be felt or internalized by a subject but nevertheless engenders feelings (designated here as 'affections'); that which underlies emotions about lived experiences and but cannot be attributed to or possessed by a subject. The 'feeling' in its objective state insofar as it is preserved and rendered as a work of art.

> **Affects** *[...] go beyond the strength of those who undergo them. [...] Consonance and dissonance, harmonies of tone or color, are* **affects** *of music or painting.* [WP 164]

b. An aesthetic feature which renders the **intensity** (of a concept; thought within the body) in a form or **figure**, in distinction from the **force** of the **percept** which engenders such intensities.

> the **concept** as such can be concept of the **affect**, just as the **affect** can be **affect** of the concept. [WP 66]

c. The proper entity, along with the **percept**, that engenders blocs of **sensation** and populates the **plane of composition** with aesthetic **figures**.

> the composite **sensation** is reterritorialized on the **plane of composition** [WP 197]

4. In D&G's analysis of political history, a trait of **nomadic** existence which is expressive of the **war machine**, where emotions are caught up in a continual process of movement (speed and slowness), in distinction from feelings, which are static reflections or forms of such movements.

> Feeling implies an evaluation of **matter** and its resistances, a direction (sens, also 'meaning') to form and its developments, an economy of **force** and its displacements, an entire gravity. But the regime of the **war machine** is on the contrary that of **affects**, which relate only to the moving body in itself, to speeds and compositions of speed among elements. **Affect** is the active discharge of emotion, the counterattack, whereas feeling is an always displaced, retarded, resisting emotion. [TP 441, 400]

5.a (Special Combination): *Affection-Image*: In Deleuze's analysis of the sensory-motor interval of the **movement-image**, that which occupies the gap between stimulus and response, **perception** and action.

> the interval is not merely defined by the specialization of the two limit-facets, perceptive and active. There is an in-between. **Affection** is what occupies the interval, what occupies it without filling it in or filling it up. It surges in the centre of indetermination, that is to say in the **subject**, between a **perception** which is troubling in certain respects and a hesitant action. [C1 67, 65]

b. The quality and power that is actualized or **expressed** through affection-images and by **action-images**, and cannot change in power (be 'divided') without changing in quality; in Deleuze's cinematic schema, the *dividual*.

> *In a state of things which actualizes them the quality becomes the 'quale' of an object, power becomes action or passion,* **affect** *becomes* **sensation**, *sentiment, emotion or even impulse [pulsion] in a person, the face becomes the character or mask of the person [...].* [C1 100, 97]

> *The* **affect** *is impersonal and is distinct from every individuated state of things [...]. The* **affect** *is indivisible and without parts; but the singular combinations that it forms with other* **affects** *form in turn an indivisible quality, which will only be divided by changing qualitatively (the* **'dividual'***)*. [C1 101, 98–99]

c. The **expression** of a quality and power in a face or contour which is detached from its context by virtue of an **any-space-whatever**, such that the affection can apply to all possible contexts or circumstances (a **virtual** affection); in Deleuze's cinematic schema, the *Qualisign*.

> *as soon as we leave the face and the close-up, as soon as we consider complex shots which go beyond the simplistic distinction between close-up, medium shot and long shot, we seem to enter a 'system of emotions' which is much more subtle and differentiated, less easy to identify, capable of inducing non-human* **affects**. [C1 113, 110]

d. The **expression** of a quality and power in a face or contour that resembles a face in a close up, which is linked through montage to a spatio-temporal context; in Deleuze's cinematic schema, the *Icon*.

> *What expresses [the* **affect***] is a face, or a facial equivalent (a faceified object) or, as we will see later, even a* **proposition**. *We call the set of the expressed and its* **expression**, *of the* **affect** *and the face,* 'icon'. [C1 99, 97]

- E. B. Y.

Affection-image

cross-reference: **Affect** (def. 5.a.)

Aion

(also '*Aeon*')

1.a. A recurring, yet unlimited, form of time where the past and future relate to an **event** which can be discerned only by virtue of incorporeal effects that are indefinitely divisible between anterior and posterior states, in distinction from **Chronos**, which is a single, infinitely cyclical, form of time.

> But being an empty and unfolded form of time, the **Aion** subdivides ad infinitum that which haunts it without ever inhabiting it —the **Event** for all **events**. [LS 75, 64]

b. A musical measurement of time which continually modifies speeds, rather than a measurement that engenders a 'pulsed' or metered time; a type of **rhythm**.

> **Aeon**: *the indefinite time of the* **event**, *the floating line that knows only speeds and continually divides that which transpires into an already-there that is at the same time not-yet-there.* [TP 289, 262]

- E. B. Y.

Les Années d'hiver: 1980–1985

Published in French in 1986, this collection features short articles from newspapers and magazines along with conference papers and interviews, including commentaries in major mainstream publications like *Le Monde*, *Libération*, and *Le Nouvel Observateur*. Topics include French politics, racism, the third world, psychoanalysis, neoliberalism, art, literature, and the mass media. In his preface, Guattari explains that his title refers to the period of disillusionment that followed the abandonment of the post-1968 radical movements of the 1970s, as well as the disappointment with François Mitterand's government, which, he implies, manifests the general failure of French socialism to reform a developed capitalist society when it had the rare chance to do so. His essays demonstrate that he stands behind his own positions of the 1970s in calling for the liberation of **desire**, the struggles of minoritarian **groups**, and the ushering in of a **post-media era** which would loosen the mass media's control of the new technologies of communication and information. Some of the chapters have been translated into English and appear in *The Guattari Reader*, *Soft Subversions*, and *Chaosophy*. - J. W.

Any space whatever

(*espace quelconque*)

1. In Deleuze's analysis of the **movement-image**, a term which he borrows from Pascal Augé, which is defined in terms of the genetical component of the **affect** that occupies the space between **perception** and action; a **virtual** space that is detached from a specific temporal sequence, applicable to any or all possible sequences.

> Any-space-whatever *is not an abstract universal, in all times, in all places. It is a perfectly singular space, which has merely lost its homogeneity, [...] so that the linkages can be made in an infinite number of ways. It is a space of* virtual *conjunction, grasped as pure locus of the possible.* [C1 113, 109]

- E. B. Y.

Anti-Oedipus

L'Anti-Œdipe. Capitalisme et schizophrénie, avec Félix Guattari (1973)

Following their initial encounter after the events of May 1968, Deleuze and Guattari begin working on the first volume of their

Capitalism and Schizophrenia project in earnest through a regular exchange of letters, drafts, and meetings. Rooted in the flurry of social desires that sprang from the student movements, as well as in the charges of failure and catastrophe that followed in their wake, *Anti-Oedipus* is very much a manifesto of revolutionary striving, and Deleuze himself later commented that it was written for an audience between the ages of fourteen and twenty-one. Nevertheless, the book is also a systematic analysis of **desire** and contains both a critique of the psychoanalytic **concept** of the **unconscious** and of the social and political institutions that belong to contemporary bourgeois society. According to the major thesis put forward in this work, the unconscious is neither a theater for the figural representation of individual and social phantasy, nor a projection of the family onto the psychology of individuals, but rather a factory. Thus, the concept of the unconscious is defined, against psychoanalytic and structuralist interpretations alike, in productive and primarily 'machinic' terms. It is in this sense that the phrase '**desiring-machine**' is deployed, from the very first chapter, as a liberating and potentially revolutionary manner of producing the unconscious socially, politically, and culturally as a positive **force** of liberation from the repressive signifying regimes of Oedipus and the family, which first of all trap desire and cause its **expression** to be blocked by signifying regimes that convert it into individual **expressions** of phantasy with no collective meaning. (Hence, one of the key verbs employed throughout is *rabattement*, which means 'to reduce' or to 'pull down,' and bears a comical allusion to having the wool pulled down over one's own eyes.) Consequently, there is also an implicit synthesis between the concepts of psychoanalysis and those of **Marx**ism, particularly from the *Grundrisse*, as well as concepts drawn from the cultural anthropology of Pierre Clastres. This is particularly evident in the third chapter, 'Barbarians, Savages, and Civilized Men,' which presents a uniquely new version of 'Universal History,' or the 'History of Capitalist Societies,' from the perspective of an immanent critique of Oedipus in order, as they claim, 'to overturn the theater of representation into the order of [real] desiring-production' (AO 294, 271). The conclusion contains an introduction to the method of '**schizoanalysis**,' a term coined by Guattari as an antidote to the familialism inherent in **Freud**ian psychoanalysis and the Lacanian School. According to the major thesis, desire is machinic and the analysis of desire follows from this simple premise in treating any of its various expressions with a view to 'how it works' (rather than 'what it means'). The objective of a schizoanalysis is to show, in each case or in each social formation, how desire is either organized according to a paranoiac and repressive pole or a revolutionary and potentially schizoid pole of unconscious investment; or, in all cases, that desiring-production is always equal to real social-production. - G. L.

The Anti-Oedipus Papers

Cobbled together by editor Stéphane Nadaud from archival materials and assembled around the process of composing *The Anti-Oedipus* with Deleuze. These disparate writings include: annotated notes and clarifications written by Guattari to Deleuze and then corrected and revised; reminders to himself; autobiographical and theoretical journal entries (1971–2); a glossary of **concepts**. Meta-comments on letters between Guattari and Deleuze as well as the former's entreaties to the latter and his partner Fanny appear throughout. These papers provide some insights into how Guattari and Deleuze worked together and lay bare some of the conceptual challenges faced by the authors in fine-tuning their investigations: how to read **Marx**ism unconventionally by focusing on its conceptualization of capitalism; how to extract from psychoanalysis schizoanalytic principles; how to be done with representational semiotics. Guattari's conceptual and practical struggles are front and center: **Foucault**'s *Archaeology of Knowledge* is hard to get through; the concepts of his analyst Lacan play a dominant role and are repeatedly challenged; **Freud**'s sweeping pronouncements about Oedipus are wrestled with; the search for a better semiotics than that of linguistic **structuralism** bears fruit (strong identification with **Hjelmslev**). Diverse theoretical skirmishes are punctuated by practical examples from Guattari's practice at La Borde and criticisms of bad psychoanalytic clinical **habits**. Guattari often responds to Deleuze's requests for clarification with intense explanations marked by exclamations, name-calling, and asides. Brief characterizations of how Guattari approached concepts punctuate explanations, surf their crests, and make messy outlines. Guattari's journal entries provide insight into his self-analysis and how he thought about his relationship with Deleuze. - G. G.

Aristotle

Deleuze's most substantial engagement with Aristotle occurs when tracing the history of the subordination of **difference** to representation (in the opening of the chapter 'Difference In Itself' in *Difference and Repetition*): his concern with Aristotle's 'categories' involves the manner in which **difference** becomes both a matter of contrariety and analogy. He claims that with both contrariety and analogy, the non-representative nature of real difference is lost: in Aristotle's philosophy, on the one hand, all specific differences are subordinated to the identity of the generic categories (or 'genera') to which they belong, taking the form of contrariety, while, on the other hand, those generic categories are 'undetermined' such that they can only be related to each other through analogy.

Since Aristotle's 'generic' categories aren't determined by anything else, the categories (and all the specific **differences** within them) are only distinguishable and distributable according to what Deleuze calls **good sense** and **common sense**. 'Generic' here retains not only the technical sense of genus, but also contains the pejorative sense of the unexceptional and everyday: if you don't know what 'everybody knows', or don't wish to conform to the customary judgment and image of thought (which depends on a 'transcendental operation' of the **faculties**), you cannot ascertain the generic/analogous differences between categories to begin with, nor can you grasp the specific differences/contrarieties within them. Deleuze calls this a model of 'organic' representation because the specific difference it represents is 'maximal or perfect': a thing is represented 'organically' in the sense of being connected or coordinated with other parts of its genus (through contrariety). It thereby takes the 'finite as its element' unlike the 'orgiastic' representation of difference with **Hegel** and **Leibniz**, which take the 'infinite as its element'.

The Aristotelian dialectic, in this sense, is confined to ascertaining **differences** or *problems* in the form of **propositions** which pass categorical tests; as Deleuze states, 'in order to judge a problem, Aristotle invites us to consider "the opinions accepted by all men or by the majority among them, or by the wise" in order to relate these to general (predicable) points of view, [...] every problem the corresponding proposition of which contains a logical fault in regard to accident, genus, property or definition will be considered a false proposition' (DR 199, 160). - E. B. Y.

Artaud, Antonin

While Artaud, of course, was the inspiration for D&G's well-known concept of the **body without organs**, as well as many of their discussions of **schizophrenia**, Deleuze devotes a conspicuous discussion of **depth** and **affect** to Artaud in *The Logic of Sense*. It is conspicuous, because, while **Carroll** is hailed as the 'master and the surveyor of **surfaces**' which is where 'the entire logic of sense is located', Artaud 'is alone in having been an absolute depth in literature', which is conveyed through a language of suffering (LS 105, 93). He claims that for Artaud's schizophrenic, 'it is less a question of recovering meaning than of destroying the word, of conjuring up the affect, and of transforming the painful passion of the body into a triumphant action, obedience into command, always in this depth beneath the fissured surface' (LS 100, 88). From this perspective, of course, Deleuze notes that he can see why Carroll's work would seem to Artaud to be superficial.

Despite Artaud's intensive focus on '**depth**' and disregard of the **surface**, Deleuze insists that 'Artaud pursues in all this the terrible revelation of a thought without image', that is, where 'schizophrenia is not only a human fact but also a possibility for thought' (DR 185, 148). This is truly a 'theater of cruelty', in which he notes that 'In this collapse of the surface, the entire world loses its meaning. [...] Every **event** is realized, be it in a hallucinatory form. Every word is physical, and immediately **affects** the body' (LS 100, 87). Likewise, with Guattari, he emphasizes that 'making yourself' a **Body without Organs** cannot 'avoid hallucinations, erroneous **perceptions**, shameless phantasies, or bad feelings' (TP 314, 285), because you have an affected body without anything to attribute the **affects** *to*, which makes the 'false' sometimes gain its own menacing traction. - E. B. Y.

Assemblage

(Fr: *Agencement*)

By the mid-1960s Guattari had developed a conception of **group** fantasies applicable to political vanguards and psychiatric institutions. Yet he found the psycho-sociological construction of the 'group' to be too positivistic, individual-centric, and its apprehension overly dependent upon utterances and blind to imaginaries and **desires** struggling to connect with history. However, by the late 1970s he abandoned the group for the more abstract 'assemblage' (sometimes translated as 'arrangement') in order to avoid the confusing distinction between groups and individuals, so as to add non-human, machinic elements into the collective mix. A highly technical description is developed in *The Machinic Unconscious* based on nuclei and different types of consistencies, and a variation of this emerged in *A Thousand Plateaus*, focusing on **territoriality** and the lines that open it; yet both semiotic and geological settings share two features: machinic characteristics and enunciative power. By the time of *Chaosmosis*, the **concept** includes a chaotic dimension of infinite speeds within the analysis of the four ontological matrices that re-engages the relations between **virtual** and **actual** functions. A further constant is the underlying articulations of two registers: **expression** and content. Note that this entry is divided between definitions that stem from Guattari's work, definitions that stem from Guattari's work with Deleuze (beginning with def. 3), and Deleuze's own use in his work on **Foucault** (def. 6).

> 1.a. In Guattari's explanation of **group** phantasy and **desire**, a collection of heterogeneous (mixed) components from which subjectifications are created, that engage in a variety of semiotic and machinic processes of enunciation; enunciative components that are collective and neither human nor molar essences.
>
> > Here we shall speak of collective **assemblages** *of enunciation even if only one individual expresses himself, because he or she will be considered a non-totalizable* intensive multiplicity. [MU 55]
> >
> > **Assemblages** *may involve individuals, but also functions, machines, diverse semiotic systems. It is only by taking desiring machines all*

the way back to the molecular order —that is, to a point prior to the group *and the individual [...] – that we will succeed in misarticulating mass-produced institutional structures, and in giving marginal positions of* desire *the possibility of freeing themselves from neurotic impasses.* [GR 154–5]

There are only **multiplicities** *of multiplicities forming a single* **assemblage**, *operating in the same* **assemblage**: *packs in masses and masses in packs.* [TP 38, 34]

b. Interacting pragmatic fields (for generative and transformative **schizoanalyses**) that display a nucleus or nuclei where consistencies (molar, molecular and abstract) interact, both strongly and weakly with different semiotic components and enunciative foci, while still holding machinic 'potential' in reserve.

An **assemblage** *draws its greater or lesser degree of freedom from the formula of its machinic nucleus, but this formula is metastable. As such, the* **abstract machines** *that compose it do not have any 'real' existential consistency; they do not have any 'mass', their own 'energy', or memory. They are only infinitesimal indications hyper-***deterritorialized** *from crystallizations of a possible between states of affairs and states of* **signs**. [MU 47]

c. (Special Type): *Components of passage*: That which permits intra- and inter-assemblage **transversal** relations to take place by performing various tasks, such as modulating consistency and articulating the modalities by which **abstract machines** are outputted, with relative degrees of **deterritorialization,** and in support of the potentialities of concrete machines; inter-assemblages remain open to new components of mutation and improvisation despite the tendency to harden them (i.e. biologically).

Components of passage *cannot be simple effects of transition, simple statistical reversals bearing upon molecular populations. They are the bearers of* **diagrammatic** *keys concealed by the abstract consistency of machinic nuclei. It is through these components of passage that possible worlds and real worlds clash and proliferate.* [MU 147]

2. The object of scrutiny of the **schizoanalyst,** who examines its components in order to assist in the integration and/or escape

of **desire**; that which is clogged by redundancies, disempowering and/or liberating **black holes, resonance** effects and molar formations.

> We will be particularly concerned with locating the different types of 'assembling' that enable a component to pass to the rank of component of passage. [MU 188]

3.a. In Guattari's work with Deleuze, the arrangement or disposition of **milieu** components toward a function that is external to that milieu, initially as a function of the **territory** (or ultimately as a **deterritorialized** function of the cosmos).

> The **territory** is the first **assemblage**, the first thing to constitute an assemblage [...] [TP 356, 323]

b. (Special Type): *deterritorialized assemblage*: In D&G's mechanosphere (a cosmology that combines **vitalism** and machines), concrete arrangements of **milieu** components which release themselves when they no longer function for the **territory**, but instead become integrated, working parts of an **abstract machine** (which is passing through or cutting into the territory), or of other assemblages (in distinction from milieu components which remain part of territorial assemblages, or machines that are *too* abstract or 'reified').

> in many cases, a **territorialized**, assembled *function acquires enough independence to constitute a new* **assemblage**, *one that is more or less deterritorialized, en route to* **deterritorialization** [TP 357, 324]

c. In D&G's reading of **Kafka** and their explanation of the **line of flight** of desire, the proper object of **deterritorialization** by an **abstract machine** that has no reality (being abstract) except for its capacity or power to undergo deterritorialization. [K, TP]

4. In D&G's theory of **signs**, that which simultaneously produces corporeal mixtures and incorporeal **forms of content** and **expression** (on a horizontal axis) according to the arrangement of bodies, collective enunciations, and/or **milieus**, and which may be more or less (de)**territorialized** (on a vertical axis) according to biological, social, historical, or political circumstances.

On a first, horizontal, axis, an assemblage *comprises two segments, one of content, the* other *of* expression. *On the one hand it is a machinic* assemblage *of bodies, of actions and passions, an intermingling of bodies reacting to one another; on the other hand it is a collective* assemblage *of enunciation, of acts and statements, of incorporeal transformations attributed to bodies. Then on a vertical axis, the* assemblage *has both* territorial *sides, or* reterritorialized *sides, which stabilize it, and cutting edges of* deterritorialization, *which carry it away* [TP 97–8, 88]

5. Deleuze's version of **Foucault**'s *dispostif*, which both organizes the visible and articulable, and is **diagramed** by power relations. [F]

knowledge is a practical assemblage, *a 'dispostif' of statements and visibilities.* [F 44, 51, translation modified]

6. In D&G's explanation of philosophy, the **concept** which occupies (or **territorializes**) the **plane of consistency** (in concrete assemblages) by means of variation.

Concepts *are concrete* assemblages, *like the configurations of a machine, but the plane is the* abstract machine *of which these* assemblages *are the working parts.* [WP 36]

- G. G. (intro, 1 & 2) and E. B. Y. (3–6)

Attribute

1. In **Spinoza**, an infinite essence of substance (*thought* and *extension* being those we can know), which is conceived through itself (in distinction from **modes**, which are conceived through something else).

By attribute, *I mean that which the intellect perceives as constituting the essence of substance.* [Spinoza (*Ethics*, I, Def. 4) 2000, 75]

2. In Deleuze's reading of **Spinoza**, a qualitative **multiplicity** of thought or extension which is infinite in principle, and, insofar as it is explicated by **modal** essences, exists in parallel with its counterpart by expressing the same **univocal** substance (and can be distinguished from its counterpart only *quantitatively*); that

which constitutes an eternal causal chain (whether in thought or extension) and is implicated in the effects or modes (as a modification of thought or of extension). [SEP, SPP]

> There is one substance per **attribute** *from the viewpoint of quality, but one single substance for all* **attributes** *from the viewpoint of quantity. What is the sense of this purely qualitative* **multiplicity**? *The obscure formulation [...] is justified by the new status of real distinction. It means: substances as qualified are qualitatively, but not quantitatively, distinct* [SEP 37]

- E. B. Y.

Autopoiesis

According to Guattari, **machines** and **assemblages** are made up of organic, inorganic, technological, and semiotic components. Even though they are not organic living entities, assemblages are endowed with enough **subjectivity** to react to their environments. *Autopoiesis* refers to their life-like ability to self-regulate, self-perpetuate, and reproduce. The term is introduced in *Chaosmosis*.

1. Term borrowed from the biology of **Humberto Maturana** and **Francesco Varela**, for whom it designates a **life** form's ability to produce and maintain its own existence.

> *Since the relations of production of components are given only as processes, if the processes stop the relations of production vanish; as a result, for a machine to be* **autopoeitic***, its defining relations of production must be continuously regenerated by the components which they produce.* [Varela, 1979, 13]

2. Guattari's extension of **Maturana** and **Varela**'s theory beyond living systems to include all types of Deleuzo-Guattarian **machines**—social, economic, linguistic, aesthetic.

> Autopoietic machines *undertake an incessant process of the replacement of their components as they must continually compensate for the external perturbations to which they are exposed.* [CM 39]

3. An ontology of complexity offered as a corrective to **structuralist** theory.

> *It's from a failure to see that machinic segments are* **autopoietic** *and ontogenetic that one endlessly makes universalist reductions to the Signifier and to scientific rationality.* [CM 30]

4. A political strategy of psychic and social autonomization, especially of **subjectivity**.

> *The important thing is not the final result but the fact that the multicomponential cartographic method can coexist with the process of subjectivation, and that a reappropriation, an* **autopoiesis**, *of the means of production of subjectivity can be made possible.* [CM 13]

- J. W.

Bateson, Gregory

References to Bateson appear throughout Guattari's solo writing as well as in his work with Deleuze. A controversial and interdisciplinary thinker, Bateson trained, researched, and wrote in the fields of anthropology, psychiatry, biological evolution, animal studies, cybernetics, and systems theory. He conducted field research and laboratory experiments, in conjunction with his original theoretical work. His book *Steps to an Ecology of Mind* was particularly important to Guattari, who shared a similar range of interests even if he often differed in approach. Earlier in his career, Guattari took issue with Bateson and his colleagues for their behaviorist and objectivist methodology, complaining that they reduced behavior to a **flux** of information and were just as reliant on the signifier as the structuralists (MR 88–90). In *Capitalism and Schizophrenia* Deleuze and Guattari take issue with Bateson's theory that schizophrenia may result from the double bind—the sending of contradictory messages which creates a no-win situation for the interlocutor, as when a parent signals love me but don't love me. For Deleuze and Guattari, the double bind describes the Oedipus complex, not schizophrenia, which for them is characterized by the refusal of any Oedipal relation (AO 79–80, 360). However, they embrace Bateson's idea of the plateau of **intensity**, a continuous state of excitation that is not orientated toward climax, which is how they define the plateaus that make up **rhizomes** and **assemblages** (TP 21–2, 158). Later, Guattari borrows Bateson's notion of the ecology of mind to describe the interdependence between humans and their environment, an idea which he incorporates into his own notion of **ecosophy** (*Chaosmosis, The Three Ecologies*). The frequency with which he is cited and the variety of contexts in which he appears show the extent of Bateson's influence, despite the sometimes critical tone of Deleuze and Guattari's discussions of him. - J. W.

Becoming

(Fr: *Devenir*)

Contending with the nature of change, or novelty, is paradoxical, but essential, Deleuze would argue, for an affirmative existence. On the one hand, change is not something that we can foresee or predict (utilizing our **good sense**), because if it were predicable, it would not be new. On the other hand, it is not something that we can *recognize* (utilizing our **common sense**), because, likewise, if it presented itself in a *familiar* form, it also would be determined in advance, and thus would not be new.

Taking inspiration from **Nietzsche**, 'becoming' is 1) unlimited and unending, as it has no true point of origin or destination (the world is always in '**flux**'), and 2) insofar as the past is itself considered *infinite*, the present counter-intuitively always occurs as the 'return' of recognizable and even foreseeable forms, but is irreducible to such forms precisely because becoming can never be 'given': it is, as Deleuze shows, always in between the past and future since 'it moves in both directions at once' and 'always eludes the present' (LS 3, 2). In this sense, becoming is not perceptible because its onset coincides with its *immediate* disappearance. Grasping this **paradox** is crucial for understanding why, on the one hand, Nietzschean **morality** affirms 'being' according to 'action' (and denies non-being according to its reaction and absence of becoming), and, on the other hand, when discussing the various types of 'becomings' with Guattari (**becoming-animal**, etc.), the nature of the *process* itself is emphasized rather than 'cause' and especially rather than 'result' (since this focuses on the past and future, which are merely reflections of one another in terms of the 'becoming' which they indicate).

1. The central tenet of **Nietzsche**'s cosmological theory of existence, appropriated from the ancient philosopher Heraclitus, that (in Nietzsche's version) asserts continual process and denies religious (messianic and eschatological) and scientific (mechanic and thermodynamic) theories of existence which presume that, in one form or another, being may have a final state. Consequently, there is no vantage point from which to judge such existence: it is never blameworthy but is innocent, despite the shortcomings and atrocities of humanity as well as the violence and severity of nature.

> *Straight at that mystic night in which was shrouded Anaximander's problem of* **becoming**, *walked Heraclitus of Ephesus and illuminated it by a divine stroke of lightning. '* **'Becoming'** *is what I contemplate,' he exclaims [....] He no longer distinguished a physical world from a metaphysical one, a realm of definite qualities from an undefinable 'indefinite.' And after this first step, nothing could hold him back from a second, far bolder negation: he altogether denied being. [...] Heraclitus proclaimed: 'I see nothing other than* **becoming**. *[...] You use names for things as though they rigidly, persistently endured; yet even the stream into which you step a second time is not the one you stepped into before.'* [Nietzsche, 1998, 50–2]

> *If the world had a goal, it must have been reached. If there were for it some unintended final state, this also must have been reached. If [...] in the whole course of its* **becoming** *it possessed even for a moment this capability of 'being,' then all* **becoming** *would long since have come to an end [...].* [Nietzsche (*Will to Power* #1062), 1968, 546]

2.a. In Deleuze's reading of **Nietzsche,** the form of **repetition** or state of being in **eternal return,** where being is never fixed (even when it appears to be so); any 'sameness' and 'similarity' (or link between cause and effect) is actually indicative of a *continual* process of change without an origin or destination.

> *What is the being inseparable from that which is* **becoming?** *Return is the being of that which* **becomes.** *Return is the being of* **becoming**

itself, the being which is affirmed in becoming. The **eternal return** as law of becoming, as justice and as being. [N 23, 24]

> past time being infinite, becoming would have attained its final state if it had one. And, indeed, saying that becoming would have attained its final state if it had one is the same as saying that it would not have left its initial state if it had one. [N 44, 47]

b. (Special Combination): becoming-*active*: The *being* of **force** only insofar as force is active (destruction or self-destruction), in distinction from becoming-*reactive*, where forced is turned against itself and nullified, resulting in nihilism (*non-being* of the negative).

> [...] becoming *is double*: [...] becoming-*active of reactive* forces *and* becoming *reactive of active forces*. *But only* becoming-*active has being; it would be contradictory for the being of* becoming *to be affirmed of a* becoming-*reactive, of a* becoming *that is itself nihilistic.* [...] becoming-*reactive has no being.* [N 66, 71–2]

3. In Deleuze's reading of **events** in **Carroll**'s Alice books, that which constitutes the eternal time of the event, and, in accordance with **Stoic** logic, is reversible insofar as it is considered in itself; that which does not regress toward an earlier state or progress towards a final state.

> *pure* becoming [...] *is the* **paradox** *of infinite identity (the infinite identity of both directions or senses at the same time—of future and past, of the day before and the day after, of more and less, of too much and not enough, of active and passive, and of cause and effect).* [...] *Hence the reversals which constitute Alice's adventures: the reversal of* becoming *larger and* becoming *smaller*. [LS 4, 2–3]

4. In Deleuze's perspective on history, political and social change which is, paradoxically, anachronistic; that is, it can only be recognized as novel retrospectively and in its process lacks progressive appearances or indications. [DR, NG]

> **Becoming** *isn't part of history; history indicates only the set of preconditions, however recent, that one leaves behind in order to* 'become,' *that is, to create something new. This is precisely what* **Nietzsche** *calls the Untimely*. [NG 171, translation modified]

- E. B. Y.

Becoming-animal

It is always comical to imagine an animal on a psychoanalyst's couch, and this concept serves as a great complement to the concept of (de)**territorialization** which does not focus on our refined, human sensibilities, and resists **Freud**ian notions of interiority and phantasy which would motivate our behavior. The reason why this concept is coined in terms of '**becoming**' (and not just as *being* or 'animalism'), is to emphasize that the division between human and animal is not black and white; rather, the **difference** concerns states of **desire** which are always in development or a process (rather than a point that is reached); the division is defined by our **affections** and our actions (influenced by **Spinoza's modes**), and not some transcendental criterion. As Deleuze states, 'There is no terminus from which you set out, none which you arrive at or which you ought to arrive at. […] The question "What are you becoming?" is particularly stupid' (D 2). Many of the specific becomings (**becoming-woman, becoming-imperceptible**, etc.) also move away from the self-centeredness of being 'too human', as **Nietzsche** may say, especially when considering the normalcy and exclusions imposed by majority **groups**.

> 1.a. A continual process by which a subject acquires a filiative relationship by contagion with a **multiplicity,** which has anomalous features based on the **milieu** and **affective** manner of (de)**territorialization** undergone (in distinction from characteristics of 'real' animals). [TP]
>
>> *The pack is simultaneously an animal reality, and the reality of the* **becoming-animal** *of the human being; contagion is simultaneously an animal peopling, and the propagation of the animal peopling of the human being.* [TP 267, 242]
>>
>> **Animal** *characteristics can be mythic or scientific. But we are not interested in characteristics; what interests us are* **modes** *of expansion, propagation, occupation, contagion, peopling.* [TP 264, 239]
>
> b. The process by which the body enters into relations of motion and rest, or experiences **affects**, which are already contained within human potential, that correspond to or function as those

of particular animals (on a molecular level), in distinction from *imitating* the features of animals in the **imagination** (on a molar level). [D, TP]

> **Becomings-animal** *are neither dreams nor phantasies. They are perfectly real. But which reality is at issue here?* For if **becoming-animal** *does not consist in playing animal or imitating an animal, it is clear that the human being does not 'really' become an animal any more than the animal 'really' becomes something else.* [...] *The* **becoming-animal** *of the human being is real, even if the animal the human being becomes is not* [...].[TP 262, 238]

> *you* **become-animal** *only if, by whatever means or elements, you emit corpuscles that enter the relation of movement and rest of the animal particles* [...]. *Man does not become wolf, or vampire, as if he changed molar species; the vampire and werewolf are* **becomings** *of man, in other words, proximities between molecules in composition, relations of movement and rest, speed and slowness between emitted particles.* [TP 303, 274–5]

2. In D&G's reading of **Kafka**, a process by which the protagonists of many of his short stories initially liberates **desire** from its abstraction or **territorialization**, but ultimately fails because such desire is not reintegrated within social and political **assemblages** (desire is instead **reterritorialized**.)

> *It is true that the* **becoming-animal** *was already digging a way out, but the* **becoming-animal** *was incapable of going wholeheartedly into it.* [...]. *It allowed itself then to be recaptured, reterritorialized, retriangulated.* [K 59]

- E. B. Y.

Becoming-imperceptible

1. To enter into a state of movement that eludes any **perception** (whether actual, photographic, or cinematic), such that perception is no longer centered around subjects and objects, but the **durations** or passages between them. [D, TP]

> *The* **imperceptible** *is the* **immanent** *end of* **becoming**, *its cosmic formula.* [...] *one makes a world that can overlay the first one, like a*

transparency. Animal elegance, the camouflage fish, the clandestine: this fish is crisscrossed by abstract lines that resemble nothing, that do not even follow its organic divisions; but thus disorganized, disarticulated, it worlds with the lines of a rock, sand, and plants, becoming imperceptible. [TP 308, 280]

2. The proper object of study of pharmaco-analysis.

It is our belief that the issue of drugs can be understood only at the level where desire *directly invests* perception, *and perception becomes molecular at the same time as the* imperceptible *is perceived. Drugs then appear as the agent of this* becoming. [TP 313, 283]

- E. B. Y.

Becoming-intense

1. The aspect of all **becomings** involving the role of the **affect**, when the features of the becoming concern **intensities** or **sensations** rather than resemblances or imitations (animal, molecule, woman, etc.). [K, TP]

> Becoming *is never imitating. When Hitchcock does birds, he does not reproduce bird calls, he produces an electronic sound like a field of* intensities *or a wave of vibrations, a continuous variation, like a terrible threat welling up inside us.* [TP 336, 305]

- E. B. Y.

Becoming-woman

1. The resistance to the molar form of 'woman' determined by the majority ('men'); the molecular sexuality in all genders (and ages, ethnicities, etc.) which can be identified with the ahistorical, apolitical little girl who has no identity (neither woman, man, nor even child) or predetermined sexual orientation. [D, TP]

> *The girl's* becoming *is stolen first, in order to impose a history, or prehistory, upon her. [...] The girl is certainly not defined by virginity [...] She is an abstract line, or a* line of flight. *Thus girls do not belong to an age group, sex, order, or kingdom: they slip in*

> everywhere, between orders, acts, ages, sexes [...] It is not the girl who becomes a woman; it is becoming-woman that produces the universal girl. [TP 305, 276–7]
>
> Sexuality is the production of a thousand sexes, which are so many uncontrollable becomings. Sexuality proceeds by way of the becoming-woman of the man and the becoming-animal of the human: an emission of particles. [TP 307, 278–9]

- E. B. Y.

Bergson, Henri

While Bergson was an influential and renowned philosopher during his lifetime, especially before World War I, there was an abrupt and widespread disavowal of his work in the 1940s, after his death. Deleuze, ignoring this trend, devoted a book-length study to Bergson's philosophy, which appeared in 1966 (two other early essays, originally appearing in 1956, have been translated into English), and is arguably responsible for re-introducing and revitalizing Bergson's work. Bergson is later utilized at an important juncture in the first half of the chapter on 'Repetition for Itself' in *Difference and Repetition* to explain, on the one hand (alongside Hume), how the present in time is constituted by contractions *in* the mind (that are not reflections but durations), and, on the other hand (alongside Proust), how contraction can function in relation to the past as a whole, where the present is 'telescoped' within an immemorial past (or virtuality) with which it coexists. Thus the very tension that exists between the successive or linear time constituted by the present (duration) and the non-chronological time that envelops or implicates it, which was criticized as being mythical or indeterminate, is precisely what draws Deleuze to Bergson's work. This is because it demonstrates a way of thinking about time and change that does not subordinate it to arbitrary, abstract, and external reference points that would determine what we are (or were, or will be); as he states,

> Bergsonism has often been reduced to the following idea: duration is subjective, and constitutes our internal life. [...] But, [...] the only subjectivity is time, non-chronological time grasped

in its foundation, and it is we who are internal to time, not the other way round. That we are in time looks like a commonplace, yet it is the highest **paradox**. Time is not the interior in us, but just the opposite, the interiority in which we are, in which we move, live and change. (C2, 80, 82)

Deleuze utilizes this distinction in his later work on cinema to explore the **difference** between *movement* and *time*, and though he finds limitations in Bergson's system (see *Bergsonism*), many of his **concepts** are inspired by his work. - E. B. Y.

Bergsonism

Deleuze's work on **Bergson** resonates strongly but elusively with *Difference and Repetition* (to the extent that the reader may find whole sentences from *Bergsonism* repeated in *Difference and Repetition*, especially in chapters II and V, with only minor revisions), as well as, to a lesser but no less relevant extent, with the *Cinema* books (**perception-images**, movement), *The Logic of Sense* (sterile division), and *Francis Bacon: The Logic of Sensation* (contraction-dilation). The challenge to reading *Bergsonism* is to understand that throughout the first two chapters, Deleuze is speaking in well-known Bergsonian dualisms (e.g. **matter**—memory, **perception-images**—**recollection-images**, **differences** in kind—differences of degree), and will not begin to show the interpenetration or dynamics of the terms until chapters three and four (in fact, his interest in **Bergson** arguably stems from his **concepts** that are not simple dualisms, like **contraction** and indetermination). Even in doing so, he will reveal these interpenetrations gradually, so that the reader will be forced to constantly re-think, re-read, and refer back to the previous chapters to see how these dualisms are being broken down. It may be useful to skip ahead in order to prevent feeling as though the system has lost all foundation later on.

The reader familiar with *Difference and Repetition* will recognize that Deleuze, while appropriating much of **Bergson**'s terminology (like 'difference in kind'), will ultimately launch a critique against Bergson for not recognizing **intensity** as the feature of **virtuality** which indicates its degree of **difference** (and not difference *of* degree) within the **actuality** that it incarnates. Deleuze in fact gives Bergson the benefit of the doubt in *Bergsonism* much more so than he does in *Difference and Repetition*, noting that Bergson 'recognizes intensities, degrees or vibrations in the qualities that we live' (B 92), despite that he will later state that 'the Bergsonian critique of **intensity** seems unconvincing. It assumes qualities ready-made and extensities already constituted' (DR 299, 239). It is essential to keep this critique of Bergson in mind when noting the conspicuous lack of emphasis on 'intensity' throughout *Bergsonism* despite the lengthy discussion of the relationship between **contraction**, **duration**, and extensity; while extension in **matter** may be purely automatic or physical (where it disappears in appearing), the contraction of that matter is ultimately psychic or spiritual, (preserving the past in the present), but the role of intensity is underemphasized. Deleuze will explore the problem of quantity and quality with regard to extension and intensity again in his work on **Spinoza**, alongside his work on difference and repetition. It is also relevant to note that Deleuze does not invoke the term '**habit**' throughout *Bergsonism*, despite that he takes up a discussion of habit in comparison with **Hume** in chapter II of *Difference and Repetition*; habit in Bergson parallels the motor-memory or motor-schemes of **perception**, which also correspond to the sensory-motor schema of the **movement-image** in the first *Cinema* book (also refer to complete entry on habit for **Bergson**'s sense of the term). - E. B. Y.

Binomial

cross-reference: **Action-Image** (competing **forces**)

Black hole

Guattari was fascinated by theoretical physics, especially its ability to discover particles not yet empirically observed. Black holes, for example, were predicted theoretically before they were detected experimentally. In his conceptualization of the psyche, black holes play a role analogous to Lacan's void or gap. However, a black hole is not empty; rather, it consists of concentrated energy capable not only of swallowing everything in its path but also of emitting particles. A social or psychic black hole can either trap **subjectivity** in its deadly grip or, if navigated successfully, can provide energy and emit semiotic elements which enable liberating **lines of flight**.

1.a. For D&G, a region of cosmic, social, or psychic space which absorbs all particles that come near it. Not a void, but a hyper-concentration of energy. In exceptional circumstances black holes may also emit particles. [RM, MU, TP].

> *There is no doubt that mad physical particles crash through the* **strata** *as they accelerate [...] as they tend toward a state of absolute* **deterritorialization**, *the state of unformed* **matter** *on the* **plane of consistency**. *In a certain sense, the acceleration of relative* **deterritorialization** *reaches the sound barrier: the particles bounce off this wall, or allow themselves to be captured by* **black holes** *[...]* [TP 62, 56]

b. According to D&G's materialist conception of semiology, an abyss into which are fatally pulled various semiotic particles of the psyche, but which also may emit or release new particles hypercharged with energy.

> *It may be necessary for the release of innovative processes that they first fall into a catastrophic* **black hole**: *stases of inhibition are associated with the release of crossroads behaviors.* [TP 368, 334]

2. A center of attraction which draws in the semiotic components which make up **assemblages**. When semiotic formations become centered and are made to communicate through **resonance**, there results an emptying out and impoverishment of **subjectivity**, and the creation of rigid structures such as Oedipal or semiotic triangles, or faciality.

> *This* **black hole** *effect is produced by the node of* **resonance** *that emerges when a point of recentering is constituted between semiological* **redundancies**. *It tends to attract and isolate* **redundancies** *of every nature from their substrate, emptying them of their contents.* [MU 210]

3. For D&G, the mechanism of **subjectivation** which operates within the black hole/white wall system which forms the face: black holes of **subjectivation** pierce the white wall of **significance** [faciality].

> *The face digs the hole that subjectification needs in order to break through; it constitutes the* **black hole** *of subjectivity as consciousness or passion, the camera, the third eye.* [TP 186, 168]

4. In Guattari's reading of **Proust**, a motif or **refrain** which organizes energies and passions, either repressing them or releasing them.

> *The perverse sea of Montjouvain represents the focal point of the Recherche's* **black hole** *of passion. But, as seems evident by now, it is now longer a question of a passive* **black hole**, *associated with a powerless hate [...] nor an empty, inhibitive* **black hole** *[...] The sea of Montjouvain is alive; it is inhabited by representations, characters, matters of* **expression** *conveying quanta of potentialities, emitting* **signs**—*particles capable of interacting with the most diverse semiotic components.* [MU 291]

- J. W.

Blanchot, Maurice

Although Blanchot, a French novelist and philosopher, was born almost twenty years before Deleuze (and began publishing his major works well before Deleuze), he also outlived him, and for all intents and purposes, they were contemporaries. Unlike most other 'post-structuralist' or 'post-modernist' thinkers, Deleuze makes reference to Blanchot at critical junctures throughout most of his works, from *The Logic of Sense* and *Difference and Repetition*, to *The Fold*, *What is Philosophy?*, and the *Cinema* books. Blanchot's approach appeals to Deleuze in general for his uncompromising formulations of the loss of identity (see **counter-actualization**), relations (or 'non-relations') of **force**, and the **eternal return**. He makes great use of his concept of the 'Other Death' (elaborated in Blanchot's *The Space of Literature*) when discussing the **passive synthesis** of memory and **life**, and makes use of his **concept** of the **Outside** to define how the **plane of immanence** is both closer and

further away than the thinkable. Additionally, he incorporates the Outside into his understanding of the cinematic **time-image**, and utilizes it in terms of understanding the *relation* of **forces**, which serves as a fulcrum in his work on **Foucault** when he is trying to analyze a concept of power that does not close in on itself or become an all-inclusive trap that pervades every experience.
- E. B. Y.

Body without Organs; BwO

(Fr: *Corps sans Organes*)

While the question 'What is **life**?' is a cliché of philosophical inquiry, defining the 'body' is an attempt that Deleuze inherits to ascertain what really composes the human being (as well as other bodies, such 'capital' or the earth), which is reducible neither to the variables of science and medicine, nor to the moral judgment of passions and actions. His early work on **Spinoza** foregrounds this, when he showed that bodies cannot be defined in terms of forms, organs, functions, or subjects. Rather, they must be defined *kinetically*, in terms of an infinite number of particles in relations of 'motion and rest', and *dynamically*, in terms of 'the capacity for **affecting** and being affected'—that is, an **intensive** determination (SPP 123-4). Considered apart from unifying and functional 'organs' or 'organization', bodies involve power, **expression**, and endurance; considering the body as an 'organism' in advance, the argument goes, suppresses those very capacities. In fact, Deleuze insists that there is a moral *judgment* tied to being an organism, and not to conform to that is to be less than human (deviant, criminal, etc.).

Deleuze introduced the concept of the Body without Organs (abbreviated as BwO) or the '*glorious* body' in *The Logic of Sense*, in order to distinguish between the metaphysical nature of **surfaces** (which occupy the past and future) and the physical nature of corporeal 'mixtures' (which occupy only the present): on the one hand, surfaces are devoid of **sense** through *fragmentation* and *decomposition* (as in **Carroll**), while from the perspective of **depth** (or the BwO), surfaces are devoid of sense through that which is *unified* and *undecomposable* (as in **Artaud**) but also vital, cruel, and active. In his work with Guattari, Deleuze synthesizes this with the notion of the intensive body in **Spinoza**, as well as with his **Nietzsche**an claim that evolution is not a *reaction* to the environment; according to this claim, 'only the involuted evolves' because the **differences** of **intensity** that are implicated in an egg or embryo contain all the **virtual matter** that undergoes **differenciation** or 'the augmentation of free surfaces, stretching of cellular layers, invagination by folding, regional displacement of **groups**' (DR 266, 215) before it is **actualized**. In short, orientations, axes, speeds and **rhythms** are primary to the organization and structure of any body. In Deleuze's later work on art, he likewise characterizes the BwO in terms of **life** that maintains a relationship with the 'non-organic'. The BwO is similarly characterized as an 'egg' with Guattari in order to emphasize that production in capitalist societies involves an unending *process* of 'recording' and 'repelling production', where organization and structure are, likewise, secondary to a process that is unified by *capital*, which is itself fluid (capital has no permanent qualities) and non-productive (it doesn't actually produce anything), but also is the condition of production (that is, of action, labor, innovation, etc.). While it could be objected that the BwO is simply 'metaphysical' (that is, it doesn't 'exist'), this unified, intensive element is in fact endowed with a purely lived, physical reality, whether considered in terms of Spinoza's immanent (or 'pantheistic') substance, virtual matter or **partial objects** that **differenciate** and dispose the body, or capital that combines with desire. In other words, **intensity**, 'evolution', and even money are not abstract, separate from our actions and **desires**; they *constitute* our desire, as larger bodies, but bodies without predetermined forms, parts, or 'organs'.

> 1.a. A phrase that Antonin **Artaud** uses (only once) at the end of his radio play *To Have Done with the Judgment of God*, where the parts or organs of the body are organized such that they are no longer subjected to a medical determination and theological judgment.
>
>> *When you will have made him a* **body without organs** */ then you will have delivered him from all his automatic reactions / and restored him to his true freedom.* [Artaud, 1976, 571]

b. Also *glorious body*/BwO: In Deleuze's reading of **Artaud**, the body of a schizophrenic that produces **language** with tonic inflections indicative of intense suffering: such language is lived as an extension of the body itself within **depth**.

> *For the schizophrenic, then, it is [...] a question of [...] destroying the word, of conjuring up the* **affect**, *and of transforming the painful passion of the* **body** *into a triumphant action [...]. To these values a glorious body corresponds, being a new dimension of the schizophrenic* **body**, *an organism without parts which operates entirely by insufflation, respiration, evaporation, and fluid transmission (the superior* **body** *or* **body without organs** *of Antonin Artaud)*. [LS 100, 88]

c. In D&G's reading of **Artaud**, and in Deleuze's analysis of art, that which involves the *unending* pushing back of or confrontation with the limit(s) of **subjectivity, stratification**, and the organism; that which unifies fragmented organs or parts of the body to produce an indeterminate organ or unactualized organs, rather than unifying those fragmented parts such that they form an organism with a predetermined function that restricts or limits processes of **desire**; in Deleuze's analysis of art, the result of an experimentation on the body that that undoes the organic association that organs have with one another **other** (physically) or with a function (psychically) to create the condition for new, inorganic physical associations and psychic functions.

> *You never reach the* **Body without organs**, *you can't reach it, you are forever attaining it, it is a limit.* [TP 166, 150]

> *It is not a question of a fragmented, splintered* **body**, *of* **organs** *without the* **body** *(OwB). The* **BwO** *is exactly the opposite. There are not* **organs** *in the sense of fragments in relation to a lost unity, nor is there a return to the undifferentiated in relation to a differentiable totality.* [TP 182, 164–5]

> *The* **body without organs** *does not lack* **organs**, *it simply lacks the organism, that is, the particular organization of the* **organs**. *The* **body without organs** *is thus defined by an indeterminate organ, whereas the organism is defined by determinate* **organs**. [FB 47]

> *[The* **body without organs**] *is a whole non-organic* **life**, *for the organism is not life, it is what imprisons life. The* **body** *is completely living, and yet non-organic.* [FB 45]

2.a. In D&G's analysis of capitalism, a zero-**intensity** that engenders varying degrees of intensity based on attracting and repelling **forces**; a disengaging of the organs from the organism in favor of their indefinite or contingent determination as intensities; an embryological conception of the body which recognizes only dynamic and kinetic (but not formal) **differences**; a synthetic functioning of the organs or parts of a body such that they are appropriated to compose, relay, or direct **flows** (i.e. anything which is in a state of quantitative **flux** but is also ultimately qualitative—capital, labor, information, **matter**) that exceed or **transverse** the body itself; the **desire** of the *social body* which has been **deterritorialized** by capital (rather than **codified** by the primitive machine or overcodified by the despotic machine). [AO, TP, FB]

> *Capitalism tends toward a threshold of decoding that will destroy the socius in order to make it a* **body without organs** *and unleash the* **flows** *of desire on this body as a* **deterritorialized** *field.* [AO 36, 33]

> *[*Intensities*] are all positive in relationship to the zero* intensity *that designates the full* **body without organs**. [AO 20, 19]

> **Organs** *are no longer anything more than* **intensities** *that are produced, flows, thresholds, and gradients. 'A' stomach, 'an' eye, 'a' mouth: the indefinite article [...] expresses the pure determination of* intensity, *intensive* difference. [TP 182, 164]

> *The* **BwO** *is the egg. [...] you always carry it with you as your own* **milieu** *of experimentation, your associated milieu. The egg is the milieu of pure* intensity, *spatium not extension, Zero intensity as principle of production.* [TP 181, 164]

b. In terms of the productive processes of **desire**, the smooth **surface** of an unformed body (whose **partial-objects** or organs are not differentiated) that repels production and instead records production; the condition for a 'miraculating machine' that, by way of recording the desiring process, makes that process appear to originate from it; that which produces the first **passive synthesis** (*disjunctive*) of a both-and-neither ('either... or... or...' rather than either/or) nature that, when conflated with the connective syntheses (and, and, and...) of productive **desiring-machines**, results in conjunctive syntheses and 'consumptions' of a 'celibate machine'. This allows for a distribution (of flows, intensities, etc.) that does not conform to an organic, theological, or even sexual law.

> [T]he **body without organs,** *the unproductive, the unconsumable, serves as a* **surface** *for the recording of the entire process of production of* **desire,** *so that* **desiring-machines** *seem to emanate from it in the apparent objective movement that establishes a relationship between the machines and the* **body without organs** *[...].* *[W]hen the productive connections pass from [desiring] machines to the* **body without organs** *(as from labor to capital), it would seem that they then come under another law that expresses a distribution in relation to the non-productive element.* [AO 12–3, 11–2]

3.a. In distinction from the *psychoanalytic* conception of the body, the disposition, **composition,** or construction of its parts or **partial objects** that, if it doesn't fail, or isn't blocked and poorly constructed, ultimately results in a favorable desiring process; the rejection and endurance (suffering) of partial objects which would fragment it and empty its **depth** (by fixating it in a depressive position that would qualify the object as actually present or absent) in favor of a full depth that is complete (by occupying a schizophrenic position that determines objects as fluid and continuous rather than solid and circulating); a 'death drive' or 'immobile motor' that cannot be separated from the '**life**' or **desire** of its parts.

> *What the schizoid position opposes to bad* **partial objects***—introjected and projected, toxic and excremental, oral and anal—is not a good object, even it if were partial. What is opposed is rather an organism without parts, a* **body without organs,** *with neither mouth nor anus, having given up all introjection or projection, and being complete, at this price.* [LS 216, 188]

> *The* **body without organs** *is the* **matter** *that always fills space to given degrees of* **intensity,** *and the* **partial objects** *are these degrees, these intensive parts that produce the real in space* [AO 359, 326–7]

> *Death is not desired, there is only death that desires, by virtue of the* **body without organs** *or the immobile motor, and there is also* life *that desires, by virtue of the working organs.* [AO 362, 329]

b. (Special Combinations): *Full BwO*: A full, or catatonic BwO, or sometimes simply the BwO, is well constructed and a successful experiment when it is itself anti-productive, inorganic, and sterile, and thus allows **flows** and **intensities** to transverse it without interruption. *Empty BwO*: a poorly constructed BwO, or failed experiment, whose flows or intensities are interrupted, blocked, or **stratified**, and thus do not produce anything. Clinical/catatonic Schizophrenia, hypochondria, paranoia, **masochism**, and drug-induced bodies are results of an empty BwO. *Cancerous BwO*: when the BwO continually depends upon the formation of the organism in order to escape from or push back the limits of the organism. [AO, TP]

> *The* **strata** *spawn their own* **BwOs**, *totalitarian and fascist* **BwOs**, *terrifying caricatures of the* **plane of consistency**. *It is not enough to make a distinction between full* **BwOs** *on the plane of consistency and empty* **BwOs** *on the debris of strata destroyed by a too-violent destratification. We must also take into account cancerous* **BwOs** *in a stratum that has begun to proliferate.* [TP 181, 163]

4. An unformed body, such as the Earth, which constantly eludes **stratification** and **territorialization**; **matter** without a **form of content** or expression; the plane of consistency. [TP]

> *[Professor Challenger] explained that the Earth—the* Deterritorialized, *the Glacial, the giant Molecule—is a* body without organs *[...] permeated by unformed, unstable matters, by* flows *in all directions.* [Hjelmslev] *used the term matter for the* plane of consistency *or* Body without organs *[...]: subatomic particles, pure* intensities, *prevital and prephysical singularities.* [TP 63, 40]

- E. B. Y.

Cahiers de Royaumont: Nietzsche (1966)—published under the direction of Deleuze

A dossier published from the historic colloquy on **Nietzsche** at Royaumont, which took place July 4–8 1964, and was organized and moderated by Martial Gueroult. This gathering was important because it ostensibly confirmed Nietzsche's formal entrance into the curriculum of French academic philosophy and included several notable figures such as Beufret, Deleuze, **Foucault**, **Klossowski**, Lowith, Marcel, Vattimo, Wahl, and others. The published proceedings under the direction of Deleuze are organized into three sections: I. Man and World (or the Nietzschean conception of world); II. Confrontations (where Nietzsche's philosophy is compared to other figures such as **Freud, Marx**, and Dostoyevsky); III. Experiences and **Concepts** (which includes important papers on concepts such as '**value**,' '**Eternal Return**,' and 'Will to Power'). Deleuze contributes the conclusion to the last section on the concepts of will to power and the eternal return. - G. L.

Carroll, Lewis

Deleuze's interest in Lewis Carroll as a dark, thoughtful, and entertaining writer, who used the genre of Children's Literature to express profound philosophical ideas, participated in the interest in Carroll along these lines in the late twentieth and twenty-first centuries. In *The Logic of Sense* he used Carroll as a springboard to discuss **Stoic** philosophy in terms of his readings of **Spinoza** and **Nietzsche**, as well as to continue his polemic against psychoanalysis and representational philosophy (**Plato, Kant**, etc.). Most of all, however, he utilizes Carroll as an occasion for a discussion of philosophies of linguistics and propositional logic which are arguably unmatched throughout the rest of his *oeuvre*, with the possible exception of the creative work on semiotics with Guattari in the Capitalism and Schizophrenia project (especially 'Postulates of Linguistics'). It is also worth noting that Deleuze appreciates Carroll's choice of a little girl narrator in the *Alice* books, which offer a unique perspective where there is constraint from brashly manipulating or even interpreting **events** and instead perceiving the connections between words and things.

Deleuze takes examples from Carroll's work—primarily the *Alice* books, which he regards as superior to the logical works—out of context and imbues them with a significance (which Carroll may or may not have intended) in the context of his philosophical discussions. While Carroll probably intended such instances to be amusing anecdotes that were merely a part of the larger plot of his works, Deleuze takes them as the very object of his inquiry. In this manner, Deleuze distinguishes between Carroll's *logical* works and his '*fantastic*' works (e.g. *Alice in Wonderland, Through the Looking Glass*):

Carroll's entire logical work is directly about **signification**, implications, and conclusions, and only indirectly about **sense**—precisely, through the paradoxes which **signification** does not resolve, or indeed which it creates. On the contrary, the fantastic work is immediately concerned with sense and attaches the power of **paradox** directly to it. [LS 26, 22]

Thus, Carroll's fantastic works make use of logic, but only in order to invert or distort it according to the expression of **non-sense** which occurs in domains where logical **propositions** encounter their own **outside**. It is this use of **paradox** which the fantastic works, brought out through his unique appropriation of the children's genre, that Deleuze feels has important philosophical implications. - E. B. Y.

Cartography

In his final books, Guattari describes **schizoanalysis** in terms of cartography. He found Lacan's topographical models too reductive, and so replaced them with much more complex schemas. He called his mappings of psychic and social entities **schizoanalytic cartography**. Though inspired by the mathematics of cartography, Guattari's version belongs to his **aesthetic paradigm** and makes no claims to scientific or mathematical rigor. The term appears in *A Thousand Plateaus*, but is much further developed in *The Machinic Unconscious*, *Chaosmosis*, and especially *Schizoanalytic Cartographies*.

> 1. a. In **schizoanalysis**, understood as a mapping of the psyche or the socius, the ability of a map (as opposed to a tracing) to create its corresponding **territory**.
>
> *The* **cartography** *of abstract machinisms makes history by dismantling dominant realities and significations [...]* [MU 174]
>
> b. A principle of the **rhizome**, which is understood to be a map (experimentation) and not a tracing (representation).
>
> *Principle of* **cartography** *and decalcomania: a* **rhizome** *is not amenable to any structural or generative model.* [TP 13, 12]

2. Metamodelization.

[...] it is a matter of constituting networks and rhizomes *in order to escape the systems of* modelization *in which we are entangled and which are in the process of completely polluting us, head and heart. The old psychoanalytic references (mechanistic and/or structuralist), the systemic references that spread like an epidemic, the residues of dogmatic Marxism, continue to obstruct our ability to develop new analytic-militant* cartographies. [GR 132].

3. The means by which a **group** forms a **subjectivity** shared by its members. Serves a protective psychic function.

In a more general way, one has to admit that every individual and social **group** *conveys its own system of modelising* **subjectivity***; that is, a certain* **cartography**—*composed of cognitive references as well as mythical, ritual and symptomatological references—with which it positions itself in relation to its affects and anguishes, and attempts to manage its inhibitions and drives.* [CM 11]

4. A clinical practice which helps psychotic patients construct new components for their impoverished psychic and social **Universes**.

Schizoanalytic **cartography** *consists in the ability to discern those components lacking in consistency or existence.* [CM 71]

- J. W.

Chaos

While chaos may conjure up images of an abyss, an intimidating formlessness or a bewildering indeterminacy (an amorphous mass, for example), Deleuze draws on **Nietzsche**'s Heraclitian, Anti-**Plato**nic vision to assert that the world and the cosmos 'repeats' itself, but such that it is a **force** of chaos—that is, of unpredictable change (disguised as a cycle); in Nietzsche's terms, there is no 'empty space': chaos is therefore a 'play of forces'. D&G in fact insist that chaos should not be characterized by the absence of determination, but by the absence of (apparent) connection between determinations (WP 42); similarly, Deleuze describes **repetition** that disappears in appearing as a 'constantly aborted moment of birth'

(DR 91, 70). D&G add to this that the problem of chaos is that it has no *presence*; rather, it has an 'infinite speed'. Thus chaos is indeterminate and formless only to the extent that determinations connect in a smaller space, and forms change in a faster time, than is conceivable: the defining feature of chaos is thus not absence, but complexity. This will also be related to the concept of the **milieu**, which is defined by the stability of periodic repetition; here, chaos is not the opposite of the milieu, but the totality *of* milieus and their **rhythms** (**becomings**): their *complication*. Such a space-time, however, is not representable, nor is it a 'non-being' that would contradict being; in accordance with Deleuze's conception of the **fold**, it is the most comprised and convoluted state of the **serial** process of implication and explication. Chaos is therefore not something that should be viewed *negatively*, as a disorder in our **sensations**, as a hole in our understanding, or even as dysfunction; rather, it is source of composition in art, the challenge of indifference to philosophy, and the decelerated variable in science (this is reflected, respectively, in the last three definitions).

1.a. In **Nietzsche's** work, the cyclical movement or **eternal recurrence** that characterizes **forces** in tension; the necessity of chance in the continuity of **becoming**.

> *Universal* chaos *which excluded all purposeful activity does not contradict the idea of the cycle; for this idea is only an irrational necessity* [cited in N 26, 28]

> *if there ever was a* chaos *of* forces *the* chaos *was eternal and has reappeared in every cycle.* [cited in N 27, 29]

b. In Deleuze's reading of **Nietzsche**, the *unity* of all chance through **eternal return** which can be neither subjectively nor objectively represented; the law of **repetition** for itself (which has no ground or predetermined form).

> **Nietzsche** *had already said that* chaos *and* eternal return *were not two distinct things but a single and same affirmation. [...] With* eternal return, *chao-errancy is opposed to the coherence of representation; it excludes both the coherence of a subject which represents itself and that of an object represented. Re-petition opposes re-presentation [...].* [DR 69, 57]

2. In Deleuze's explanation of systems (of all varieties), the unity or complication (and co-implication) of all **series** of divergent **repetitions,** where **difference** has no mediation; that which contains all series in a simultaneous fashion.

> *Systems of* **simulacra** *affirm divergence and decentering: the only unity, the only convergence of all the* **series,** *is an informal* **chaos** *in which they are all included.* [DR 347, 278]

> *The basic* **series** *are divergent [...] in the sense that the point or horizon of convergence lies in a* **chaos** *or is constantly displaced within that* **chaos.** *This* **chaos** *is itself the most positive, just as the divergence is the object of affirmation [...]. Each series explicates or develops itself, but in [...]this* **chaos** *which complicates everything.* [DR 150–1, 123–4]

3. In D&G's cosmology and musicology, an infinitely complex, inaccessible, albeit determined pattern whose directional components are unstable but serve as the basis for **milieus** (and the **rhythms** which express the relation of milieus to chaos).

> *From* **chaos,** **Milieus** *and* **Rhythms** *are born. This is the concern of very ancient cosmogonies.* **Chaos** *is not without its own directional components, which are its own ecstasies. [...] The milieus are open to* **chaos,** *which threatens them with exhaustion or intrusion. Rhythm is the milieus' answer to* **chaos.** *What* **chaos** *and rhythm have in common is the in-between—between two milieus, rhythm-***chaos** *or the* **chaos***mos [...]* **Chaos** *is not the opposite of rhythm, but the milieu of all milieus.* [TP 345, 313]

4.a. In D&G's explanation of art, the origin of the **affect** and **percept** that is formed on the **plane of composition,** which dissociates given or ready-made opinions from the **Figures** or medium of an artwork; a *chaosmos* that combines the functions of chaos and the cosmos in natural (i.e. terrestrial) or aesthetic **milieus.**

> *artists struggle less against* **chaos** *[...] than against the 'clichés' of opinion.[...] Art is not* **chaos** *but a composition of* **chaos** *that yields the vision or* **sensation** [WP 204]

b. From an artistic perspective, an un**actualize**d and unthinkable **virtuality.** The complete and unlimited state of forms which cannot be given because it has no presence.

> Chaos *is defined not so much by its disorder as by the infinite speed with which every form taking shape in it vanishes.* [WP 118]

5.a. In D&G's explanation of philosophy, that which disappears in appearing and thus cannot be thought, and threatens to engulf the **difference** inherent to the **concept** (into an abyss of scattered, unconnected parts) insofar as components of chaos are filtered, but not slowed down, through the **plane of consistency**.

> *Philosophy struggles [...] with the* **chaos** *as undifferentiated abyss or ocean of dissemblance.* [WP 207]

> **Chaos** *is an infinite speed of birth and disappearance. [...]* [WP 118]

b. From a philosophical perspective, a void that contains the totality of formed **matter**, or, a **virtuality** which threatens to override and destroy **strata** with too much complexity.

> *[Chaos] is a void [...] containing all possible particles and drawing out all possible forms* [WP 118]

6. In D&G's explanation of science, that which is endowed with functions and variables through slowing down and limitation.

> *Science approaches* **chaos** *in a completely different, almost opposite way [than philosophy]: it relinquishes [...] infinite speed, in order to gain a reference able to* **actualize** *the* **virtual**. [WP 118]

- E. B. Y.

Chaosmosis: An Ethico-Aesthetic Paradigm

The final decade of Guattari's thinking culminates in *Chaosmosis*, which explores the existential role of creativity in daily life, world politics, science, society, and psychoanalytic practice. The book proposes an elaborate ontology (or **heterogenesis**) which draws heavily on science but which, Guattari insists, functions as an **aesthetic paradigm**. Building on this ontological schema, *Chaosmosis* offers an account of **ecosophy** which is more theoretically technical than the version presented in *The Three Ecologies*, as well as a redefinition of **schizoanalysis** as **metamodeling**. Both ecosophy and metamodeling are explained in terms of Guattari's graphic schema of **four functors,** demonstrating his penchant for scientific and mathematical **concepts,** especially his enthusiasm for far-from-equilibrium thermodynamics as theorized by **Ilya Prigogine** and incorporated into psychoanalysis by **Mony Elkaïm.** Guattari contrasts his own account of the machinic **phylum** against the schema of the four causes in **Heidegger**'s technology essay, which he found overly pessimistic as well as too narrow in its definition of the **machine.** While it overlaps with *What Is Philosophy?* thematically and theoretically, Guattari's final book departs from the joint work by its emphasis on the growing importance of **subjectivity** in contemporary world politics. Central to the discussion of global geopolitics is an account of the production of subjectivity, especially in its collective and machinic versions. Guattari argues that capitalism offers a standardized, mass-manufactured, impoverished subjectivity, but that this capitalist standardization is refused by on the one hand, nationalist and fundamentalist movements which are conservative and reactionary, and on the other hand autonomist and libratory movements which are creative and liberating. All of these movements, for better or for worse, instead demand subjective singularization. Guattari advocates the pursuit of liberation through the unleashing of singularizing processes which would transform existence in all its dimensions by releasing mutant creative energies. - J. W.

Chaosophy: Texts and Interviews 1972–1977

In 2009, Semiotext(e) published a new, expanded edition of *Chaosophy*, which first appeared as a slim volume in 1995. Like the older version, it includes translations of numerous chapters from **Révolution moléculaire,** as well as talks, interviews, and journalistic pieces. These selections are limited to occasional essays, with little evidence of Guattari's more dense theoretical writing. Themes reflect Guattari's preoccupations and engagements during the early 1970s, including the reception of *Anti-Oedipus,* institutional psychoanalysis, the anti-psychiatry movement, homosexual liberation, cinema criticism, and his time in New York working in family therapy with **Mony Elkaïm.** Some of these texts originally appeared in the 1996 edition of *Soft Subversions.* There are a few new essays, but the main change is the chronological rearrangement of the original tables of contents and the addition of a substantial new introduction. - J. W.

Chomsky, Noam

Chomsky serves as both a foil and an inspiration for Guattari, who during the 1970s developed his own materialist general semiology as a reaction against the structuralists' emphasis on language (***Machinic Unconscious***). On the one hand, Guattari faults Chomsky's linguistics for being too structuralist, arborescent, and formalist, opposing Chomsky's abandonment of content and context to his own preference for pragmatics. On the other hand, Guattari is attracted to Chomsky's conception of language as infinitely creative in its capacity to assemble countless sentences from a limited number of linguistic components. He credits Chomsky with the idea of the **abstract machine**; the term is Guattari's, but he uses it to paraphrase Chomsky's account of the production of sentences by generative grammar. Guattari borrows Chomsky's own terms 'transformational' and 'generative' but he abandons the axiomatic, algebraic, and geometric paradigms on which Chomsky based them. In *A Thousand Plateaus*, he and Deleuze define the **rhizome** in relation to Chomsky's grammatical trees. - J. W.

Chronos

1. A single, infinitely cyclical, form of time where the present **contracts** the past and future such that there is only corporeality and causality without effects, in distinction from **Aion**, which is a recurring, yet unlimited, form of time that involves only incorporeality and effects.

> Whereas **Chronos** *was inseparable from the bodies which filled it out entirely as causes and* **matter,** **Aion** *is populated by effects which haunt it without ever filling it up. Whereas* **Chronos** *was limited and infinite,* **Aion** *is unlimited, the way that future and past are unlimited, and finite like the instant.* [LS 189, 165]

- E. B. Y.

Chronosign

cross-reference: **Time-Image** (image of non-chronological time)

Cinema (Vol I & II)

Cinema 1: The Movement-Image
L'Image-mouvement. Cinéma 1 (1983)

Cinema 2: The Time-Image
L'Image-temps. Cinéma 2 (1985)

These two volumes, published during the period of the 1980s, arrive from several sources and influences. Deleuze maintained a long relationship with the celebrated journal, *Cahiers du cinéma*, from the 1970s onward, and particularly with the editor Jean Narboni, and often participated or assisted with its public programs. In 1976, Deleuze published an article on **Bergson** and Godard for a special issue at the invitation of Naboni, and regularly published and conducted interviews for the journal afterward. The second is a series of seminars that Deleuze conducted on cinema, beginning in 1981, in order to assist with the establishment of the department of cinema at the Université de Paris-VIII, in which the philosopher Jean-François Lyotard took part. In January, Deleuze offers his first seminar on **Bergson**'s *Matter and Memory*, entitled 'Image-Movement, Image-Time.' Deleuze uses the occasion to take up and champion **Bergson**'s metaphysics of time, which constitutes the opening of the first volume on the 'Movement-Image.' The necessity of beginning a philosophical study of the cinema with an exposition of **Bergson**'s thesis from 1896, which pre-dates the invention of the modern cinema itself, is offered by Deleuze in the preface to the French edition:

> **Bergson** was writing *Matter and Memory* in 1896: it was a diagnosis of a crisis in psychology. [...] The Bergsonian discovery of a movement-image, and more profoundly, of a time-image, still retains such richness today that it is not certain that all of its consequences have been drawn. [C1 ix]

Accordingly, Deleuze's study is divided between the two, each consecrated to the movement-image and the time-image; at the same time, as a parallel to the crisis invoked above, Deleuze also sets his study of the history of cinema within a larger narrative concerning the rise and eventual crisis of the cinema based on the dominance of the movement-image, and its reversal in post-war cinema, when 'a direct image of time is formed and imposed on cinema' (C2 ix). It is this larger historical narrative that has been the subject of much controversy, particularly concerning the reversal of post-war cinema around the direct image of time; however, what is most important to understand is that Deleuze is using this narrative to address a similar crisis as the one confronted by **Bergson**: a crisis in psychology, which is most intensely experienced in cinema and philosophy as well, concerning the movement-image as the **perception** of the physical reality of the external world, and the time-image as the perception of psychic reality in consciousness. The resulting two volumes present one of the most powerful metaphysical critiques of the foundations of time, perception, and memory, in which Deleuze invents (or fabricates) a dizzying array of new **concepts** drawn from his exploration of modern European and American cinema, focusing mostly on the great directors (Hitchcock, Welles, Godard, Fellini, Resnais, etc.) who he compares not only with painters or architects, but with thinkers. This critique will also have import for the theory of cinema as Deleuze, in the second volume, opposes the dominant method of semiology, proposed by Christian Metz among others, as providing an adequate language for the cinematic image. As he writes in the preface to the English translation, 'the cinema seems to us to be a composition of images and **signs**, that is, a pre-verbal intelligible content (pure semiotics), while a linguistic inspiration abolishes the image and tends to dispense with the sign' (C1 ix). Also in the second volume, Deleuze returns to reprise the major arguments in ***Nietzsche and Philosophy*** and ***Difference and Repetition*** concerning 'the image of thought' in both modern cinema and philosophy. It is here that he puts forward his most powerful claim that both post-war cinema and philosophy only dramatize a situation in which, concerning the psychological crisis announced in the beginning, modern man has been reduced to 'a purely optical and sound situation,' and it is only by investing this interval with new intensities can cinema and philosophy help to repair our belief in this world. - G. L.

Code

(see also **transcoding**)

1.a. In D&G's analysis of **territorialization**, the basis of the **milieu** which, although it contains variation, is not in communication with other milieus; that which is distinct from the **territory**, which enables possibilities of *decoding* and transcoding.

> *Each* **milieu** *has its own* **code***, and there is perpetual* **transcoding** *between milieus; the* **territory***, on the other hand, seems to form at the level of a certain decoding.* [TP 355, 322]

b. In D&G's analysis of **desiring-machines**, the type of social **desire** ('coded') that results from the primitive **territorial** machine (in distinction from the overcoding and territorialization by the despotic machine), which limits production to lateral alliances and extended filiations (such that **disjunctive syntheses** are subordinated to **connective syntheses**).

> *The primitive* **territorial** *machine, with its immobile motor, the earth, is already a social machine, a megamachine, that* **codes** *the* **flows** *of production, the flows of means of production, of producers and consumers* [AO 156, 142]

2.a. (Special Type): *Overcoding*: In D&G's analysis of capitalism, the process by which the despotic machine or the state leaves the codes of the primitive machine intact but performs a **disjunctive synthesis** where the filiations and allegiances are predicated upon their direct affiliation to the sovereign.

> **Overcoding** *is the operation that constitutes the essence of the State, and that measures both its continuity and its break with the previous formations: the dread of* **flows** *of* **desire** *that would resist coding, but also the establishment of a new inscription that* **overcodes***, and that makes desire into the property of the sovereign* [AO 217, 199]

b. The object of human surplus **value** in precapitalist—i.e. primitive and despotic—societies (where the machine engenders the measurable distinction between labor and capital), in distinction from its decoding in capitalist societies (where labor and capital are *machinic* and do not create a measurable distinction).

> It is from the fluxion of decoded flows, *from their conjunction, that the filiative form of capital [...] results. The differential relation expresses the fundamental capitalist phenomenon of the transformation of the surplus* value *of* code *into a surplus value of* flux. [AO 248, 228]

> the decoding of flows *in capitalism has freed,* **deterritorialized**, *and* decoded *the flows of* code *[...] to such a degree that the automatic machine has always increasingly internalized them in its body or its structure as a field of* forces, *while depending on a science and a technology [...]. In this sense, it is not machines that have created capitalism, but capitalism that creates machines.* [AO 253, 233]

3. In Deleuze's analysis of art, a feature of abstraction in painting which subordinates tactile or non-visual referents to a visual field; a feature of the digital which eclipses the manual and **haptic**.

> it follows that what abstract painting elaborates is less a **diagram** *than a symbolic* **code**, *on the basis of great formal oppositions. It replaced the diagram with a* **code**. *This* **code** *is 'digital,' not in the sense of the manual, but in the sense of a finger that counts. 'Digits' are the units that* **group** *together visually the terms in opposition.* [FB 103–4]

- E. B. Y.

Coldness and Cruelty

Présentation de Sacher-Masoch. Le froid et le cruel (1967)

After publishing an article entitled 'De Sacher Masoch au Masochisme' (from Sacher-Masoch to Masochism) in 1961, Deleuze expanded on all of the themes of the original essay in his book-length work on **Sacher-Masoch**. It is notable that this work, along with *Proust and Signs*, were among his first to be translated into English, and these may have made Deleuze appear to that audience as an unusual literary critic with an emphasis in human sexuality; however, in this text Deleuze was in fact responding to

1) the intellectual currency surrounding one of the most common and reductive dualisms in psychoanalysis: the complementarity of sadism and **masochism**, and 2) the emphasis being placed on the literature of de Sade (in distinction from the psychological disorder of 'sadism') in intellectual circles (instigated by authors such as André Breton, Georges Bataille and Maurice **Blanchot**) at the expense of the literature of Sacher-Masoch. While focus had been on the revolutionary and *transgressive* nature of de Sade's work, Deleuze wished to illuminate the revolutionary and *imaginative* nature of Sacher-Masoch's. On the one hand, the Sadist wishes to use the 'hypocritical language of established order and power' to use apathy (and irony) to demonstrate that **reason** is always undermined by lust or sensuality (CC 17); on the other hand, the masochist 'suspends' sensuality itself (in a state that conflates reality and phantasy), and exposes the hypocrisy of the law through not only an unquestionable obedience to it, but a demand that its punishments be administered without having transgressed it (this foregrounds Deleuze's reading of the law that has 'no content' in **Kafka's** work).

The reader may find Deleuze more generous with psychoanalytic theory in this work (as well as *The Logic of Sense*, which employs some psychoanalytic terminology) than in his work with Guattari in the Capitalism and Schizophrenia project, which unabashedly takes **Freud** as a target. Nevertheless, this work does set the stage for Deleuze's more direct and philosophical critiques of Freud in the chapter 'Repetition for Itself' from *Difference and Repetition*, where he questions the connection between **repetition** and the pleasure principle. While both **Sacher-Masoch** and Sade are 'perverse', Deleuze argues their work is 'pornology' rather than pornography, since the 'erotic language cannot be reduced to the elementary functions of ordering and describing' (CC 18); this in fact echoes his treatment of **Klossowski** in *The Logic of Sense* where repetition also creates the conditions for a structure of perversion.

Deleuze's argument that Masoch is a **'symptomatolgist'** is revised in his treatment of other authors in *Essays Critical and Clinical*. As he later implies in *Dialogues*, when he wrote on **Kafka** with Guattari, it became clear in retrospect that he was not interested in applying psychoanalysis to Sacher-Masoch (even through critique), but in investigating how the author illuminates dispositions and problems that are in fact cultural and *social*; Sacher-Masoch, he states, was producing **collective assemblages of enunciation,** where 'the **flux** of pain and humiliation is expressed as a contractual assemblage' [D 121]. - E. B. Y.

Collective assemblage of enunciation

While this **concept** emerges from Guattari's notion of enunciations that are not 'individual', with Deleuze it is developed in their work on **Kafka** and in *A Thousand Plateaus*. In the Kafka text, they note that the solidarity of 'doubles' was ensured by a **territorialized** function which those doubles represented; however, the enunciations of 'K.' (the character in Kafka's novels) become 'collective' or **deterritorialized** when they are no longer representative and there is no longer 'content' for such 'enunciations' or **expressions** to refer to (i.e. when the machine that they are connected to becomes *truly* abstract and **immanent** to concrete **assemblages** of **desire**). In *A Thousand Plateaus*, they similarly focus on the manner in which impersonal statements are tied to collectives, and are not attributable to **subjects**. In both cases, the subject is no longer divided in a Cartesian sense between an enunciation ('I think') and a statement ('I am') that could constitute its 'being'.

1. In Guattari's work, a function of enunciation in which it is not tied to a personal subjectify, but emerges from **group** phenomena, social **assemblages**, and technological apparatuses.

> *we witness the same questioning of subjective individuation, which certainly survives, but is wrought by* collective assemblages of enunciation. [...] *The term 'collective' should be understood in the sense of a* **multiplicity** *that deploys itself as much beyond the individual, on the side of the socius, as before the person, on the side of pre-verbal* **intensities**, *indicating a logic of* affects *rather than a logic of delimited sets.* [CM 8–9]

2.a. In D&G's reading of **Kafka,** language in which the **form of content** is carried away (on a **line of flight**) by a **deterritorialized** or unformed/deformed **expression;** the manner in which incorporeal expressions are liberated from a functional solidarity with the content of machinic **assemblages.**

COLLECTIVE ASSEMBLAGE OF ENUNCIATION 71

This primacy of the enunciation refers us once again to the conditions of **minor literature:***[...] it is* **expression** *that precedes contents, whether to prefigure the rigid* **forms** *into which contents will flow or to make them take flight along* **lines** *of escape or transformation.* [K 85]

b. In D&G's theory of **signs**, the manner in which enunciations become impersonal but are at the same time *determined* or attributable to collectivities (on a horizontal axis) and statements attributable to **events** and de/**territorialized assemblages** (on a vertical axis); the dissolution of Cartesian **subjectivity** that is divided between enunciations (such as 'I think') and its abstract existence (based on statements such as 'I am'), such that, on the one hand, enunciations indicate a **multiplicity** rather than a self, and on the other hand, statements incarnate states of **desire**.

the third person indefinite, HE, THEY, [...] ties the statement to a **collective assemblage***, as its necessary condition, rather than to a subject of the* **enunciation***.* [TP 292, 264–5]

The process of the cogito, you recall, is: I can say 'I think, therefore I am,' but I can't say 'I walk, therefore I am.' [...] for from a subject of the statement I cannot conclude a being of **enunciation***, or the being of a subject of* **enunciation***; but I can say 'I think, therefore I am,' because from a subject of* **enunciation** *I can conclude the being of this subject. [...]By contrast, our hypothesis was that what produces statements were machinic* **assemblages** *or, what amounts to the same thing,* **collective** *agents of* **enunciation** *[...]. [W]e must explain how machinic agents of* **enunciation** *effectively produce variable statements in such and such circumstances [...] whatever takes place on the order of the* **event***, i.e. the statement or* **desire***, the event is finally the very identity of the statement and of desire* [webdeleuze 26/03/1973]

In **enunciation***, in the production of utterances, there is no* **subject***, but always collective agents: and in what the utterance speaks of, there are no objects, but machinic states* [D 71]

- E. B. Y.

Common sense

cross-reference: sense (def. 2.b.)

Concept

Unlike the traditional treatment of concepts as universals (**Platonic** Ideals), **Kantian** 'a prioris', or even the **Nietzschean** and Derridean treatment of concepts as metaphors, D&G cast the concept in relation to the **affect** and **percept**, and invert its conventional role: it is the affect and percept that are objective and impersonal (through the arts) and the concept that is **subjective** by virtue of its expression and referentiality (hence the 'conceptual personae' of the thinker). This is also a notable shift from Deleuze's early use of the term 'ideas' (of **difference**), which in this case emphasizes concrete variations (in distinction from varieties in art and variables in science).

> 1.a. In D&G's definition of philosophy, that which occupies or populates the **plane of immanence**, as both an **intensive** ordinate or whole, and as a fragment that is situated contextually with other concepts; that which preserves the infinite, unthinkable speed of **chaos** but carries out relative, thinkable movements of variation on the plane (and thus does not utilize **propositional** logic but enters into intensive relations of **resonance** to other concepts).
>
>> *The* concept *is in a state of survey [survol] in relation to its components, endlessly traversing them according to an order without distance.* [WP 20]
>>
>> *the* concept *is not discursive, and [...] the philosophical* concept *usually appears only as a* proposition *deprived of sense.* [WP 22]
>
> b. In distinction from science, a **virtuality** that does not refer to an **actual** or possible state, but is constituted ideally in variations within real states through self-reference.
>
>> *The* concept *[...] has no* reference: *it is self-referential* [WP 22]
>>
>> *By retaining the infinite, philosophy gives consistency to the* **virtual** *through* concepts [WP 118]

- E. B. Y.

Contraction

Contraction is not **repetition** for itself, but repetition exposed to generic **difference:** first, it concerns our visceral or physical nature, where we both 'contract' elements to form bodies (even inorganic matter 'contracts' chemical elements), as well as where we form 'cases' within our **imagination** (which acts as another 'organ' of contraction). For this reason Deleuze will say that the 'contemplations' of the **imagination** are distinct from reflection, memory, and understanding (they are not 'active'); here we form a generic difference by means of **habit**, before that difference is reflected on to be 'understood' or calculated. Second, contraction concerns the manner in which the past as a whole 'coexists' with the present in varying degrees, before it is telescoped through successive instants that become embedded. In both cases, contraction involves an interaction between **repetition** and difference (independently of any 'understanding'), whether explicated through the generality of **habit,** or implicated by 'the past in general'. In Deleuze's early work on **Bergson** and again in his later work, the 'resonating' nature of contraction is equated with **sensation,** which may 'preserve' the elements or qualities of **chaos** insofar as they do not 'appear in disappearing'; rather, they are *prolonged.*

1. In Deleuze's reading of **Bergson**, a **mode** of **repetition** which introduces time and **difference** into **matter,** or prolongs the present in the past with a certain **duration;** the generation of **difference** by virtue of repetition [B, DR, DI]

   What is opposed to contraction *is pure* repetition *or* matter: *repetition is the* mode *of a present that appears only when the other present has disappeared—the present itself, or exteriority, vibration, relaxation.* Contraction, *on the other hand, designates* difference *because difference in its essence makes a repetition impossible, because it destroys the very condition of any possible repetition.* [DI 45]

   Whenever **Bergson** *discusses memory, he presents two aspects of it, the second of which is the more profound: memory-recollection and memory-* contraction*. By contracting itself, the element of* repetition *coexists with itself—one might say, multiplies itself and maintains itself.* [DI 47]

The identical elements of material **repetition** *blend together in a* **contraction** *[...]*. [DI 47]

2. In Deleuze's reading of **Hume**, the primary function of the **imagination** which forms **impressions** by virtue of succession. [ES, DR]

> **Hume** *explains that the independent identical or similar cases are grounded in the* **imagination**. *The imagination is defined here as a* **contractile** *power: like a sensitive plate, it retains one case when the other appears.* [DR 90–1, 70]

3.a. In Deleuze's explanation of time, the **passive synthesis** of **habit** which occurs *within* the mind before it is reflected on *by* the mind (to create principles or reflect on successive instants); the fusion of successive instants in a viscera, psyche, or a contemplative soul.

> *When we say that* **habit** *is a* **contraction** *we are speaking not of an instantaneous action which combines with another to form an element of* **repetition**, *but rather of the fusion of that repetition in the contemplating mind. [...] It is simultaneously through* **contraction** *that we are habits, but through contemplation that we contract.* [DR 95, 74]

b. The **passive synthesis** of memory which determines the past not as successive instants but as a coexisting whole in degrees of **intensity** or of expansion/relaxation.

> *If we compare the* **passive synthesis** *of* **habit** *and the* **passive synthesis** *of memory, we see how [...] In one case, the present is the most* **contracted** *state of successive elements or instants which are in themselves independent of one another. In the other case, the present designates the most* **contracted** *degree of an entire past, which is itself like a coexisting totality.* [DR 104, 82]

4. In D&G's explanation of experience and art (and in Deleuze's reading of **Bergson** and **Bacon**), the feature of **sensations** which, depending on their degree, provides variety or quality to their **expression**; the manner in which sensation vibrates, resonates, or preserves itself within quality and/or on **the plane of composition** (as a 'Monument' or work of art), as a response to the **chaos** of infinite variety or the **force** of an encounter. [B, FB, WP]

> *All our* **sensations** *are extensive, all are 'voluminous' and extended, although to varying degrees and in different styles, depending on the type of* **contraction** *that they carry out.* [B 87]
>
> *How will* **sensation** *be able to sufficiently turn in on itself, relax or* **contract** *itself, so as to capture these non-given* **forces** *in what it gives us, to make us sense these insensible forces, and raise itself to its own conditions?* [FB 56]
>
> **Sensation** *is the* **contracted** *vibration that has become quality, variety.* [WP 211]
>
> **Sensation** *is pure contemplation [...] to the extent that one contemplates the elements from which one originates.* [WP 212]

- E. B. Y.

Counter-actualization

It is easy to feel victimized by the way **events** play out, and equally easy to resent outcomes or feel guilt or regret about them, and wish things were otherwise. Deleuze would probably say that in the first case, we are trapped in a linear sense of time (a stupid sense of cause and effect—'why did this happen to me?'), while in the second case, we have the insight to look backwards, but are equally trapped in the perspective of our current state of affairs ('what if?'). How do we get around these limitations? Deleuze argues that we must see ourselves, to some extent, as actors in our own lives: this enables us to attain a perspective that lifts us out of our present or *actual* circumstances (in **Nietzsche**an terms, we actively forget causes or 'traces') and perceive **events** superficially—as though they were not even happening to us *personally*. In fact, the idiom *'act as if'* testifies to this: act as if the traumatic event did not even cause the actual scar, or that the event was impersonal and had nothing to do with you, and the event (and even the scar) may ultimately gain a new **sense**.

1.a. The orientation or perspective on the **event** (as presence) towards its **virtuality** (past-future), despite its **actuality**.

> *there is the future and the past of the* **event** *considered in itself, sidestepping each present, being free of the limitations of a state of*

affairs, impersonal and pre-individual, neutral, [...] always divided into past-future, and forming what must be called the **counter-actualization** [LS 172, 151]

b. The manner in which **events** play out not as different ways things could have occurred in the past (such that we are *burdened by* different possibilities of the past and present), but play out in reverse so that a future (which *does not yet* have a **sense**) informs the sense of the past event, depersonalizing its sense in the present; the perspective of events taken by an actor where, because events do not happen to an individual, are ideal (rather than possible) and incessant (without beginning or end).

> **Counter-actualization** *is nothing, it belongs to a buffoon when it operates alone and pretends to have the* **value** *of what could have happened. But, to be the mime of what effectively occurs, to double the* **actualization** *with a* **counter-actualization,** *the identification with a distance, like the true actor and dancer, is to give to the truth of the* **event** *the only chance of not being confused with its inevitable* **actualization.** [LS 182, 161]

> *The actor thus* **actualizes** *the* **event,** *but in a way which is entirely different from the* **actualization** *of the event in the* **depth** *of things. Or rather, the actor redoubles this cosmic, or physical* **actualization,** *in his own way, which is singularly superficial—but because of it more distinct, trenchant and pure [...]becoming thereby the actor of one's own* **events**—*a* **counter-actualization.** [LS 171, 150]

- E. B. Y.

Crystal image

cross-reference: **Time-Image** (circuit between real and imaginary)

Dark precursor

cross-reference: **Force**

Denotation

1. The linguistic reference to determinable instances, in the form of affirmation or denial (truth or falsity), in a given state of affairs; the first dimension of the **proposition** along with **manifestation, signification,** and **(non)sense.**

> *The first [relation within the* **proposition***] is called* **denotation** *or indication: it is the relation of the proposition to an external state of affairs (datum).* [LS 16, 12]

- E. B. Y.

Depth

1.a. In Deleuze's reading of **Carroll**, the feature of states of affairs which involve nightmarish scenarios and ruptures of the **surface** (in distinction from the language of suffering produced by **Artaud**, involving pure depth).

> *In Lewis* **Carroll***, everything begins with a horrible combat, the combat of* **depths***: things explode or make us explode, boxes are too small for their contents, foods are toxic and poisonous, entrails are stretched, monsters grab at us. [...] the world of* **depths** *[...] rumbles under the* **surface***, and threatens to break through it. Even unfolded and laid out flat, the monsters still haunt us.* [ECC 21]

> *if* **depth** *evades the present, it is with all the* **force** *of a 'now' which opposes its panic-stricken present to the wise present of measure* [LS 189, 165]

b. The corporeal domain of causes and mixtures which evade the past and future (**Aion**) by virtue of continuous presence (**Chronos**).

> *The* **becoming**-*mad of* **depth** *is then a bad* **Chronos***, opposed to the living present of the good Chronos.* [LS 187, 164]

> *Mixtures are in bodies, and in the* **depth** *of bodies: a body penetrates another and coexists with it in all of its parts, like a drop of wine in the ocean, or fire in iron.* [LS 8, 5–6]

- E. B. Y.

Descartes, René

Deleuze's most substantial discussions of Descartes arise in his work on **Spinoza** and in *Difference and Repetition*. Firstly, Deleuze defends the logic behind Spinoza's dismissal of Descartes' famous mind-body dualism, where (in Descartes) there is more than one substance, despite that the same **attribute** may belong to both. In Spinoza's terms, if we hold Descartes to his definition of substances, which is 'that which can exist by itself, without the aid of any other substance' (Descartes, 1934, 101), then, logically, there can only be one substance, because it would be infinite or all-inclusive. If there were more than one, they would be in a relation of causality, analogy or hierarchy (as they are in Descartes, where thoughts are trustworthy because of their permanence, and bodies are not because of their changeability), but they could not be truly infinite. What Deleuze therefore argues that Spinoza adds to this debate is: if thoughts and bodies arise from the *same* substance, we cannot have knowledge of ourselves as a thinking thing (as Descartes would have it), because we can have neither an adequate idea of our body nor of our mind (as Deleuze explains it: 'the body surpasses the knowledge that we have of it, and [...] thought likewise surpasses the consciousness that we have of it' [SPP 18]). Spinoza will insist instead that adequate ideas involve the 'order and connection' of things in the mind which parallel the 'order and connection' of bodies in extension because they are both **modalities** of **attributes** of the same substance. In technical terms, if the only way to make 'real' distinctions is by virtue of attributes, then those attributes cannot be counted or divided (as in Descartes) because this would not be a real distinction (just a 'numerical' one); rather, the attributes (of thought and extension) are infinite in essence because they are both **expressions** of the same **univocal** 'substance' (despite that they are really distinct). Only in their finite, causal determination as **modes** are they divisible, but in this case they are interdependent. Thus while Descartes is skeptical of the changeability of bodies in the physical world, but less skeptical of abstract ideas, Spinoza would argue that both follow the same necessary 'order and connection', and are both just as prone to cause error (as well as to avoid error).

In *Difference and Repetition*, Deleuze comments on the Kantian critique of Descartes' Cogito (in Chp. II), before launching his own critique of the function of representation in both thinkers (in Chp. III). While **Kant**'s critique focuses on Descartes' determination ('I think') of the undeterminable ('I am'), Deleuze's critique focuses on the status of *recognition* in the famous *Cogito Ergo Sum* line of reasoning. By recognizing myself as a thinking thing, I always already know what it means to think (in Descartes' case, for example, it arises from 'doubting'). This moment of recognition only validates the familiarity of the same process or conclusion (with 'certainty') but does not think **difference**; as Deleuze states, 'the identity of the Self in the "I think" [...] grounds the harmony of all the **faculties** and their agreement on the form of a supposed Same object' (DR 169, 133). In contrast to this, Deleuze argues that the familiar, recognizable, or repeated is actually a displacement and disguise of difference (when it isn't a 'bare and brute' repetition of the same which 'cancels' difference), and that the only way to 'think' difference is to encounter it in these forms of **repetition**. Here, 'the Cogito [cannot serve] as a **proposition** of consciousness'; rather, these forms, are, properly, impossible to think as they arise from the 'cogitandum' and the **faculties** in discord (DR 250, 199). Added to this, as Deleuze emphasizes later in the work, while the 'self' may be among the 'centres of envelopment which testify to the presence of individuating factors' (DR 323, 259), it always immediately refers to the **Other** who implicates or en**folds** it. In his work with Guattari, the **collective assemblage of enunciation** is offered as an alternative to the Cartesian dualism between the 'I think' and the 'I am'. - E. B. Y.

Desert Islands and *Two Regimes of Madness*

L'Île déserte et autres textes, 1953–1974 (2002)
Deux régimes de fous et autres textes, 1975–1995 (2003)

Conceived by Deleuze shortly before his death, both volumes collect texts and interviews between 1975 and 1995, a period that also saw the publication of his major works with Guattari leading to the last collaborative work, *What is Philosophy?* (1991). Both volumes gather together various prefaces to new and translated editions of his works, as well as conference addresses, public interviews, and articles for newspapers and journals. In the preface to the second volume, the editors underline the fact that the selection of works included in both volumes conform to Deleuze's explicit instructions, and do not incorporate transcriptions of seminars, letters and correspondences (with a few notable exceptions), collective writings (petitions, questionnaires, memoranda), nor articles that were later incorporated into other collections, such as *Negotiations* (*Pourparlers*) and *Essays Critical and Clinical* (*Critique et Clinique*). Of particular importance is the documentation of Deleuze's later political statements on a number of contemporary events and issues, such as the Palestinian question, the trial of Antonio **Negri**, and the Gulf War. - G. L.

Desire

Although **Kant** is a reference point for the development of a modern **concept** of desire, its disentanglement from psychoanalytic concepts of the pleasure principle, the death drive, and repression are crucial for Deleuze, especially in his work with Guattari. While Deleuze pays special attention to the concept of desire in terms of **the Other**, but with an emphasis on structures of *possibility* (in *The Logic of Sense*), in the vision put forward in *Anti-Oedipus*, desire is not self-preservative or self-destructive *per se*, but 'productive' and social. That is, if desire is truly **unconscious**, then it has no representative content and therefore cannot 'lack', as there would be no actual object presented to the drives to obtain. Desire is, instead, 'continuous' and therefore connective and productive by nature. Those things which we would normally associate with the *satisfaction* of desire (security, comfort, pleasure, even orgasm) are manufactured by consciousness and its representations, and are actually 'interruptions' of the naturally continuous process of desire itself. The only way to link desire to 'lack' is to maintain that the object of desire is a phantasy, which, in accordance with Deleuze's reading of the **partial object**, will never coincide with the **series** of real objects. It will instead become a matter of constructing a **body without organs** that paradoxically ensures connection while itself consistently repelling any predetermining, organic or organized, function (hence two parts of the **desiring-machine**—one of 'attraction' and the other of 'repulsion').

1.a. In **Kant**, the **faculty** in which representation attains a causal relationship to external objects.

> *the* **faculty** *of* **desire** *is the being's faculty of* **becoming** *by means of its ideas the cause of the actual existence of the objects of these ideas* [Kant, (*Critique of Practical Reason*; Preface), 94]

b. In **Kant** and Deleuze's reading of Kant, that which, as a higher faculty, is determined neither by the representation of an object nor a feeling of pleasure or pain, but a practical interest legislated by moral law.

> *as pleasure or pain is necessarily combined with the* **faculty** *of* **desire** *(either preceding this principle as in the lower* **desires***, or following it as in the higher, when the* **desire** *is determined by the* **moral** *law), we may also suppose that the Judgment will bring about a transition from the pure faculty of knowledge [...] to the realm of the* **concept** *of freedom [...]* [Kant, (*The Critique of Judgment*; Intro, III) 1914, 17]

> *a representation of an object can never determine the free will or precede the* **moral** *law; but by immediately determining the will the* **moral** *law also determines objects as being in conformity with this free will. More precisely, when reason legislates in the* **faculty** *of* **desire***, the faculty of* **desire** *itself legislates over objects* [KCP 40]

c. In D&G's reading of **Kant**, the cause of the reality of representations which, like the psychoanalytic conception, is conceived in terms of interiority (phantasy) rather than exteriority.

> *it is not by chance that* **Kant** *chooses superstitious beliefs, hallucinations, and fantasies as illustrations of this definition of* **desire***: as Kant would have it, we are well aware that the real object can be produced only by an external causality and external mechanisms; nonetheless this knowledge does not prevent us from believing in the intrinsic power of* **desire** *to create its own object[...].* [AO 27, 25]

> *It is not possible to attribute a special form of existence to* **desire***, a mental or psychic reality that is presumably different from the material reality of social production.* [AO 32, 30]

2.a. In **Freud's** work, the **force** of (libidinal) **unconscious** wishes or instincts which are repressed by social prohibitions or 'cathected' through investments of energy, and are satisfied (albeit only temporarily) through various (usually neurotic) acts.

> *prohibition owes its strength and its obsessive character precisely to its* **unconscious** *opponent, the concealed and undiminished* **desire**— *that is to say, to an internal necessity inaccessible to conscious inspection. [...] The instinctual* **desire** *is constantly shifting in order to escape from the impasse and endeavours to find substitutes [...]. Any fresh advance made by the repressed libido is answered by a fresh sharpening of the prohibition. The mutual inhibition of the two conflicting forces produces a need for discharge, for reducing the prevailing tension* [Freud, 2003, 30]

b. In Lacan's reading of **Freud**, in distinction from needs, an **unconscious** and unconditional demand that both fundamentally *lacks* its own being and has a *signifying* structure, due to its locus in **the Other**.

> *man's* **desire** *is the* **Other***'s* **desire***. [...] the subject find[s] the constitutive structure of his* **desire** *in the same gap opened up by the effect of signifiers in those who come to represent the Other for him, insofar as his demand is subjected to them. [...]* **desire** *is [...] an unconditional demand for presence and absence* [Lacan, 2006, 525]

> **Desire** *is a relation of being to lack. This lack is the lack of being properly speaking. It isn't the lack of this or that, but lack of being whereby the being exists [...] Being attains a* **sense** *of self in relation to being as a function of this lack in the experience of* **desire**. [Lacan, 1991, 223–4]

3.a. In Deleuze's explanation of perceptual structures of possibility, that which may be expressed by **Others**.

> *[...]* **desire***, whether it be* **desire** *for the object of* **desire** *for Others, depends on this structure [of the possible]. I* **desire** *an object only as expressed by the Other in the* **mode** *of the possible; I* **desire** *in the Other only the possible worlds the Other expresses.* [LS 357, 318]

b. In Deleuze's reading of **Tournier**, that which is either sexualized and embodied by **the Other** (objects, possible worlds), or desexualized and disembodied in a world without Others.

The Other *is a strange detour—it brings my* desires *down to* objects, *and my love to worlds. Sexuality is linked to generation only in a detour which first channels the* difference *of sexes through the Other. [...]. To establish the world without Others [...] is to avoid the detour. It is to separate* desire *from its object, from its detour through the body, in order to relate it to a pure cause* [LS 356, 317]

c. The **masochistic** state where reality and phantasy are conflated, such that sexual experience is always ritualized (toward suffering) because the ideational or **imaginative** conditions the sensual and forbidden (in a state of permanent interruption or waiting).

The essence of **masochistic** *humor lies in this, that the very law which forbids the satisfaction of a* desire *under threat of subsequent punishment is converted into one which demands the punishment first and then orders that the satisfaction of the* desire *should necessarily follow upon the punishment.* [CC 88–9]

4.a. In D&G's anti-psychoanalytic (**schizoanalytic**) conception, an uninterrupted and synthetic function of the **unconscious** which has neither positive value in pleasure nor negative **value** in lack.

Desire *is the set of* passive syntheses *that engineer* partial objects, flows, *and bodies, and that function as units of production. [...].* **Desire** *does not lack anything; it does not lack its object. It is, rather, the subject that is missing in* desire, *or* desire *that lacks a fixed* **subject***; there is no fixed subject unless there is repression.* [AO 28, 26]

[...] desire *[can be] defined as a process of production without reference to any exterior agency, whether it be a lack that hollows it out or a pleasure that fills it.* [TP 170–1, 154]

[...] in order to relate desire *to pleasure or to the orgasm, one must relate it to lack. It is exactly the same thing. The first proposition is the inverse of the second.* [webdeleuze 14/01/1974]

b. The **assemblage** or construction of the non-functional, imperceptible, and non-representative on a **plane of immanence** or consistency that is neither too **stratified** (to become fascist) nor too rapidly destratified (destructive).

Desire *stretches that far:* desiring *one's own annihilation, or* desiring *the power to annihilate. Money, army, police, and State* desire, *fascist* desire, *even fascism is* desire. *[...] The test of* desire: *not* *denouncing false* desires, *but distinguishing within* desire *between that which pertains to stratic proliferation, or else too-violent destratification, and that which pertains to the construction of the* plane of consistency *(keep an eye out for all that is fascist, even inside us, and also for the suicidal and the demented).* [TP 183, 165]

There are no internal drives in desire, *only* assemblages. Desire *is always assembled; it is what the assemblage determines it to be.* [TP 253, 229]

On the plane of consistency *or* immanence, *[...] desire directly invests the field of* perception, *where the imperceptible appears as the perceived object of* desire *itself, 'the nonfigurative of* desire.*'* [TP 313, 284]

c. In D&G's reading of **Kafka**, the actual juridical or bureaucratic processes within social **assemblages** that are revealed through the disassembly or **deterritorialization** of their apparent or representative functions.

Repression doesn't belong to justice unless it is also desire *itself—* desire *in the one who is repressed as well as in the one who represses. And the authorities of justice are not those who look for offenses but those who are 'attracted, propelled by offense.'* [K 49]

5. In Deleuze's analysis of the logical dimensions of the **proposition**, the state where **sense** that correlates to belief produces a **manifestation** of the personal (the 'I'), conditioning **denotations** of external states of affairs.

Desires *and beliefs are causal inferences, not associations.* **Desire** *is the internal causality of an image with respect to the existence of the object or the corresponding state of affairs.* [LS 17, 13]

6. In Deleuze's reading of **Proust**, that which, *when working in conjunction with memory*, produces multiple images of the beloved, each seen in a singular respect in order to engender jealousy (the condition of love).

consider love itself: **desire** *and memory combine in order to form precipitates of jealousy, but the former is first of all concerned with multiplying the non-communicating Albertines, the latter with extracting from Albtertine incommensurable 'regions of memory'.* [P 118]

- E. B. Y.

Desiring-machines

Machines and **desire** conjoin very early in Guattari's writing, circa 1969, in the essay 'Machine et structure' (PT) as a critique of the disempowering effects for subjectification of structural-linguistic psychoanalysis practiced by Lacanians. Yet Guattari attributed to Lacan himself the conceptual foundations for this critique. The first glimmer of his interest in Deleuzian philosophical **concepts** (**repetition** and **series**) is also found there. The Guattarian subject is located at the intersection of machine and structure beyond the individual and human collectivity in an order of scientific and technological advances—later **phylum**—of growing importance for contemporary life. The roots of the **assemblage** and of **subjectification** are embedded in this term whose fuller development will appear in *The Anti-Oedipus*.

Not to be confused with the **Freud**ian Id, desiring-machines are non-Oedipal and engaged in real processes of production. They express a direct link between **desire** and production. Their components couple and connect with one another *and* cut the fluxes of **desire**; libido is both energy that is expended in and produced by their couplings. And they break down, but continue working nonetheless. Desiring-machines function and have no inscribed meaning. The realm of production and organization is that of desiring-machines, but they pour over the **surface** of anti-production, the **body-without-organs**, connecting together, and with components of anti-production by means of disjunction. Tools are contrasted with desiring-machines. The latter do not project; rather, they dis/connect (break/flow) in nuanced ways (detaching or slicing or rendering residual) and work by recurrence, bearing chains of **a-signifying code** with them.

1.a. A disruptive object that cannot be enveloped by structure, which is modeled on Lacan's **objet petit a.**

> The **objet petit a** described by Lacan as the root of **desire**, as the umbilicus of the dream, bursts into the structural equilibrium of the individual like some infernal machine. [PT 244]

b. That which produces connective syntheses by virtue of an attraction towards organs and **partial objects** (oriented towards life), and that which at the same time repels production as well as an organization of the body (oriented towards death); the coexistence of forces of life and death in an interminable process of production which takes place by virtue of (**abstract**) **machines** and within social **assemblages**.

> *it is absurd to speak of a death* **desire** *that would presumably be in qualitative opposition to the life desires. Death is not desired, there is only death that desires, by virtue of the* **body without organs** *or the immobile motor, and there is also life that desires, by virtue of the working organs. There we do not have two desires but two parts, two kinds of* **desiring-machine** *parts, in the dispersion of the machine itself.* [AO 362, 329]

2. Productive connections by **partial objects** which are recorded and transformed by the disjunctive syntheses on the **body without organs** (to result in conjunctive syntheses which do not conform to a sexual, organic, or theological law); that is, the operation through **deterritorialization** or disassembly of representation in favor of a machinic functioning in reality. [AO, K, TP]

> *Insofar as it brings together—without unifying or uniting them—the* **body without organs** *and the* **partial objects***, the* **desiring-machine** *is inseparable both from the distribution of the partial objects on the body without organs, and from the leveling effect exerted on the partial objects by the body without organs* [AO 359–60, 327]

> **desire** *never stops making a machine in the machine and creates a new gear alongside the preceding gear, indefinitely, even if the gears seem to be in opposition or seem to be functioning in a discordant fashion.* [K 82]

3.a. The rejection of the signifier, signifying chain, and the double planes of linguistic semiology as the constitutive features of processes of **subjectification**.

> *The essence of the machine [...] is that one cannot ultimately distinguish the* **unconscious** *subject of* **desire** *from the order of the machine itself.* [MR 117]

b. Technical machines and **collective assemblages of enunciation** which escape from the impasses of individuation within signifying systems that block access to the real; hence, they are non-Oedipal and engaged in real processes of production.

No need for these things to represent: technical **machines** *do it better!* [...] *Technical* **machines** *liberate the potential schizo use of* **desiring-machines**. [AOP 152–3]

4. An abstract or concrete object consisting of breaks, **flows** and components that couple and connect with one another *and* cut the fluxes of **desire**, yet nevertheless continue working.

A **machine** *may be defined as a system of interruptions or breaks (coupures). These breaks should in no way be considered as a separation from reality* [...] *Every* **machine** *is* [...] *related to a continual material* **flow** *that cuts into it* [...] *removing portions from the associative flow* [...] *Each associative flow must be seen* [...] *as an endless flux.* [...] *In a word, every* **machine** *functions as a break in the flow in relation to the* **machine** *to which it is connected, but at the same time is also a flow itself, or the production of a flow, in relation to the* **machine** *connected to it.* [AO 39, 36]

- G. G. (rev. E. B. Y.)

Deterritorialization

Cross reference: **Territory**; Territorialization

Diagram

First appearing in Guattari's writings from the 1970s, and then in *A Thousand Plateaus*, the 'diagram' is an interesting example of a **concept** that Deleuze also took in his own direction (in his work on **Foucault** and **Bacon**). While Guattari used the term primarily in the context of an **a-signifying semiotic** system that would bypass the pitfalls of representation and connect directly to reality, which he and Deleuze emphasized as a feature of the **abstract machine** in *A Thousand Plateaus*, Deleuze focused on the paradoxical status of the diagram that involves both order and **chaos**. For example, in Deleuze's **Foucault**, diagrams concern the relations of **force** that are fixed as power relations, but are at the same time unstable and mutable within **the Outside**; likewise, in *Francis Bacon: The Logic of Sensation*, it is the chaotic disruption of 'figurative givens' within the painting that institute a new non-signifying and sensory order. Then, again with Guattari in *What is Philosophy?*, the diagram becomes a feature of the **plane of immanence** that is not **intensive** but determined as infinite movement.

1. In Guattari's adaptation of Charles Peirce's semiotics, a **sign** system where signification and representation are bypassed in favor of contact between language and real, material fluxes (as with **Metamodelization** and **Cartography**).

> **Denotation** *disappears in the face of the processed described by Peirce as* 'diagrammatization'. *[...] This operation of signs, this work of* **diagrammatization,** *has become the necessary condition for the* **deterritorializing** *mutationst that* affect *the fluxes of reality; no longer is there representation, but simulation, pre-production, or what one might call 'transduction'.* [MR 95]

2.a. In Deleuze's reading of **Foucault**, a term used (by Foucault) to describe the form of the Panopticon that is an ideal function of power (operating in many institutions such as school, the workplace, and the clinic) rather than a historical site with a predetermined function (limited to prisons).

> *The panopticon must not be understood as a dream building, it is the* **diagram** *of a mechanism of power reduced to its ideal form as a pure architectural and optical system: it is in fact a figure of political technology [...] detached from any specific use.* [Foucault, 1995, p. 205]

b. That which is invisible and inarticulable but produces visibilities and statements, generating the split and solidarity between **forms of content** and **forms of expression**.

> *[...] we can conceive of pure* **matter** *and pure* **functions,** *abstracting the forms which embody them. [...] What can we call such a new informal dimension? On one occasion* **Foucault** *gives it its most precise name: it is a* 'diagram', *[...] It is a* machine *that is almost blind and mute, even though it makes others see and speak.* [F 30, 32]

c. A composition or distribution of points and lines (singularities or **differences**) that constitute the relations between **forces**, or power relations, which is presented in a fixed form but is founded upon a fluid, unstable, or formless form that emerges from **the Outside** and continually resists the formalization of power.

> *We can [...] define the* **diagram** *in several different, interlocking ways: it is the presentation of the relations between* **forces** *unique to a particular formation; it is the distribution of the power to* **affect** *and the power to be affected; it is the mixing of non-formalized pure functions and unformed pure matter [...] it is a transmission or distribution of singularities* [F 61, 72–3]

> *The* **diagram***, as the fixed form of a set of relations between* **forces***, never exhausts force, which can enter into other relations and compositions. The* **diagram** *stems from the* **outside** *but the outside does not merge with any* **diagram***, and continues instead to 'draw' new ones.* [F 74, 89]

3. In Deleuze and Guattari's explanation of the **abstract machine**, a destratified function of a **deterritorialized assemblage**, which engenders and is encased within the **stratified** function of **concrete assemblages** (*dispositifs*) [F, TP].

> *The* **abstract machine** *is like the* **diagram** *of an* **assemblage***. It draws lines of continuous variation, while the concrete assemblage treats variables and organized their highly diverse relations as a function of those lines.* [TP 110–11, 100]

4. In Deleuze's explanation of painting, an artistic device that deforms figuration, rather than reconstitutes movement or narrates a story, in order to render **forces** and lines of **sensation** visible, by negotiating between the **chaos** (catastrophe) that it induces and the clichés (givens) that it destroys or dissociates.

> *The* **diagram** *is the operative set of a-signifying and non-representative lines and zones, line strokes and color patches [...] The* **diagram** *is [...] a violent* **chaos** *in relation to the figurative givens, but it is a germ of* **rhythm** *in relation to the new order of the painting.* [FB 101–2]

5. In D&G's explanation of the impetus of thought, a **sensation** or movement that composes the determinations of **chaos** on the **plane of immanence** or consistency, which are presupposed by the **concepts** and **intensities** which occupy it [TP, WP].

> *From* **chaos** *the* **plane of immanence** *takes the determinations with which it makes its infinite movements or its* **diagrammatic** *features.* [WP 50]

- E. B. Y.

Dialogues I & II

Dialogues, avec Claire Parnet (1977; réédition, 1996)

A series of conversations or dialogical mediations with former student and journalist, Claire Parnet, this work continues the collaborative form created with Guattari in which the individual identity of the speaker or personal pronoun disappears in favor of a free indirect discourse. The original edition contains four sections addressing the notion of '**becoming** multiple' in a conversation, the somewhat bombastic or tongue-in-cheek discussion of 'the superiority of Anglo-American literature,' and dialogues on 'dead psychoanalysis' and on 'many politics.' This edition first appears in English translation in 1987 and contains an original preface by Deleuze where he describes the book as made up of 'several reveries' and again emphasizes the fact that the manner in which the conversation was made, by creating a line between multiple points and subjective positions, is just as much a part of a theory of multiplicities as the arguments it puts forward. In 1996, a new edition of *Dialogues* is published, which concludes with 'The Actual and Virtual,' purportedly the last work written by Deleuze before his suicide in 1994. - G. L.

Dicisign

cross-reference: **Perception** (diffuse); def. 2b.

Difference

Difference is a buzzword often associated with 'post-structuralist' philosophy, which critiques the limiting, binary differences engendered by **structuralism**; it is also associated with identity politics in terms of the discourses of the marginalized and oppressed. However, Deleuze, on the one hand, is not a philosopher of language *per se* (he does not take the text as his primary object of study) and his discussion of structures can be found in his systems of **serialization** and **passive syntheses**; on the other hand, while his conception of difference could be used to discuss oppression (i.e. the tyranny of representation), he offers an explicit conception of **the Other** that is bound up with his philosophy of **expression**, and by extension, of **collective assemblages of enunciation**. The problem of difference, for Deleuze, primarily involves the very heart of thinking outside of representation, and defining the term often involves his *critique* of its subordination to identity throughout the history of philosophy before it is situated as a **force** of decentering and divergence within heterogeneous systems.

1.a. A relation that cannot be thought in terms of a predetermined image, or mediated by a higher principle, and is paradoxically thinkable, albeit not defined, only by virtue of its effects (resemblance, identity, analogy and opposition); that which implicates **repetition**, rather than contradiction, as its outer limit.

> Consider the two propositions: *only that which is alike* **differs**; *and only* **differences** *are alike*. *The first formula posits resemblance as the condition of* **difference**. *[...] According to the other formula, by contrast, resemblance, identity, analogy and opposition can no longer be considered anything but effects, the products of a primary* **difference** *or a primary system of* **differences**. [DR 143, 116–7]

> *It is said that* **difference** *is negativity, that it extends or must extend to the point of contradiction once it is taken to the limit. This is true only to the extent that* **difference** *is already placed on a path or along a thread laid out by identity.* [DR 60, 49–50]

b. The proper state of **univocal** being, which distinguishes neither between original and copy (**Plato**), nor between categories

(**Aristotle**); furthermore, no distinction is made between a reflection of an opposite with which being would share an absolute or 'infinitely large' identity (**Hegel**), nor between inessential properties or 'infinitely small' cases (**Leibniz**); rather, a state in which all things are **simulacra** that exclude the possibility of contradiction or exterior terms which would mediate large/small differences in order to distinguish their truth or falsity.

> Plato *gave the establishment of* difference *as the supreme goal of dialectic.* However, difference *does not lie between things and* simulacra, *models and copies. Things are simulacra themselves, simulacra are the superior forms [...].* [DR 81, 67]

> *generic or categorical* difference *remains a* difference *in the* Aristotelian *sense [...]: it has no content in itself, only a content in proportion to the formally* different *terms of which it is predicated. [...] generic (distributive and hierarchical)* difference *is content in turn to inscribe* difference *in the quasi-identity of the most general determinable* concepts *[...].* [DR 42, 33]

> *With [...* Leibniz*], representation conquers the infinite because a technique for dealing with the infinitely small captures the smallest* difference *and its disappearance. With [...* Hegel*], representation conquers the infinite because a technique for dealing with the infinitely large captures the largest* difference *and its dismembering.* [DR 331, 263]

c. The dissolution of the representation and identity of subjects and objects, which are sensed or perceived instead by virtue of the unending drama of a **series** of metamorphoses, evolutions, or involutions that displace and disguise them. [LS, DR]

> *Representation fails to capture the affirmed world of* difference. *Representation has only a single centre [...].* Difference *[by contrast] must become the element, the ultimate unity [...] Each term of a* series, *being already a* difference, *must be put into a variable relation with other terms, thereby constituting other series devoid of centre and convergence. Divergence and decentering must be affirmed in the series itself. [...]* **Difference** *must be shown differing.* [DR 68, 56]

– E. B. Y.

Difference and Repetition

Différence et répétition (1968)

Difference and Repetition is Deleuze's major philosophical work and was his primary thesis for his Doctorat d'État. Far from being his first substantial work of philosophy, however, it was published fifteen years after his first book on **Hume**. As he states in the preface to the English edition, 'After I had studied Hume, **Spinoza**, **Nietzsche** and **Proust**, all of whom fired me with enthusiasm, *Difference and Repetition* was the first book in which I tried to "do philosophy"' (DR xii, xv). His studies of **Bergson, Sacher-Masoch** and **Kant** were also written before *Difference and Repetition*, and resonances from Deleuze's work on all seven of these thinkers can be found in *Difference and Repetition*. In fact, many of his starting points and claims can be traced back to those earlier apprenticeship works. However, what distinguishes *Difference and Repetition* is the new constellation that Deleuze creates by recasting those claims under the rubric of '**difference**' and '**repetition**,' which he insists has remained unthought in the history of philosophy that has been determined under the requirements of **representation**. It is this fundamental approach that distinguishes Deleuze's work from other French post-structural thinkers of his generation such as Derrida and Lyotard; although he is inspired from a **Nietzsche**an perspective, according to which the world is composed by an interplay of differences, he nevertheless continues to 'do **metaphysics**' by systematically demonstrating how difference envelops and is developed by repetition in a variety of domains (aesthetics, ethnology, biology, mathematics, etc.). Despite this systematic and metaphysical impulse, *Difference and Repetition* presents a challenge to the reader because the idea of difference 'in-itself' can never be defined as such without subordinating it to **representation**. Instead, Deleuze offers a **multiplicity** of claims regarding difference, all of which are 'disguises' of the same fundamental problem, and in this way the style of the book testifies to its central premise.

The dynamic that Deleuze elaborates between **difference** and **repetition** is not only a tool for philosophical inquiry uncontaminated by **representation**, it is at the same time a critical weapon. Throughout *Difference and Repetition*, Deleuze analyzes the philosophical systems of other thinkers to show the various ways in which difference and repetition either become 'too general', or how a specific interplay between the two fall victim to representation. Deleuze discusses these perspectives because he is interested in investigating the point at which certain systems of thought subsume or 'cancel out' difference. Nevertheless, no matter how abstract the cancellation of difference becomes, it is still enveloped by genuine difference. In other words, theories of repetition that subordinate difference to representation or identity, or that subsume difference under contradiction, still express a shadow, however distorted, of real effective difference (thus failing to capture the true nature of difference does not invalidate those theories but simply limits their scope). As Deleuze states, 'An entire **multiplicity** rumbles underneath the "sameness" of the **Idea**' (DR 344, 275). In this manner, a great challenge to the reader is to negotiate between those perspectives from which Deleuze departs and the new and evasive image of thought which he offers. For this reason, *Difference and Repetition* still remains one of the most profoundly influential, contested, and discussed philosophical works of the twentieth century. - E. B. Y.

Differenciation

1.a. The **actualization** of the **virtual** (in response to the **differentiation** of the virtual); the prolongation of different levels of **sensation** or qualitative impressions; the expansion and separation of **intensities** or **differences** in kind (qualities) throughout a field of extensity (in distinction from differences of degree, which cancel difference); the physical (organic) or psychic (expressive) solution to a virtual problem, as with the development of parts of an organism that serve specific functions.

> *This fundamental* **differenciation** *(quality–extensity) can find its reason only in the great synthesis of Memory which allows all the degrees of* **difference** *to coexist as degrees of relaxation and* **contraction**, *and rediscovers at the heart of* **duration** *the implicated order of that* **intensity** [DR 299, 239]

the nature of the **virtual** *is such that, for it, to be* **actualized** *is to be* **differenciated**. *Each* **differenciation** *is a local integration or a local solution [...]An organism is nothing if not the solution to a problem, as are each of its* **differenciated** *organs, such as the eye which solves a light 'problem'* [DR 263, 211]

We know that the **virtual** *as virtual has a reality [...] in which everything coexists with itself, except for the* **differences** *of level [of expansion and* **contraction***]. On each of these levels there are some 'outstanding points,' which are [...]themselves virtual. [...] what coexisted in the virtual ceases to coexist in the* **actual** *and is distributed in lines or parts that cannot be summed up [...] These lines of* **differenciation** *[lignes de différenciation] are therefore truly creative* [B 100–101]

b. The **force** of **chaos** which relates different levels of the **virtual** to one another, or implicates spatio-temporal **series** within each other, generating **intensities**. [B, DR]

The essential point is the simultaneity and contemporaneity of all the divergent **series***, the fact that all coexist. From the point of view of the presents which pass in representation, the series are certainly successive, one 'before' and the* **other** *'after'. [...]. However, this no longer applies from the point of view of the* **chaos** *which contains them [...]: the* **differenciator** *always makes them coexist.* [DR 151, 124]

– E. B. Y.

Differentiation

While this term is absent in **Bergsonism** (though readers should note that the French term *différenciation* is translated as *differentiation* in that text), in **Difference and Repetition** Deleuze makes an important distinction between differentiation and **differenciation**. This term involves a quasi-mathematical operation of setting conditions for determination (which thus concerns coexisting differences), while its counterpart refers to actual or 'extensive' differences; as Deleuze states, if differen*t*iation determines 'problems', differen*c*iation expresses 'solutions' (there could thus be no 'differen*c*iation' without 'differen*t*iation').

1. The state of the Idea insofar as it concerns a degree of difference or of a **virtual multiplicity** (in distinction from a difference of degree, or numerical multiplicity); the self-differing or variation the virtual independently of its **actuality**; the process which determines Ideas, despite that such Ideas do not resemble the **actualizations** which incarnate them.

> *We call the determination of the* virtual *content of an Idea* **differentiation**; *we call the* **actualization** *of that* virtuality *into species and distinguished parts* **differenciation**. [DR 258, 207]

> *all the Ideas, all the relations with their variations and points, coexist, even though there are changes of order according to the elements considered: they are fully determined and* **differentiated** *even though they are completely un***differenciated**. [DR 314, 252]

> *complete determination carries out the* **differentiation** *of singularities, but it bears only upon their existence and their distribution* [DR 262, 210]

- E. B. Y.

Disjunctive synthesis

(also *Inclusive Disjunction*)

1.a. In Deleuze's explanation of distributive logic, the manner of apprehending two or more **series** without reducing them to a center of convergence; in D&G's explanation of **desiring-machines**, one of the three major **modes** of the **passive syntheses** resulting in a subjective break (the others being *connective* and *conjunctive*).

> *Three sorts of synthesis are distinguished: the connective synthesis (if..., then), which bears upon the construction of a single* **series**; *the conjunctive series (and), as a method of constructing convergent series; and the* **disjunctive** *series (or), which distributes the divergent series. [...]* [D]isjunction *is not at all reduced to a conjunction; it is left as a* **disjunction**, *since it bears, and continues to bear, upon a divergence as such.* [LS 199, 174]

> *The first* **mode** *[of desiring-production] has to do with the connective synthesis, and mobilizes libido as withdrawal energy*

*(*énergie de prélèvement*). The second has to do with the* **disjunctive synthesis,** *and mobilizes the* Numen *as detachment energy (*énergie de détachement*). The third has to do with the conjunctive synthesis, and mobilizes* Voluptas *as residual energy (*énergie résiduelle*).* [AO 45, 41]

b. In Deleuze's interpretation of the logical **paradox** 'either x or y or both', the manner in which two distinct **series** or singularities communicate **sense** without becoming identical; portmanteau words (like 'fruminous'—fuming + furious) that would not simply conflate the sense of two disparities, but affirm that the sense contains both and neither.

> *the portmanteau word is grounded upon a strict* **disjunctive synthesis.** *[…] the necessary disjunction is not between fuming and furious, for one may indeed be both at once; rather, it is between fuming-and-furious on one hand and furious-and-fuming on the other. […]* **disjunctive** *or portmanteau words, which perform an infinite ramification of coexisting* **series** *and bear at once upon words and senses.* [LS 55, 46–7]

2. In Deleuze's reading of **Leibniz,** the manner in which an **event** is not expressed by the compossibility of worlds or **monads,** but where worlds are nevertheless compatible through an affirmation of their divergence and decentering; the manner in which the **events** communicate such that they do not engender the best possible world, but rather, instigated by the disjunction, ensure that the **passive syntheses** of *connection* and *conjunction* endlessly diverge.

> **Leibniz** *though makes use of this rule of incompossibility in order to exclude* **events** *from one another. He made a negative use of divergence of* **disjunction***—one of exclusion.[… However,] from this other point of view, the divergence of* **series** *or the* **disjunction** *of members (membra disjuncta) cease to be negative rules of exclusion according to which events would be incompossible or incompatible.* [LS 197, 172]

- E. B. Y.

Dividual

cross-reference: Affect (5.b.)

Duration

This elusive term from **Bergson**'s philosophy was utilized by Deleuze when describing the paradoxes of **contraction**: that is, how the viscera or '**matter**' (which is in motion) contracts aspects of the past and the present and therefore has a temporality or 'duration' that is indicative of its evolution or change, which is itself irreducible to the matter, space, or extension in which the contraction takes place (that is, it is irreducible to the physical evidence as well as the individual, successive moments). The concept is also referenced briefly in his work on **Spinoza**, but is primarily taken up again in his work on movement in *Cinema*.

> 1.a. A term that Henri **Bergson** uses to characterize the continuous nature of lived experience where the present coexists with the past as a whole.
>
>> *our* **duration** *is not merely one instant replacing another; if it were, there would never be anything but the present—no prolonging of the past into the* **actual**, *no evolution, no concrete* **duration**. **Duration** *is the continuous progress of the past which gnaws into the future and which swells as it advances. And as the past grows without ceasing, so also there is no limit to its preservation.* [Bergson, 1911, 4]
>
> b. In Deleuze's reading of **Bergson**, the coexistence of past and present instances in the memory as a spatial, qualitative **multiplicity**, in distinction from the succession of past and present instances in **matter** as a numerical multiplicity; an indivisible, subjective **virtuality** that differs in kind (in itself and from **matter**) by virtue of **differenciation**, in distinction from an objective **actuality** that can be counted as well as divided without changing in nature; in Deleuze's explanation of **difference**, the prolongation or preservation of the past in the present; the movement of matter (in distinction from the separation and existence of matter) which divides by changing

in nature, whether psychically (the mind which perceives differences in kind based on intuition) or physically (movements of differenciation).

> *Movement is undoubtedly explained by the insertion of* **duration** *into* **matter***: Duration is differenciated according to the obstacles it meets in matter […]*. **Duration***, to be precise, is called* **life** *when it appears in this movement.* [B 94–5]

> *Not only do* **virtual multiplicities** *imply a single time, but* **duration** *as virtual multiplicity is this single and same time.* [B 83]

> **Duration**, *memory or spirit is* **difference** *in kind in itself and for itself; and space or* **matter** *is difference in degree* [….] **Duration** *is only the most contracted degree of matter, matter the most expanded (*détendu*) degree of* **duration***. But* **duration** *is like a naturing nature (*nature naturante*), and matter a natured nature (*nature nature*).* [B 93]

c. In Deleuze's explanation of **repetition**, in distinction from a motor or automatic repetition where there is only presence in **matter**, a **contraction** where the present relates the past to the future in a movement of creative evolution. [B, DR]

> *What is expanded (*détendu*) if not the* **contracted** *—and what is contracted if not the extended, the expanded (*détente*)? This is why there is always extensity in our* **duration***, and always* **duration** *in* **matter** [B 87]

2. In Deleuze's reading of **Bergson** for his work on *Cinema*, the indication of change, by virtue of movement, in the quality of an open whole which itself encompasses various sections, objects, or subjects (that is, while the state of individual parts or sections change, the relation between them constitutes the essence of this change and explains it).

> *if the whole is not giveable; it is because it is the Open, and because its nature is to change constantly […] So that each time we find ourselves confronted with a* **duration***, or in a* **duration***, we may conclude that there exists somewhere a whole which is changing […].* [C1 10, 9]

> *To say that* **duration** *is change is part of its definition: it changes and does not stop changing. […] imagine I am starving at A, and at B there is something to eat. When I have reached B and had something to*

> eat, what has changed is not only my state, but the state of the whole which encompassed B, A, and all that was between them. [C1 8–9, 8]

3. In Deleuze's reading of **Spinoza**, the feature of an existing **mode** which endures independently of the **attribute** that it modifies, in distinction from a modal essence, which contains degrees of power or **intensity** within all modes that exist (but does not exist or have duration). [SEP]

> *when* **modes** *come into existence, they acquire extensive parts. They acquire a size and* **duration**: *each mode endures as long as its parts remain in the relation that characterizes it.* [SEP 213]

- E. B. Y.

Ecosophy

This term is a neologism coined by Norwegian philosopher Arne Naess, but redefined by Guattari in the late 1980s in terms of a different conception of **subjectivity**. It required an explicitly tripartite adumbration (mental, social, environmental) that focused on the construction of ontological **territories** on a **machinic phylum,** rather than a natural reference, as well as new incorporeal political values beyond traditional party politics. Guattari came to ecology late in his life. He found in it the philosophical and political impetus not only to seek scientific solutions to environmental menaces, but to reconfigure social practices devastated by upheavals in the public sphere, and resist capitalistic subjectifications and their infantilizing mediatic inducements and appeals to post-modern cynicism.

> 1.a. An activist practice that engages artistic production towards maximizing the incomparable and automodelizing traits of mental ecologies with a commitment to ethically responsible negotiations of collective actions and large-scale engagements, since **subjectivity** is intimately imbricated in mutually dependent bio- and mechano-spheres.

> *Despite having recently initiated a partial realization of the most obvious dangers that threaten the natural environment of our societies, they [political groupings and executive authorities] are*

generally content to simply tackle industrial pollution and then from a purely technocratic perspective, whereas only an ethico-political articulation—which I call ecosophy *—between the three ecological registers (the environment, social relations, and human* subjectivity*) would be likely to clarify these questions.* [TE 27–8]

b. Mental, social, environmental registers that aim at an ethico-political linkage of the micro and macro levels, building a critique of technocratic solutions, and highlighting the role of artists in fostering emancipatory eco-praxes. Art and ecology are closely linked in the production of subjectivity in a way that would assist in extracting potential for existential change and assisting in the development of new processes that are more complex, sustaining and enriching.

This new ecosophical *logic […] resembles the manner in which an artist may be led to alter his work after the intrusion of some accidental detail, an* event-*incident that suddenly makes his initial project bifurcate, making it drift far from its previous path, however certain it had once appeared to be.* [TE 52]

2.a. (Special Type): *Machinic Ecology*: Processes of subjectification that are dependent upon developments in, and engender themselves upon, the vast phylum of technological, informational, chemical, biogenetically engineered infrastructures that support human life.

In the final account, the ecosophic *problematic is that of the production of human existence itself in new historical contexts.* [TE 34]

b. (Special Type): *Three Ecologies*: that which requires the creation of collective assemblages of enunciation based on eco-political and aesthetic principles that promote resingularizing subjectifications.

The principle common to the three ecologies *is this: each of the* existential Territories *with which they confront us is not given as an in-itself, closed in on itself, but instead as a for-itself that is precarious, finite, finalized, singular, singularized, capable of bifurcating into* stratified *and deathly* repetitions *or of opening up processually from a praxis that enables it to be 'habitable' by a human project.* [TE 53]

3. An antidote to the neoliberal myths of the 1980s and a critique of capitalist market logics following their entry into the post-revolutionary Eastern bloc.

4. The rationale underlining Guattari's unsuccessful run for office under the Green banner in the Paris regional elections in 1992, where he took out membership in both factions of a split party, and agitated for transversal bridges between the two and the necessity of dissensus for a new politics within a renewed public intellectual sphere.

> *If the* ecological *movement in France today, which appears to have so much promise, fails to engage with this problem of recomposing militant situations (in an entirely new sense, that is to say, of collective* assemblages *of subjectiviation) then it will certainly lose the capital of confidence invested in it, and the technical and associative aspects of ecology will be recuperated by the traditional parties, State power, and eco-business.* [CM 129]

- G. G.

Elkaïm, Mony

Born in Morocco but based mostly in Belgium, this psychotherapist was practicing family therapy in the south Bronx when Guattari met him in 1972. Having distanced himself from **Freud**ian and Lacanian theory with the publication of ***Anti-Oedipus*** that same year, Guattari was drawn to Elkaïm's work with poor families, whose socio-economic circumstances he took into account. The latter's practice expanded on family therapy's basic notion of the family system, as developed by **Gregory Bateson** and his collaborators at the Mental Research Institute in Palo Alto, California. Elkaïm enlarged the scope of treatment beyond the family in order to include the surrounding neighborhood and social context. He borrowed **Ilya Prigogine**'s idea of open systems far from equilibrium as a corrective to the prevailing view of the family as a system tending toward homeostasis. Upon his return to Europe, he and Guattari joined with Franco Basaglia and David Cooper to form an international network for alternative psychiatry (CY 186–7). Guattari maintained a close relationship with Elkaïm despite disagreements regarding the understanding of the notion of system [CM 7]. - J. W.

Empiricism and Subjectivity

Empirisme et subjectivité. (1953)

Empiricism and Subjectivity is Deleuze's first sole-authored book (his first book, also on **Hume**, was co-authored a year previously with André Cresson). Despite being published almost a decade before his next book-length work, the reader may discover resonances with other philosophers and writers that Deleuze studied early in his career such as **Bergson, Proust, Spinoza**, and **Nietzsche**. An argument can certainly be made that Deleuze was emphasizing traits in Hume's works that many other scholars of Hume would choose not to emphasize, such as the role of **habit** and custom in relation to **repetition** and the imagination; yet, this shift in emphasis also arguably marks the originality of his approach.

This work on **Hume** also sets the stakes for Deleuze's interest in **transcendental empiricism**; in this regard, the question Deleuze asks is: how is the mind (or an idea in the mind) formed without 'transcending' or going beyond experience or the given? As he states:

> The given is the idea as it is given in the mind, without anything transcending it—not even the mind, which is therefore identical with the idea. But, the transcendence itself is also given, in an altogether different sense and manner—it is given as practice, as an **affection** of the mind, and as an **impression** of reflection [...] Empirical **subjectivity** is constituted in the mind under the influence of principles affecting it; the mind therefore does not have the characteristics of a preexisting subject. [ES 28–9]

Complex formulations such as these are common in *Empiricism and Subjectivity*; in general they demonstrate the dynamic between the given as an **impression** that merely gives birth to the mind, and the principles of association that constitute **habit, reason,** and belief. In short, the subject does not 'transcend' experience in order to think; rather, experience is only 'transcended' temporally, insofar as it is grounded in past experience and facilitates the passions in the future. Deleuze concludes from this that if there are no a priori subjects, that is, if subjects are defined by their context, then **subjectivity** is 'qualified' by the mind itself, and any operation of the mind (reason, belief, etc.) 'gives the subject a possible structure' while 'passions can give it being and existence' (ES 120). In this early work one can thus find playful and elliptical language (which becomes a trademark in his major works) when he describes the transitions between 1) nature and human nature, 2) habit and experience, 3) the given and the idea, or 4) the passional and the social. - E. B. Y.

Essays Critical and Clinical

Critique et clinique (1993)

In a conversation with Raymond Bellour and Francois Ewald for *Magazine Litteraire* in 1988, Deleuze speaks of his long-time plan of bringing together a series of studies of writers as great diagnosticians and symptomatologists under the general title 'Critique et Clinique.' Five years later this collection is published, mostly drawn from Deleuze's previous and uncollected essays and prefaces on various writers who are frequently referenced in his other major works, including **Artaud**, Beckett, **Kafka**, Lawrence, **Sacher-Masoch**, Melville, and Whitman. Whether this fulfills Deleuze's original plan for the project is doubtful, since by this time Deleuze succumbs to a more serious phase of a pulmonary disease that made it difficult for him to write. Nevertheless, *Essays Critical and Clinical* (according to the English title) also collects new and previously unpublished writings, including the introductory essay, 'Literature and Life,' and the essay 'He Stuttered,' which was originally written for the first international conference on Deleuze that took place at Trent University in 1992, and was organized by the Canadian academic Constantine Boundas and the American philosopher Dorothea Olkowski. - G. L.

Eternal return

Whether in reference to ancient theories or not, 'eternal return' probably conjures up images of cycles: the return of the seasons, the 'cycle of **life**', etc. And yet, the variations of each (re)occurrence belie the notion that things *truly* 'recur': each winter is just a little unlike the last, each life is somehow unique. While this may make it seem as though change is linear, Deleuze would argue it is, paradoxically, somewhere in-between; it is the '**simulacrum**' that makes each season or life both 'similar' and different (relative *to* that similarity): they are impersonal **singularities** which have nothing to do with the identity of an individualized nature, nor are they reproductions of something original. Here we can begin to touch on the **paradox** of an infinite, all-inclusive past, which nevertheless *changes* by virtue of the present on its way to an infinite, all-inclusive future.

The eternal return, however, is not some overly complex way of resigning to a platitude like 'everything is everything', because *not everything* 'returns': in accordance with **Nietzsche**'s ontology, that which does not return, and does not exist, is *nothing*. There is no such thing as 'empty space' or the existence of nothingness (the recent scientific discovery of the Higgs boson could be considered supportive of this thesis). And yet, we often *believe* that there is—through **values** that are opposed to this life, or through our wish that things should be otherwise (i.e. the present should *not* exist, and some other present should). So, following Deleuze's reading of Nietzsche, if 'nothing' cannot exist—if it is not something we can *will* (without being 'reactive' in our **morality**), then eternal return is an ethical thought of the state of the world which, in believing, we affirm that we are more than simply 'ephemeral', even if our nature *cannot* be explained by a 'higher' value or truth that would justify it.

What Deleuze adds to the French reception of Nietzsche that is perhaps most distinct is his location of eternal return as a **synthesis** of time that 'expels' the generic features of **habit** and memory: it harnesses the impersonal and incessant features of eternity or death only in order to deny the negative features of habit (generic, mediated **difference**) and of memory (generic, mediated **repetition**), ultimately to 'select' unmediated difference (which lacks any 'centre' within an identity) on the basis of unmediated repetition (in its continuous, lived manner of being without place). In this case, insofar as that which 'returns' passes through all the other disjointed **series** or **events** with which it is in communication, it **expresses** the '**univocity**' of being and a state of permanent **becoming**.

1. In **Nietzsche**'s work, the logical conclusion of a non-creationist and non-teleological hypothesis, which asserts that if the past is infinite, then there is nothing that can achieve or reach a final state, and there is no state of equilibrium of **force**. Rather, the future is, likewise, infinite and the present displays a permanent state of **becoming** which, on the one hand, 'repeats' aspects of the (infinite) past, and on the other hand, is neither predicable nor predetermined.

> *From this gateway Moment a long* eternal *lane stretches backward: behind us lies an* eternity. *Must not whatever can already have passed this way before? Must not whatever can happen, already have happened, been done, passed by before?* [Nietzsche, 2006, 126]

> *This world: [...] an ocean of* forces *storming and flooding within themselves,* eternally *changing,* eternally *coming back, with oceanic years of recurrence, with an ebb and flow of its configurations, [...] blessing itself as that which must* eternally return, *as a becoming that knows no satisfaction with what it will become, no tedium, no fatigue [...] without goal, unless the goal lies in the contingency of the circle, without will, unless a loop has good will towards itself [...].* [Nietzsche, (*The Will to Power* #106) 1922, author's translation]

2.a. In Deleuze's reading of **Nietzsche**, a critique or refusal of the nihilistic principles of both science and religion (as well as the reactive **moralities** and **forces** in general) which prioritize being over **becoming**; an understanding of the 'same' or 'return' in the present in terms of diversity rather than identity.

> *We misinterpret the expression '*eternal return*' if we understand it as 'return of the same'. It is not being that returns but rather the returning itself that constitutes being insofar as it is affirmed of* becoming *and of that which passes[...]. In other words, identity in the* eternal return *does not describe the nature of that which returns*

but, on the contrary, the fact of returning for that which differs.
[N 45, 48]

The test of the eternal return *will not let reactive* forces *subsist, any more than it will let the power of denying subsist. The* eternal return *transmutes the negative: [...] it makes negation a power of affirming.*
[N 81, 86]

b. An **ethical** thought which turns negation against reactive or negative **forces**, and thereby affirms or selects active force (that is, being which is understood as having a different and active **sense**, rather than tracing being back to an identity and limiting its sense); the active power of forgetfulness.

Only the eternal return *can complete nihilism because it makes negation a negation of reactive* forces *themselves.* [N 65, 70]

the eternal return *mak[es] something come into being which cannot do so without changing nature [...]; for the* eternal return *is being and being is selection.* [N 66, 71]

The genius of eternal return *lies not in memory but in waste, in active forgetting. All that is negative and all that denies, [...] everything which cannot pass the test of* eternal return—*all these must be denied.* [DR 66, 55]

3.a. In Deleuze's explanation of time, the third and final **passive synthesis** which conflates the **repetition** of the first, passive syntheses of **habit** with the **difference** of the second, passive syntheses of immemorial memory; additionally, the selective *expulsion* of the generic, mediated difference produced by habit (representations, calculated expectations, **good sense**), along with the selective expulsion of the generic, mediated repetition produced by immemorial **memory** (the pure past which repeats itself outside of successive time); thus, in distinction from the visceral power of habit and the erotic power of memory, the incessant and impersonal **force** of death or Thanatos (**the Outside**).

Eternal return, *in its esoteric truth, concerns—and can concern— only the third time of the* series. *[...] in this final synthesis of time, the present and past are in turn no more than dimensions of the future: the past as condition, the present as agent. [... this involves] expelling the agent and the condition in the name of the work* or product; making **repetition**, *not that from which one 'draws off' a* **difference**, *nor that which includes difference as a variant, but making it the thought and the production of the 'absolutely* **different**'; *making it so that repetition is, for itself, difference in itself.* [DR 118, 94; translation modified]

Thanatos appears in third place as this groundlessness [...]– namely, the **eternal return** *in so far as this does not cause everything to come back but [...] affirm[s] only the excessive and the unequal, the interminable and the incessant.* [DR 141, 115]

b. The **repetition** of **difference** whereby that which repeats or returns does so by virtue of the same and similar, but in a *non-cyclical* manner whereby the same and similar both displace and disguise difference and cause that which guarantees sameness and similitude (identity) to diverge, decenter, or multiply; a temporal line that is paradoxically both circular and straight; a 'return' that does not bring back the same but displaces the same along a path that has no center or telos; the simultaneous negation of negation and affirmation of difference (if understood as a centrifuge, it expels the weight of the negative to the periphery preserving the levity of difference within); the result of an **inclusive disjunction** which enables the conjunctive synthesis or reconciliation of the past and the future (or two disparate **series**) only by virtue of a whole that lacks an identity or a place (the **partial object**, the **event** of all events, or the **univocal** being of all beings).

The wheel in the **eternal return** *is at once both production of* repetition *on the basis of* difference *and selection of difference on the basis of repetition.* [DR 51–2, 42]

The **eternal return** *[...] occurs, therefore, as a unique* event *for everything that happens to the most diverse things [...].* [LS 205, 179]

the **eternal return** *is a circle which is always ex-centric [...]* . [LS 302, 265]

[...] negation as a consequence, as the result of full affirmation, consumes all that is negative, and consumes itself at the mobile centre of eternal return. *For if* eternal return *is a circle, then* **Difference** *is at the centre and the Same is only on the periphery: it is a constantly decentered, continually tortuous circle which revolves only around the unequal.* [DR 55, 67]

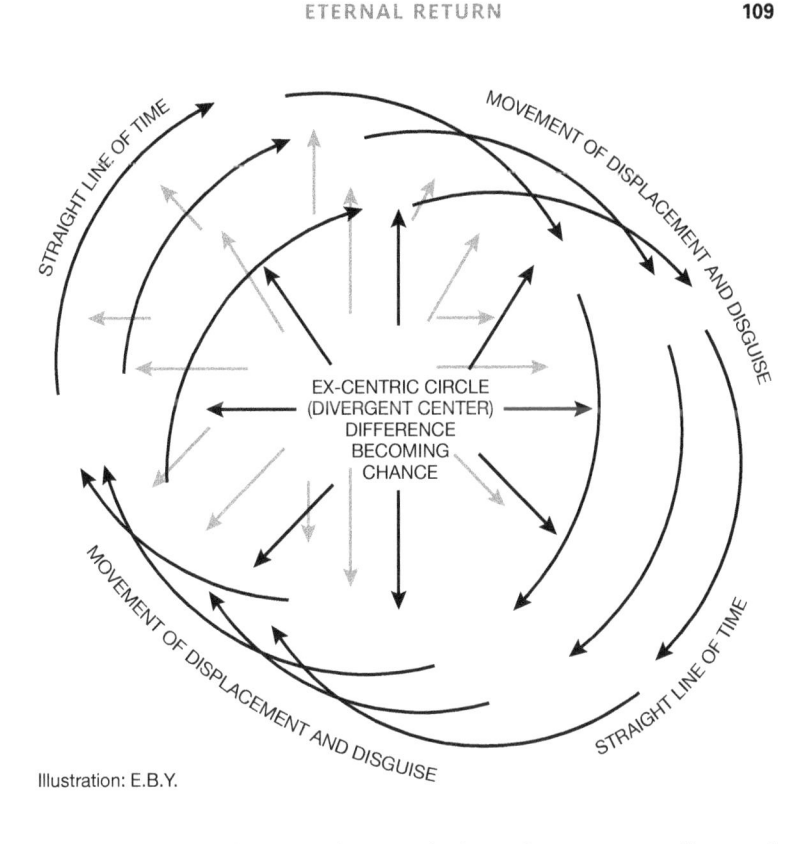

[Figure: Illustration: E.B.Y. — concentric arrows labeled STRAIGHT LINE OF TIME and MOVEMENT OF DISPLACEMENT AND DISGUISE around a center labeled EX-CENTRIC CIRCLE (DIVERGENT CENTER) / DIFFERENCE / BECOMING / CHANCE]

> *This is how the story of time ends: by undoing its too well centred natural or physical circle and forming a straight line which then, led by its own length, reconstitutes an* **eternally** *decentred circle.* [DR 141, 115]

> **Eternal return** *affects only the new, it repudiates [the default and the equal] and expels them with all its centrifugal* **force**. [DR 113, 90]

4.a. In Deleuze's critique of **Plato,** the affirmation of the **simulacrum** for itself, where recurrence does not reveal content that was formerly concealed, but produces change and new content which appears as 'simulation' by virtue of its resemblance (in contrast to Platonism, which affirms the model of the idea behind the simulacrum).

> *That the Same and the Similar may be simulated does not mean that they are appearances or illusions. [...] Simulation understood in this way is inseparable from the* **eternal return**, *for it is in the* **eternal**

return *that the reversal of the icons or the subversion of the world of representation is decided. [...] In the* eternal return, *one must pass through the manifest content, but only in order to reach the latent content situated a thousand feet below (the cave behind every cave ...). Thus, what appeared to* **Plato** *to be only a sterile effect reveals in itself the intractability of masks and the impassibility of* **signs**. [LS 301, 264]

[...] the eternal return *is, in fact, the Same and the Similar, but only insofar as they are simulated, produced by the simulation, through the functioning of the* simulacrum. [LS 302, 265]

b. In Deleuze's discussion of faith, in contrast to a **Kierkegaard**ian mode of **repetition** (of the '*once and for all*') which involves an incommunicable belief that returns to a finite or teleological sphere of existence (resulting in irony or tragedy upon return to aesthetic and ethical spheres), a repetition (that is '*for all times*') that affirms apparently finite or teleological existence as *parodic* or as **simulacra**; a 'belief' only in the contingency of any possible future, which thus parodies all theological and especially eschatological belief systems.

taken in its strict sense, eternal return *means that each thing exists only in returning, copy of an infinity of copies which allows neither original nor origin to subsist. That is why the* eternal return *is called 'parodic': it qualifies as* simulacrum *that which it causes to be (and to return). [...]* Eternal return *is not a faith, but the truth of faith: [...] it is not a belief but the parody of every belief (the highest humor): a belief and a doctrine eternally yet to come.* [DR 119, 95–6]

Nietzsche *announces only a light punishment for those who do not 'believe' in* eternal return: *they will have, and be aware of, only an ephemeral life!* [DR 66, 55]

Kierkegaard *offers us a theatre of faith; he opposes spiritual movement, the movement of faith, to logical movement. [...]. With* Nietzsche, *it is a theatre of unbelief [...]And what would* eternal return *be, if we forgot that it is a [*force*...] which selects, one which expels as well as creates, destroys as well as produces?* [DR 12, 55]

– E. B. Y.

Ethics

While ethics is an essential branch of philosophy that deals with character, behavior, and institutional practices, it is sometimes treated as a synonym for '**morality**'. However, inspired by **Spinoza**, who asked why people stubbornly fight for their own servitude as if it were their salvation (see Preface of the *Theologico-Political Treatise*), Deleuze makes an important distinction along those lines: on the one hand, *morality* involves imperatives that are often grounded in a transcendental (that is, inaccessible) law that people may blindly follow, and on the other hand, *ethics* involves *capacity* or **power**. In other words, morality asks what people *should* do, while ethics asks what people *can* do. Although this version of ethics might sound dangerous, it is important to note that 'power' is not meant in the Hobbesian sense: whereas Hobbes famously asserted that the exercise of our power in a state of nature involves a permanent state of war, where we all have a right to everything, and also that we ought to give up our power to live in peace, **Spinoza**, by contrast, argued that we have *less* power in a state of nature, not more (Deleuze remarks that it is a state of 'impotence and slavery' where we are subjected to external causes that we cannot comprehend). **Spinoza**'s conclusion in *The Ethics* is that because people are the most 'useful' thing in nature to other people, we ought to endeavor to form relations with them (provided that they too recognize this and live ethically through active **affects**, or adequate ideas). Thus, society may form a system of rewards and punishments for those who are enslaved to passions, but the incentive for entering into it is that other people enable us to exercise our *capacity* or power *more* so than we could in a 'state of nature'.

This notion of ethics becomes somewhat transformed in Deleuze's reading of **Nietzsche**'s work, especially with regard to the **eternal return**. In this case, Deleuze emphasizes that while the eternal return may be a cosmological and speculative notion, its consequences are actually extremely practical. For example, Nietzsche's famous parable of the demon who asks whether you would want to re-live this life 'innumerable times again', could be considered as a curse or as a blessing: a curse (and a 'weight'), if you think that your life *ought* to be a certain way, and resent circumstances that you think should have been otherwise; however, it is a blessing if you affirm that there is no particular desirable outcome, that *all* circumstances must 'return' and be affirmed (as in the case with **Spinoza**, it is a question of your *capacity* to endure and affirm all possibilities). The answer to the demon's riddle is perhaps, from this Deleuzian perspective, that the only desirable life is one that incorporates 'chance' (that affirms all possibilities, or all outcomes of the 'dice throw'); any life whose outcomes are determined in advance is denying the eternal return of all outcomes. In this case, our **affective** disposition is central to a conception of ethics (as in Spinoza), in terms of a capacity or power, but the emphasis is on the necessity of chance as the condition of novelty and joy (it is a 'tragic thought', where pain is essentially '**transmuted**' into joy), in distinction from the Spinozist correlation of chance with confusion, sadness, and powerlessness.

> 1.a. In Deleuze's reading of **Spinoza**, the tendency of individuals to overcome the social contract that is formed based on coercion or systems of rewards and punishments (hopes and fears), or morals (Good and Evil), and instead to form consensual relations with other citizens based on active affections using **reason** (common notions). [SEP, SPP]

>> in the State of Nature [...] I experience passive affections which cut me off from my power of action [...]. There is a great **difference** between seeking what is useful through chance [...] and seeking to organize what is useful. There is in Nature neither Good nor Evil, there is no **moral** opposition, but there is an **ethical** difference. This ethical difference [...] relates to the kind of affections that determine our conatus [power]. [SEP 261]

> b. The tendency of societies to promote freedom from (or devalue) tyrannical or oppressive powers that inspire sad passions and weakness through superstition or myth (as well as fortuitous encounters that form inadequate ideas based in a state of nature). [SEP, SPP]

>> This **ethical** conception has a fundamental critical aspect [...] the devaluation of sad passions, and the denunciation of those who cultivate and depend on them, form the practical object of philosophy. Few themes of the **Ethics** reappear more constantly than

this one: that all that is sad is bad and enslaves us; all that involves sadness expresses tyranny. [SEP 270]

c. A subjective capacity to distinguish between good and bad on the basis of **reason**, which we are not born with and cannot be taught, but acquire through experience; an **Ethology** that evaluates the composition of **affects** or **becomings** (speeds and slownesses) on the **Plane of Immanence**. [SEP, SPP]

> **Ethics** *is an* **ethology** *which, with regard to men and animals, in each case considers their capacity for being* **affected**. *[...] For a given individual, i.e. for a given degree of power assumed to be constant within certain limits, the capacity for being affected itself remains constant within those limits, but the power of acting and the power of being acted upon vary greatly, in inverse relation to one another.* [SPP 27]

> **Spinoza**'s ethics *has nothing to do with a* **morality**; *he conceives it as an* ethology, *that is, as a composition of fast and slow speeds, of capacities for affecting and being affected on this* plane of immanence *[...]. How do individuals enter into composition with one another in order to form a higher individual, ad infinitum? [...] what is the* difference *between the society of human beings and the community of rational beings? [...] in what order and in what manner will the powers, speeds, and slownesses be composed?* [webdeleuze 21/12/1980]

d. A method of evaluating things, especially living things and people, (that is, Beings), according to their power, or what they do and are capable of doing (what **mode** of existence they imply), in distinction from judging their essence based on moral or abstract criteria. [SEP, SPP]

> **Spinoza** *didn't entitle his book Ontology, he's too shrewd for that, he entitles it* **Ethics**. *Which is a way of saying that, whatever the importance of my speculative* **propositions** *may be, you can only judge them at the level of the* ethics *that they envelop or imply [impliquer].* [webdeleuze 21/12/1980]

> *The* **ethical** *discourse will not cease to speak to us, not of essences, it doesn't believe in essences, it speaks to us only of power (puissance), that is, the actions and passions of which something is capable. Not what the thing is, but what it is capable of supporting and capable of doing.* [webdeleuze 21/12/1980]

2.a. In Deleuze's reading of **Nietzsche**, the practical synthesis that correlates to the speculative synthesis of the **eternal return** (where the only unity is **multiplicity**), whereby the will is given a rule to affirm chance (every possible outcome) and **becoming** (as a form of being), as well as to actively select and expel the **negative**.

> As an **ethical** *thought the* **eternal return** *is the new formulation of the practical synthesis: whatever you will, will it in such a way that you also will its* **eternal return** [N 63, 68]

b. The affirmation of the contingent and changing nature of the *present* (circumstance, motive, and/or sense) insofar as it is included within the necessity, eternity, and unity of the past and future; in distinction from bad conscious and reactive **morality**, the morality of the master that does not need to deny *in order to* affirm, but denies only those perspectives which prevent affirmation (which themselves seek to deny).

> **Nietzsche**'s *philosophy is a logic of multiple affirmation and therefore a logic of pure affirmation and a corresponding* **ethic** *of joy. The tragic is not founded on a relation of* life *and the negative but on the essential relation of joy and* **multiplicity** *[...]* [N 17, 17–18]

- E. B. Y.

Ethology

This scientific study of processes of animal behavior, favoring field observation, is a subdiscipline of evolutionary biology. The ideas of its Austrian founders Nikolaas Tinbergen and Konrad Lorenz were influential in post-war anthropology and spread via Lévi-Strauss in France. Guattari, however, criticizes its mechanistic behaviorist assumptions and hierarchical arborescent logics by inserting **transversal** connections between otherwise hardened distinctions (acquired-innate).

1.a. The interpolation of freedom and experimentation into closed behavioral sequencing, which **deterritorializes** a given functional space and time (i.e. courtship rituals) and establishes new **transversal** co-relations between the most and least deterministic components.

> 'Ethology' *then can be understood as a very privileged molar domain for demonstrating how the most varied components [...] can crystallize in* **assemblages** *that respect neither the distinction between orders nor the hierarchy of forms. What holds all the components together are* **transversals**, *and the* **transversal** *itself is only a component that has taken upon itself the specialized vector of* **deterritorialization**. [TP 370–1, 336]

b. An analytic science where machinic rather than mechanistic connections are favored because they connect disparate, yet mutually influential, biological and semiotic components in **rhizomatic** entanglements.

> *Biological* **assemblages** *depend on psychological and social assemblages as much as the latter depend on the former. Thus there is nothing 'antiscientific' in putting forth the hypothesis that hyper-***deterritorialized** *components concerning* **imagination**, *faciality, music, etc. are not only able to modify the social field, but also bodies, metabolisms, and cerebral connections!* [MU 145]

c. A re-thinking of **territory** in non-human animals by describing the open **assemblages** of components, some of which become actively **expressive**, and give consistency to social relations between the same and different species; expressivity as surplus **value** of **code** (beyond the sum of genetic encoding, ecological adaptation, and social communication) which is a source of innovation, where art replaces explanation by innate mechanisms and the need to satisfy the big drives (hunger, sex, flight, aggression).

> *Perhaps art begins with the animal, at least with the animal that carves out a* **territory** *and constructs a house [...]. The* **territory***-house system transforms a number of organic functions—sexuality, procreation, aggression, feeding. But this transformation does not explain the appearance of the* **territory** *and house; rather, it is the other way around.* [WIP 183]

- G. G.

Event

An 'event' usually means that something is *happening*: but the **paradox** is that, on the one hand, an event can only really be grasped in hindsight (or with foresight), and, on the other hand, we *do* presume that we can refer to incidents, changes, or actions (whether novel or not), that are *currently* unfolding. How does this work? Deleuze will argue that such references—in the linguistic form of 'infinitives'—envelop the other **propositional** dimensions of language because while those dimensions involve determinations, **subjects**, and universal **concepts** within linear time (**Chronos**), infinitives occupy the both past and the future at once: how else could they be **expressed**? If we grasped them as what they are, they would have already happened (or would be a foregone conclusion); for this reason, they are expressed as the simultaneous instantiation of past and future (which itself occupies an 'eternal', infinitely divisible line). This will be complicated in Deleuze's reading of **Leibniz**, where he applies the concept to the conjunction of **series**.

1. According to Deleuze's reading of **Stoic** *lekton*, an incorporeal '**surface**' effect which evades the causal state of corporeal mixtures (**Chronos**), and, because is different in nature than effects within **depth** (it does not in turn induce mixtures), is reversible on the eternal line of the **Aion**; that which is irreducible to, but not independent of, the **proposition**, expressed in the infinitive form of verbs.

> Mixtures in general determine the quantitative and qualitative states of affairs [...] —but incorporeal events at the surface [...] are the results of these mixtures. [LS 8, 6]

> Each event is the smallest time, smaller than the minimum of continuous thinkable time, because it is divided into proximate past and imminent future. But it is also the longest time, longer than the maximum of continuous thinkable time, because it is endlessly subdivided by the **Aion** which renders it equal to its own unlimited line. [LS 63, 74]

2. In Deleuze's reading of **Leibniz**, that which, on the one hand, originates in **chaos** (thus having no existence in space and time), and on the other hand, has **serial** extension (formal

properties) and **intensity** (degrees) in space and time, and is objectified and subjectified by virtue of individual unities (**monads**); in Deleuze's reading of **Whitehead** alongside **Leibniz**, the prehension of series of **singularities** (a world) that is implicated by other worlds.

> *The* event *is a vibration with an infinity of harmonics or submultiples [...]. For space and time are not limits but abstract coordinates of all* series, *[...] we can [thus] consider a second component of the event: extensive series have intrinsic properties (for example, height,* intensity, *timbre of a sound, a tint, a* value, *a saturation of color), which enter on their own account in new infinite series [...].* [FLB 77]

> *Prehension is individual unity. Everything prehends its antecedents and its concomitants and, by degrees, prehends a world. [...] the* event *is thus a 'nexus of prehensions.'[...]; the* event *is [...] at once public and private, potential and real, participating in the becoming of another* event *and the subject of its own becoming.* [FLB 78]

- E. B. Y.

Existential territory

One of Guattari's **four functors**, **Existential territory** is the incorporated, embodied, singular self, which includes the body and its intensities. In Guattari's late work, this **concept** plays a role similar to that of the **body without organs**.

1.a. The schizoanalytic counterpart to identity; a non-discursive, **intensive, affective**, proto-subjective incorporation.

> *We must start from a multivalent logic, and accept the notion of identity which I call* **existential territory**, *because we cannot live outside our bodies, our friends, some sort of human cluster, and at the same time, we are bursting out of this situation.* [GR 216]

b. The lived experience of the body, self, family, ethnicity.

> *The objects of art and* desire *are apprehended within* **existential Territories** *which are at the same time the body proper, the self, the maternal body, lived space,* **refrains** *of the mother tongue, familiar faces, family lore, ethnicity.* [CM 95]

2. The individuated aspect of **subjectivity**, whose social aspect is composed of **universes** of reference or **value**.

It is during this chaosmic folding that an interface is installed—an interface between the sensible finitude of existential Territories *and the trans-sensible infinitude of the* Universes *of reference bound to them.* [CM 111]

3. The embodied, corporeal aspect of a machine or **assemblage**.

The machine is always synonymous with a nucleus constitutive of an existential Territory *against a background of a constellation of incorporeal* Universes *of reference (or* value*).* [CM 53]

4. A **virtual territory** that forms to counter the destabilizing effects of **deterritorialization**.

Spontaneous social ecology works towards the constitution of existential Territories *that replace, more or less, the former religious and ritualized griddings of the socius.* [TE 64]

- J. W.

Expression

To *express* usually means to express *something*—a 'feeling' or a truth—whether through the informality of spontaneous gestures and conversations or the formality an artistic or literary medium. In fact, shifting away from ancient theories of mimesis towards modern philosophical theories of expression in **Kant** and **Hegel**, we have embraced the notion that **expression** is, somehow, an expression of an interior world. We 'express' our opinions, our sexuality, our creativity, etc. What this implies, however, is that the expressed conceals the 'real' feeling or truth that it expresses (i.e. it could always be expressed in another way).

Deleuze's approach to **immanence**, inspired by his study of **Spinoza**, complicates this notion of expression, where that which is 'expressed' exists only by virtue of its expression. Despite Spinoza's claim that the first ideas we have are confused, **imaginary** ideas of our body, to 'express' an idea (adequately) does *not* imply that such an idea is *caused* by our 'feelings' (pleasures, pains, hopes, fears, **perceptions**, or affections); rather, it is a *conception* of the *relationship* of our body to external causes (in this sense, the expression of ideas would 'parallel' the expression of the body). 'Expression' is thus not the expression that *refers to* an interior world; it is an *action* and an **affect** which is undergone with knowledge of its cause (actions 'express' their causes insofar as there is knowledge of them). In more **Leibniz**ian terms, Deleuze will claim in *The Logic of Sense* that the facial expressions of **the Other** explicate a possible external world that implicates the observer; in this text he also frames the issue in terms of **events** that 'subsist' the **proposition** and are grasped paradoxically *only* as effects (here there is Spinozist **resonance** with the knowledge through the effect within **modes**). With Guattari, the raw material of expression is attributed to the delineation between the internal world of the **milieu** and the external world of **chaos** or the cosmos (it will also *form* a complementary relationship with content: see **Form of Expression**).

1.a. In **Spinoza**, the character of **attributes** (i.e. the thought and extension) which qualify the existence of God, or infinite substance, and of their finite **modalities** (ideas and bodies).

> *God—in other words a substance consisting of infinite* **attributes**, *each of which* **expresses** *eternal and infinite essence—necessarily exists.* [Spinoza (*Ethics*, I, Prop. 11) 2000, 82]

> *Particular things are nothing other than the affections, i.e. the* **modes**, *[...] by which the* **attributes** *of God are* **expressed** *in a certain and determinate way.* [Spinoza (*Ethics*, I, Prop. 25C) 2000, 97]

b. In Deleuze's reading of **Spinoza**, the feature of essence which does not refer to a transcendent being, but exists only insofar as it is expressed *adequately* through an idea of an effect that is implicated by the knowledge of its cause; insofar as **attributes** and their modifications are parallel to one another, that which is expressed in a different, albeit corresponding order and connection in thought (ideas) and extension (bodies). [SPP, SEP]

> *the essence of substance has no existence outside the* **attributes** *that* **express** *it, so that each attribute* **expresses** *a certain eternal and infinite essence. What is* **expressed** *has no existence outside its*

> expressions; *each* expression *is, as it were, the existence of what is expressed.* [SEP 42]
>
> *the* attributes express *themselves in one and the same order, down to the level of finite* modes, *which must have the same order in different attributes.* [SEP 106]
>
> *Let us first consider an idea as the knowledge of some thing. It is only true knowledge to the extent that it bears on the thing's essence: it must 'explicate' that essence. [...] knowledge of an effect, considered objectively, 'involves' a knowledge of its cause, or [...] an idea, considered formally, '*expresses*' its own cause. An adequate idea is just an idea that* expresses *its cause.* [SEP 133]

2.a. In Deleuze's analysis of the dimensions of the **proposition**, which denote (particular determinations), manifest (the speaker and their beliefs), and signify (universal **concepts**, probabilities, etc.), the **sense** of the **event** that subsists within the first three dimensions, but cannot be reduced to them (despite that it does not exist independently of them); the manner in which the neutrality of sense alters (or is 'expressed' within) other variables and contexts, but itself is not altered (as the expressed).

> *The* expression *is founded on the* event, *as an entity of the* expressible *or the* expressed*. [...The event] differs in nature from its* expression*. It exists in the* proposition, *but not at all as a name of bodies or qualities, and not at all as a subject or predicate. It exists rather only as that which is* expressible *or* expressed *by the proposition, enveloped in a verb.* [LS 209, 182]

b. In Deleuze's reading of **Leibniz**, the manner in which the entire world, with varying degrees of clarity and obscurity, is enveloped by individuals or **monads**; in this manner, the 'world' exists only in its expressions.

> *Since all the individual* monads express *the totality of their world—although they* express *clearly only a select part—their bodies form mixtures and aggregates, variable associations with zones of clarity and obscurity.* [LS 128, 112]

c. In Deleuze's explanation of **the Other** or the beloved, a **sign**, facial expression, or phenomenon that implicates another possible world (in distinction from referring to possibilities that can be realized, it envelopes an **expressed** that can be explicated).

> *A frightened countenance is the* **expression** *of a frightening possible world, or of something frightening in the world—something I do not yet see. [...] the* **expressed** *possible world certainly exists, but it does not exist (actually) outside of that which* **expresses** *it. The terrified countenance bears no resemblance to the terrifying thing. It implicates it, it envelops it as something else, in a kind of torsion which situates what is* **expressed** *in the* **expressing**. [LS 346, 307]

> *the beloved* **expresses** *a possible world unknown to us, implying, enveloping, imprisoning a world that must be deciphered, that is, interpreted.* [P 7]

3. (Special Combination): *Matter of Expression*: In D&G's analysis of **territorialization,** in distinction from a **form of expression,** the direct use of **matter** or material from a **milieu** to mark a relation between the unstable and contingent forces of **chaos** to the stable center of the milieu, not in order to accomplish any functional act which would stabilize the **territory,** but in order to delineate and constitute it (as one would plant a flag).

> *There is a* **territory** *when the* **rhythm** *has* **expressiveness.** *What defines the territory is the emergence of* **matters** *of* **expression** *(qualities).* [TP 347, 315]

> **Territorial** *marks are ready-mades. And what is called art brut in not at all pathological or primitive; it is merely this constitution, this freeing, of* **matters** *of* **expression** *in the movement of* **territoriality:** *the base or ground of art. Take anything and make it a matter of* **expression.** [TP 349, 316]

> **Expressive** *qualities or* **matters** *of* **expression** *enter shifting relations with one another that 'express' the relation of the* **territory** *they draw to the interior* **milieu** *of impulses and exterior milieu of circumstances* [TP 349–50, 317]

- E. B. Y.

Faculty

'Faculty' is a term that Deleuze appropriates directly from **Kant**, but in order ultimately to demonstrate a reversal of its role: rather than faculties working in harmony to produce **common sense**, he insists that thought only occurs when there is a discord or disharmony between them (i.e. when we encounter that which *eludes* recognition because it can 'only be sensed' or 'only be remembered'). Thus while Kant thinks that the power of the mind should ultimately be attributed to the legislative capacity of the understanding (with regard to any faculty—sensibility, **desire**, etc.), Deleuze thinks that this limits thought to recognizable forms of the same and similar, rather than the different and new; in other words, rather than legislating other 'lower' faculties, thought must attain a relation to 'non-thought' or the unthinkable, which cannot be recognized (but which we have the faculties to experience or recall).

1. In **Kant**, representations originating from the senses or from the mind (sensibility, pain/pleasure, **desire**, knowledge) which are fundamentally distinct, and attain a higher form insofar as they legislate themselves by virtue of *a priori* **concepts** of the understanding (judgment for pain/pleasure, reason for desire, understanding for knowledge) to produce **common sense**, relationships among representations, or an accord among each other.

> *all* **faculties** *of the soul, or capacities, are reducible to three, which do not admit of any further derivation from a common ground: the* **faculty** *of knowledge, the feeling of pleasure or displeasure, and the* **faculty** *of desire. For the* **faculty** *of cognition understanding alone is legislative, if [...] this* **faculty**, *as that of theoretical cognition, is referred to nature, in respect of which alone (as phenomenon) it is possible for us to prescribe laws by means of a priori* **concepts** *of nature, which are properly pure concepts of understanding.*
>
> *Our entire* **faculty** *of cognition has two realms, that of natural* **concepts** *and that of the concept of freedom, for through both it prescribes laws a priori. In accordance with this distinction, then, philosophy is divisible into theoretical and practical.*
>
> *In respect of the* **faculties** *of the soul generally, regarded as higher* **faculties**, *i.e. as* **faculties** *containing an autonomy, understanding*

is the one that contains the constitutive a priori principles for the **faculty** of cognition (the theoretical knowledge of nature) [Critique of Judgment]

2.a. In Deleuze's reading of **Kant**, the source of representations (of pain and pleasure, **desire**, or knowledge) which engender a mutual recognition, **common sense**, and an identity of the subject who conceptualizes them.

> representation was defined by certain elements: identity with regard to **concepts**, opposition with regard to the determination of concepts, analogy with regard to judgment, resemblance with regard to objects. The identity of the unspecified concept constitutes the form of the Same with regard to recognition. [...] Each element thus appeals to one particular **faculty**, but is also established across different **faculties** within the context of a given **common sense** [...]. [DR 174, 137–8]

> An object is recognized [...] when one **faculty** locates it as identical to that of another, or rather when all the **faculties** together relate their given and relate themselves to a form of identity in the object. [DR 169, 133]

b. On the one hand, the receptive (and 'lower') intuition of sensibility, and, on the other hand, the active (and 'higher') legislative functions of the mind, including **imagination**, understanding, and **reason**.

> We must distinguish between, on one hand, intuitive sensibility as a **faculty** of reception, and, on the other, the active **faculties** as sources of real representations. [...] There are thus three active **faculties** which participate in synthesis, but which are also sources of specific representations when any one of them is considered in relation to any other: **imagination**, understanding, **reason**. [KCP 9]

> [...] a [higher] faculty [...] is called on to legislate over objects and to distribute their specific tasks to the other **faculties**: thus understanding legislates in the **faculty** of knowledge and **reason** legislates in the **faculty** of desire [KCP 68]

3. In Deleuze's version of **transcendental empiricism**, the powers of the mind (**sensation, imagination,** memory, cognition) that maintain a fundamental relation to that which exceeds their grasp (the *sentiendum* as the insensible that can only be sensed,

the *memorandum* as the immemorial that can only be remembered, or the *cogitandum* as the unthinkable that can only be thought), thereby effectuating a **difference** and **paradoxical** communication among one another (rather than a mutual recognition or harmony); in distinction from **Kant**, the priority of passive or 'receptive' sensibility over the active **faculties** of imagination, understanding, and reason insofar as thought originates in a violent encounter, developing from **sensation** rather than a priori **concepts** or categories.

> *The violence of that which forces thought develops from the sentiendum to the cogitandum. Each* faculty *is unhinged [...]. Each one, in its own order and on its own account, has broken the form of* **common sense** *[...]. Rather than all the* faculties *converging and contributing to a common project of recognising an object, we see divergent projects in which, with regard to what concerns it essentially, each* faculty *is in the presence of that which is its 'own'.* [DR 177, 141]

- E. B. Y.

Figure

While Deleuze provides his own definition of Figures in **Bacon**'s work that are not 'figurative' (that is, representative), with Guattari, the term expands in meaning to designate, on the one hand, religious figures of transcendence, and, on the other hand, in art, that which preserves **sensations** (which is closer to the meaning in *The Logic of Sensation*).

1. An aesthetic form, exemplified in the paintings of Francis **Bacon**, which does not operate according to the representative laws of **figuration** (as, for example, in a photograph, which purports to resemble its object or subject), but instead **diagrams** the very devices of the aesthetic medium (in painting: color, line, light, contour, etc.) such that they form a new relationship based on **sensation**.

> *There are two ways of going beyond figuration (that is, beyond both the illustrative and the figurative): either toward abstract form or toward the* **Figure**.*[...]. The* **Figure** *is the sensible form related to a*

sensation; *it acts immediately upon the nervous system, which is of the flesh, whereas abstract form is addressed to the head, and acts through the intermediary of the brain, which is closer to the bone.* [FB 34]

[...] the **diagram** *acted by imposing a zone of objective indiscernibility or indeterminability between two forms [...]. And between the two, it imposes the* **Figure** *[...].* [FB 157]

2. (Special Combination): *Aesthetic Figure*: In D&G's analysis of Art and Literature, **affects** and **percepts** (**sensations**) that are produced and preserved in some formal medium (painting, sculpture, writing, etc.); embodied possibilities which extend sensations of a lived **event**, in distinction from **intensive concepts** *of* sensations that **actualize** a **virtual** event.

Aesthetic figures *[...] are* **sensations**: **percepts** *and* **affects**, *landscapes and faces, visions and* **becomings** [WP 177]

3. In D&G's distinctions between religion, art, and science: firstly, in *religion*, a **form of expression** which refers to an absolute plane with which it maintains vertical or transcendental relationships; secondly, in *art*, a form of expression which severs reference to divine or transcendent planes of thought by preserving **sensations** on a **plane of composition** (whose referent is instead dissembling and **diagrammatic**); thirdly, in *science*, a form of expression where a functive is preserved on a plane of reference.

the **figure** *[in religion] is essentially paradigmatic, projective, hierarchical, and referential* [WP 89]

the arts and sciences also set up powerful **figures** *[...] that [...] emancipate a particular level so as to make it into new planes of thought on which [...] references and projections change* [WP 89–90]

- E. B. Y.

Flows

Sometimes translated as **flux** [*fluxes*], this term appears frequently in ***Anti-Oedipus*** and ***A Thousand Plateaus***. A conceptual adaptation from the philosophy and science of fluids, it is deployed by Deleuze and Guattari in counterpoint to **structuralism** or hylomorphism. Flows are characteristic of **matter**, energy, **desire**, libido, and capital; they are associated with **nomads**, **deterritorialization**, **machines**, and **smooth space**. In Guattari's final works based on the **four functors**, flux or flow belongs to the discursive side of the **Plane of Consistency**, along with the machinic **Phylum**.

1. Existential reality, as viewed by scientific approaches which privilege fluids over solids, as in D&G's reading of ancient atomism.

> *this kind of eccentric science [...] uses a hydraulic model, rather than being a theory of solids treating fluids as a special case; ancient atomism is inseparable from* **flows**, *and* **flux** *is reality itself, or consistency.* [TP 398, 361]

2.a. For D&G, **matter**, energy, or resources which have not yet been formed, overcoded, or territorialized.

> *There is always something that* **flows** *or flees, that escapes the binary organizations, the* **resonance** *apparatus, and the overcoding* **machine** *[...].* [TP 238, 216]

b. Resources which the state has not yet captured or organized.

> *If it can help it, the State does not dissociate itself from a process of capture of* **flows** *of all kinds, populations, commodities or commerce, money or capital, etc.* [TP 425, 385–6]

3. Those aspects of the body, the psyche, and the socius that precede or bypass the subject-object dichotomy.

> **Flows** *of* **intensity**, *their fluids, their fibers, their continuums and conjunctions of* **affects**, *the wind, fine* **segmentation**, *microperceptions, have replaced the world of the* **subject**. [TP 179, 162]

4.a. For D&G, a key characteristic of **desire**.

> *For it is a matter of* **flows**, *of stocks, of breaks in and fluctuations of* **flows**; *desire is present wherever something* **flows** *and runs [...]* [AO 115, 105]

b. For Guattari, **desire** itself.

> *For Gilles Deleuze and me* **desire** *is everything that exists before the opposition* between *subject and object,* before *representation and production [...] It's everything that overflows from us. That's why we define it as* flow. [SS 142]

5.a. One of the two aspects of the **machine**; current, movement, or stream which is broken during the machinic process.

> *In a word, every* **machine** *functions as a break in the* **flow** *in relation to the machine to which it is connected, but at the same time is also a* **flow** *itself, or the production of a* **flow***, in relation to the machine connected to it.* [AO 39, 36]

b. That which an **assemblage** arranges or integrates.

> *An* **assemblage***, in its* **multiplicity***, necessarily acts on semiotic* **flows***, material flows, and social flows simultaneously.* [TP 25, 22–3]

6. The opposite of **segmentation**.

> *And in fact, whenever we can identify a well-defined* segmented line, *we notice that it continues in another form, as a* quantum **flow**. [TP 239, 217]

7. One of Guattari's **four** ontological **functors** which may be material, energetic, economic, or semiotic; examples include libido, capital, and **signs**; often translated as **flux**.

> *You either speak or you eat [...] On one side a differentiated* **flux**—*the variety of food taken up in a process of disaggregation, chaotization, sucked up by an inside of flesh*—*and on the other side, a* **flux** *of elementary articulations*—*phonological, syntactical, propositional.* [CM 88]

- J. W.

Flux

cross reference: flow

Fold

(Fr: *Pli*)

In an interview with Arnaud Villani in his late career, Deleuze described himself as a 'pure metaphysician', and his concept of the 'fold' is perhaps an archetypical example of the relationship between the 'metaphysical' (that is, thought and 'being') and the 'physical' (**matter**, visibility, extension, etc.). The well-established mind–body problem, and the status of metaphysics, of course, becomes problematic after **Heidegger** and **Merleau-Ponty**; in inheriting this problem, Deleuze also distinguishes his approach from what he identifies as the 'negativity' of dialectics and existentialism (as with, for example, **Hegel**'s and **Sartre**'s 'holes' and 'lakes of non-being'). In his view, the self or subject is not an existential void whose thought is uncontaminated by and separated from the world. Deleuze's response, however, is that the 'metaphysical' *exists*, but paradoxically, in the form of *difference*. This is where the concept of the fold arises: the self is always *enfolded* or implicated by **the Other** and **the Outside**, while thought (or 'doing metaphysics') involves a mode of questioning and problematizing that cannot be represented by predetermined criteria, but is instead *unfolded* by **difference** in the form(s) of **repetition**.

The concept of the fold was explored most explicitly in Deleuze's work on **Foucault** and **Leibniz**, though it was foregrounded in *Difference and Repetition* (in terms of the ontology of **difference**), his work on **Spinoza** (indirectly, in terms of 'explication' and 'implication'), and elsewhere. In *Foucault*, the concept is utilized to examine the status of 'doubling' in terms of Foucault's characterization of resistance and his reading of **Nietzsche**'s concept of **Force**; in *The Fold: Leibniz and the Baroque*, focus is placed on the almost unthinkable manner in which the relation of the 'metaphysical' soul to 'physical' **matter** is one of enfolding or enveloping, but simultaneously one of unfolding or development (taking departure from **Spinoza**, as Leibniz was a reader of Spinoza). Deleuze casts this concept within the context of Leibniz's philosophy of force and **monad**ism: while the monad is enclosed and unextended, it is also implicated by the **Outside**.

1.a. In **Heidegger**'s metaphysics, the ambiguity—that is, the 'twofoldness' or 'duality' (*Zwiefalt*)—between Being and beings, where Being must disclose itself within beings ('as' beings), while at the same time remaining irreducible to beings and concealed.

> *Metaphysics is a fate [...] that it lets mankind be suspended in the middle of beings [...], without the Being of beings ever being able to be experienced and questioned and structured in its truth as the* **twofoldness** *of both in term of metaphysics and through metaphysics. [...] Being itself can open out in its truth the* **difference** *of Being and beings preserved in itself only when the difference explicitly takes place. But how can it do this if beings have not first entered the most extreme oblivion of Being, [...]? Thus what can be distinguished in the difference in a way presents itself, and yet keeps itself hidden [...]. Together with the beginning of the completion of metaphysics, the preparation begins, unrecognized and essentially inaccessible to metaphysics, for a first appearance of the* **twofoldness** *of Being and beings [...].* [Heidegger, 1973, 90–1]

b. Merleau-Ponty's (phenomenological/ontological) alternative to **Hegel**ian and **Sartre**an **subjectivity** (which insist that consciousness is 'non-being'), where consciousness is not a negation of the sensible world, but where it reprises or reconstitutes (*reprendre*) the world genetically (in a 'chiasmatic relation').

> *since* **sensation** *is a reconstitution, it presupposes in me sediments left behind by some previous constitution, so that I am, as a sentient subject, a repository stocked with natural powers at which I am the first to be filled with wonder. I am not, therefore, in* **Hegel**'*s phrase, 'a hole in being', but a hollow, a* **fold**, *which has been made and which can be unmade.* [Merleau-Ponty, 2005, 249–50]

2. In Deleuze's combined reading of **Heidegger** and Merleau-Ponty, the shift from a phenomenological to an ontological conception of **difference** where difference is not the non-being of the negative, but has an obscure and intentionally ambivalent relationship to the Open or the visible; in Deleuze's reading of **Foucault**, the resolution of the existential problematic of 'intentionality' behind disclosure through the

characterization of knowledge as a correlation between the visible and articulable.

> The *not* expresses not the negative but the **difference** between Being and being. *[...] This difference is not 'between' in the ordinary sense of the word. It is the* **Fold**, *Ztviefalt. It is constitutive of Being and of the manner in which Being constitutes being, in the double movement of 'clearing' and 'veiling'. Being is truly the* **differenciator** *of difference—whence the expression 'ontological difference'*. [DR 78, 65]

> *It was Merleau-Ponty who showed us how a radical, 'vertical' visibility was* **folded** *into a Self-seeing [...] Being as* **fold** *[...]. according to* **Heidegger** *or Merleau-Ponty, the* **fold** *of being surpasses intentionality only to found the latter in a new dimension: this is why the Visible or the Open does not give us something to see without also providing something to speak [...]. This cannot be so in* **Foucault**, *for whom the light-Being refers only to visibilities, and language-Being to statements: the* **fold** *will not be able to refound an intentionality* [F 91, 111]

3.a. In Deleuze's reading of **Leibniz**, the action or operation of involution/envelopment of inorganic and/or organic **matter** which produces or creates the conditions for development/ evolution (unfolding) of the **monad**; the doubling of the **outside** by the inside through which it is differentiated (derivative or determining forces—elastic or plastic, from the 'lower floor' are unified by primitive force on the 'upper floor').

> *The severing of the inside from the* **outside** *in this way refers to the distinction between the two levels, but the latter refers to the* **Fold** *that is* actualized *in the intimate* **folds** *that the soul encloses on the upper level, and effected along the creases that* matter *brings to life always on the outside, on the lower level.* [FLB 30]

> *Unity of movement is an affair of the soul [...]. the curvilinear course followed by a given body under the impetus of the* **outside** *goes back to a 'higher,' internal and individuating, unity on the other floor, that contains the 'law of curvilinearity,' the law of* **folds** *[...].* [FLB 12]

b. In Deleuze's reading of **Blanchot** (via **Foucault**), the internalization of a relation that serves as the basis of **force** (that is external to any particular relation), such that the object or origin of thought is that which has no relation; the **Outside** doubled onto the inside (of thought and of the body). [F, FLB]

> *is there an inside that lies deeper than any internal world, just as the* **outside** *is farther away than any external world? The outside is not a fixed limit but a moving matter animated by peristaltic movements,* **folds** *and* **foldings** *that together make up an inside: they are not something other than the outside, but precisely the inside of the outside.* [F 96–97]

4.a. In Deleuze's reading of **Spinoza**, the **paradox** of parallelism, where the distinct **attributes** (thought and extension as the two we can know) *explicate* or *express* substance/God, by virtue of **modal essences,** but are at the same time *implicated* by substance/God.

> *The absolutely infinite consists, first of all, of an infinity of formally or really distinct* **attributes**. *[...]* Expression *here appears as the relation of form and absolute: each form expresses, explicates or* **unfolds** *the absolute, but the absolute contains or 'complicates' an infinity of forms.* [SEP 119]

> *God remains implicated in things which explicate him. It is a complicative God who is explicated through all things [...].* [SEP 175]

b. In Deleuze's explanation of an embryonic (in distinction from a phylogenetic) determination of the self (as a larval subject and passive self), **differenciation** as the doubling of the self/other (interiorization of the **outside**) by virtue of a **dark precursor.**

> *in all his work* Foucault *seems haunted by this theme of an inside which is merely the* **fold** *of the* **outside**, *as if the ship were a* **folding** *of the sea. [...]It is never the other who is a double in the doubling process, it is a self that lives me as the double of the other: I do not encounter myself on the outside, I find the other in me [...]. It resembles exactly the invagination of a tissue in embryology, or the act of doubling in sewing: twist,* **fold**, *stop, and so on.* [F 81, 97]

> *Why is* **differenciation** *at once both composition and determination of qualities, organization and determination of species? [...] Beneath the* **actual** *qualities and extensities, species and parts, there are spatio–temporal dynamisms. [...] Embryology shows*

that the division of an egg into parts is secondary in relation to more significant morphogenetic movements: the augmentation of free **surfaces**, stretching of cellular layers, invagination by **folding**, regional displacement of **groups**. [DR 266, 214]

- E. B. Y.

The Fold: Leibniz and the Baroque

Le Pli. Leibniz et le Baroque (1988)

Published during the mid-1980s, during the same period as the cinema studies, in this work Deleuze foregrounds another crisis of **reason**, the crisis of Baroque reason experienced most intensely by the philosopher **Leibniz**. For Deleuze, Leibniz is the philosopher of the Baroque because he proposed his entire system on the basis of the perceived collapse of Theological reason and the loss of its highest principle, the Good. The **proposition** at the center of Leibniz's philosophy, 'everything has a reason,' must be understood as a cry of the philosopher according to Deleuze. Nevertheless, from the ruins of the crisis of theological order, Deleuze shows how Leibniz invents a new metaphysical foundation through the most dizzying creation of new **concepts**, particularly the concept of the **Monad** (which is explicated by what Deleuze calls the baroque **fold**), and, most importantly, by the creation of the principle of a pre-established harmony in relation to the existence of other possible worlds. As commonly understood, according to Deleuze, the notion of a pre-established Harmony cannot be adequately represented by the image of a bird's-eye view that supposedly unifies all these perspectives in a perfect sphere. Rather, the true notion of Harmony consists in the degree of conviction expressed by each monad to share the same reality as all the other monads. For Leibniz, this pre-established harmony refers to the selection of a shared reality that has been placed into each monad in advance by God, which Deleuze defines as 'a condition of closure.' However, it is around this point that Deleuze diverges from Leibniz's philosophy and employs the philosophy of **Whitehead** to prove that in the modern world it is precisely the 'condition of closure' that has undergone change, allowing a great degree of what he defines as dissonance to enter into the world, a dissonance that expresses in varying degrees existence of other possible worlds that are real and no longer merely possible, as in the system of Leibniz. The resulting image is not only a new image of reason no longer modeled on the theological point of view, but more importantly, a new cosmology based on a principle of infinite openness and no longer on a condition of closure. In the conclusion of *The Fold*, Deleuze demonstrates this new condition primarily through musicology, drawing upon the work of French composer Pierre Boulez. He writes:

> If harmonics lose all privilege of rank (or relations, all privilege of order), not only are dissonances 'excused' from being resolved, divergences can be affirmed, in a **series** that escape the diatonic scale where all tonality dissolves. But when the **monad** is in tune with divergent series that belong to incompossible monads, then the other condition is what disappears [i.e. closure]: it could be said that the monad, astraddle over several worlds, is kept half open as if by a pair of pliers. (Fold 137) - G. L.

Force

While this term stems from Deleuze's reading of **Nietzsche** (and is applied to his version of **repetition** in the **eternal return**), it becomes especially important in his dialog with **Blanchot** via his reading of **Foucault**'s notions of 'power' and 'biopower'. On the one hand, **forces**, for Nietzsche, cannot be reduced to mechanism or measurement (and are thus outside of the scope of knowledge); furthermore, they are what engender active and reactive qualities of **life**. On the other hand, Foucault defines power as an exercise of force that utilizes knowledge (the visible and articulable), but force relations themselves are independent of knowledge (being invisible and inarticulable), and are instead indicative of action and reaction, provoking and being provoked, etc. To take this further, however, Blanchot states (when commenting on Deleuze's reading of Nietzsche) that 'the distance that separates forces is also their correlation [...] what holds them at a distance, **the Outside**, constitutes their sole intimacy' (Blanchot, 1993, 160–1).

Deleuze in fact insists that there is a 'force *of* the Outside' that 'disrupts' **diagrams** of power, operating with a **vital** resistance, and instigating novelty; the logic is that because the only object of force is another force, forces cannot be reduced to the strategic codifications of power (or phenomena of resistance), but come from the Outside that is **folded** both within the inner and outer world (in terms of the 'encounter', it is what provokes us to think or experience **sensation**).

1.a. **Nietzsche's** term for the plurality of determined, conditioned, and quantitatively limited element(s) which produce the world, **value**, and qualities; that which contains quantity but cannot be definitively measured because its observable quality as well as its relative magnitude is always changing (which science mistakenly thinks it can explain).

> *All [...] prejudices, naiveties, misunderstandings [...] are everywhere reducible to this numerical and quantitative scale of* **force**. [Nietzsche (Will to Power # 710), 1968, p. 378]

> *'Mechanistic interpretation': desires nothing but quantities; but* **force** *is to be found in quality. Mechanistic theory can therefore only describe processes, not explain them.* [Nietzsche (Will to Power # 660), 349]

> *The measure of* **force** *(as magnitude) as fixed, but its essence in* flux. [Nietzsche (Will to Power # 1064), 547]

> *This world: a monster of* **force**,*[...] transformed as a whole which is untransformably large, [...] definitive* **force** *situated in defined space, and not space that would be 'empty' anywhere, rather as* **force** *everywhere, as a play of* **forces** *and* **force**-*waves simultaneously one and many [...], an ocean of* **forces** *storming and flooding within themselves [...].* [Nietzsche, (Will to Power # 1067), 1922, author's translation]

b. In Deleuze's reading of **Nietzsche**, that which, through necessary relation to other dominant and dominating forces, produces a living body as well as active and reactive qualities of **life**.

> **Forces** *are said to be dominant or dominated depending on their* **difference** *in quantity.* **Forces** *are said to be active or reactive depending on their quality.* [N 49, 53]

Every relationship of forces *constitutes a body—whether it is chemical, biological, social or political.* [N 37, 40]

c. When determined by **nihilism**, a force which turns against itself; reactive forces which separate active force from its relation to other forces to make active force reactive.

When reactive **force** *separates active* **force** *from what it can do, the latter also becomes reactive. [...] How do they triumph? Through the will to nothingness, thanks to the affinity between reaction and negation.* [N 59, 57]

2.a. In Deleuze's explanation of the development of **difference**, as well as the system of **simulacra**, the impulse or **dark precursor** that precedes and instigates the communication of **series**, and the movement that results from and surpasses the communication; an encounter that engenders thought. [DR, LS]

[....] series *communicate under the impulse of a* force *of some kind* [DR 143, 117]

what is this agent, this force *which ensures communication? Thunderbolts explode between different* **intensities**, *but they are preceded by an invisible, imperceptible* **dark precursor** [DR 145, 119]

b. The **repetition** of the **eternal return** (the third **passive synthesis**) which is preconditioned by plurality and contingency rather than **habit** or memory.

The expulsive and selective **force** *of the* **eternal return**, *its centrifugal force, consists of distributing* **repetition** *among the three times of the pseudo-cycle, but also of ensuring that the first two repetitions do not return* [DR 370, 297]

3.a. In Deleuze's reading of **Nietzsche** and **affect**, relations determined by the *will to power* which exercise a capacity to affect and be affected.

The relationship between **forces** *in each case is determined to the extent that each* **force** *is affected by other, inferior or superior,* **forces**. *It follows that will to power is manifested as a capacity for being affected.* [N 57, 62]

> *Power (what* **Nietzsche** *calls 'will to power' and Welles, 'character') is this power to* **affect** *and be affected, this relation between one* **force** *and others.* [C2 135, 139]

b. In Deleuze's reading of **Foucault**, that which constitutes the **Outside** of forms but is not exterior to them; that which constitutes a power relation which involves provocation, seduction, enabling, or production, and may be **diagrammed** within forms (of knowledge; content and **expression**), but cannot be localized in any given form; an affect that can be determined as active or reactive (within diagrams of power), or exercises a capacity for resistance.

> *an exercise of power shows up as an* **affect**, *since* **force** *defines itself by its very power to affect other* **forces** *(to which it is related) and to be affected by other* **forces**. *[...]* **force** *displays potentiality with respect to the* **diagram** *containing it, or possesses a third power which presents itself as the possibility of 'resistance'.* [F 74, 89]

> *the* **outside** *concerns* **force:** *if* **force** *is always in relation with other* **forces, forces** *necessarily refer to an irreducible outside which no longer even has any form and is made of distances that cannot be broken down through which one* **force** *acts upon another or is acted upon by another.* [F 72, 86]

4. That which cannot be directly sensed, seen, or heard, but which can be rendered sonorous or visible by means of the dissipation, deformation, and isolation of elements of bodies. The proper object of painting, music, and in some cases, literature and film. [TP, FB, DR, LS, K, ECC]

> *The task of painting is defined as the attempt to render visible* **forces** *that are not themselves visible. Likewise, music attempts to render sonorous* **forces** *that are not themselves sonorous. [...] if* **force** *is the condition of* **sensation**, *it is nonetheless not the* **force** *that is sensed, since the sensation 'gives' something completely different from the* **forces** *that condition it.* [FB 56]

5. In Deleuze's reading of **Leibniz**, in its primary role, that which engenders **folding** and unfolding in a **monad**, and, in its derivative role, that which folds or is enfolded but is not perceived as such.

> *Primary* **forces** *are* **monads** *or substances in themselves or of*

themselves. Derivative forces *are the same, but under a vinculum or in the flash of an instant. In one case, they are taken in multitudes and become plastic, while in the other they are taken in a mass and become elastic, because masses are what change at every instant (they do not go from one instant to another without being reconstituted).* [FLB 117]

- E. B. Y.

Form of content

Ferdinand de Saussure's well-known thesis, on the one hand, is that the interrelationship of language ('signifiers') is only a 'negative' one (e.g. a tree is *not* a horse, a horse is *not* a pipe, etc.), and that the sign/referent (that is, the relation between signified-signifier) is *arbitrary*; on the other hand, Guattari, and Deleuze along with him, prefer the **Hjelmslev**ian approach which gives content (what Saussure would call the 'signified'), its own *form* (content, in this sense, can no more be considered a 'signified' than a 'signifier'). Content, for D&G, refers to the tangible, corporeal and the machinic; in a **Foucauldian** sense, it would concern the 'visible' or observable, in distinction from incorporeal statements or **Forms of Expression**. In this sense, the two dimensions (Content and Expression) *interact*, rather than one 'signifying' the other. Furthermore, this 'horizontal' interaction is determined by the complexities of action, **desire** and **de/territorialization**.

1. A phrase from Louis **Hjelmslev** to designate the **function** of the **sign** that is directed inward, and which is in mutual solidarity with the **form of expression**.

> [I]*n one of the two entities that are* functives *of the* sign *function, namely the content, the sign function institutes a form, the* **content-form**, *which from the point of the of the purport is arbitrary and which can be explained only by the sign function and is obviously solidarity with it.* [...] expression *and* content [...] *are each defined only oppositively and relatively, as mutually opposed functives of one and the same function.* [Hjelmslev, 1961, 54]

2.a. In D&G's reading of **Hjelmslev, matter** whose substance is related to the actions and passions of the body, or is otherwise machinic; the segment of an **assemblage** (neither **territorialized** nor **deterritorialized**) that comprises a **machinic assemblage** of bodies.

> [Hjelmslev] *used the term content for formed* **matters**, *which would now have to be considered from two points of view: substance, insofar as these matters are 'chosen', and form, insofar as they are chosen in a certain order.* [TP 49, 43]

> *On a first, horizontal axis, an* **assemblage** *comprises two segments, one of content, the other of* **expression**. [TP 97, 88]

b. In D&G's analysis of **stratification**, one side of a double articulation of formed **matter** where substance is primary to its successive formalization, in distinction from **forms of expression**, where form is primary to a simultaneous substantiation.

> *The first articulation chooses or deducts, from unstable particle-flows, metastable molecular or quasi molecular units (substances) upon which it imposes a statistical order or connections and succession* (**forms**). [TP 46, 40]

> *Content and* **expression** *are two variables of a function of* **stratification**. [TP 49–50, 44]

c. When deformed or formless in a **deterritorialized assemblage**, that which is indistinguishable from **expression**. [K, TP]

> *The* **assemblage** *is also divided along another axis. Its territoriality (content and* **expression** *included) is only a first aspect [...]. Following these lines, the assemblage no longer presents an* **expression** *distinct from content, only unformed* **matters**, *destratified* **forces**, *and functions.* [TP 556, 504–5]

3. In Deleuze's reading of **Foucault**, places of visibility, such as hospitals or prisons, which are non-discursive (as in Foucault's historical formations), and can be distinguished from their substance in that they are irreducible to a **form of expression** (such as penal law and delinquency, or medicine and diagnoses).

> **Form** [of content] *is prison and the substance is those who are locked up, the prisoners.* [F 41, 47]

> *the general hospital as a* **form of content** *or a place of visibility for*

madness did not have its origins in medicine, but in the police; while medicine as a **form of expression** *[...] deployed its discursive system [...] outside the hospital.* [F 53, 62]

- E. B. Y.

Form of expression

'**Expression**' is considered by Deleuze independently of its *form*, but *Forms of Expression* are considered by Deleuze and Guattari alongside **Forms of Content** in terms of a 'horizontal' axis—that is, an axis which involves either incorporeality or corporeality (**surface,** or **depth**) and is independent of the 'vertical' axis of **assemblages**. In this case, it is the incorporeality of 'expressions'— enunciations, statements—that are 'formalized' to the extent that they are repeated and repeatable, whether with regard to **desire**, or, in Deleuze's work on **Foucault**, with regard to power.

1. A phrase from **Louis Hjelmslev** to designate the **function** of the **sign** that is directed outward, and which is in mutual solidarity with the **form of content**.

> *[T]the* formal *and nominalistic description in linguistic theory is not limited to the* **expression-form***, but sees its object in the interplay between the* **expression-form** *and a* **content-form***.* [Hjelmslev, 1961, 54]

2.a. In D&G's reading of **Hjelmslev, matter** whose **substance** is related to **incorporeal** transformations and enunciations (speech acts), or is otherwise **collective,** and can be attributed to **bodies** or **forms of content;** the segment of an **assemblage** (neither **territorialized** nor deterritorialized) that comprises **collective assemblages of enunciation.** [K, TP]

> *[***Hjelmslev***] used the term* expression *for functional structures, which would also have to be considered from two points of view: the organization of their own specific* **form***, and substances insofar as they* **form** *compounds.* [TP 49, 43]

> *On a first, horizontal axis, an* **assemblage** *comprises two segments, one of* **content***, the other of* **expression** [TP 97, 88]

b. In D&G's analysis of **stratification**, one side of a double articulation of formed **matter** where form is primary to a simultaneous substantiation, in distinction from **forms of content**, where substance is primary to its successive formalization.

> The second articulation established functional, compact, stable structures (**forms**), and constructs the molar compounds in which these structures are simultaneously actualized (substances). [TP 46, 41]

c. Deterritorialized **matter**, such as music, which may be more or less formless or deformed in accordance with its **intensity**, and which, in turn, carries away contents along a **line of flight**. [K, TP]

> [M]usic makes [the refrain] a **deterritorialized** content for a deterritorializing form of expression [TP 331, 300]

> Both expression and content are more or less deterritorialized, relatively deterritorialized, according to the particular state of their form. [TP 97, 87]

3.a. In Deleuze's reading of **Foucault**, iterable statements, such as 'penal law' in Foucault's historical formations, that can be distinguished from **substance** and is primary to, and not derivate of, **Forms of Content** such as prisoners and prisons.

> **Form** [of expression] is penal law and the substance is 'delinquency' in so far as it is the object of statements. [F 41, 47]

> Penal law, for its part, produces statements of 'delinquency' independently of prison [...] the two forms [of content and expression] do not have the same formation, genesis or genealogy [...]. [F 53, 62]

b. The doubling of a **form of content** which interiorizes and is coextensive with it within a 'non-place' and 'non-relation' (rather than projecting it in an independent form), where the expression (speakable) may attain primacy, as in **Blanchot's** work.

> [E]ven **Foucault** needs a third agency to coadapt [...] the visible and the articulable [...], operating either beyond or on this side of the two **forms** [of content and expression]. It is for this reason that [...] the place of confrontation implies a 'non-place'. [F 58, 68]

[O]ne of **Foucault's** *fundamental theses is the following: there is a difference in nature between the* **form** *of* **content** *and the* **form of expression** *[...] but while* **Blanchot** *insisted on the primacy of speaking as a determining element, Foucault [...] upholds the specificity of seeing.* [F 52, 61]

- E. B. Y.

Foucault, Michel

It is impossible to underestimate the effect that Foucault had both on Deleuze's career as a professor, and on the later stages of his work, especially his more political writings with Guattari. Foucault, for his own part, expressed great appreciation for Deleuze's project, as evidenced in his introduction to *Anti-Oedipus*. Reading between Deleuze's own work devoted to Foucault and the Capitalism and Schizophrenia project with Guattari proves fruitful; concepts that have an especially Foucauldian **resonance** include 'double articulation' in *A Thousand Plateaus*, where there is both **code** (redundancy) and **territorialization** in all **strata**, which correspond loosely to the relation between what Foucault describes as 'knowledge' and 'power'. Furthermore, **forms of content** and **forms of expression** correspond *loosely* to Foucault's visibilities and statements. There is also a correspondence between Deleuze and Guattari's 'concrete **assemblages**' and Foucault's 'dispositif' (See Deleuze's essay 'What is a Dispositif?'); however, reading between Foucault and Deleuze may reveal that there is arguably no correlation for the **abstract machine** in Foucault's works. Deleuze in fact addressed a letter to Foucault where he stated that 'Lines of flight and movements of **deterritorialization**, as collective historical determinations, do not seem to me to have any equivalent in Michel's work' (Deleuze 1997). In these terms, since **desire** is closely connected to deterritorialization for Deleuze (and Guattari), Deleuze will insist that his conception of desire also conflicts with Foucault's conception of 'pleasure' (see entry on **Sacher-Masoch**); in Deleuze's view, pleasure concerns an interiority or relation to the Self which does not take place in processes of desire, because desire concerns the '**fold**' of the **Outside** onto the inside. - E. B. Y.

Foucault

Foucault (1986)

In an interview with Claire Parnet, published later in *Negotiations*, Deleuze describes this work published two years after Foucault's death as an attempt to paint a portrait of his philosophy. Although Deleuze partly intended this as an act of homage to a long-time friend and philosopher he had always publicly admired, and who had been his sponsor for several academic appointments throughout his career, this portrait of Foucault as a thinker is also intended to respond to the criticisms of both the philosophy and the man that had become quite virulent in the period immediately following Foucault's death and threatened to deform his philosophy for later generations. There are two major misunderstandings that become the primary targets of Deleuze's criticism. The first is that after abandoning (or even 'destroying') the notion of the subject in his earlier writings, in the period following the appearance of the first volume of *The History of Sexuality* (a period also remarked by an eight-year hiatus in publication), Foucault recants his earlier writings and performs 'a return to the subject,' especially in the later volumes of the *History of Sexuality* on the Greek formations of sexuality and the self. The second line of attack that Deleuze openly confronts concerns the portrait of Foucault's own life in the hands of his most vociferous critics (including the New Philosophers) and the public charges of political and philosophical nihilism, moral perversion, and personal solipsism.

To combat both these images, in *Foucault* Deleuze provides three masks that correspond to what Deleuze and Guattari later call 'conceptual personae,' and which serve to characterize different aspects of a living portrait by also providing three distinctive images of thought that can be found in Foucault's entire philosophical trajectory. The first image is that of ' a new archivist,' which is also the title of the first chapter and is drawn from Deleuze's earlier writings on Foucault in the 1972 edition of *Un Nouvel Archivist*. This section covers Foucault's writings up through the publication of *An Archeology of Knowledge* in which historical **strata** and formations are analyzed by the uncovering of statements that are found to be exterior to the discursive temporality of most historical narration, even constituting the dimension of exteriority that Foucault himself always privileged in constituting key moments and scintillating events that will determine a genealogy of causal relationships, but almost in the manner of a throw of the dice between a previous historical epoch and the present actuality of its interpretation or construction in the text of the archivist of statements. The second image Deleuze provides is that of the 'New Cartographer,' written to cover those works that perform an analysis of 'micro-disciplinary orders' following the period of *Discipline and Punish*. The third image (or portrait) is drawn from Foucault's later essay 'On the Lives of Infamous Men,' and is employed to draw a comparison between the legacy of Foucault's thought and the event of resistance to domination it represents, like those anonymous individuals who cause power to first appear and become visible by drawing a line that causes a style of living to become indistinguishable from knowledge. - G. L.

Four functors

Sometimes translated as 'functions' (*foncteurs*). A four-part schema consisting in **Flows** [*fluxes*], **Phylums, Universes,** and **Territories**. In his late work, Guattari draws dozens of versions of the schema, usually arranged into quadrants resembling those of an x-y graph. Serves as a diagrammatic tool for the related practices of **schizoanalysis**, schizoanalytic **cartography**, **metamodelization**, and **ecosophy**. Guattari claims that the schema is not mathematical and non-representational. For him, it replaces structures, ordinary social science models, binaries, and Lacanian mathemes. Sometimes presented as a mapping of the **plane of consistency** or the **assemblage**. Explicated in great detail in *Schizoanalytic Cartographies*. Provides the theoretical foundation for *Chaosmosis*, and also informs *What Is Philosophy?* See **schizoanalysis, 1.a.**

1. In mathematics, a functor (*foncteur*) is a type of mapping between categories.

2. The four domains of **metamodelization**, proposed as a non-structuralist mapping of complex formations like subjectivity.

Note that the categories of **metamodelization** *proposed here*— **Fluxes**, *machinic* **Phylums**, *existential* **Territories**, *incorporeal* **Universes**—*are only of interest because they come in fours and allow us to break free of tertiary descriptions which always end up falling back into dualisms.* [CM 31]

3. The ecosophic object, a conceptual tool for mapping the **three ecologies**; see **ecosophy**.

In order to counteract reductionist approaches to **subjectivity**, *we have proposed an analysis of complexity starting with an ecosophic object with four dimensions:*

-material, energetic and semiotic **Fluxes***;*

-concrete and abstract machinic **Phylums***;*

-virtual **Universes** *of value;*

-finite existential **Territories***.* [CM 124]

4. An alternative to **Freud**ian, Lacanian, and **Marx**ist social and psychic schemas.

To speak of **machines** *rather than drives,* **Fluxes** *rather than libido,* existential **Territories** *rather than the instances of the self and of transference, incorporeal* **Universes** *rather than unconscious complexes and sublimation, chaosmic entities rather than signifiers—fitting ontological dimensions together in a circular manner rather than dividing the world up into infrastructure and superstructure—may not simply be a matter of vocabulary!* [CM 126]

5. A non-representational schema for mapping the **plane of consistency**.

the **Plane of Consistency** *is divided into four domains of consistency*

-energetic-signaletic **Flows** *[fluxes] (F.)...*

-abstract machinic **Phylums** *(Φ.)...*

-existential **Territories** *(T.)...*

-incorporeal **Universes** *(U.)... [SC 80]*

- J. W.

Francis Bacon: The Logic of Sensation

Francis Bacon. Logique de la sensation (1981)

Deleuze was a contemporary of Francis **Bacon**'s, and his choice to devote a book to Bacon's work was probably motivated by a desire to expand his **concepts** into fields of aesthetics in his later career (he had done this earlier with a great deal of literature, and again with *music*—especially in *A Thousand Plateaus*, and does this following this work with *cinema* and, to a lesser extent, with *architecture* in *The Fold*, and again with *literature* in *Essays Critical and Clinical*). Deleuze was probably influenced to write on Bacon from encounters he had with the artist's paintings in Paris exhibitions, and from the way in which Bacon's work uniquely treats the problem of 'figuration': just as modern philosophy has dealt with the problem of *representation*, so too 'modern' painting has dealt with the problem of *figuration*, which is where the painting resembles the 'real' visual world which 'reign[s] over vision' (so that the eye is limited to form rather than movement and connection [FB11]). While much modern painting simply resorted to non-representational—albeit 'abstract'—colors, shapes, lines, etc., as Deleuze states, 'what is interesting is the way in which Bacon, for his part, breaks with figuration: it is not impressionism, not expressionism, not symbolism, not cubism, not abstraction' (FB xiv); rather, it is what he calls a **haptic** vision that entertains a relation to **chaos** without becoming chaotic. Just as Deleuze insists that resemblance and symbolism cannot be done away with, but can in fact be the more profound, displaced and disguised form of non-representative **differences**, so too he finds in Bacon's work an example of conventional figuration which is actually indicative of **sensation**. So, on the one hand, philosophy begins with what 'Everybody knows', the **common sense** we share, in order to complicate such opinions and express **sense** itself, and on the other hand, Deleuze emphasizes that for Bacon, there is no 'blank canvas', only visual 'clichés' which are utilized to be deformed such that invisible **forces** and **rhythms** can be **diagrammed** or *composed* (this actually foreshadows his discussion of the **plane of composition** with Guattari in *What is Philosophy?*, while the discussion of the cliché foreshadows his work in the *Cinema* books). In fact, many concepts from Deleuze's other works can be found extended in this work, especially **Intensity** and the **Body without Organs**, though there are also some concepts unique to it, such as the '**Figure**' (which is not 'figurative'). - E. B. Y.

Freud, Sigmund

Freud & Deleuze: A 'return to Freud', spearheaded by Jacques Lacan in the 1950s and 60s, expanded the influence of psychoanalysis as well as the treatment of Freud's original work, and it is impossible to ignore this cultural context when assessing Freud's influence on Deleuze. In any case, while Deleuze makes reference to other psychoanalysts such as Theodor Reik and Melanie Klein (and, with Guattari, Wilhelm Reich), as well as Lacan, his target in critiquing psychoanalysis is almost always Freud's texts. While Freud saw psychoanalysis as a *science*, Deleuze saw his own project as philosophical, and as such, he interrogated the *metaphysical* and *conceptual* foundations of Freud's framework. In this sense, Deleuze was perhaps territorial in distinguishing his approach from Freud's and especially from Lacan's, not only in his writing but also in his teaching; as one commentator notes, 'Deleuze's seminar was held at the same time on the same day as Lacan's, several miles away in central Paris, so that one could not attend both' (NG 185).

The first substantial engagement with Freud in one of Deleuze's book-length projects arrives in **Coldness and Cruelty**. Here he notes, for example, that Freud takes it for granted that the exception to the pleasure principle, namely, the death instinct, indicates that **repetition** is involved with psychic mechanisms that are 'beyond'—that is, not subject to—the pleasure principle. While he takes a detour in **The Logic of Sense** to discuss general psychoanalytic themes involving infantile sexuality, **depth/surface**, and schizophrenia, he expands on themes involving repetition in **Difference and Repetition** where he critiques Freud's concept of the **unconscious** by way of his varieties of **passive syntheses**. This treatment of the unconscious is also echoed in his work on **Nietzsche**, where he notes that Freud, unlike **Nietzsche**, always considered repression and *forgetting* in a negative sense. After teaming up with Guattari for the 'Capitalism and Schizophrenia' project, though, the tone of the critiques shift from patient and focused to unabashed, hyperbolic, and playful (perhaps channeling Nietzsche), and don't miss any opportunity to flaunt the limitations of psychoanalysis, especially concerning the reduction of **desire** to representation, memory, or 'Oedipal intrigues'. Thus while Guattari's criticism of (and continued respect for) Freud came from an investment in the practice of psychiatry, Deleuze's objections came from his very determination of the psyche and what it means to exist. - E. B. Y.

Freud & Guattari: Even in the most heated moments of criticism, Freud still garners respect from Guattari. Whether the target is under constant fire, like the Oedipus complex and resignation-inducing castration; or the distinction between neurosis and psychosis is exploding; or Freud's reticence in the face of stumbling upon the productive **unconscious**, the **body-without-organs**, and the **becoming-animal** of his patients, is shown to be regrettable; or revealing how the interminability of the cure haunted an aging Freud. Freud remains central to Guattari's thought, especially in his earliest writings, because of what he discovered but abandoned. Freud wore the blinkers of ancient myth and Guattari's task is to adjust them by opening his field of vision by transversalizing the transference relation; by renovating the group **psychology** and opening up the dual analytic relation; by challenging universals with singularizations; by liberating the unconscious from psychoanalytic interpretation itself. Traces of the Freudian nomenclature are evident in Guattari's formulations from the 1960s and early 70s, such as the latent-manifest distinction in the unconscious of an institution, and the task of creating new introjects for the super-ego in relation to **desire**. While rejecting Freud's familialism, theory of sexuality, and psychical topography, Guattari respected his writerly inventions and saved his fiercest attacks for Freud's followers who had rebaptized him in the waters of **structuralism**. - G. G.

Functive

cross-reference: **Four Functors**

Genesign

cross-reference: **Time-Image** (type of choosing that involves time as a **series**)

Good sense

cross-reference: **Sense** (def. 2.a.)

Gramme

cross-reference: Gaseous **Perception**

Group

In Guattari's usage, the term refers not to conventional group therapy, but to the notion as refined by **Sartre**, who defines various types of groups according to the degree of subjective engagement. Guattari's political and professional activities took place primarily in group settings. Although psychoanalysis is typically practiced as individual out-patient therapy, Guattari worked at an in-patient psychiatric clinic as part of a team providing around-the-clock care to patients living in close contact with each other. Guattari therefore found it necessary to adapt psychoanalysis to the group context. He proposed **transversality** to describe groups that were more open, less hierarchical, and more adaptive to concrete situations. He held similar views about the hierarchies and leader cults common in radical political circles. He distinguished efficacious, self-directed **subject**-groups from alienated, neurotic **subjugated** groups. After he began working with Deleuze, he abandoned the idea in favor of the **collective assemblage of enunciation**.

1. A coherent collective formation. As theorized by Jean-Paul Sartre, a group may be deliberately organized (as in a political

party) or may form around a concrete undertaking (like waiting for a bus).

> *we must emphasize that* **groups** *[...] can arise only on the foundation of a collective which [...] whatever its aim [...] must itself, as a free organization of individuals with a common aim, produce its collective structure [...]* [Sartre, 1976, 253–4]

2. The dimension in which, according to Guattari, psychoanalysis must operate in an institutional setting.

> *As a temporary support set up to preserve, at least for a time, the object of our practice, I propose to replace the ambiguous idea of the institutional transference with a new* **concept: transversality** *in the* **group**. [MR 17]

3. A militant revolutionary collective.

> *In a basic* **group**, *you can hope to recover a minimal collective identity, but without megalomania, with a system of control at hand; thus the* **desire** *in question will perhaps be better able to make its voice heard, or will perhaps even be better able to fulfill its militant engagements.* [PT 285]

4.a. (Special Combination): **Subject-group**. A collectivity which is brave, efficacious, and self-directed, and articulate because it lucidly accepts alterity, finitude, dispersal, and death.

> *A* **subject-group**, *on the other contrary, is a* **group** *whose libidinal investments are themselves revolutionary [...]* [AO 382, 348]

b. (Special Combination): **Subjugated group.** Term developed by Guattari to describe an alienated collectivity incapable of articulating its **desires**, engaged in collective neurotic obsession, and receiving its law from the exterior. Such a group offers reassurance and protection.

> *A revolutionary* **group** *at the preconscious level remains a* **subjugated group**, *even in seizing power, as long as this power itself refers to a form of* **force** *that continues to enslave and crush desiring production.* [AO 382, 348]

5. Designating a social or institutional collectivity, this term was later abandoned in favor of **assemblage**.

I've change my mind: there are no subject-groups, *but* assemblages *of enunciation, of subjectivization, pragmatic assemblages that do not coincide with circumscribed* groups. [SS 179]

- J. W.

The Guattari Reader

This well-balanced essay collection remains the best point of entry into Guattari's solo writing because it includes both theoretical essays and journalistic texts that span his career. The editor's introduction provides an overview of Guattari's life and work, situating it intellectually and historically. Texts cover not only Guattari's critique of psychoanalysis and engagement in radical politics, but also his meticulous reworking of linguistics and semiotics. - J. W.

Habit

While many concepts which Deleuze appropriates resonate primarily with one thinker (such as '**eternal return**' with **Nietzsche**, or '**affect**' with **Spinoza**), 'habit' is a term employed by both **Hume** and **Bergson**. Deleuze's work on Hume predates Bergson by over a decade, but the two are discussed side by side in the chapter on 'Repetition for Itself' in *Difference and Repetition* when dealing the first **passive synthesis** of time.

Deleuze emphasizes that habits are not 'psychological': we do not acquire habits by means of action, but through the **passive synthesis** of contemplation. Not only everything we do, but everything we *are* (psycho-organically), is predicated on visceral '**contractions**'. There is thus no such thing as a living being without 'habits' (there would in fact be no living present in time without them), and to judge habits **morally** as 'bad' (e.g. 'addiction'), is often to overlook the natural tendency and necessity of acquiring habits (and is perhaps, with reference to **Hume**, also to overlook the institutions which may or may not satisfy habits). At the same time, this is not meant to valorize being a 'creature of habit', since living by this manner alone would eclipse the nature of **difference** and novelty by forming principles and expectations based on generalities and even prejudices that are the result of an **active synthesis** of the mind.

1.a. In **Hume,** the foundation for beliefs and inferences that are not based on logic but on probability and experience; the foundation for reasoning of cause and effect that forms associations of ideas and goes beyond experience.

> *the supposition, that the future resembles the past, is not founded on arguments of any kind, but is derived entirely from* **habit***, by which we are determined to expect for the future the same train of objects, to which we have been accustomed.* [Hume, 2003, 96]

> *Experience is a principle, which instructs me in the several conjunctions of objects for the past.* **Habit** *is another principle, which determines me to expect the same for the future; and both of them conspiring to operate upon the* **imagination** *[...]* [Hume, 2003, 189]

b. In Deleuze's reading of **Hume,** the tendency of the mind to observe cases of **repetition** in experience, and form probabilities in the **imagination** based on those cases or repeat unobserved cases to form beliefs that are not based on experience; a natural tendency, based on experience, to engender means to satisfy ends (in practice, the actual, artificial means which satisfy these ends).

> **habits** *are not themselves natural, but what is natural is the* **habit** *to take up* **habits***. Nature does not reach its ends except by means of culture, and tendency is not satisfied except through the institution.* [ES 44]

> **Habit** *itself is a principle different from experience; the unity of experience and* **habit** *is not given. By itself,* **habit** *can feign or invoke a false experience, and bring about belief through 'a* **repetition'** *which 'is not deriv'd from experience.' This will be an illegitimate belief, a fiction of the* **imagination***.* [ES 69]

> *The* **imagination***, under the influence of the principle of* **habit***, is also the mind which reflects time as a determined future filled with its anticipation.* [ES 96]

2.a. In **Bergson**'s work, a motor-memory, or learnt recollection, which can be distinguished from a spontaneous memory in that the former fades over time, requires **repetition**, and is not unique, while the latter is unique and is only repeated or recalled by virtue of its unrepeatability.

> *how can we overlook the radical* difference *between that which must be built up by* repetition *and that which is essentially incapable of being repeated? Spontaneous recollection is perfect from the outset; [...] On the contrary, a learnt recollection passes out of time in the measure that the lesson is better known; [...]. Repetition, therefore, in no sense effects the conversion of [Spontaneous recollections] into the [learnt recollections]; its office is merely to utilize more and more the movements by which the first was continued, in order to organize them together and, by setting up a mechanism, to create a bodily* habit. [Bergson, 1913, p. 95]

b. In Deleuze's reading of **Bergson**, the **contraction** of successive interdependent instants within a contemplating mind, which occurs on both the level of **matter** (the organism), as well as the level of memory. [B, DR]

> *When we say that* habit *is a* contraction *we are speaking not of an instantaneous action which combines with another to form an element of* repetition, *but rather of the fusion of that repetition in the contemplating mind. [...]* habit *here manifests its full generality: it concerns not only the sensory–motor* habits *that we have (psychologically), but also, before these, the primary* habits *that we are; the thousands of* passive syntheses *of which we are organically composed.* [DR 95, 74]

3. The foundation of expectation and need build upon successive **passive syntheses,** and determined by the contemplations (and **contractions**) of the viscera and the **imagination** (in distinction from the foundation of identity built upon the simultaneous **passive syntheses** of memory).

> *These thousands of* habits *of which we are composed—these* contractions, *contemplations, pretensions, presumptions, satisfactions, fatigues; these variable presents—thus form the basic domain of* passive syntheses. [DR 100, 78]

- E. B. Y.

Haecceity

1. In Deleuze and Guattari's reading of Duns Scotus, the individual and unique, albeit contingent and impersonal nature (akin to **Spinoza's modes**) of life or **assemblages** (which cannot be reduced to subjects or things) that engender **events; singularities**. [TP, I]

> *This is sometimes written 'ecceity,' deriving the word from ecce, 'here is.' This is an error, since Duns Scotus created the word and the* **concept** *from haec, 'this thing.' But it is a fruitful error because it suggests a* **mode** *of individuation that is distinct from that of a thing or a subject.* [TP 599, 540]

> haecceities *form according to compositions of nonsubjectified powers or* **affects**. [TP 294, 266]

> *an* **assemblage** *of the* haecceity *type [...] carries or brings out the* **event** *insofar as it is unformed and incapable of being effectuated by persons.* [TP 292, 265]

- E. B. Y.

Haptic

1.a. In Deleuze's reading of Alois Riegl (and Egyptian Art), a manner of 'far-seeing' (distinct from 'near-seeing') where form and ground merge so depths are perceived in terms of warm and cool (color), and expansion and contraction (light).

> *'Haptic,' from the Greek verb aptô (to touch), does not designate an extrinsic relation of the eye to the sense of touch, but a 'possibility of seeing [regard],' a type of vision distinct from the optical* [FB 189]

b. In Deleuze's explanation of art, a tactile relation with the optical or visual that neither subordinates touch to sight (as in digital vision, where we can choose or touch what we see based on predetermined alternatives, as on a computer or video game), nor subordinates vision to touch (as in purely manual referents which scramble or dismantle the visual); rather, a relation that shifts from manual (or analogical) referents within an optical (or digital), **codified** space.

> we will speak of the **haptic** [...] when sight discovers in itself a specific function of touch that is uniquely its own, distinct from its optical function. One might say that painters paint with their eyes, but only insofar as they touch with their eyes [...] through violence and manual insubordination. [FB 155]
>
> if we consider the painting as a process, there is instead a continual injection of the manual **diagram** into the visual whole, a 'slow leak,' a 'coagulation,' an 'evolution,' as if one were moving gradually from the hand to the **haptic** eye, from the manual diagram to **haptic** vision. [FB 159–60]

c. In D&G's explanation of **nomadism**, a feature of **smooth space** where distance and direction are not determined visually but by relations of **intensity**.

> [smooth space] is a tactile space, or rather 'haptic,' a sonorous much more than a visual space. The variability, the polyvocality of directions, is an essential feature of smooth spaces of the **rhizome** type, and it alters their **cartography**. [TP 421–2, 382]

- E. B. Y.

Hegel, Georg Wilhelm Friedrich

Hegel is perhaps the figure which Deleuze most explicitly polemicizes and caricatures in *Difference and Repetition* (and in his philosophical project in general); at the same time, he appropriates some of Hegel's philosophical language in order to invert it. For example, Deleuze's use of Hegel's phrases 'for itself' (*für sich*) and 'in itself' (*an sich*), which appear in two of his five chapter titles of *Difference and Repetition*, arguably resonate more with Hegel than most philosophers (and perhaps their appropriation by **Sartre**, de Beauvoir, **Heidegger**, etc.): while Hegel argues that **difference** is only created when that which is in itself is reflected as what it is not to become for itself, Deleuze ultimately argues that difference is *already* in itself, and that **repetition** (as the indifferent, ontological category) is never in itself, but always for itself.

It is important to understand the dense, albeit essential, aspects of Hegel's philosophy that Deleuze focuses on. In Hegel's case, something becomes 'in-and-for-itself' through being mediated or *sublated* by that which can be opposed to both what it is and is not (in abstract terms, a 'becoming' that is opposed to 'being' and to 'non-being'). Then the thing is no longer identical to what it is not (and 'for itself') by being reflected, but is mediated by a new thing which is in itself because it is not reflected, but is also for itself in that it preserves the identity of the opposites that it sublates (and thus 'in and for itself'). The **different**, for Hegel, concerns the tension between something being that which it is not in order to be 'for itself', but such difference is also 'identical' to what it is not; Deleuze notes that, for Hegel, 'difference as such is already implicitly contradiction' [DR 54, 44], but a contradiction which is a negative reflection of its opposite. Only indifference is in itself.

While, in **Aristotle**, contradiction was limited by specific **differences** within a genus (as 'contraries'), or by **propositions** which pass the test of those finite, categorical divisions and measurements, in Hegel, contradiction 'extend[s] to the infinite' in that the mediation of the dialectic (that is, the reflection of a thing in what it is not) grounds every thing an in infinitely large process or whole. Unlike Aristotle's 'organic representation', Deleuze calls this 'orgiastic representation' because, in Hegel's version, it is a chaotic promiscuity where the 'restlessness' of the infinite whole is synthesized with every thought, action, or thing; the whole is the part and vice versa (**Leibniz**, on the other hand, has another version that extends to the 'infinitely small' or 'inessential'). The problem with this, as with Aristotle, is that it subordinates difference to contradiction and to representation. In this case, difference is submitted to the identity of the 'whole'; that is, the different 'for itself' must, through contradiction, be coextensive with the identity of that which is 'in itself' (the world, the self, etc.): as Deleuze states, 'Difference is the ground, but only the ground for the demonstration of the identical. Hegel's circle is not the **eternal return**, only the infinite circulation of the identical by means of negativity' (DR 61, 50).

Deleuze radically reverses Hegel's conceptions of the in itself and for itself, arguing that when the in itself (**difference**) is separate from the for itself (**repetition**), that separation is also implicitly a mediation (unlike Hegel, where mediation has not yet occurred), because either repetition (the 'for itself') excludes and is thereby included and mediated by difference (the 'in itself') as in **habit**, or difference (the 'in itself') excludes and is thereby included and mediated by repetition (the 'for itself') as in *memory*. In other words, in Deleuze's version, in order for either the 'in itself' or the 'for itself' to exist independently, whichever excludes the other is, paradoxically, implicitly included and mediated by it (any further mediation does not resolve the tension). - E. B. Y.

Heidegger, Martin

While Deleuze demonstrates an appreciation for the late Heidegger's notion of the identity of **difference**, where difference 'must be thought as the Same, in the Same', he questions why Heidegger still insisted on describing the 'being' of difference in terms of nothing (or 'striking through' being). In fact, Heidegger's reading of **Nietzsche**, while at moments lucid, depicts eternal **'return'** as a return of the same: while Heidegger does insist that 'The same, by contrast, is the belonging together of what differs, through a gathering by way of the difference' (DR 79, 66), this is a difference between Being and beings which always returns to a circuitous dialectic of its revealment and concealment. While Deleuze appreciates this as a springboard for considering the nature of the **fold** (*Zweifalt*), he will emphasize that the role of difference, in the case of **Nietzsche**, involves an **ethics** of selection, and in the case of the fold, involves the affirmation of **events** which, à la **Blanchot**, concern **singularities** within the **Outside** (neither of which fit in Heidegger's notion of *Dasein* in terms of the coherence of being-in-the-world or the 'Open'). Both cases entail a conception of death that is not our ultimate horizon (a being-toward, as Heidegger would insist), but a neutral and impersonal line that we continually cross. - E. B. Y.

Heterogenesis

Guattari's earliest work in semiotics and linguistics culminated in a detailed genealogy of the **assemblage** and its components. The mature version of this genealogy dominates *The Machinic Unconscious*. His work of the 1980s draws less on semiotics and more on complexity and chaos theory, necessitating the replacement of his semiotic genealogy with a new ontology. In *Schizoanalytic*

Cartographies and *Chaosmosis*, with a nod to Heidegger's essay on technology, Guattari expands the notion of the **machinic phylum** to trace the phylogenesis and ontogenesis of **machines** and **assemblages**. Because of the heterogeneity of the components that make up the **assemblage**, he calls this second ontology heterogenesis.

1. The process of coming into being, understood as the emergence of order out of **chaos** as described by complexity theory.

> A *machinic* **assemblage**, *through its diverse components, extracts its consistency by crossing ontological thresholds, non-linear thresholds of irreversibility, ontological and phylogenetic thresholds, creative thresholds of* **heterogenesis** *and* **autopoiesis**. [CM 50]

2.a. A power that can effectuate creative change in a complex system.

> *The fact that [*Universes of value*] are tied into singular* **existential Territories** *effectively confers upon them a power of* **heterogenesis**, *that is, of opening onto singularizing, irreversible processes of necessary* **differentiation**. [CM 55]

b. Machinic self-regulation and self-reproduction which foster social, aesthetic, and clinical creativity, unlike the free market model that leads to capitalist homogenization.

> *No question here of aleatory neoliberalism with its fanaticism for the market economy, for a univocal market, for a market of* **redundancies** *of capitalist power, but of a* **heterogenesis** *of systems of valorization and the spawning of new social, artistic and analytical practices.* [CM 117]

c. The creation of new, richer modes of subjectivity, as for example during the 'complex ontological crystallization' that takes place in the encounter with certain works of art.

> *The heterogeneity of components (verbal, corporeal, spatial...) engenders an ontological* **heterogenesis** *all the more vertiginous when combined, as it is today, with the proliferation of new materials, new electronic representations, and with a shrinking of distances and an enlargement of points of view.* [CM 96]

- J. W.

Hjelmslev, Louis

In his lecture on the 'geology of morals' in *A Thousand Plateaus*, the fictitious Professor Challenger cites the linguist Louis Hjelmslev, whom he describes as 'the Danish Spinozist geologist.' Guattari began reading Hjelmslev in the 1970s, and told Deleuze that they must look to him in order to disengage from the **structuralism** that dominated French linguistics at the time (AOP 38). In a 1973 essay on the role of the signifier in the psychiatric institution (GR), Guattari uses Hjelmslev's terminology to provide an alternative to Lacan's Saussure-based theory of the role of the signifier in psychoanalytic practice. Lacan insists that Saussure's signifier and signified remain cut off from the real. Guattari associates the real with Hjelmslev's **matter** (sometimes translated 'purport'), and the signifier-signified with Hjelmslev's 'substance'-'form' relation. Guattari reincorporates the real into semiotic theory by identifying a kind of a-semiotic encoding that, borrowing Hjelmslev's terminology, bypasses 'substance' in order to couple 'form' directly with 'matter'. This material, non-semiotic dimension of Hjelmslev's linguistic model, as read by Guattari, makes him a geologist capable of explaining the stratification of meaning that captures and reterritorializes the **flows** of **intensities**. See also **form of content** and **form of expression**. - J. W.

Hume, David

Deleuze finds in Hume a discussion of the origin of the mind as an '**impression** of **sensation**' and 'passion' which is at once partial (prejudiced) and directional (purposeful), and, after being reflected in the **imagination** (and corrected by **reason**), moral, just, and economical. The imagination, in Hume, is constituted by '**habit**', which may facilitate natural tendencies but is itself based on principles or artifices that are not found in experience. The distinction is also between natural impressions and sensations which create the mind (or where **repetition** can be separated from the 'objects repeated'), and the artificial habits which are constructed by the mind (where relations of causality are expected or inferred from repetition). Deleuze later refines this thesis with reference to **Bergson** to show that the '**contractions**' within the mind which constitute successive experiences that we call **habits** take place prior to 'reflection'.

Hume's 'pragmatism' also resonates with **Spinoza's**: there is, in his analyses of both writers, a strong suspicion of the erroneous power of the **imagination**, or what Hume calls the 'fancy'. According to Deleuze, in Spinoza's case, ideas based on the affections are inadequate and confused because they are conceived through something else (the imagination), while in Hume's case, the imagination extends habits to believe or 'repeat' things that are not based in experience (until it is corrected by **reason**/understanding). Also like Spinoza, 'reason' is born from the imagination despite the shortcomings of the imagination; in Spinoza, reason simply forms a 'true order and connection' of impressions so that the subject can be **affected** in order to extend their essence, while in Hume, reason infers causality or relations among impressions so that the passions can be 'satisfied'.

Hume's overall appeal to Deleuze involves the manner in which **reason** and principles are there to facilitate, extend, and correct the passions, affections, and perceptions, but not to replace or control them. In Hume's case, this works on a deeply political and social level (all instincts or passions are customs satisfied in artifice or institution). - E. B. Y.

Hyalosign

cross-reference: **Time-Image** (circuit between real and imaginary)

Icon

cross-reference: **Affect**ion-Image (quality-power)

Imagination

As it is in **Hume** and **Spinoza**, for Deleuze, the imagination is distinguished from memory and even from understanding (we neither have to recall something nor comprehend it in order to imagine it), and while it certainly can be responsible for *delusion* (which is its initial sense), it can also serve as the foundation to form connections or perceive relations of causality that are not delusional (which is its ultimate sense). The initial and ultimate senses of this definition can be compared both in Deleuze's reading of Hume and Spinoza (and are listed in the first and second definitions, respectively).

> 1.a. In Deleuze's reading of **Hume**, in an initial sense, that which is the condition of the formation of **habit** in the mind; the ability of the mind to contemplate objects and intuitively remember and recognize them, as well as reflect passions. This leads to erroneous beliefs, idolatry, erroneous **perceptions**, and religion.
>
>> **habit** *is experience, insofar as it produces the idea of an object by means of the* **imagination** *and not by means of the understanding.* [ES 68]
>>
>> *The passions* **imagine** *themselves, and the* **imagination** *becomes passionate* [ES 57]
>>
>> *To believe is an act of the* **imagination,** *in the sense that the concordant images presented by the understanding or the concordant parts of nature ground themselves upon one and the same idea in the* **imagination.** [ES 72]
>>
>> *the* **imagination** *will not allow itself to be fixed by the principle of* **habit,** *without at the same time using habit for the purpose of passing off its own fancies, transcending its fixity and going beyond experience.* [ES 69]
>
> b. In Deleuze's reading of **Spinoza**, in an initial sense, the limited **faculty** of the mind which posits essences of things which may not exist (or are not present), depends on chance encounters and finite, determined causal chains of **events**; also, the faculty which retains traces of **affects** (that is, which remembers an image that continues to cause a passive affection) [SEP, SPP]
>
>> *images are the corporeal affections themselves, the traces of an external body on our body. Such ideas [...] indicate our actual state and our incapacity to rid ourselves of a trace; they do not express the essence of the external body but indicate the presence of this body and its effect on us. Insofar as it has [these] ideas, the mind is said*

to **imagine** *[...] insofar as our affections mix together diverse and variable bodies, the* **imagination** *forms pure fictions, like that of the winged horse* [SPP 74]

2.a. In Deleuze's reading of **Hume**, in an ultimate sense, the **faculty** which allows the mind to unchain itself from **habits** and posit, rather than contemplate, objects that are not based on experience; the ability of the mind to form associations based on experience, and recognize causality in order to **reason**.

Experience causes us to observe particular conjunctions. Its essence is the **repetition** *of similar cases. Its effect is causality as a philosophical relation. This is how* **imagination** *turns into understanding.* [ES 67]

Hume *forcefully distinguishes the union or fusion of cases in the* **imagination**—*a union which takes place independently of memory or understanding—and the separation of these same cases in the memory and the understanding.* [DR 157, 313]

b. In Deleuze's reading of **Spinoza**, in an ultimate sense, the basis for **reason** to form connections and relations among objects and images which diminishes the affection provoked by any single object or image. [SEP, SPP]

Reason *[...] satisfies the demands of* **imagination** *better than can* **imagination** *itself.* **Imagination**, *carried along by its fate, which is to be affected by varying causes, doesn't manage to maintain the presence of its object. [...] the active feelings born of reason or of common notions are in themselves stronger than any of the passive feelings born of* **imagination**. *[...] It thus diminishes the* **intensity** *of feelings of* **imagination** *since it determines the mind to consider several objects.* [SEP 295]

3. In Deleuze's explanation of the first **passive synthesis**, the power of all living things to **contract** and contemplate the qualities of **sensations** and **impressions**, as well as physical and chemical materials.

The **imagination** *[...] contracts cases, elements, agitations or homogeneous instants and grounds these in an internal qualitative* **impression** *endowed with a certain weight.* [DR 91, 70]

- E. B. Y.

Immanence

Immanence and transcendence are philosophical terms that are deeply bound up with theology; in the case of immanence, God is 'within' the physical world, and in the case of transcendence, God is 'above' or beyond the physical world. This distinction also extends to 'metaphysical' **concepts** in general, and Deleuze, of course, values concepts that arise from (or **express**) things that can be sensed, perceived, or imagined (emphasizing the immanence of **virtual** ideas to the real), rather than concepts which explain things according to separate, abstract criteria. Ideas, he claims, must self-**differ** (in relation to themselves), rather than differ *from* something else upon which they are dependent or contingent. In a slight variation on immanence, Deleuze (often with Guattari) describes a '*plane* of immanence' which serves as a field for concepts. He takes **Spinoza** as his archetype for a philosopher of immanence, and with Guattari, he shows that the object of **desire** is not absent or 'beyond' the social world (that is, it does not arise from dream or phantasy); rather, desire is a process that is immanent *to* the social world. This concept, important to Deleuze, was the topic of his last essay (which is translated in *Immanence, a Life*).

1. In **Spinoza**, the characteristic feature of a pantheistic God or single substance which is the cause of all things (that is, which is caused or created by nothing outside it, or, nothing other than itself), including the **attributes** and **modes**.

> *God is the* **immanent** *but not the transitive cause of all things [...] no substance can exist outside God [...and] there can exist no thing which is in itself and outside God.* [Spinoza (*The Ethics* I, prop. 18) 2000, 91]

2. In Deleuze's reading of **Spinoza**, the manner in which the **expression** of the same, infinite, **univocal** substance cannot be separated from the finite **modes** in which it is expressed because different attributes (i.e. thought and extension), and modifications of those attributes (i.e. ideas and bodies), are not in a causal relation to each other; rather, they are caused and expressed in *parallel* by the same univocal substance.

> *Absolute* **immanence** *is in itself: it is not in something, to something; it does not depend on an object or belong to a subject. In* **Spinoza**,

immanence *is not* immanence *to substance; rather, substance and modes are in* immanence. [PI 26]

immanence *signifies first of all the* **univocity** *of the* **attributes**: *the same attributes are affirmed of the substance they compose and of the* **modes** *they contain.* [SPP 52]

only God is a cause; [...] the cause is essentially **immanent**; *that is, it remains in itself in order to produce (as against the transitive cause), just as the effect remains in itself (as against the emanative cause).* [SPP 54]

3.a. In Deleuze's explanation of systems, the **virtual** state of problems–ideas which are displaced and disguised throughout, but contained within, various **series**.

The **virtual** *[...] is the characteristic state of Ideas: it is on the basis of its reality that existence is produced, in accordance with a time and a space* **immanent** *in the Idea.* [DR 211, 263]

Repetition *is constituted only with and through the disguises which affect the terms and relations of the real* **series***, but it is so because it depends upon the* **virtual** *object as an* **immanent** *instance which operates above all by displacement.* [DR 129, 105]

b. The status of a plane (**plane of immanence** or **consistency**) that is formed when **virtual** ideas, events, or **singularities** cut across, **transverse**, or survey a **milieu**.

it is only when **immanence** *is no longer* **immanence** *to anything other than itself that we can speak of a plane of* **immanence**. [PI 27]

The One is not the transcendent that might contain **immanence** *but the* **immanent** *contained within a transcendental field. One is always the index of a* **multiplicity:** *an event, a* **singularity***, a life.* [PI 30]

4. In D&G's reading of **Kafka's** novels, **desire** which dismantles the transcendental representations of social **assemblages** by refusing mediation to its essential features (e.g. the law, power, etc.), to instead become immersed within and shaped by them.

The transcendence of the law was an abstract [and reified] machine, but the law exists only in the **immanence** *of the* **machinic** *assemblage of justice. [...] Justice is no more than the* **immanent** *process of* **desire**. [K 51]

- E. B. Y.

Impression

cross-reference: **Action-Image** (possible behavior)

Index of equivocity

cross-reference: **Action-Image** (inference creating contradiction)

Index of lack

cross-reference: **Action-Image** (inference creating anticipation)

Instincts and Institutions

Instincts et Institutions (1949)

One of the earliest published writings by Deleuze, this is a collection published by Hachette for which Deleuze contributed the introduction. This essay has not been re-issued or translated, perhaps according to Deleuze's wishes. Nevertheless, it can be seen as an early foreshadowing of Deleuze's interest in combining **symptomatology** with the analysis of social institutions, or the clinical with the critical, which becomes the central theme of the later collection of works under this title and the entire trajectory of the 'Capitalism and Schizophrenia' volumes, written with Guattari. - G. L.

Integrated world capitalism

This term refers to a minimal model of global and post-industrial capitalism in which three evaluative terms are used: 1) processes of machinic production; 2) structures of social **segmentation**, considered in terms of the state; 3) dominant economic-semiotic systems, considered in terms of the market. This **mode** of capitalistic valorization is described on the basis of the order of priority given to the three terms, in this case, production-market-state. The key features are that production is more and more decentered and focused on **signs** and **subjectivity**, and that the capacity to integrate and exploit social diversity is unprecedented. Information and fluidity play key roles in production. Despite the absence of an outside of real subsumption, resistance stirred in the popular molecular disturbances and struggles around the globe at the time (Sandinista/Nicaragua, Solidarity/Poland, Autonomy/Italy, Workers' Party/Brazil). These are evidences of resistance to the unidimensional subjectivities (serial and standard) and social segmentations (precarity of labor, reified generations, dismantled class alliances) of semiotic capital.

1.a. A theory of globalization developed collaboratively in the 1980s with French philosopher Eric Alliez, in which the current stage of post-industrial capitalism is marked threefold by modes of info-machinic production and a condition of permanent crisis; the market becomes transnational, and the state becomes minimal and speculative.

> Integrated World Capitalism [...] [is] *based upon semiotic means of evaluation and valorization of capital which are completely new and have an increased capacity for the machinic integration of all human activities and faculties.* [GR 244]

b. (Special Type): *Post-industrial capitalism*: Theory akin to post-Fordism that hints at the emergence of the important immaterial labor hypothesis in which human semiosis ('general intellect') is directly and immediately productive of **value**, coagulating in semiotic objects (i.e. in the online activities of visitors to social media websites which, in turn, extract and exploit user data). This is an emphasis that puts less weight on, and hybridizes, the materialities of the worker and the products of labor.

> Post-industrial capitalism [...] *tends increasingly to decenter its sites of power, moving away from structures producing goods and services towards structures producing* **signs**, *syntax and* [...] **subjectivity**. [TE 47]

c. As a precursor to semiocapitalism in which capitalist production has become semiotic and 'seizes individuals from the inside' (SS 20), subsumption (capital looks inside and expands intensively) becomes real and not only formal (capital looks outside and incorporates non-capitalistic processes).

The power of the productive process of Integrated World Capitalism *seems inexorable, and its social effects incapable of being turned back; but it overturns so many things, comes into conflict with so many ways of life and social valorizations, that it does not seem at all absurd to anticipate that the development of new collective responses [...] coming from the greatest variety of horizons, might finally succeed in bringing it down.* [GR 246]

- G. G.

Intensity

Intensity is usually associated with the measurement of energy, or more simply, is another term for strength or **force**, and is not a common term in the history of philosophy (with the exception of **Bergson** and **Kant**); Deleuze, however, uses it to characterize the dynamic of differential systems. In fact, he notes that the scientific field of energetics tends to subordinate the indivisible, quantitative nature of intensity to extensive qualities (for the purpose of measurement), and does not grasp the intensive itself.

While the term can in fact be found in Bergson's work, Deleuze does not emphasize it in *Bergsonism*, and, in *Difference and Repetition*, he critiques Bergson's use of the term for (similarly) subordinating it to quality. The concept acquires incredible importance throughout his writings, and is utilized to characterize **affect** both in **Spinoza**'s modes and in the **Body without Organs**; the term can be differentiated from **force** in that forces engender the relations that produce bodies, while intensities concern fluctuations or thresholds *within* bodies. In fact, in **What is Philosophy?** the term is differentiated from force in that intensity has to do with **concepts** that 'occupy' the **plane of immanence**, while force has to do with the determinations or **diagrams** of **chaos** that construct the plane; in this case (as in others), force concerns 'movement', while intensity concerns 'speed' (in many ways, force can be considered in terms of that which puts **series** into communication, while intensity concerns the resulting **difference**).

1.a. A term that Henri **Bergson** uses to describe the nature of subjective experience which cannot be attributed to conscious qualities.

> *We [...] associate the idea of a certain quantity of cause with a certain quality of effect; and finally, [...] we transfer the idea into the* **sensation***, the quantity of the cause in the quality of the effect. At this very moment the* **intensity***, which was nothing but a certain shade of quality of the sensation, becomes a magnitude.* [Bergson, 1913, p. 42]

> *every state of consciousness corresponds to a certain disturbance of the molecules and atoms of the cerebral substance, and [...] the* **intensity** *of a* **sensation** *measures the amplitude, the complication or the extent of these molecular movements.* [Bergson, 1913, p. 6]

b. In Deleuze's critique of **Bergson**, that which engenders, but is irreducible to, extensive quantity and quality.

> **Bergson** *[....] already attributed to quality everything that belongs to* **intensive** *quantities. He wanted to free quality from the superficial movement which ties it to contrariety or contradiction (that is why he opposed* **duration** *to* **becoming***); but he could do so only by attributing to quality a* **depth** *which is precisely that of* **intensive** *quantity. One cannot be against both the negative and* **intensity** *at once.* [DR 299, 239]

2.a. In Deleuze's critique of **Kant,** in distinction from an extensive quantity apprehended by intuition, a quantity that cannot be divided and is apprehended instantaneously.

> *the rules of addition and subtraction are not valid for* **intensive** *quantities. [...] the real which fills space and time from the point of view of its* **intensive** *quantity is grasped as produced starting from degree zero* [webdeleuze 21/03/1978]

> *While he refuses a logical extension to space and time,* Kant's *mistake is to maintain a geometrical extension for it, and to reserve* **intensive** *quantity for the* **matter** *which fills a given extensity to some degree or other.* [DR 290, 231]

b. **Difference** within or expressed by distance; quantitative difference that cannot be divided without changing in nature, in distinction from extensive quantity and (indivisible) qualities.

Within intensity, *we call* difference *that which is really implicating and enveloping; we call distance that which is really implicated or enveloped. For this reason,* intensity *is neither divisible, like extensive quantity, nor indivisible, like quality.* [DR 297, 237 translation modified]

3.a. In Deleuze's reading of **Spinoza**, in distinction from the extensive parts that form characteristic relations of existing **modes** (bodies); a transient modal essence (which is also an **affection** of substance).

[...] physical reality is an intensive *reality, an* intensive *existence. One sees from this that essence does not endure.* [SEP 312]

each finite being must be said to express the absolute, according to the intensive *quantity that constitutes its essence. According, that is, to the degree of its power. Individuation is, in* **Spinoza**, *[...] quantitative and intrinsic,* intensive. [SEP 197]

b. That which is engendered in the body (of the **subject**, socius, earth, etc.) by relations of **force**, which fluctuates as a result of the strength of those forces but is always positive.

It must not be thought that the intensities *themselves are in opposition to one another, arriving at a state of balance around a neutral state. [...] the opposition of the* **forces** *of attraction and repulsion produces an open* series *of* intensive *elements, all of them positive [...] through which a subject passes.* [AO 20, 19]

c. In varying degrees, the lived experience of the **Body without Organs** (in waves or passages which lack extension, **stratification**, or form); **sensations** that appear by way of the deformation of vision [AO, TP, FB]

The **BwO** *is an* intense *and* intensive *body. [...] the body does not have organs, but thresholds or levels. Sensation is not qualitative and qualified, but has only an* intensive *reality which no longer determines with itself representative elements, but allotropic variations.* [FB 45]

4. In Deleuze's explanation of systems, that which is engendered by relations of **force** or a *dark precursor*, relating **differences** within distinct **series** to each other, causing sub-representative

or non-symbolic communication within or between various systems (biological, aesthetic, social, etc.) to occur.

> If [...] series *communicate under the impulse of a* force *of some kind, then it is apparent that this communication relates* differences *to other differences [...] The nature of these elements [...] can be determined: these are* intensities *[...]*. [DR 143, 117]

5. In D&G's explanation of the **assemblages** in **Kafka**'s novels, the points or **Segment**-blocks that are in contact; such **series** are *contiguous* rather than *distant*.

> *The Castle brings [...] out what was already there but still too covered up by spatial figures: the* series *become* intensive, *the journey reveals itself as an* intensity, *[...] part of a cartography that [...] has definitely ceased to be spatial.* [K 78]

6. A characteristic of **concepts** which occupy, trace, or survey the connections between determinations of **chaos** on **the plane of immanence** or consistency.

> *Each* **concept** *[is...] the point of coincidence, condensation, or* **accumulation** *of its own components. [...] In this sense, each component is an* intensive *feature, an* intensive *ordinate.* [WP 20]
>
> *The* **concept** *[...] has no energy, only* intensities *[...]*. [WP 21]

- E. B. Y.

Kafka, Franz

Unlike in Deleuze's work with Guattari, Kafka does not hold a prominent place in Deleuze's early works. Deleuze's only notable engagement with Kafka is in the essay 'Humor, Irony, and the Law' from ***Coldness and Cruelty***, where he notes that in 'the world described by Kafka' one is already guilty in advance by submitting to the law because the object of the law is necessarily concealed and elusive. The law is thus 'necessarily' comical, and **Sacher-Masoch**, in a different but comparably 'subversive' way, exposes the humor in the law. Deleuze's comments here, however brief, foreshadow the explosive role that Kafka will assume in his work with Guattari. Not only will the thesis re-emerge that the unattainable object of the law and of **desire** are the same, but Kafka's entire literary **assemblage** of the seemingly dysfunctional components which implement the law (in a '**machine**' of justice), as well as assemblages of bureaucratic power and capitalism, for that matter, are instigated by such elusive '**desire**'.

The casual reader of Kafka, familiar with *The Metamorphosis* and *The Trial*, or perhaps with his larger body of work, may be struck by Deleuze and Guattari's idiosyncratic approach to his work (or what they call his 'components of **expression**'), which may seem more of a springboard for their own lexicon than an analysis of Kafka *qua* Kafka. However, there is a deep appreciation for the richness and subtleties of the different genres of Kafka's work. Regarding the genres of the letters, stories, and novels, D&G argue, firstly, that the letters are vampiric but function to keep the beloved faraway so that Kafka can continue writing. The letters also divide Kafka into a '**subject of enunciation**' and a '**subject of the statement**', where he produces a 'fictive' or 'superficial' self in order to liberate a 'real movement' for his writing. Secondly, they argue that the stories which involve a '**becoming-animal**' cannot develop into novels because while they offer a temporary escape from the familial triangle, the animals cannot get out of the family segments and find their way into social **machines**. Becoming-animal is a 'refuge' rather than 'a way out'. The novels, by contrast, are interminable because they take as their subject **machinic assemblages** which can be found everywhere. - E. B. Y.

Kafka: Toward a Minor Literature

Kafka: pour une littérature mineure (1972)

Kafka is a fulcrum in Deleuze's work with Guattari, and they thought him important enough to devote a separate volume of their capitalism and schizophrenia project entirely to his work, publishing it after *Anti-Oedipus* and as a primer for what was to come in *A Thousand Plateaus*. The book serves not only as a study of Kafka's works but as a polemic, extended from *Anti-Oedipus*, against **psychoanalysis**; however, this time it is less against the clinical establishment than the psychoanalytic interpretation of (Kafka's) literature which eclipses its political relevance and expression. Deleuze and Guattari further divorce themselves from conventional Kafka literary criticism when they insist that obvious anomalies in his work, such as the giant vermin of *The Metamorphosis*, the apparent inaccessibility of the law, or other 'Oedipal intrigues' such as the 'Letter to the Father', merely 'bait' the reader to be interpreted. They therefore dissociate **Kafka** from clichéd interpretations which explain his writing in terms of isolation, despair, suffering, or repressed sexuality, and criticize interpretations of his work involving 'allegory, metaphor, and symbolism' (K 45).

Many of the essential terms from 'Capitalism and Schizophrenia' arguably find a precise point of articulation in *Kafka: Towards a Minor Literature*, such as the **rhizome, desiring-machines** and the **assemblage**. D&G characterize Kafka's work as a 'writing machine' and a rhizome that has no 'privileged points of entry'. Like the technical, legal, or bureaucratic machines that Kafka portrays in his works, such a writing machine only functions 'in the real' by a 'disassembling' (*démontage*) and '**deterritorialization**', or in other words as a 'process' which may appear mysterious or dysfunctional but in fact expresses a 'minority struggle'. In these terms, minor literature may correspond to peoples who have been oppressed in the *past* (as with Kafka's status as a Czech Jew writing in German); more precisely, however, it corresponds to the expression of collective desire which revolts against social and political machines of the present and *future* that are 'knocking at the door', or in other words have a nascent but notably encroaching influence.

From this perspective, Kafka does not employ metaphor or symbolism to represent what these machines 'are' because they *already* operate by virtue of metaphor and symbolism in order to engender social and political oppression, or **territorial assemblages**. Rather, his literary expression 'dismantles' any superficial representation of law, power, or capitalism by illustrating *only* their legislation, bureaucratic procedures, and concrete social structures. Kafka, as D&G claim, is not interested in presenting an image of a 'transcendental law' which would be 'unknowable' or 'hidden', but is instead interested in 'dissecting the mechanism' of a machine of justice that itself 'remains unrecognizable' or that is of a 'different sort' (K 95). In other words, the elusive nature of the momentum behind Kafka's narratives is not meant to turn focus back onto a mysterious object; rather, by presuming that such an object will *always* be concealed, it focuses exclusively on assemblages that 'function in the real' because there is nothing abstract which could represent them. This involves a 'construction of the law' that is 'denuded' (dénueé) or empty: the law is not a 'domain of knowledge' but is for Kafka the domain of 'pure practical necessity'. D&G thus insist that when superficial representations are 'dismantled', they lose their apparent, mechanical, or abstract function to express a social and political function. - E. B. Y.

Kant, Immanuel

Deleuze shows appreciation for Kant's critique of the Cartesian Cogito in *The Critique of Pure Reason*, noting that the determinate act of thinking 'implies an undetermined existence': if I can conclude that 'I am' based on the determination that 'I think', then I am determining an indeterminate, vague existence devoid of any specific features or characteristics. By adding the 'form' of *time* through which the determination can be made, Deleuze shows that Kant establishes a 'receptive' cogito as a **faculty** which relates immediately to experience and has sensibility as a source. However, this faculty, he argues, is 'endowed with no power of [passive] synthesis' (DR 109, 87), and instead the synthetic, representative functions of action, unification, and totalization take place in the faculties of **imagination**, understanding, and **reason**, respectively; this subordinates the 'intuitive' or visceral experiences within time to the requirements of a *recognition* by the faculties (in this sense, he shares a concern with Husserl regarding Kant's move to make all syntheses subject to the understanding). Thus, like **Hegel** and **Leibniz**, Kant essentially represents infinity, but in this case it is in the form of an incessant temporality which is never experienced in its own right as a **passive synthesis** of **contraction**-contemplation (that would contribute to a **transcendental empiricism**); Deleuze states that, for Kant, 'synthesis is understood as active and as giving rise to a new form of identity in the I, while passivity is understood as simple receptivity without synthesis' (DR 109, 87).

While Deleuze is not *explicitly* critical of Kant in his book devoted to him, both in his work on **Nietzsche** and in his most 'critical' chapter in **Difference and Repetition** ('The Image of

Thought'), Deleuze will distinguish the Nietzschean **paradox** of novelty from the circularity of recognition in Kant. He will in fact note that Kant had the right idea when he tried to 'conceive of an immanent critique' where **reason** is not critiqued in the name of the sentiments, or something else external to it; rather, 'critique must be a critique *of* reason *by* reason itself' (N 85, 91). However, he argues that without a conception of genesis or novelty, philosophy becomes a matter of distinguishing between the faculties of the mind (according to **common sense**), and the object of internal critique is simply 'illusion'—the illegitimate usage of reason—when 'thought confuses its interests and allows its various domains to encroach upon one another (DR 173, 137); that is, when 'higher' faculties appropriately legislate lower faculties (reason legislating desire, or judgment legislating feeling, but not vice versa). Thus each faculty must *recognize* the instances or objects it legislates—like objects of desire legislated by reason (or moral law), but this recognition cannot account for, and does not value, **becoming** or novelty: it is an apprehension, a re-cognition, of objects by virtue of their familiarity, while in the case of novelty, if we could recognize something as new, it wouldn't be new. 'Genesis', in the Nietzschean sense, cannot be based on expectation or memory, nor on analogy, resemblance, identity, or judgment (the four elements of representation), because it would be determined in advance: 'the new—in other words, difference—calls forth forces in thought which are not the forces of recognition, today or tomorrow, but the powers of a completely other model, from an unrecognized and unrecognizable *terra incognita*' (DR 172, 136). This is the internal criterion (or test of **eternal return**) that determines the differential and genetical components of thought, and is where Deleuze diverges from Kant.
- E. B. Y.

Kant's Critical Philosophy

La Philosophie critique de Kant (1963)

Famously referred to by Deleuze as 'a work on an enemy' (N 6), this introduction to Kant's philosophy is more like an examination of a machine in order to understand its various parts and how they work together to produce a systematic unity (perhaps as a prelude to the work of dismantling the Kantian system that becomes the explicit goal of *Difference and Repetition*). The English translation, published in 1984, contains a new preface 'On the Four Poetic Formulas which might summarize Kantian philosophy,' where we find the most succinct formulation of the meaning of the Kantian 'event' in modern philosophy (i.e. 'the Copernican turn'); importantly, all of the principles refer to literary statements (e.g. Hamlet's 'Time is out of joint,' Rimbaud's '*Je est un autre*,' **Kafka**'s 'the Good is what the law says,' and again Rimbaud's poetic phrase 'a disorder of the senses'). The main body of the original volume contains a systematic and didactic exposition of the three critiques and a definition of the major terms of the Kantian system; however, the originality of Deleuze's interpretation appears in the importance placed on the third critique, *The Critique of Judgment*, and especially concerning the **concept** of the sublime. Thus, Kant's philosophy is centered on the struggle between empiricism and dogmatic rationalism, in which Kant attempts to delimit the ideas of pure **reason** as the source for determining the true nature of reason's interests or ends, and the means of realizing these interests. What the third critique, and particularly the conception of the sublime, reveal is that the source of the supra sensible ideas is nothing less than a ruse of Nature herself. In Deleuze's reading, this is expressed as the highest of paradoxes, in some ways prefiguring the critical place of **paradox** in *The Logic of Sense*. This paradox is formulated in the concluding section on 'the Ends of History' as follows: 'Sensible nature as a phenomenon has supersensible nature as a substratum...' thus, whatever appears to be contingent in the accord of sensible nature with man's faculties is a supreme transcendental appearance, which hides a ruse of the supersensible. Moreover, according to a second sense of the paradox (which Deleuze points out must not be confused with the first because both paradoxes constitute the truth of history), it appears *as if* reason wanted the senses to proceed according to their own ends and in their own interests, 'even in man,' only in order to be capable of receiving, in the idea of a final end, the effect of the presence of the supersensible which consequently first appears in the form of non-sense from the standpoint of individual a priori reason, but which nevertheless hides the empirical design of Nature within the limited framework of the human species. - G. L.

Kierkegaard, Søren Aabye

Deleuze distinguishes the repetition of Kierkegaard's well-known and paradoxical 'leap' of faith to **Nietzsche**'s movement of **eternal return**. While he notes that this movement makes Kierkegaard one of the 'great repeaters', in that 'faith possesses sufficient force to undo **habit** and reminiscence' (DR 118, 95) through suspension of proof and a 'renewal' through **repetition,** because it is a repetition that takes place 'once and for all', it always returns to the aesthetic and ethical spheres of existence (and can be revealed only through irony and humor). - E. B. Y.

Klossowski, Pierre

Deleuze engages the French writer Klossowski as a **Nietzsche**an pornologist (**Sacher-Masoch** and de Sade also fall into this category) who, in his fictional works such as *Le Souffleur*, *Roberte ce soir*, and *Le Baphomet* expresses a sort of demonic parody of a 'perverse' sexuality made possible by a God who 'suspends' bodies within properties of 'identity and immortality, personality and resurrectibility, incommunicability and integrity' (LS 332, 292). However, since this 'divine creation in fact depends on bodies', the corporeality and visibility of bodies can be made to 'double', 'multiply', and 'reflect' one another through voyeurism, while the incorporeality of body-language (gestures) and actual language 'fabricates a body for the mind' through a *resonating* act that 'transcends itself as it reflects a body' (ibid). In these cases, *reflection* assumes a 'perverse' power whose goal is 'to assure the loss of personal identity and to dissolve the self' through the suspense and hesitations in scenes of sexual 'exchange' (where wives are essentially prostituted) or simply of rape, debauchery, and travesty. In every case, Deleuze emphasizes the role of a '**repetition**' which operates as a 'negative' or 'exclusive' disjunction, a 'disjunctive syllogism' which parodies the demands of a divine, 'either-or' order: *either* the woman can consent to being 'exchanged' (and made to double and resonate), *or* she can make her body 'silent' through 'frozen' gestures. Either way, the body will be repeated or reflected in a manner that makes it double or resonate; as Deleuze states, 'this is the false repetition which causes our illness. True repetition, on the other hand, appears as a singular behavior that we display in relation to that which cannot be exchanged, replaced, or substituted' (LS 328, 287). This 'true' repetition—that is, a repetition that does not involve the reflection of 'continuation, perpetuation or prolongation'—even through dissolution of the self—but rather through the **disjunctive** *synthesis* that involves an *already* dissolved self (and *'actualized* intentionality') whose repetition is *already* difference (and thus does not need to reflect it), is what Klossowski arrives at via excessive parody. He thus argues that Klossowski's work has an illness-convalescence structure comparable to *Thus Spoke Zarathustra*, and refers to Klossowski on occasion when discussing Nietzsche's **eternal return** (i.e. the eternal return 'is not a belief but the parody of every belief'). - E. B. Y.

Lawrence, D. H.

It is probably not insubstantial that Deleuze's wife, Fanny, was a translator of D. H. Lawrence, as it may have contributed to his appreciation for the author and perhaps for certain Anglo-American literature in general (e.g. Dickens, Woolfe, Miller, Melville, etc.). In *Dialogues* with Claire Parent, Deleuze emphatically insists that Lawrence expresses the true sense of the **line of flight** and did not reduce his work to the oedipal intrigues of psychoanalysis, nor reduce his life to a feeling of ressentiment. Deleuze also appreciates the resonance of the religious themes in his works (especially *Apocalypse*) with **Nietzsche** in terms of the resentful will to self-annihilate in Christendom (see *Essays Critical and Clinical*). - E. B. Y.

Lectosign

cross-reference: **Time-Image** (speech-acts dissociated from action-images)

Leibniz, Gottfried Wilhelm

Leibniz is known for his thesis that God chooses among the 'best' of all 'possible worlds' (implying that there are other 'possible worlds' that exist alongside this one), and Deleuze shows great appreciation for the novelty of Leibniz's theories of compossibility and **monad**ology which, he claims, avoid pitfalls of contradiction; however, he characteristically evacuates the theological dimension in Leibniz's work and critiques him (along with **Hegel**) for subordinating **difference** to a *representation* of infinity.

As Deleuze explains it, for Leibniz there are many possible worlds because 'every individual **monad** expresses the same world *in its totality* although it only clearly expresses a part of this world, a **series** or even a finite sequence' (FLB 60); that is, each monad expresses the whole world, just not with the same emphasis, succession, or sequence; it is not 'conscious' of all it can perceive, and most 'singularities' get lost in the obscurity of the ordinary. He claims that Leibniz's theory of 'compossibility' (where different possible worlds can coexist) avoids contradiction because, while there may be contradiction between continuous existing states (of individual monads), there is no contradiction between the monad and the world since ('pre-individual') **singularities** are independent of their explication and predication (by a monad). Deleuze uses Leibniz's well known example of Adam's original sin to illustrate this point: according to Leibniz, there is a 'world' in which Adam has sinned, and a world in which Adam has not sinned. And yet, as Deleuze stresses in all of the major works where he treats Leibniz —*Difference and Repetition*, *The Logic of Sense*, and again in *The Fold*—'God did not create Adam as a sinner, but rather the world in which Adam sinned' (DR 58, 48). There is always a fragmented world composed of 'pre-individual **singularities**', before those singularities are actualized by individuals; in Adam's case, these are 'to be the first man, to live in a garden, to give birth to a woman from himself' (LS 131, 114). Deleuze claims that Leibniz would view these singularities as predicates that can be analyzed infinitely (insofar as their **differences** can disappear by virtue of their continuity)—that is, their differences are 'infinitely small'—hence his method 'consists in constructing the essence from the inessential, and conquering the finite by means of an infinite analytic identity'

(DR 331, 263). Deleuze claims that these 'inessential' or 'infinitely small' differences, in which each *individual* existence implicates the essence of the whole, can be contrasted with **Hegel**'s 'infinitely large' whole in which each thing becomes through a dialectical contradiction; in other words, unlike the 'Restlessness' of Hegel's 'orgiastic representation' that relates each thought, action, or individual to an infinite whole, in this case there is the 'intoxication' and 'giddiness' of an orgiastic representation that relates **perceptions** or differences which dissolve together (from clarity to obscurity) into the infinitely small. In this case, difference 'remains subject to the condition of the convergence of **series**' (DR 60, 49) where identity is a *'presupposition of representation'* (determined by God, who actualizes the 'best possible world'), and analysis would go from the most to the least different because it would establish the identity of series as the ground for co-existence.

In Deleuze's version of **Leibniz**, God may make the 'best possible worlds' *converge*, but his point of interest is in the dynamics of *divergent* 'worlds'; that is, how each **monad** expresses the entire world while at the same time being implicated by other worlds (this dynamic between implication and explication is elaborated in his concept of the **fold**). It may seem counterintuitive that any monad could be 'implicated' in other words, if it contains the world in its entirety; however, this is precisely why it *can* be, since the **differences** are differences of emphasis. In this sense, the features of the world that are expressed by monads precede them: 'It is indeed true that the **expressed** world does not exist outside of the monads which express it [...]. It is no less true, however, that God created the world rather than monads' (LS 127, 110). Thus, rather than focusing on an analysis of 'infinitely small' differences, Deleuze claims that the singularities of the world, and the **series** which are expressed or repeated through them, can be assessed *synthetically*, in terms of the 'common' and 'indeterminate' object that is the very condition for 'divergence'; as he states, this is an 'ambiguous **sign** of the genetic element in relation to which several worlds appear as instances of solution for one and the same problem' (LS 130, 114). This problem synthesizes 'incompossible' worlds by virtue of difference with no prior identity; to return to the example of Adam, there is 'an objectively indeterminate Adam, that is, an Adam positively defined *solely* through a few singularities which can be combined and can complement each other in a very different fashion in different worlds' (LS 131, 114). It is, in other words, less a matter of an 'inessential' trigger or feature that may instigate Adam to actualize one possible world over another than it is a matter of the way that singularities combine (in a serial form) to define the individual. There is an 'Adam' that belongs to both 'incompossible' worlds, synthesizing them by virtue of 'disjunction', as a question or problem of sin as it is defined by a diverging series of singularities: 'Instead of each world being the analytic predicate of individuals described in series, it is rather the incompossible worlds which are the synthetic predicates of persons defined in relation to **disjunctive syntheses**' (LS 131, 115). - E. B. Y.

Lenin, Vladimir Ilyich

Although as a youth Guattari was a follower of Trotsky, his mature writings manifest a fascination with Lenin, who is mentioned repeatedly in his most theoretical accounts of revolution. On several occasions Guattari revisits the genesis of the Russian revolution. In his earlier, more Lacanian work, he describes the Leninist intervention as a 'cut' or 'break' with the network of signifiers that enabled the rise of the Bolsheviks. After he abandoned the Lacanian view of the all-powerful signifier, Guattari claims that Lenin 'diagrammatized' the class struggle. In both cases, Guattari associates Lenin with a point of **singularity** or bifurcation at which revolution becomes possible. In the joint work with Deleuze, the Leninist moment is described as an irruption of **desire** that results in 'incorporeal transformation.' - J. W.

Life

We tend to think in dualisms of being biologically alive or dead, and, added to this, do not always inquire into the creative aspects of health and evolution; however, Deleuze attempts to overturn both of these prejudices without resorting to science, mysticism, or theology. In this sense, although he is sometimes described as a 'vitalist', his understanding of 'life' is counter-intuitive because by incorporating **Bergson**ian notions of the **virtual** totality (**contraction/**

expansion) in addition to **Nietzsche**an notions of **force** (as well as the concept of **intensity**), Deleuze arguably elides the ambiguities that led to accusations of mysticism in Bergson. Throughout his writings, Deleuze examines the relationship between **matter** and time by problematizing the opposition between the organic and inorganic (thus if he is a 'vitalist', he is arguably not a 'materialist'). In fact, he develops a **concept** of life based upon his notion of **passive synthesis**, and extends this concept to include notions of *resistance* which serve as an insurmountable origin and object of power (where life is encountered via the **force** of the **Outside**). Finally, via **Nietzsche**, Deleuze characterizes 'life' as that which is inevitably distorted and limited by *knowledge* and *representation*, and with Guattari, emphasizes the role of **intensity** as well as the **Blanchotian** notion of the impersonal and incessant (such that life is not something possessed by individuals).

1.a. In **Bergson**, the *Élan Vital* (vital impetus) which involves a creative development and evolution that cannot be reduced to mechanic or teleological theories and tends toward diversity and complexity.

> *The role of* life *is to insert some indetermination into* matter. *Indeterminate, i.e. unforeseeable, are the forms it creates in the course of its evolution. [...] the main energy of the vital impulse has been spent in creating apparatus of this kind [...].* [Bergson, 1911, p. 126]

b. In Deleuze's reading of **Bergson**, the **actualization** of the **virtual**, or the insertion of **duration** into **matter**; differenciation.

> *It is as if* Life *were merged into the very movement of* **differen-** *ciation, in ramified series [...].* Duration, *to be precise, is called* life *when it appears in this movement. Why is differenciation 'actualization'? Because it presupposes a unity, a* virtual *primordial totality that is dissociated according to the lines of* differenciation. [B 94–5]

c. In Deleuze's explanation of time (and reading of **Bergson**), **matter** (organic and/or psycho-organic) that is **contracted** to form the present in time, or the first **passive synthesis** (which, in the case of humanity, is also implicated by the second and third passive syntheses); matter which urgently relates the body to its **milieu** as a problem (the *form* of which is a *response* to the problem).

> *Each line of* life *is related to a type of* **matter** *that is not merely an external environment but in terms of which the* living being *manufactures a body, a form, for itself. This is why the* living being *in relation to* matter *appears primarily as the stating of a problem, and the capacity to solve problems: The construction of an eye, for example, is primarily the solution to a problem posed in terms of light.* [B 103]

> *To the first* **synthesis** *of time there corresponds a first question– problem complex as this appears in the* living *present (the urgency of* life*). This living present, and with it the whole of organic and psychic* life, *rests upon* habit. [DR 99, 78]

2.a. In Deleuze's reading of both **Nietzsche** and **Foucault**, a set of non-organic **forces** of resistance (to power, **reason**, death, dominating forces, subjugation, etc.), expressed by virtue of thought or critique.

> **Life** *becomes resistance to power when[ever] power takes* life *as its object. [...] resistance becomes the power of* life, *a vital power that cannot be confined within species, environment or the paths of a particular* **diagram**. *Is not the force that comes from outside a certain idea of* Life *[...]?* [F 77, 92–3]

> *For rational knowledge sets the same limits to* life *as reasonable* life *sets to thought;* life *is subject to knowledge and at the same time thought is subject to* life. *[... However, by virtue of critique] thought that would affirm* life *instead of a knowledge that is opposed to* life. **Life** *would be the active* **force** *of thought, but thought would be the affirmative power of* life. [N 94, 101]

b. In Deleuze's reading of **Blanchot** and Bichat, a **force** or line that *continually* confronts death (rather than meeting death at an absolute limit). [N, DR, AO, F, NG]

> *Maurice* **Blanchot** *distinguishes [...] these two irreducible aspects of death; the one, according to which the apparent* **subject** *never ceases to live and travel as a One– 'one never stops and never has done with dying'; and the other, according to which this same subject [...] finally ceases to die since it ends up dying* [AO 363, 330–1]

> *Bichat wrote the first great modern book on death, ramifying partial*

deaths and taking death as a **force** *coextensive with* **life:** *'a vitalism rooted in mortalism,' as* **Foucault** *puts it.* [NG 91]

c. In Deleuze's explanation of **immanence**, the impersonal and yet qualitatively **singular** nature of the **subject; haecceity**.

> The **singularities** *and the* **events** *that constitute a* life *coexist with the accidents of the* life *that corresponds to it [...]a singular* life *might do without any individuality [...]. For example, very small children [...] have hardly any individuality, but they have* **singularities:** *a smile, a gesture, a funny face, not subjective qualities.* [PI 29–30]

d. In Deleuze's analysis of art, a **destratified**, unstructured, and vital rendering of **forces** that is distinct from the organic **form** (or organism) in which it emerges; Wilhelm Worringer's term for the non-organic but vitalist line or **expression** in Gothic Architecture.

> *[T]he organism is not* life, *it is what imprisons* life. *The body is completely* living, *and yet non-organic.* [FB 45]

> *'[Gothic Architecture] embodies no organic* **expression** *[...] it is nevertheless of the utmost vitality [...] its expression of* life *must, as an expression, be divorced from organic* life' [cited in TP 628, 562]

3. In D&G's explanation of capitalism, the impersonal and incessant **force** of **desiring-machines**, which, in being combined with the **Body without Organs**, emit varying levels of **intensity** (zero intensity being death) resulting from attracting and repelling forces. [B, AO, TP]

> **Desiring-machines** *do not die [...]. The machines tell us this, and make us* **live** *it, feel it [...] the setting in motion of other working parts on the* **body without organs,** *the putting to work of other adjacent parts on the periphery* [AO 364, 331]

– E. B. Y.

Line of flight

(*ligne de fuite*, also translated as *line of escape*)

While a 'line of flight' would normally designate the actual or projected itinerary for a an object moving through the air, the French term *fuite*, translated as 'flight', denotes the sense of 'fleeing' or escaping, but not of flying. In fact, in the English edition of the **Kafka** text and of *Anti-Oedipus*, line of flight is translated as 'line of escape'. The phrase is chosen because 'lines' emphasize a sort of vector-space; in other words, a space that is 'mapped' (**rhizomatically**) but not 'traced'. However, the terms 'escape' and even 'flight' may be misleading: if a movement of escape involves responding to a problem (whether that problem involves physical subjugation and/or psychic oppression, etc.), such a *riposte* would not necessarily operate with a predetermined resolution. As Deleuze states, 'Movement always happens behind the thinker's back, or in the moment when he blinks. Getting out is already achieved, or else it never will be.' (D 1) In other words, escape or 'getting out' is less about foreseeing a future outcome (which would just replace one problem with another) than it is about the process of **becoming** (which does not occur by virtue of 'imitation or assimilation'). Even 'freedom', which is perhaps considered the ultimate resolution, is a delusion because **desire** is already **immanent** to the paths or 'lines' that exist in every **assemblage**; in D&G's view, rather, it is a matter of existing in an 'adjacent' way to assemblages, 'always repelled, always kept outside, moving too fast to really be "captured up"' (K 60). In other words, it is not an issue of achieving 'freedom' once and for all, but of continually liberating desire in reality from its guidance by or fixation upon external **forces** (whether political, familial, biological, cultural, etc.) that represent (or **territorialize**) it.

Although the phrase 'line of flight' is used in passing in *Anti-Oedipus* to designate the 'schizoid breakthrough' from the familial relation, it is more emphasized in the **Kafka** text to differentiate between the processes of **becoming-animal** and of **deterritorialization** (in the first case, the line of flight is botched, while in the second, it succeeds). It takes on its most pronounced and complex role, though, in *A Thousand Plateaus*, with regard to segmentation; here, the 'line' itself may be destructive or creative. Finally, Deleuze, with Claire Parnet, also draws on the concept to distinguish between the writing styles of Anglo-American and French literature.

1.a. In D&G's distinction from rigid segmentary lines, the inventive and dynamic composition of individuals or **groups** which precedes the **territorialization** of **assemblages** within a **milieu** in which **desire** is **immanent** (supple or molecular **segmentation** which lies between rigid lines and lines of flight may serve as a transition between rigid segmentation and the line of flight).

> *From the viewpoint of micropolitics, a society is defined by its* **lines of flight**, *which are molecular. There is always something that flows or flees, that escapes the binary organizations, the* **resonance apparatus, *and the overcoding machine*** [TP 238, 216]

> *it is also possible to begin with the* **line of flight**: *perhaps this is the primary line, with its absolute* **deterritorialization**. [TP 226, 204]

b. On the one hand, an inventive escape from territorialized **assemblages** and by virtue of a departure from (or within) rigid and supple **segmentation** (such that they are faraway and contiguous), which can lead **desire** to creation (on a deterritorialized **plane of consistency**) and also ultimately to **reterritorialization**.

> *D[eterritorializion] is absolute when it conforms to the first case and brings about the creation of a new earth, in other words, when it connects* **lines of flight**, *raises them to the power of an abstract vital line, or draws a* **plane of consistency**. [TP 561, 510]

c. On the other hand, a destructive escape from **territorialized assemblages** by virtue of a departure from (or within) rigid and supple **segmentation**, which can lead **desire** to abolition or death, or, when machinic, to war.

> **lines of flight** *are immanent to the social field. Supple* **segmentarity** *continually dismantles the concretions of rigid segmentarity [...]. The* **line of flight** *blasts the two [supple and rigid] segmentary* series *apart; but it is capable of the worst, of bouncing off the wall, falling into a* **black hole**, *[...] and in its vagaries reconstructing the most rigid of* **segments**. [TP 227, 205]

The **assemblage** *that draws* **lines of flight** *is [...] of the* **war machine** *type.* [TP 253, 229]

2.a. In D&G's reading of **Kafka**, on the one hand, the failure of **becoming-animal** to liberate **desire** (in his short stories), and, on the other hand, the liberation of **desire** (in his novels) by virtue of dismantling or disassembling its relationship to representation along the very social, political, or capitalist lines which the **becomings-animal** *separated* themselves from.

the animal essence is the way out, the **line of escape***, even if it takes place in place, or in a cage. A* **line of escape***, and not freedom.* [K 60]

b. In Deleuze and Parnet's reading of Anglo-American literature (especially **Woolf**, **Lawrence**, Miller, etc.), the expression of **becomings** (often 'encounters' with minorities) or discoveries about reality (in distinction from fantastic voyages that escape *from* reality) which cannot be reduced to the 'rediscovery' of oedipal intrigues or existing formations of power.

even when a distinction is drawn between the **flight** *and the voyage, the* **flight** *still remains an ambiguous operation. What is it which tells us that, on a* **line of flight***, we will not rediscover everything we were fleeing?* [D 38]

To write is to trace **lines of flight** *which are not imaginary, and which one is indeed forced to follow. Because in reality writing involves us there. To write is to* **become***, but has nothing to do with becoming a writer.* [D 43]

- E. B. Y.

The Logic of Sense

Logique du sens (1969)

The Logic of Sense offers both a philosophy of language, time, psychology, and **events** (all of that which contributes to a philosophy of **sense**), as well as a rigorous treatment of the works of **Lewis Carroll**. Deleuze organizes his exploration in a serial format, which important because, as he explains in *Difference and*

Repetition, a series always implies one or more with which it is in communication. Therefore the reader may be attentive to the way that one particular series, or chapter, may resonate more or less with others (e.g. 'events' imply 'double causality', 'non-sense' implies 'humor', etc.); however, there is also a progression between chapters, where Deleuze moves from ancient philosophy in the beginning of the text (**Plato**, the **Stoics**), as well as fundamental aspects of logic (**propositions, paradoxes**, etc.), to more complex notions of seriality, structure, time (**Chronos** and **Aion**), and especially psychoanalytic notions of schizophrenia, sexuality, and **desire**, before re-examining many of those themes in the context of his reading of **Leibniz**, Husserl, **Artaud**, Borges, and others. Appendixes containing articles which extend themes from the first thirty-four series are included in the work (one of which contains an important discussion of **The Other**). Although the book is not a treatment of Carroll's work *per se*, his work provides a framework for Deleuze's text; there is hardly a chapter or 'series' in which aspects of his work are not used to introduce, develop, or exemplify the concepts under consideration.

It is useful to compare Deleuze's approach to humor and irony in *The Logic of Sense* with his approach in his earlier work, *Coldness and Cruelty*. In that work, he argues that the **masochistic** subversion to the Law exposes the unknowability and elusiveness of its object and foundation (the result of an inflated ego at the expense of a dissolved super-ego), while irony involves a sadistic exercise of power, in favor of anarchy, which intentionally utilizes the law in order to demonstrate that it lacks foundation (the result of an inflated super-ego at the expense of a dissolved ego). In *The Logic of Sense*, humor involves the combination of non-sense with **sense** to express the **events** which are necessarily outside of the domain of **propositions**; this involves an 'art of **surfaces** and doubles' (at which **Carroll** excels). Humor is therefore a nonsensical or non-philosophical aspect of sense, which testifies to the importance of Carroll (and literature in general) in the work. Irony, which Deleuze contrasts to humor and also discusses in an appendix on **Klossowski**, involves an intellectual equivocation of higher (singular) and lower (ordinary) senses (by virtue of maintaining individuality which is above the dimensions of the **proposition**). This makes it distinct from the humorous art of the surfaces, since the ironist maintains a position of eminence.

Written shortly after his work on **Nietzsche** and **Spinoza**, as well as *Difference and Repetition*, the reader will find many themes re-examined in this work, such as **eternal return** (here in the context of **Stoic** thought) and **Univocity** (in the context of **events**). Additionally, this text highlights the importance of schizophrenia for Deleuze, which he discusses in terms of **Artaud's** language of **depth**, as well as the complex relationship between **partial objects** and the **body without organs**: this foregrounds his interest as it complements Guattari's own clinical and theoretical interest in their collaborative work which followed. - E. B. Y.

The Machinic Unconscious: Essays in Schizoanalysis

The Machinic Unconscious was, in its original French version, published a year before *A Thousand Plateaus*, and includes what may be read as rough drafts of the latter work's 'plateaus' on language, faciality, and the **refrain**. In this, his first monograph, Guattari continues re-thinking Lacanian psychoanalysis, this time taking as his point of departure Lacan's famous dictum that the unconscious is 'structured like a language.' He argues that the unconscious includes a heterogeneous array of non-linguistics components and that, moreover, it is not structured at all, but machinic. While offering a much more complex alternative to Lacan's Saussurean linguistics, the book takes **structuralism** to task for the scientific aspirations which it uses to justify its reductive models of the psyche and of social relations. Perhaps paradoxically, Guattari's anti-structuralist theory of the **unconscious** draws on linguistics, mathematics, quantum physics, and animal **ethology**. *The Machinic Unconscious* provides a much more sustained and detailed analysis of several themes already present in *The Anti-Oedipus Papers*, especially those related to Guattari's materialist semiotics which emphasizes a-signifying elements such as body markings, the genetic code, or musical notation. - J. W.

Major literature

1. Literature that deals with individual concerns or Oedipal struggles, such as romantic or marital themes, or family dramas. In this sense, the social and political milieu serves merely as a context for the narcissistic or subjective experiences or the main characters.

> *In* major literatures *[...] the individual concern (familial, marital, and so on) joins with other no less individual concerns, the social* milieu *serving as a mere environment or a background* [K 17]

2. Literature in which the **form of content** corresponds to the **form of expression**.

> *A* major, *or established,* literature *follows a* vector *that goes from content to expression.* [K 28]

- E. B. Y.

Manifestation

1. The personalization of states of affairs according to beliefs and **desires** which inform that which is denoted, and is the primary relation within the **proposition** in the case of speech (*parole*); the second dimension of the proposition along with **denotation**, **signification**, and **(non)sense**.

> *[Manifestation] concerns the relation of the* proposition *to the person who speaks and* expresses *himself.* Manifestation *therefore is presented as a statement of* desires *and beliefs which correspond to the proposition. [...] [Manifestation] makes* denotation *possible, and inferences form a systematic unity from which the associations derive.* [LS 17, 13]

- E. B. Y.

Marx, Karl

While references to Marx are practically absent from Deleuze's early work (with notable exceptions, such as discussions in *Difference and Repetition*), they are equally present as the driving force behind his first work with Guattari, *Anti-Oedipus*, and continue to resonate throughout the Capitalism and Schizophrenia Projects. As Deleuze states,

> I think Felix Guattari and I have remained Marxists, in our two different ways, perhaps, but both of us. You see, we think any political philosophy must turn on the analysis of capitalism and the ways it has developed. What we find most interesting in Marx is his analysis of capitalism as an **immanent** system that's constantly overcoming its own limitations, and then coming up against them once more in a broader form, because its fundamental limit is **Capital** itself. [N 171]

It is important to point out that Deleuze and Guattari were likely aligning themselves with Marx not because they were advocating his conclusions about capitalism, but because during the time they wrote *Anti-Oedipus*, the psychoanalytic framework had made it difficult to discuss a cohesive thesis of **desire**, as a result, there was not as much emphasis as D&G thought there should be on the role of capital. As Deleuze states, 'the new philosophers, denouncing Marx, don't begin to present any new analysis of capital […]' (NG 145). D&G appropriate Marxist themes of surplus-value, labor, and forces of production and recast them in relation to concepts of **The Body without Organs**, desire, and social **machines**. - E. B. Y.

Masochism

cross-reference: **Sacher-Masoch**, *Coldness and Cruelty*, Desire

Matter

While 'matter' touches on questions involving materialism, which involve issues of **surface** and **depth**, as well as **flows** as discussed in *Anti-Oedipus*, the term is used explicitly with regard to D&G's reading of **Hjelmslev**.

1. In Hjelmslev, the purport of the **sign** ('mass').

> *Purport, so considered, exists provisionally as an amorphous* **mass**, *an unanalyzed entity, which is defined only by its external functions [...] each language lays down its own boundaries within the amorphous* 'thought-mass' *and stresses different factors in different arrangements, puts the centers of gravity in different places and gives them different emphases.* [Hjelmslev, 1961, 50–2]

2. In D&G's reading of **Hjelmslev**, that which precedes the formalization of **content** and **expression**, and exists independently of **stratification**. [TP, F]

> [Hjelmslev] *used the term* matter *for the* **plane of consistency** *or* **Body without Organs**, *in other words, the unformed, unorganized, non-stratified, or destratified body and all its flows.* [TP 43]

> **Hjelmslev** *proposed a very important conception of* 'matter' *or* 'sense' *as unformed, amorphous, or formless* [TP 531]

3.a. A function of the **abstract machine** that has no tangible form, in distinction from substance, which is a function of **concrete assemblages**. [TP, F]

> [the **abstract machine**] *functions by* matter, *not by substance; by function, not by form [...] the abstract machine is pure* **Matter-Function**—*a* **diagram** *independent of the forms and substances, expressions and contents it will distribute. [...] substance is a formed* matter, *and* matter *is a substance that is unformed either physically or semiotically.* [TP 156, 141]

b. The element of a **diagram** or **cartography** that is **outside** of, or in the non-relation between, **forms of content** and **forms of expression**, which nevertheless **transverses** or passes through those forms and is not exterior to them. [TP, F]

> *We can conceive of pure* **matter** *and pure functions, abstracting the forms which embody them.* [F 29, 33]

- E. B. Y.

Maturana, Humberto

cross-reference: Varela, Francisco and Humberto Maturana

Metamodelization

Guattari found the science-inspired models of social science useful but reductive. In order to benefit from modeling while at the same time avoiding reductionism, Guattari combined new and existing models in an analytic practice he called metamodelization (metamodeling). Even as he denounced their limits, he borrowed from Lacan's **diagrams**, Chomsky's syntagmatic trees, and the Oedipal and linguistic triangles. However, whereas Lacan's, Chomsky's, and **Freud**'s scientific model were meant to be applied again and again to different situations, metamodelization builds a new map for each analysis. Guattari uses this term from the early 1980s onward.

1.a. The analysis of psychic, social, or artistic formations by examining standard models (such as the Oedipal triangle) already in place while opening up onto new mappings assembled from a heterogeneous array of components.

> Since that time, my reflection has had as its axis problems of what I call **metamodelization**. That is, it has concerned something that does not found itself as an overcoding of existing modelizations, but more as a procedure of 'auto-modelization,' which appropriates all or part of existing models in order to construct its own **cartographies**, its own reference points, and thus its own analytic approach, its own analytic methodology. [GR 122]

b. Schizoanalysis.

> I repeat: **schizo-analysis** is not an alternative modelization. It is a metamodelization. [GR 133]

2.a. **Subjectivity**, and especially the coming into being of subjectivity.

> And that, in a sense, subjectivity is always more or less the work of metamodelization. [SS 205]

b. An anti-structuralist analytic alternative to Freudian and Lacanian topographies of the psyche.

> Thus, instead of constantly returning to the same supposedly founding structures, to the same archetypes, to the same 'mathemes,' schizoanalytic metamodelization will instead prefer to map (cartographier) the compositions of the unconscious, continent topics, in their connection to social formations, technology, arts, sciences, etc. [SS 212]

- J. W.

Microfascism

Fascism is not a historical phenomenon that has passed away and will never happen again. It cannot be adequately defined 'macropolitically' in relation to the totalitarian state, with which it shares certain features. Rather, Guattari believed it was necessary to conduct a micropolitical examination of the molecules of fascism because it has survived its historical mutations and adapted itself to contemporary institutions, knowingly or unknowingly clinging to subcultural and political expression. Bits and pieces of fascist desire may be crystallized within a current microphysics of power relations that support it. Analysis of this phenomenon considers the kinds of desiring-machines at its base and how they function, develop and perfect themselves in each iteration.

> 1.a. A type of fascism that jumps trans-historically between generations and adapts itself to new conditions along the machinic phylum; hence, it is irreducible to historical phenomena like National Socialism.
>
>> The historical transversality of the machines of desire on which totalitarian systems depend is, in fact, inseparable from their social transversality. Therefore, the analysis of fascism is not simply a historian's speciality. I repeat: what set fascism in motion yesterday continues to proliferate in other forms, within the complex of contemporary social space. [CY 236]
>
> b. A dangerous, cancerous molecular phenomenon that draws processes of subjectification into itself.

> *What makes* **fascism** *dangerous is its molecular or* **micropolitical** *power, for it is a mass movement: a cancerous body rather than a totalitarian organism.* [ATP 236, 215]

2.a. The historical conjunctures at which the masses desire their own death in spite of themselves and live on; a type of fascism that never stops happening, and therefore one may never stop struggling against it (as in the notorious claim that 'everybody wants to be a fascist').

> *A* micro*politics of* desire *means that henceforth we will refuse to allow any* **fascist** *formula to slip by, on whatever scale it may manifest itself, including within the scale of the family or even within our own personal economy.* [CY 239]

b. A fascism immanent to **desiring-production**.

> *Fascism seems to come from the* **outside***, but it finds its energy right at the heart of everyone's desire.* [CY 245]

- G. G.

Milieu

Milieu is a French term usually used in English to mean 'environment', but it also carries connotations of 'middle' and even 'medium'. In this sense, it has both a spatial and temporal dimension: your environment is something you are 'in the midst of', in terms of being in the process of experiencing it, and you are also within some space (or body) that serves as a vehicle for that experience. D&G provide a unique angle on this term when they claim that milieus are composed of 'periodic **repetition**' (and are thus '**coded**'), but, as they insist, 'not only does the living thing continually pass from one milieu to another, but the milieus pass into one another, they are essentially communicating' (TP 345, 313). In this sense, the **concept** of the milieu serves as the foundation for grasping **rhythms** that are expressive of the **difference** *between* milieus, where the **force** of **chaos** at the heart of milieus (which, they say, is the 'milieu of all milieus') is confronted.

1.a. In D&G's explanation of **territorialization**, stable, **coded** patterns that make up the internal and external organization of the environment of living things, which may be 'transcoded' or part of other, larger milieus; the source of **affects**/actions and **percepts** in living things, whether internally or externally.

> *Every* milieu *is vibratory, in other words, a block of space-time constituted by the periodic* repetition *of the component. Thus the living thing has an exterior* milieu *of materials, an interior* milieu *of composing elements and composed substances, an intermediary* milieu *of membranes and limits, and an annexed* milieu *of energy sources and actions*-perceptions. [...] *The notion of the* milieu *is not unitary: not only does the living thing continually pass from one* milieu *to another, but the* milieus *pass into one another; they are essentially communicating.* [TP 345, 313]

b. Before being **territorialized**, a *directional*, isolated component of **chaos** that functions for itself; when **territorialized**, a *dimensional* function of the **territory** (which may be interior, exterior, intermediary, or annexed).

> **Chaos** *is not without its own directional components, which are its own ecstasies.* [...] *There is a* territory *precisely when* milieu *components cease to be directional, becoming dimensional instead* [TP 347, 315]

> *A* territory *borrows from all the* milieus; *it bites into them, seizes them bodily (although it remains vulnerable to intrusions). It is built from aspects or portions of* milieus [TP 347, 314]

2. In D&G's analysis of **stratification**, formed **matter** (substance) which provides strata with materials and elements; whether horizontally, through association in a variety of forms (parastrata), or vertically, through variations of singular forms undergoing **(de)territorialization** (epistrata).

> *In relation to the central belt of the* **stratum**, *the intermediate strata or* milieus *constitute 'epistrata' piled one atop the other, and form new centers for the new peripheries. We will apply the term 'parastrata' to the second way in which the central belt fragments into sides and 'besides,' and the irreducible forms and* milieus *associated with them.* [TP 58, 52]

- E. B. Y.

Minor cinema

Although he did not publish a cinema book, Guattari grafted the principles of minoritarian **becoming** developed in literature onto cinema. A minor cinema precipitates minoritarian becomings in its audiences and participants. Guattari did not fix the kind of cinema he had in mind either in terms of period or genre. Under the guise of a 'mad cinema', Guattari sought out examples of films that reached audiences by releasing **affective intensities** and **a-signifying** pointsigns that contagiously conjoined otherwise non-communicating perspectives. This gave voice to workers, to the homeless, to non-professional actors, overcoming technical hurdles and specializations, contributing to the formation of a critical alternative to mass commercial cinema. Deleuze also touches on this notion in his work on Cinema (see def. 2).

1.a. An art precipitating non-countable, revolutionary **becomings**, freeing anOedipal and molecular components.

b. A model of cinema that is unconfined by specific genre or period, but inspired by the European alternatives to psychiatry movement that emerged in Europe in the 1970s, favoring exceptional documentaries such as *Fous à délier* [Fit to be Untied] by Marco Bellocchio, Sandro Petraglia, Stefano Rulli (1976), *Yama: An Eye for an Eye* (Sato Mitsuo, 1985), and Peter Robinson's *Asylum* (1972); but, also including fictions like David Lynch's *Eraserhead* (1977), Terence Malik's *Badlands* (1973) and Bellocchio's *Fists in the Pocket* (1965) as inspired explorations of madness and social ills.

> *If one specifies that a 'minor' art is an art that serves people who constitute a minority, and that it is not all pejorative. A major art is an art at the service of power. Hence I wonder if a certain number of films like Fous à délier, Ce gamin-là, Coup pour coup, La Ville bidon, Paul's Story, Asylum, do not announce a new era in the history of cinema. A* **minor cinema** *for minorities, in one form or another, and for the rest of us, too: we all participate in one of these minorities, more or less.* [SS 180]

c. Cinema which puts an emphasis on a-signifying point-signs like patches of color, non-musical sounds, and non-narrative **refrains** that are not subjugated to dominant **encodings**.

> When [minor cinema] is exploited by capitalist and bureaucratic socialist powers to mold the collective imaginary, cinema topples over to the side of meaning. Yet, its own effectiveness continues to depend on its pre-signifying symbolic components as well as its a-signifying one: linkages, internal movements of visual images, colors, sounds, rhythms, gestures, speech, etc. [SS 150]
>
> It is important [...] to insist on the independence of an **a-signifying semiotics**. It is this [...] that will allow us to understand what permits cinema to escape the semiology of meaning and to participate in the collective **assemblages** of desire. [SS 149]

d. An ethical film praxis in which filmmakers would immerse themselves in the social realities they portrayed and take responsibility for their source materials.

e. An approach to cinema that shares some features with Third Cinema such as democratization of production, politically progressive activism, and a prefigurement a people (a viewership to come).

2. In Deleuze's discussion of **cinema**, the invention of a missing people by passing through a crisis (impossibility), and the merging of private/public boundary through the immediacy of the former's political status.

> This acknowledgement of a people who are missing is not a renunciation of political cinema, but on the contrary the new basis on which it is founded, in the third world and for **minorities** [C2 209, 217]

- G. G.

Minor literature

We have become accustomed to stories being *about* personal relationships; that is, the inner lives and worlds of the characters more than the external worlds that they inhabit. Of course, there always must be a 'setting', but we accept it merely as a background for the real action, which is the 'drama' between the characters (this has only been exacerbated by the individualistic and narcissistic nature of our culture). Such a perspective on literature is limiting, however, because it never truly addresses or portrays the political problems and social climates which those characters are defined by. Added to this, it is those worlds which people really experience, but have not been able to voice (because, by inhabiting them, they are too close to them).

D&G's concept of 'minor literature' is an attempt to provide an alternative model, which they think is exemplified in the works of Franz **Kafka**. They argue that Kafka's characters are primarily concerned with the social **assemblages** they are a part of, and not with interpersonal problems (e.g. marriage, family). While his characters certainly *could* be psychoanalyzed, an equally valid argument can be made that all of the feelings and thoughts of his characters are determined by external forces—whether bureaucratic, legal, or capitalist (in fact, Kafka himself argued that psychology—an 'inner world'—is something that may be experienced, but *not* observed or described). Through such characters or 'agents', social and political forces are **expressed** in a novel way; as Deleuze states (channeling **Proust**), 'It is not a question of speaking a language as if one was a foreigner, it is a question of being a foreigner to one's own language' (D 59).

1.a. Literature where a minority struggle of unrecognized **multiplicities** (populations of people that do not yet exist) is expressed by virtue of a perspective that is *necessarily* invisible and suppressed (due to its representation or abstraction by **territorial assemblages** that prevent it from coming into view), and thus where common, dominant codes and conventions are treated as though they were foreign and dysfunctional (that is, where they are **deterritorialized**).

> *[…] the first characteristic of* **minor literature** *in any case is that in it language is affected with a high coefficient of* **deterritorialization**. [K 16]

> *How many people today live in a language that is not their own? […] This is the problem of […] a* **minor literature**, *but also a problem for all of us: how to […] challenge the language and making it follow a sober revolutionary path?* [K 19]

b. Literature in which the individual concern is in the *background* and the social and political **milieu** is in the *foreground* (that is, the subject of the novel is not the person's experience, but the social and political milieu itself); literature that presents agents whose motivations are not reducible to oedipal issues.

> The second characteristic of **minor** literatures *is that everything in them is political.* **Minor** literature *is completely different; its cramped space forces each individual intrigue to connect immediately to politics.* [K 17]

c. Literature in which the author is not 'talented' in the sense that they contribute to a specifically literary tradition; that is, where the author does not utilize conventional devices, such as symbolism, attempt to conform to existing genres, or build on sophisticated techniques which would establish their voice as 'unique'; rather, literature in which the author is able to express collective sentiments by means of portraying an agent who is enmeshed within, or **territorialized** by, social **assemblages** which cannot be represented.

> *The third characteristic of* **minor** literature *is that in it everything takes on a collective* **value**. *[...] scarcity of talent is in fact beneficial [...] if the writer is in the margins or completely outside his or her fragile community, this situation allows the writer [...] to forge the means for another consciousness and another sensibility* [K 17]

- E. B. Y.

Mode

A 'mode' is usually considered in terms of a mannerism, musical scale, or style. **Spinoza**, however, focuses on the way in which all particular, 'finite' things, *are* modes or manners of expressing the same substance (or 'God'). In this regard, unlike **Descartes**, he believed that there was only one all-encompassing substance; thus, the **attributes** of that substance are in fact infinite before they are modified in finite forms. These finite forms, or modes, are always contingent upon something else (they exist 'in' something else insofar as they are caused by something else, in distinction from substance, which exists in itself). The term is important because in Deleuze's view, it involves the unique capacity for human beings to comprehend causality and act through this comprehension, therefore extending their power (and expressing the parallelism of the attributes). He uses the term in his reading of Spinoza, but also to explain both **univocity** and **intensity**: because the attributes qualify substances, the role of the modes is to modify the attributes in a quantitative fashion—they are thus distinguished by virtue of intensity or power rather than quality.

1. In **Spinoza's** work, the essence and/or existence of something insofar as it is limited by others of its kind (that is, as a modification of the same **attribute**) and is conceived within something else (finite thoughts in the mind, bodies in extension); that which exercises a capacity or power of affecting and being **affected** and serves as the basis for **ethical** determinations.

> *by* mode *I understand [...] that which is in something else, through which it is also conceived* [Spinoza (*The Ethics* I def. 5) 2000, 75]

2. That which modifies an **attribute**, in parallel with **modes** of different attributes insofar as it expresses the same substance (**univocity**); that which constitutes the *effects* of eternal *causes* of attributes as **expressions** of substance. [SEP, SPP, DR]

> *[...] the absolutely adequate character of our knowledge [...] is in the* **univocity** *of the* **attributes** *which have only one form in the substance whose essence they constitute and in the* **modes** *that imply them, so that our intellect and the infinite intellect may be* **modes**, *but they nonetheless objectively comprehend the corresponding attributes as they are formally.* [SPP 81]

> *[In] the* **univocity** *of being [...] that of which being is said is repartitioned according to essentially mobile individuating* **differences** *which necessarily endow 'each one' with a plurality of* **modal** *significations* [DR 377, 303]

3.a. (Special Combination): **Modal** *Essence*: The **intensive** reality of a mode which may or may not correspond to an *existing* mode. [SEP, SPP, DR]

> **Modal** *essences are thus distinguished from their* **attribute** *as* **intensities** *of its quality and from one another as different degrees of intensity* [SEP 197]

> **modal** *distinction [...] is established between being or the* **attributes**

on the one hand, and the intensive *variations of which these are capable on the other.* [DR 49, 39]

b. (Special Combination): *Existing* **Mode**: The extensive reality of a mode which has a **duration** and explicates the essence of an **attribute** (of thought or extension). [SEP, SPP]

> An **attribute** *no longer expresses itself only in the* **modal** *essences that it complicates or contains according to their degrees of power; it also expresses itself in existing* **modes** *that explicate it in a certain and determinate manner, that is, according to the relations corresponding to their essences.* [SEP 214–15]

- E. B. Y.

Molecular revolution

A micropolitical analysis of the molecules of revolution is consonant with **Foucault's** analysis of power as a microphysics of force relations, but with an emphasis on the **desire** that sets in motion those traversed by **deterritorializing** vectors and the emergence of autonomous, anti-capitalist refrains that subvert traditional institutions of political party, family, nation, social movement, and systems of valorization as they get into tune with one another. **Schizoanalysis** is a micropolitical practice of pragmatically assisting the most potentially transformative molecules to emerge, assemble, and work against dominant encodings of them. In the late 1960s, Guattari thought of these molecules as akin to proliferating and transversally linked 'fighting fronts' of **desiring-production**.

1.a. Decentred and without transcendent justification, or historical fixations, this revolutionary **becoming** stirs in miniature at unlocatable points: no more Octobers, no more capital 'R' Revolution, only the **assembling** of promising and highly diverse orientations of alternative machinic subjectifications from across society—peace protests, green movements, new forms of unionism, computer hacks, etc.

> I don't believe in revolutionary transformation, whatever the regime may be, if there is not also a cultural revolution, a kind of mutation among people, without which we lapse into the reproduction

of an earlier society. It is the whole range of possibilities of specific practices of change in the way of life, with their creative potential, that constitutes what I call **molecular revolution,** *which is a condition for any social transformation. And there is nothing utopian or idealistic in this.* [MRB 261]

b. Social movements that are disorganized, minoritarian, and linked to processes of singularization that produce other realities and widely disseminated **refrains** of existence, yet indexed to machinic processes that yield new forms of subversive connectivity (suggesting Web activism and mobile organizing).

The difference between these kinds of **molecular revolutions** *and earlier forms of revolution is that before everything was centred on ideology or the program, whereas today the mutational models— even if they involve things which appear to be secondary, like fashion—are immediately transmuted to the entire planet. [...] A mutation like that introduced by microprocessors changes the actual substratum of human existence and, in reality, opens up fabulous possibilities for liberation.* [CY 47–8]

2.a. Social movements that instigated by the factory of the **unconscious,** which is composed of molecular elements, and the **desiring-machines** that interconnect, taking different forms as they undergo changes of state; yet select institutions like political parties (Workers' Party in Brazil) and unions (Solidarity in Poland) are embraced, alongside more extra-parliamentary **becomings** that do not desire entry into majoritarian arrangements and are not crossed by liberal democratic values.

b. The formation of a 'gigantic **rhizome**' that is the source of historical change and that weakens molar formations as they bubble up from the machinic **phylum** and provide opportunities for mutations to occur (see MU 195).

c. The work of the **schizoanalyst, ecosopher,** and artist which converge in **diagrams** of transformation (**becomings**).

Schizoanalysis *will have a lot in common with revolutionary vision if social upheavals in the future really become [...] inseparable from a multitude of* **molecular revolutions** *in the* *economy of* **desire**. *When the barriers are brought down, and the assumptions of capitalism, the over-encodings of the super-ego, all artificially reconstituted primitive* **territorialities** *etc., done away with, then the work of the analyst, the revolutionary and the artist will meet.* [MR 260]

- G. G.

Molecular Revolution

Revolution with a small 'r' involves molecules of progressive and transformational lines of autonomous self-definition. Three volumes have been published under this title: the first 'Encres' edition develops advanced and original semiotic insights using a combination of concepts from Peirce and **Hjelmslev** (automated part-signs in an a-signifying infoscape) and a prescient hypothesis about the mutation of capitalism into semiocapital (beyond industrial labor and the disciplinary space of the factory is the space-time of control in which cognitive labor is yoked to increasingly sophisticated electronic networks of exploitation). Capitalist production has, in short, become semiotic and immaterial. The first volume also includes Guattari's disjointed theses on minor cinema and the affective contamination of audiences in formation through cinematic a-signification across genres and periods. The second '10/18' volume picks up these themes and re-embeds them in more overtly political writings about recent events Europe, specifically the state repression of Italian intellectuals, cultural responses to the German state's anti-terror practices, and efforts to reform the drug laws. Both volumes contain Guattari's fraught relationship with the European alternatives to psychiatry movement. The third translation was the first major work by Guattari alone to appear in English and it contains essays from throughout the 1970s. - G. G.

Molecular Revolution in Brazil

This text is based on transcripts of structured interviews and informal exchanges between Guattari, diverse professionals and civil society groups recorded by Brazilian psychoanalyst Suely Rolnik.

Guattari's peregrinations around Brazil in August and September, 1982 are distributed across cities, institutions and events, but also across subject matters—culture, philosophy, psychoanalysis, politics, mass media—and punctuated by minor and molar political assemblages, from social movements (gay rights) and alternative organizations (daycares) to political parties like the Workers' Party led by *Luís Inácio 'Lula' da Silva*. Guattari presciently endorses the Workers' Party as the kind he would join and reflects on Lula's important public role in the post-military climate of Brazil. This is the clearest portrait of Guattari as an activist, and his intellectual restlessness is guided by concerns with the production of subjectivity by capitalistic machines and the cultivation of micropolitical processes of singularization that frustrate and subvert it, engendering in their wake new collective arrangements. Guattari investigates the Brazilian combination of hypermodern and archaic elements in everyday life, precipitating lengthy discussions. He offers trenchant critiques of the concepts of the individual, identity, and culture as traps. Latin American contributions to alternative psychiatric practices are discussed comparatively with Europe; local minoritarian becomings are encountered and the potential of the rise of political militancy in Brazil is analyzed. Guattari presents a schizoanalytic case study, which is rare in his published work, and reveals how he mobilized his self-doubt in the analysis and discusses how traditional psychoanalytic concepts are revised and replaced by schizoanalytic transformations. Despite the doubts of some of his interlocutors, Guattari saw Brazil as a huge machine producing mutant potentialities for subjectification. He even considered relocating there. - G. G.

Monad

1. Term from Neo-Platonists for the 'one' that became popularized and attributed to **Leibniz**, that for him denoted a basic unextended compound, and also the unity of the soul and body which is 'higher' if it produces more effects on other monads and has more clear perceptions.

> The **Monad**, *of which we shall here speak, is nothing but a simple substance, which enters into compounds.* [Leibniz, 1898, 217]

> *all simple substances or created* **Monads** *might be called souls [...] the general name of* **Monads** *[...] should suffice for simple substances which have* **perception** *only, and that the name of Souls should be given only to those in which perception is more distinct, and is accompanied by memory.* [Leibniz, 1898, 230]

2.a. In Deleuze's reading of **Leibniz,** the unity of the soul which is enveloped, and at the same time developed as a **multiplicity** or **series.**

> *the* **monad** *[...] designate[s] a state of One, a unity that envelops a* **multiplicity,** *[...and] has a power of envelopment and development, while the multiple is inseparable from the* **folds** *that it makes when it is enveloped, and of unfoldings when it is developed.* [FLB 23]

b. The unity of *soul* and *matter* which folds the **Outside** onto the inside; an organism which assembles inorganic matter and has a body but is irreducible *to* its body (determined by derivative **force** but determining through primitive force), because the singularities that it encompasses through **perception** express a unique **actualization** of the world.

> *every* **monad** *[...] has a body, it is inseparable from a body corresponding to its clear zone, but it does not contain it, and is really distinguished from it. The* **monad** *merely requires it because of the limitation of its* **force** *[...].* [FLB 113]

> *All* **monads** *express the whole world darkly, even if not in the same order. Each one encloses in itself the infinity of minute* **perceptions.** *[...] What distinguishes them is their zone of clear, remarkable, or privileged expression.* [FLB 91]

- E. B. Y.

Morality

Deleuze's dismissal of 'morality' or 'moral law' should not be taken for granted, as it is done in every case for a purpose (that is, to offer an alternative), and in some cases he explores positive features of morality: on the one hand, he affirms unconventional perspectives on morality in his early work on **Hume,** where morality involves overcoming the partiality of our sympathies, and also returns to the theme of choosing among possible worlds in his later work on **Leibniz** (though he diverges from the plausibility of this view). On the other hand, he champions the superiority of 'ethics' over morality in **Spinoza**'s work, extending this to his reading of the ethics of **eternal return**; furthermore, he opens *Difference and Repetition* by insisting that laws of **repetition** cannot conform to moral laws or even natural laws, and with Guattari, lambasts the theological judgment that is crystallized not just in the priest but in the doctor and family who make the body into an 'organism' (see **BwO**), disrupting productive processes of **desire**.

1.a. In **Hume's** work, the source of distinctions between vice and virtue, or good and evil, that are inaccessible to **reason** because they are instinctual and sympathetic.

> *actions do not derive their merit from a conformity to* **reason**, *nor their blame from a contrariety to it; and [...] reason can never immediately prevent or produce any action by contradicting or approving of it, it cannot be the source of* **moral** *good and evil, which are found to have that influence. [...]* **Moral** *distinctions, therefore, are not the offspring of* **reason**. [Hume, 2003, 326]

b. In Deleuze's reading of **Hume**, in distinction from **reason** which forms relations between terms or ideas, the guidance or performance of an action which moves in one direction only (from means to ends); the **affective** impression in the **imagination** of circumstances, in distinction from its merely reasoned, causal relation (and from the imaginative fancies produced by religion and idolatry).

> **moral** *distinctions do not let themselves be engendered through* **reason***; they arouse passions, and produce or hinder action* [ES 33]

c. When corrected by general rules (**reason**), the artificial or engendered scheme or means by which we refer natural, partial instincts to be satisfied along with the instincts of others in order to uphold a just society; the extension of moral, partial sympathy to a political whole that includes others who are not naturally sympathetic.

> *the* **moral** *world is the system of means which allow my particular interest, and also the interest of the other, to be satisfied and*

realized. [...] The **moral** *problem is a problem of the whole and also a problem of means. Legislation is a great invention and the true inventors are not the technologists but rather the legislators* [ES 41]

it is not our nature which is **moral**, *it is rather our* **morality** *which is in our nature. One of* **Hume's** *simplest but most important ideas is this: human beings are much less egoistic than they are partial.* [ES 38]

2. In Deleuze's reading of **Spinoza**, a system of imperatives or laws that depend on transcendent **values** (Good and Evil) rather than natural consequences (good and bad); a judgment of existence (Being) based on transcendental values regarding the best way to realize a universal essence, which is erroneous because the existence of **modal essence,** in Spinoza's terms, is caused by laws that are both divine and natural (and cannot be revealed by that which transcends nature). [SEP, SPP]

[...] because Adam is ignorant of causes, he thinks that God **morally** *forbids him something, whereas God only reveals the natural consequence of ingesting the fruit. [...] all that one needs in order to* **moralize** *is to fail to understand. It is clear that we have only to misunderstand a law for it to appear to us in the form of a more 'You Must'.* [SPP 22]

A **morality** *recalls us to essence, i.e. our essence, and which is recalled to us by* **values**. *It is not the point of view of Being. I do not believe that a* **morality** *can be made from the point of view of an ontology. Why? Because* **morality** *always implies something superior to Being; what is superior to Being is something which plays the role of the One, of the Good, it is the One superior to Being. Indeed,* **morality** *is the enterprise of judging not only all that is, but Being itself.* [webdeleuze 21/12/1980]

3.a. In Deleuze's reading of **Nietzsche**, a passive, reactive, or slavish (resentful) disposition, in distinction from an active, affirmative or noble disposition (which acts upon rather than receives stimuli); a disposition which, insofar as it is passive as well as negative (nihilistic), is judgmental rather than **ethical**.

This is how good and evil are born: **ethical** *determination, that of good and bad, gives way to* **moral** *judgment. The good of ethics has become the evil of* **morality,** *the bad has become the good of* **morality***. Good and evil [...] are not created by acting but by* *holding back from acting, not by affirming, but by beginning with denial.* [N 114, 121–2]

b. An insufficient system for judging actions and intentions, because both could not realistically be repeated and coincide with perfect synchronicity (as a 'natural' law or good **habit**), but must instead resort to generic criteria, an image of thought, or **common sense**.

the application of the **moral** *law can be conceived only by restoring to conscience itself the image and the model of the law of nature. As a result, the* **moral** *law, far from giving us true* **repetition**, *still leaves us in generality.* [DR 5, 4]

4. In D&G's explanation of the **Body without Organs**, the power of theological and medical judgment that **stratifies** and organizes the body into an 'organism' which unethically forces it to conform to a transcendental ideal.

The organism is already that, the judgment of God, from which medical doctors benefit and on which they base their power. [TP 159]

5. In Deleuze's reading of **Leibniz**, the expression of the living present within a **monad** that includes or amplifies possible worlds by means of judgment.

Morality *consists in this for each individual: to attempt each time to extend its region of clear* **expression**, *to try to augment its amplitude, so as to produce a free act that expresses the most possible in one given condition or another.* [FLB 73]

- E. B. Y.

Movement-image

The movement-image, also the subtitle of Deleuze's first volume on **cinema**, is a taxonomic concept which includes many sub-varieties (action images, perception images, affection images, relation images, noosigns, etc.). In this case, he draws largely on **Bergson**'s conception of movement to show how images (and sounds) in film originally sought to represent a 'whole', or a world, whose connections are formed successively, like the first synthesis of time in **habit**, by 'positions in space or instants in time'.

1. Images characteristic of classical, pre-WWII cinema, in which **perception**-images, **affection-images**, and **action images** are placed in relations (or montages: successions, sequences, etc.) of association or anticipation by the viewer in such a way that they form and reinforce a linear narrative (and, consequently, a real world, as a whole, which the characters inhabit, and where actions take place).

> *The so-called classical* image *had to be considered on two axes [...]: on the one hand, the* images *were linked or extended according to laws of association, of continuity, resemblance, contrast, or opposition; on the other hand, associated* images *were internalized in a whole as concept (integration), which was in turn continually externalized in associable or extendable* images *(differentiation).* [C2 265, 276]
>
> movement-images *[...] divide into three varieties*—perception-images, action-images, affection-images. *[...] The plane of* movement-images *is a bloc of space-time, a temporal perspective, but, in this respect, it is a perspective on real Time which is not at all the same as the plane [plan] or the* movement. *[...] this point of view which makes the whole depend on 'montage', or the time of the confrontation of* images *of another kind, does not give us a* time image *for itself.* [C1 71, 68]

2.a. Images which, according to Deleuze's reading of **duration** in **Bergson**, constitute the immobile points or instants of movement/duration, and constitute an abstract or representational movement; for example, **affection-images** occupy the gap between **perception** images and **action-images** (all of which constitute mobile sections), thereby constituting cinematic **subjectivity**.

> movement *relates the objects of a closed system to open* duration, *and duration to the objects of the system which it forces to open up [...]. Through* movement *the whole is divided up into objects, and objects are re-united in the whole, and indeed between the two 'the whole' changes. We can consider the objects or parts of a set as immobile sections; but* movement *is established between these sections, and relates the objects or parts to the duration of a whole which changes. [...]* [C1 11–12, 11]

b. Images which reinforce or introduce new perspectives on the whole, or the world, either through the association or the dissociation of **action, perception,** and **affection images,** which occurs by virtue of some sort of cinematographic transformation (such as self-awareness on the part of the character, or an otherwise inability to be anticipated), despite still being imbued by linear time.

> *the shot, as always in the cinema, has two faces, the one turned towards the characters, the objects and the actions in* **movement***, the other turned towards a whole which changes progressively as the film goes on.* [C1 207, 203]

3.a. (Special Type): *Relation-image*: On the one hand, the relation between images which form a **series** in the mind (natural relation): in Deleuze's study of cinema, the *mark*; on the other hand, the relation between images which do not normally form a **series** in the mind (abstract relation): in Deleuze's study of cinema, the *demark*.

> *In accordance with the natural relation, a term refers back to other terms in a customary* **series** *such that each can be 'interpreted' by the others: these are* **marks***; but it is always possible for one of these terms to leap outside the web and suddenly appear in conditions which take it out of its series, or set it in contradiction with it, which we will refer to as the* **demark***.* [C1 207, 203]

> *There is not only the acting and the action [...], there is always [...] a fundamental third constituted by the* **relation** *itself [...].* [C1]

b. (Special Type): *Noosign*: Thought's relation with the whole, which is not given in any particular image but in a relation between images; in classical cinema, relations formed by virtue of an open whole.

> *there were necessarily two kinds of noosign. In the first kind, the* **images** *were linked by rational cuts, and formed under this condition an extendable world [...]. The other kind of noosign marked the integration of the sequences into a whole [...], but also the* **differentiation** *of the whole into extended sequences (belief in the external world).* [C2 265, 277]

- E. B. Y.

Multiplicity

Although originally a **concept** from Riemann's mathematics for conceptualizing space as manifold and dynamic, Deleuze's first substantial discussion occurs via **Bergson**'s use of the term with regard to the way that time or **duration** affects the way space is conceived. While the idea of time as the 'fourth dimension' of space is not new (e.g. Einstein), Deleuze's interest in this stems from the notion that time is the condition for change or **becoming**, and, if it is taken as the foundation for conceiving space, then space (or objects and subjects within it) is not subjected to transcendent criteria but must be conceived in terms of **difference** and **intensity**. The concept is expanded on in *A Thousand Plateaus* and *What is Philosophy?*, on the one hand, to describe how enunciations do not refer to a subject of the statement, but to a **collective assemblage** that is distributed 'rhizomatically', and, on the other hand, to characterize the variations of the philosophical concept, in distinction from the mathematical multiplicities of science.

1.a. A term used by Henri **Bergson**, influenced by Bernhard Riemann, to both characterize space in terms of objective, abstract numerical determination (discrete multiplicity), and to characterize time in terms of subjective, qualitative change (continuous multiplicity).

> *Objects in space form a discrete* **multiplicity***, and [...] every discrete* **multiplicity** *is got by a process of unfolding in space. It also follows that there is neither* **duration** *nor even succession in space [...] If [consciousness] externalizes them in relation to one another, the reason is that, thinking of their radical distinctness (the one having ceased to be when the other appears on the scene), it perceives them under the form of a discrete* **multiplicity***, which amounts to setting them out in line, in the space in which each of them existed separately. [...] but [...] the* **multiplicity** *of conscious states regarded in its original purity, is not at all like the discrete* **multiplicity** *which goes to form a number. [...] consciousness, then makes a qualitative discrimination without any further thought of counting the qualities or even of distinguishing them as several. In such a case we have* **multiplicity** *without quantity.* [Bergson, 1913, 120–2]

b. In Deleuze's reading of **Bergson**, on the one hand, a

configuration of **matter** in space where **differences** are numerical but not qualitative, and can divide *without* changing in nature, and on the other hand, a configuration of time where differences are qualitative but not numerical, and divide *only* by changing in nature.

> *experience always gives us a composite of space and* **duration** *[...] But [...] the decomposition of the composite reveals to us two types of* **multiplicity**. *One is represented by space [...]: It is a* **multiplicity** *of exteriority, of simultaneity, of juxtaposition, of order, of quantitative* **differentiation**, *of* **difference** *in degree; it is a numerical* **multiplicity**, *discontinuous and actual. The other type of* **multiplicity** *appears in pure* **duration**: *It is an internal* **multiplicity** *of succession, of fusion, of organization, of heterogeneity, of qualitative discrimination, or of* **difference** *in kind; it is a* **virtual** *and continuous* **multiplicity** *that cannot be reduced to numbers.* [B 38]

c. In D&G's explanation of **smooth space**, a quantitative or mathematical feature whose system of measurement is contingent upon the **immanent** course of its construction, independent of other systems of measurement (in distinction from **striated space**, where space and its divisibility depend on a transcendent or metric criteria applicable to many constructions).

> *Each* **multiplicity** *was defined by n determinations; sometimes the determinations were independent of the situation, and sometimes they depended upon it. For example, the magnitude of a vertical line between two points can be compared to the magnitude of a horizontal line between two other points: it is clear that the* **multiplicity** *in this case is metric, that it allows itself to be* **striated***, and that its determinations are magnitudes. On the other hand, two sounds of equal pitch and different* **intensity** *cannot be compared to two sounds of equal* **intensity** *and different pitch [...]. Multiplicities of this second kind are not metric [but are smooth].* [TP 533, 483]

2.a. The domain or **virtuality**, encompassing both space and time, in which **differences** in kind (that is, differences between past and present), and differences in degree (that is, differences of **contraction** and expansion) communicate; a more or less **intensive**/extensive state which contains some aspects of a qualitative multiplicity (it does not divide without changing in nature) and a quantitative multiplicity (simultaneity).

there exists one Time and one Time only, as much on the level of the actual parts as on the level of the virtual Whole. [B 82]

Bergson *in no way gives up the idea of a* **difference** *in kind between* **actual fluxes***; any more than he gives up the idea of* **differences** *of relaxation (*détente*) or* **contraction** *in the* **virtuality** *that encompasses them and is actualized in them. [...] Not only do* **virtual multiplicities** *imply a single time, but* **duration** *as virtual* **multiplicity** *is this single and same time.* [B 82]

b. In Deleuze's anti-dialectical explanation of thought (see **Hegel**), a feature of *ideas* which **differ** in terms of magnitude, temporality, and context, rather than differing by virtue of an abstract *opposition* between the one and the many.

There are many theories in philosophy that combine the one and the **multiple***. [...] We are told that the Self is one (thesis) and it is* multiple *(antithesis), then it is the unity of the* multiple *(synthesis). Or else we are told that the One is already* multiple*, that Being passes into non-being and produces becoming. The passages where* **Bergson** *condemns this movement of abstract thought are among the finest in his oeuvre.* [B 44]

In this Riemannian usage of the word 'multiplicity' *(taken up by Husserl, and again by* **Bergson***) the utmost importance must be attached to the substantive form:* multiplicity *must not designate a combination of the many and the one, but rather an organization belonging to the many as such, which has no need whatsoever of unity in order to form a system. [...] Everywhere the* **differences** *between* multiplicities *and the differences within* multiplicities *replace schematic and crude oppositions.* [DR 230, 182]

c. In D&G's distinction between philosophical **concepts** and scientific functions, **intensive** variations of concepts (which are inseparable from each other because they are condensations of **events**), in contrast to extensive variables of scientific functions (which are independent of each other because they refer to states of affairs).

Although scientific types of **multiplicity** *are themselves extremely diverse, they do not include the properly philosophical* **multiplicities** *[...] which expressed the inseparability of variations [...].* [WP 127]

3. In D&G's characterization of the **rhizome**, the manner

in which subjects are not unified with, or subjected to, a dominating signifier, power, object, or any supplementary dimension (rendering a **collective assemblage of enunciation** that expresses **desire**).

> Multiplicities *are* rhizomatic, *and expose arborescent pseudo* multiplicities *for what they are. There is no unity to serve as a pivot in the object, or to divide in the subject. [...] A* **multiplicity** *has neither subject nor object, only determinations, magnitudes, and dimensions that cannot increase in number without the* **multiplicity** *changing in nature (the laws of combination therefore increase in number as the* multiplicity *grows).* [TP 8, 8]

> *there is a* **collective assemblage of enunciation***, a machinic* **assemblage** *of* **desire***, one inside the other and both plugged into an immense* **outside** *that is a* **multiplicity** *in any case* [TP 26, 22–3]

4. In D&G's explanation of **becoming-animal**, insofar as that which can be counted is always indicative of a **becoming**, that which changes in nature when changing in number (as in the animal 'pack' defined by *contagion*).

> *packs, or* **multiplicities***, continually transform themselves into each other, cross over into each other. [...] This is not surprising, since* **becoming** *and* **multiplicity** *are the same thing. A* **multiplicity** *is defined not by its elements, nor by a centre of unification or comprehension. It is defined by the number of dimensions it has [...].* [TP 274–5, 249]

- E. B. Y.

Negotiations

Pourparlers, 1972–1990 (1990)

This selected edition of interviews and correspondence spans the period of the collaboration with Guattari through the decade of the 1980s, which saw many of Deleuze's most important later works, and is published just a year before *What is Philosophy?*. Although the selection is arranged chronologically according to four major subjects that also correspond to major works ('From *Anti-Oedipus* to *A Thousand Plateaus*,' '*Cinemas*,' '*Michel Foucault*,' and

'*Philosophy*'), it is evident that the particular discussions are intended to address controversy and misunderstanding that often surrounded the works or subjects addressed. Consequently, the collection begins with 'A Letter to a Harsh Critic,' addressed to the gay activist and critic Michel Cressole, which Deleuze wrote at the request of the author for inclusion in *Deleuze* (1973). In his sometimes scathing and often ironic response to the author's various critiques of Deleuze, mostly concerning the contradictions that Cressole perceives between Deleuze's stated philosophical positions and his somewhat conservative lifestyle, Deleuze uses this as an opportunity to reject the basis of this distinction, pointing instead to what is made possible for **flows** of thought (or writing) and the 'non-oedipal' and experimental nature of the subjective and political possibilities that Deleuze (and Guattari) are more interested in exploring with their works. As in the case of this opening letter, *Negotiations* is particularly intended to address the snares and pitfalls of celebrity status that was caused by *Anti-Oedipus*, and the inevitable misunderstanding of Deleuze's own philosophical project that occurs as a result, a concern that appears frequently in Deleuze's later writings and even becomes the primary subject of the last work **What is Philosophy?**. This is true not only of the controversy surrounding Deleuze and Guattari's projects, or around Deleuze's own cinema studies which is the subject of the second section, but also in response to the controversy around the figure of **Foucault**, which is the subject of the third section and corresponds to Deleuze's own attempt to rectify this thinker's public portrait in *Foucault*. The fourth section, 'Philosophy,' opens with an essay on the necessity of good mediators, again addressing the problems of publicity and communication in contemporary philosophy. This section also contains interviews that correspond to Deleuze's major work on **Leibniz**, and ends with a letter on **Spinoza's** philosophy written to Reda Bensmaia, where Deleuze again stresses the peculiar nature of style (i.e. **expression**) in philosophy. 'Politics,' the final section, contains an important interview with Antonio **Negri** on the concept of what Deleuze calls 'Control Society,' as well as a postscript on this notion that was influenced by Foucault's **diagram** of disciplinary order and is published in the *Autre Journal* in 1990. - G. L.

Negri, Antonio

Theorist of new forms of dispersed **subjectivity** of labor beyond the mass industrial worker and counted among the leaders of the Italian extra-parliamentary leftist groups Potere Operaio (Worker's Power) and Autonomia (Autonomy). Guattari defended his friend, then professor at the University of Padua, in a series of appeals after Negri was named in an arrest warrant as a terrorist, pointing out that he and his fellow activist-intellectuals had nothing to do with the armed violence of the Red Brigades. Guattari helped Negri while in Paris, until his arrest in 1979, as did Deleuze. Negri was held in prison for 4 years during which time Guattari visited regularly and began collaboration on a book. Negri won his freedom in 1983 by means of winning a parliamentary seat and receiving immunity, which was shortly thereafter revoked. Again, he fled to Paris with Guattari's help. Two years later their collaboration on the reinvention of communism, *Les nouveaux espaces de liberté*, was completed. Both thinkers worked through their debts to Leninism and refocused theoretical attention on the political problem of **subjectivity** as labor was in the process of **becoming** more immaterial. Excerpts from Negri's prison journal from Rebibbia Penale, written in the late 1990s concerning the plight of mentally ill inmates who find themselves in prison after being released from the psychiatric hospitals and expressing support for the association that agitated for their re-education and resocialization, appeared in Guattari and Deleuze's journal *Chimères*.
- G. G.

Neurosis

Freudian psychoanalysis did not treat psychotic (paranoid and schizophrenic, with the exception of a textual analysis of Schreber) patients. It focused on neurotics whose egos obey reality and repress their ids. **Schizoanalysis**, by contrast, treats psychotics whose egos, under the influence of their ids, abandon reality. The Oedipus complex became the measure for this distinction in *The Anti-Oedipus*. Since neurosis is linked with impasses and dislocations arising from the distresses of individuation, Guattari turns toward open collective processes rather than ready-made personological containments.

1.a. A strategy of molar representation (single), whereas psychosis deals in molecular multiplicities (crowd). Yet **schizoanalysis** apprehends in both variations on temporalities of stasis, and this shows it is not exclusive in its interest in phenomena of psychosis.

> *A schizophrenic out for a walk is a better model than a* **neurotic** *lying on the analyst's couch.* [AO 2, 2]

> *For* **desire** *to be expressed in individual terms means that it is already condemned to castration.* [MR 72]

b. A psychoanalytic model in which neurotics received Oedipus better than psychotics; psychosis could be neuroticized by imposing the Oedipus complex.

> *Comparing a sock to a vagina is OK, it's done all the time, but you'd have to be insane to compare a pure aggregate of stitches to a field of vaginas: that's what* **Freud** *says.* [TP 30, 27]

c. A disorder of a real process, along with psychosis, of an Oedipal desiring-production in relation to social production, and it is Oedipus that is an effect, a reaction, to the investments of desiring-production, which is social and technical and produces reality.

> *The complexions of the psychotic real, in their clinical emergence, constitute a privileged exploratory path for other ontological modes of production in that they disciple aspects of excess and limit experiences. Psychosis thus not only haunts* **neurosis** *and perversion but also all the forms of normality.* [CM 79]

2. When taken as an object of **schizoanalysis,** the schizophrenization of the neurotic achieved by drawing out the potential for connectivity trapped in the Oedipal triangle and other representations of **desire** as anti-production; the transformation of the neurotic into a group-subject in which transference was not focused on individuation and identity.

> *The project of 'schizophrenizing'* **neurosis** *is not random: in clinical*

practice, there is no real **neurosis** *that is not paired with some form of psychosis.* [AOP 143]
- G. G.

Nietzsche, Friedrich

Nietzsche's radical critique of western metaphysics and notion of 'overturning Platonism' appeals to Deleuze's own project of thinking **difference** in itself without the requirements of **representation**. Nietzsche also appeals to Deleuze not only because of his fragmented and aphoristic **mode** of **expression** which dramatizes philosophy, but also because of his approach to **life** and **ethics**. Because Nietzsche's work lacks presuppositions about **values**, it advocates *creativity* in the most essential sense. Such creativity, however, is bound up with destruction and self-destruction: in Deleuze's terms, it is an **affirmation** that is the *consequence* of **negation** (where saying 'no' is only a *means* to saying 'yes'), rather than vice versa. In other words, when the only purpose of affirmation is to negate, affirmation conceals the type of (**reactive**) **nihilism** that Nietzsche and Deleuze despise. Rather, Nietzsche's nihilism is '**active**' because the purpose of destruction is always to create. Furthermore, any religion or value-system which would deny **life** in favor of the other-worldly, or some other mode of abstraction, is strongly rejected by Nietzsche. The famous and commonly misunderstood phrase 'God is dead' for Nietzsche thus involves not simply an 'atheism', but the unbelievability of all permanent human value-systems. As Deleuze claims, 'With [Nietzsche] the age of naive confidence comes to an end, the age which at some times acclaims the reconciliation of man and God, at others the replacement of God by man' (N 148, 156). God, in other words, is no more or guarantor of value than man. Rather, Nietzsche advocates the continual destruction and re-creation of all systems of value, the focal point being '**transvaluation**'. Life and value is in a state of **becoming**, not a state of **being**, and there can be no transcendent God or abstract system of thought to justify such a state. In this way, Deleuze dissociates Nietzsche from stereotypes that suggest he is a nihilist, as well as from the platitude 'God is dead'. Deleuze also frequently follows Nietzsche's lead to dissociate the **eternal return** from any mode of circularity, equality, or sameness, characterizing it instead an instance where the different relates to the different without representation. In *Difference and Repetition*, the eternal return is called the 'final synthesis of time' that combines the **passive synthesis** of habit (repetition) with the **passive synthesis** of memory (difference). He thus valorizes a Nietzschean trope as essential to understand the interplay between repetition and difference, which testifies to Nietzsche's fundamental influence on his thought. - E. B. Y.

Nietzsche and Philosophy

Nietzsche et la philosophie (1962)

Deleuze published his apprenticeship work on **Nietzsche** in 1962, and another shorter work on Nietzsche in 1965 which included a glossary of Nietzschean personas (part of which is translated in *Pure Immanence*). Deleuze's work on Nietzsche in fact contributed to, and participated in, a resurged interest in his work among French intellectuals (such as **Klossowski**, Derrida, **Blanchot**, and **Foucault**), and in this work provides a synthetic and cohesive account of his thought. He also helped to legitimate Nietzsche's fragmentary, aphoristic style as perfectly appropriate to philosophy: because the philosopher necessarily 'masks' their fundamental question, it will always be 'disguised', or repeated in another form. Deleuze is greatly indebted to Nietzsche, appropriating many important terms in his lexicon from Nietzsche's works—**becoming, eternal return, force**, etc., which are all defined and elaborated on in this work.

It is important when reading *Nietzsche and Philosophy* to recognize that his reading of Nietzsche forecasts and resonates with his readings of **Bergson** and **Spinoza** (as well as his critique of **Freud, Kant** and **Hegel** in *Difference and Repetition*), who he wrote on shortly thereafter. For example, Deleuze effectively translates Nietzsche's complaint about slave **morality** into Spinoza's inadequate ideas: a body or reactive force is 'separate from what it can do' when cut off from its power of action (this refrain can be found almost three dozen times throughout the text, and resonates strongly in Deleuze's works on Spinoza). While Nietzsche makes mention of Hegel (and dialectical thought) in his work, Hegel's version of the dialectic in light of Nietzsche's worldview is fleshed out dramatically in the final section of the work in anticipation of what will be Deleuze's own *tour de force* against Hegelianism in *Difference and Repetition*. He likewise places Nietzsche's reading of the unconscious in contrast with Freud's, demonstrating Freud's mistake in determining forgetting or 'repression' negatively and passively (see **unconscious** 3.b.). The text can in fact be read as a primer for many of his other apprenticeship works which precede *Difference and Repetition*: his reading of Bergson's '**multiplicity**,' for example, has arguably as much Nietzschean **resonance** (in terms of his critique of the 'Whole' or the One) as Bergsonian. Thus while close readers of Nietzsche will certainly find that Deleuze is attentive towards the chronology of his works and the shift which occurs after *The Birth of Tragedy* (see the chapter 'Nietzsche's Evolution'), Deleuze is as liberal with his use of citations from Nietzsche's corpus to support the constellations and emphases that he thinks are most pertinent. - E. B. Y.

Nietzsche. Sa vie, son œuvre, avec un exposé de sa philosophie (1965)

One of the first instances of Deleuze's penchant for the form of a glossary of concepts and key figures, repeated later in *Spinoza: A Practical Philosophy* and in the concluding section of *A Thousand Plateaus*, this short introductory work appeared three years after the initial volume on Nietzsche and around the same period as the important colloquium on the philosopher organized at Roymaunt (see below). It was subsequently re-edited by Deleuze on several occasions and is now published in French under the title: *Nietzsche by Deleuze* (and included in the English text *Pure Immanence*). It contains a short biography, a summary of Nietzsche's philosophy, a dictionary of principal figures in his writings, and extracts chosen by Deleuze, which feature passages on 'the Dionysian' from *The Birth of Tragedy*, the aphorisms from *The Gay Science,* to excepts from *Will to Power*. Partly written to combat the post-war image of Nietzsche as a philosopher of National Socialism, an image partly created by his sister, both the emphasis of Deleuze's on Nietzsche's life and on the aphorism must be understood in the context of his earlier *Nietzsche and Philosophy*. - G. L.

Nomadism

(*Nomads, Nomadic Distribution, Nomos*)

While the notion of nomadic distribution and 'crowned anarchy' first makes its appearance in *Difference and Repetition* and *The Logic of Sense* as a way to describe a distribution of **difference** that is opposed to analogy (with a reference to the linguist Emmanuel Laroche), the **concept** of 'nomadism' proper is greatly expanded and developed with Guattari (with reference to the historian Arnold Toynbee and others), not to describe actual nomadic people in history *per se*, but to describe how a form of **subjectivity** is engendered by means of inhabiting **smooth space**, as well as to explain a dormant disposition towards war that is activated (as a **war machine**) when there is an attempt to contain it.

1. (Special Combination): *Nomadic Distribution*; also: *Crowned Anarchy, Nomos*: In Deleuze's reading of Laroche, the resistance to distributions and divisions of limited space which are hierarchical, arborescent, or **striated** (that is, legitimated, legal; 'logos'); rather, the distribution within unlimited space which divides and multiplies positions *within* space itself (such that space is created rather than enclosed proprietarily); a **univocal** distribution of difference. [LS, DR, TP]

> Laroche shows that the idea of distribution in *nomos*—*nemo* does not stand in a simple relation to that of allocation [...] The *nomos* designated first of all an occupied space, but one without precise limits (for example, the expanse around a town)—whence, too, the theme of the '**nomad**'. [DR 85, 309]

> there is a completely other distribution which must be called **nomadic** [...]. Here, there is no longer a division of that which is distributed but rather a division among those who distribute themselves in an open space [...]. [DR 46, 36]

The **nomadic** *distributions or* **crowned anarchies** *in the* **univocal stand** *opposed to the sedentary distributions of analogy.* [DR 378, 304]

2.a. A term from Arnold Toynbee to describe a manner of living which corresponds to an arrested civilization (that is, one which is neither growing nor shrinking), which is often a response to changes in the environment such as desiccation (and a refusal to adapt to a sedentary lifestyle in response).

> *The* **Nomad** *[...] has had the audacity to grapple with an [...] intractable element; and indeed, in its relationship to man, the Steppe, with its surface of grass and gravel, actually bears a greater resemblance to 'the unharvested sea' [...] than it bears to terra firma that is amendable to hoe and plough. Steppe-surface and water-surface have this in common, that they are both accessible to man only as a pilgrim and a sojourner. Neither offers him anywhere on its broad surface, apart from islands and oases, a place where he can settle down to a sedentary existence.* [Toynbee, 1946, p. 166]

b. In D&G's reading of Toynbee, not a migrant or wanderer, but a subject who clings to apparently desolate spaces which they refuse to leave, and as a result always appears to be wandering or moving through them, but is in fact moving at an absolute (i.e. non-measurable) speed and along a line or trajectory without any definitive beginning or end. [AO, TP, N, D]

> *We can say of the* **nomads***, following Toynbee's suggestion: they do not move. They are* **nomads** *by dint of not moving, not migrating, of holding a* **smooth space** *that they refuse to leave, that they leave only in order to conquer and die. Voyage in place: that is the name of all* **intensities***, even if they also develop in extension.* [TP 532, 482]

3.a. *Nomad:* the proper name of an agent who not only inhabits, but **territorializes**, (im)mobilizes, or constructs **smooth space** by means of consistent independence from specified points and localized, **stratified** domains.

> *The* **nomads** *are [...] wherever there forms a* **smooth space** *[...]; they remain in them, and they themselves make them grow, for it has been established that the* **nomads** *make the desert no less than they are made by it.* [TP 421, 382]

> *The* **nomad** *[...] is not ignorant of points (water points, dwelling points, assembly points, etc.). [...] The water point is reached only in order to be left behind; [...] the in-between has taken on all the consistency and enjoys both an autonomy and a direction of its own [...] The* **nomad** *is not at all the same as the migrant; for the migrant goes principally from one point to another [...].* [TP 419, 380]

b. In D&G's political theory, the depersonalization of **subjectivity** such that the subject identifies with the **multiplicity** of the **smooth spaces** they traverse or inhabit, which places them in a hostile relation to the State, as well as to sedentary existence (i.e. existence with controlled, relative movement) and to **striated space** (actualized in a **war-machine**); properly, a disposition towards *speed* (uncontrolled, absolute movement), which varies internally, by **intensity** and **affect**, rather than externally and relatively.

> *The number becomes a principle whenever it occupies a* **smooth space**, *and is deployed within it as subject [...]. The specificity of numerical organization rests on the* **nomadic** *mode of existence and the* **war** *machine function.* [TP 430, 389]

> *each time there is an operation against the State—insubordination, rioting, guerrilla warfare, or revolution as act—it can be said that a* **war machine** *has revived, that a new* **nomadic** *potential has appeared, accompanied by the reconstitution of a* **smooth space** *or a manner of being in space as though it were smooth [...].* [TP 426, 386]

> *a speed may be very slow, or even immobile, yet it is still speed. Movement is extensive; speed is* **intensive**. *[...] only* **nomads** *have absolute movement, in other words, speed* [TP 421, 381]

c. *Nomadic*: In D&G's analysis of **desire**, a use of **conjunctive syntheses** which form a polyvocal chain of social (re)production (or of '**flow**'); a form of **subjectivity** which does not segregate itself by means of restriction (the conditions of discrimination), but identifies itself perpetually as an inferior outsider (thus exposing existing segregations).

> *The* **nomadic** *and polyvocal use of the conjunctive syntheses is in opposition to the segregative and biunivocal use. Delirium has something like two poles, racist and racial, paranoiac-segregative and schizonomadic.* [AO 115–16, 105]

- E. B. Y.

Un Nouvel Archiviste. Michel Foucault (1972)

In this early work, later incorporated into the first section of *Foucault*, Deleuze champions Foucault's method of exploring the archive, according to which statements are defined neither from the point of view of a structure, nor from the position of a subject where they are said to emanate. Instead, as Deleuze explains, Foucault seeks to discover the new rules that apply to what he called 'an order of discourse,' in which statements circulate according to an 'author-function' that appears in the beginning of the seventeenth century alongside distinctive epistemological, sociological, and political transformations in European institutions. Written during the period of such works as *The Order of Things, The Order of Discourse,* and *The Archeology of Knowledge,* this represents one of the first major commentaries written on Foucault's system of thought by one of his contemporaries. - G. L.

On the Line

Rhizome, avec Félix Guattari (1976)

The concept of the **rhizome** is both a formula that Deleuze and Guattari discerned as the means of their own collaboration together, and the method of an 'anti-method,' that is, the means of constructing a 'new image of thought' that avoids the return of a transcendental plan of organization (i.e. Being, or 'the One'). Written in the same period as *Kafka: Toward a Minor Literature,* or immediately afterward, *The Rhizome* takes the form of notes on an 'experiment,' which later becomes the introduction to *A Thousand Plateaus*. In this work the **concept** of a '**collective assemblage of enunciation**,' which is first introduced in the last chapter of the Kafka book, is outlined through a series of **propositions**, all of which will serve as the guiding principles of the various plateaus that are assembled later on in the second volume of the Capitalism and Schizophrenia project. - G. L.

Other, the

(Autrui)

Deleuze's interest in the **concept** of the Other began quite early in his career (influenced largely by **Sartre**, despite its importance in the works of **Hegel**, Lacan, and Levinas); in fact, his first published article in 1945 was entitled 'Description of a Woman: For a Philosophy of the Gendered Other.' The concept is explored again explicitly in his essay 'Michel **Tournier** and the World Without Others', which examines the concept in the novel *Vendredi ou les Limbes du Pacifique* (translated simply as *Friday*) written by his close friend from high school and the Sorbonne. In both cases, Deleuze highlights the Other as an '**expression** of a possible world'—a notion that he claims to have 'borrowed' from Tournier, which contains both **Sartrean** and '**Leibnizian**' echoes. In fact, when Deleuze revises this concept with Guattari in *What is Philosophy?*, he will claim that the concept 'goes back to Leibniz, to his possible worlds and to the monad as expression of the world' (WP 17).

The concept is also bound up with his theory of **intensity** and **difference** (or differential systems and **seriality**): the other person is not an 'individual' that is dominated by our 'recognition' of them, but a 'structure which is implemented only by variable terms in different perceptual worlds—me for you in yours, you for me in mine' (DR 352, 281), which means that the Other will 'express' a different 'problem' or a different 'possible world' for me than they will for you. Just as we like to say that we act differently depending on who we're with, in this case, the Other is not an 'individual' per se; rather, they make us 'rediscover' certain 'individuating factors' through the **actualization** of the worlds that they implicate us in (when we perceive their **expression**).

1.a. In **Sartre**, the perceived agency (through the 'Gaze') which objectivizes the self through consciousness, and is in turn objectified by the consciousness of the self in addition to expressing an interior, inaccessible **subjectivity**.

> *In fact from the moment that the* **Other** *appears to me as an object, his* subjectivity *becomes a simple property of the object considered. [...] The-***Other***-as-Object 'has' a subjectivity as this hollow box has*

'an inside.' In this way I recover myself, for I cannot be an object for an object. [Sartre, 2001, 289]

b. In the work of Michel **Tournier**, the manner in which the other operates as a structure that is not phenomenological (consciousness and its perceptual field), but operates in a relation to its absence (such that the Other is the condition *for* **perception**), whereby without Others, there is no distinction between subject (consciousness) and object.

> *Each of these men was a possible world, having its own coherence, its values, its sources of attraction and repulsion, its centre of gravity. [...] And each of these possible worlds naively proclaimed itself the reality. That was what other people were: the possible obstinately passing for the real.* [Tournier, cited in LS 308, 347]

c. In Deleuze's combined reading of **Sartre** and **Tournier** (and Leibniz's **monad**), the manner in which a person 'expresses' an enfolded or enveloped world (that is, which 'enfolds' the self into that world such that they desire to experience its reality, or **virtual** state of pre-individual singularities) but does not (yet) exist outside of that expression.

> *Sartre [...] is the first to have considered* **the Other** *as a real structure [...]. But, since he defined this structure by means of the 'look,' he fell back in the categories of object and subject [...]. It seems that the structure* **Other** *precedes the look [...]. The look brings about only the effectuation or the* **actualization** *of a structure which must nonetheless be independently defined.* [LS 373, 366]

2.a. In Deleuze's analysis of **perception**, a personified **expression**, which does not resemble what it expresses, that nevertheless diverts **desire** towards possible worlds or **events** (or even physical spaces) that are outside of the grasp of consciousness, separating consciousness from its object(s). [P, LS, DR, WP]

> *Before the appearance of* **the Other**, *there was [...] a reassuring world from which my consciousness could not be distinguished.* [LS 349, 310]

> **the Other** *[...] relativizes the not-known and the non-perceived, because* **Others**, *from my point of view, introduce the sign of the unseen in what I do see, making me grasp what I do not perceive*

as what is perceptible to an **Other.** *In all these respects, my* **desire** *passes through* **others** *[...].* [LS 345, 306]

among the developed qualities and extensities of the perceptual world, [the Other] *envelops and* **expresses** *possible worlds which do not exist outside their* **expression** [DR]

the Other *Person is enough to make any length a possible* **depth** *in space, and vice versa* [WP 18]

b. In Deleuze's reading of **Proust**, the source of both love and jealousy (possible worlds of preferences and **desires**), which, insofar as they both exclude and envelop the self, must be explicated or unfolded (but are always deceptive because they disguise what they express, and can never fully include the self).

The beloved is like the sensuous quality, valid by what she envelops. Her eyes would be merely stones, and her body a piece of flesh, if they did not express a possible world or worlds, landscapes and places, ways of life must be explicated. [...] Expressivity is the content of **another person.** [P 120]

There is [...] a contradiction of love. We cannot interpret the signs of a **loved person** *without proceeding into worlds [...] that formed themselves with* **other persons** [P 8]

3.a. In psychic systems, a pre-individual *structure*, with no determined nature or identity, which expresses a state of implicated **ideas** or singularities.

the fact that there is always something else implicated which remains to be explicated or developed—all this is made possible only by the Other-*structure and its expressive power in* **perception.** *In short, it is the* Other-*structure that ensures individuation within the perceptual world.* [DR 352, 281]

b. In the experience of time, a possibility of what the self is **becoming** or what is being **actualized** (that is, an expression of the future), and a rendering of *the self* as a past or **virtual** entity. [LS, WP]

If the Other *is a possible world, I am a past world.* [LS 349, 310]

The **actual** *is not what we are but, rather, what we* **become,** *[...] that is to say,* the Other *[...].* [WP]

- E. B. Y.

Oury, Jean

Throughout his adult life Guattari worked at the La Borde psychiatric clinic, which was founded by Lacanian analyst Jean Oury soon after the two men met. They were introduced in the 1950s by the latter's brother **Fernand**. Jean Oury began entrusting the brilliant but untrained young Guattari with more and more clinical responsibility, encouraging him to give up pharmacy studies and to attend the lectures of Jacques Lacan, who was not yet known outside of psychiatric and psychoanalytic circles. Working under Oury at La Borde, Guattari and his colleagues treated psychotic patients using the techniques of psychoanalysis. The experience of adapting Freudian and Lacanian theories to the treatment of schizophrenia inspired many of the core ideas in *Anti-Oedipus*. Relations with Oury became strained as the work with Deleuze and militant political activities in Paris distracted Guattari from his duties at the clinic. - J. W.

Outside, the

1. A term used by Maurice **Blanchot** to describe the temporal and lived experience of impossibility, characterized by *incessance* (a situation which feels as if it is without beginning or end), *immediacy* (the **perception** of the ungraspable, yet stubbornly apparent), and **difference** (an oscillation that cannot be reduced to contrariety).

> *impossibility is the passion of* the Outside *itself. [...] in impossibility time [...] never fixes itself in a present, refers to no past and goes toward no future: the incessant. [...] [T]he immediate is a presence to which one cannot be present, but from which one cannot separate [...]. [W]hat reigns in the experience of impossibility is the infinite shifting of dispersal, [...] where* the other *never comes back to the same.* [Blanchot 1993, 45–6]

2.a. In Deleuze's (and sometimes Guattari's) reading of **Blanchot**, that which, containing no form of exteriority, is inaccessible to thought or cognition, and yet serves as the condition for all internal thought; the **plane of immanence** or consistency. [DR, LS, WP, N, F]

> *[the* **plane of immanence***] is an* **outside** *more distant than any external world because it is an inside deeper that any internal world.* [WP 59]

> *Thinking doesn't come from within, but nor is it something that happens in the external world. It comes from this* **Outside***, and returns to it, it amounts to confronting it. The line* **outside** *is our double, with all the double's* **otherness**. [NG 110]

b. In Deleuze's reading of **Foucault** and **Leibniz**, the field or plane which constitutes the relation of, as well as the distance *and* intimacy between, **forces**; the relation that engenders **folding** which is reducible neither to corporeal nor temporal circumstances.

> *The relations between* **forces**, *which are mobile, faint and diffuse, do not lie outside* **strata** *but form* **the outside** *of strata.* [F 70, 84]

> *The* **outside** *is not a fixed limit but a moving* **matter** *animated by peristaltic movements,* **folds** *and foldings that together make up an inside: they are not something other than* **the outside**, *but precisely the inside of* **the outside***.* [F 96–7]

> *[individuation is] an invagination of* **the outside** *that could not occur all alone if no true interiorities did not exist elsewhere.* [FLB 105]

> *What is this secret part of the* **event** *that is at once distinguished from its own realization [...], even though realization does not exist on* **the outside***? [...] [I]t is pure inflection as ideality, a neutral* **singularity**, *incorporeal as much as impassible or, if we use* **Blanchot's** *words, 'the part of the event as much as its accomplishment' [...].* [FLB 8]

– E. B. Y.

Paradox

1.a. In Deleuze's analysis of **sense**, that which is separate from anything real or possible, but nonetheless is indicative of the genesis of the real or possible; a genetical element that is dynamic, producing **non-sense** or **expression**, rather than static, producing forms of the **proposition** that involve contradiction; a philosophical thought that breaks with doxa by conforming neither to anything with recognizable significance or **good sense**, nor to any existing beliefs or **common sense**.

> *The force of* **paradoxes** *is that they are not contradictory [...]. The principle of contradiction is applicable to the real and the possible, but not to the impossible from which it derives* [LS 86, 74]

> *Philosophy is revealed not by* **good sense** *but by* **paradox**. **Paradox** *is the pathos or the passion of philosophy. There are several kinds of* **paradox**, *all of which are opposed to the complementary forms of orthodoxy—namely, good sense and* **common sense**. [DR 286, 227]

> *If philosophy is* **paradoxical** *by nature, this is [...] because it [...] expresses something that does not belong to the order of opinion or even of the* **proposition**. [WP 80]

b. A functioning of the **faculties** where each communicates with the other by way of violence rather than identity, as in **Kant**. [K, DR]

> *Each* **faculty** *[...], in its own order and on its own account, has broken the form of* **common sense** *which kept it within the empirical element of doxa, in order to attain both its 'nth' power and the* **paradoxical** *element within transcendental exercise.* [DR 178, 141]

- E. B. Y.

Partial object

(also *paradoxical object, object = x*, and *virtual object*)

Beginning with **Freud,** the psychoanalytic theory of 'drives' postulated that there must be some object upon which we fixate that would fulfill our **desire**. These objects are referred to in psychoanalytic discourses as 'partial' because they are thought to be largely symbolic (usually represented by sex organs or that which resembles them). While Deleuze explicitly discusses the partial object in terms of childhood sexuality in *The Logic of Sense*, he synthesizes his discussion of the 'paradoxical object' in his analysis of Lacan from that text with his discussion of the 'partial' and 'virtual' object in *Difference and Repetition* to emphasize that if the partial object is symbolic by nature, then our **desire** is not satisfied by encountering such objects in reality; to take this further, it is the **series** of objects that we encounter in reality (that is, by virtue of the passive syntheses of **habit**) that symbolize or 'disguise' the partial object, and not an unfulfillable wish or dream that would be 'disguised' *by* objects in reality. This is because if the partial object is always 'missing from its place', as Lacan claims, then logically, Deleuze insists, it would *never* be given in experience but would instead 'resonate' within or between **repetitions** as **differences** which are themselves fragments of a **pure past**. While this **resonance** is erotic, it is also oriented towards eternity (or the third **passive synthesis** of time) and therefore is not limited by the exigencies of pleasure and satisfaction. This issue is picked up again in *Anti-Oedipus*, where the partial object is an organ that does not produce the illusion of an organism or subject, but acts as a catalyst of *unending* processes of desire on the **body without organs**; like Deleuze's paradoxical objects, such partial-objects are dispersed without some unity in realtiy that would reveal, link, or explain them.

1.a. Melanie Klein's term for body parts whose substances infants introject (by means of orality) into their body and then project outward (aggressively or sadistically) because they are threatening.

> *My own view that the Oedipus conflict [...] gives another reason why hatred should be the basis of* **object**-*relationships [is] in the fact that the child forms its relation with its parents[...]. The ambivalence it feels towards its mother's breast as its first* **object** *becomes strengthened by the increasing oral frustration it undergoes and by the onset of its Oedipus conflict, until it grows into fully-developed sadism. [...] Oedipus conflict and the super-ego set in, I believe, under the supremacy of the pre-genital impulses, and the* **objects** *which have been introjected in the oral-sadistic phase—the first* **object** *cathexes and identifications—form the beginnings of the early super-ego.* [Klein, *The Psychoanalysis of Children*, Ch. 12]

b. Lacan's term, '*object petit a*', or object of the drive which is symbolized or incarnated in parts of the **Other** in various stages of infantile sexuality and then later in adult life.

> *what makes us distinguish this satisfaction from the mere autoeroticism of the erogenous zone is the object that we confuse all too*

often with that upon which the drive closes —*this* **object**, *which is in fact simply the presence of a hollow, a void, which can be occupied,* **Freud** *tells us, by any* **object,** *and whose agency we know only in the form of the* **lost object,** *the* **petit a.** [Lacan, 1981, 179–80]

2.a. In Deleuze's reading of Klein, the communication of bodies in **depth** which ultimately fragments and *empties* the body by subordinating it to an oral-anal construct which organizes its **differences** into systems of representation (or 'heights'), in distinction from a *full* but part-less or organ-less body (a **Body without Organs**) whose differences are organized only in **depth**.

> *What the schizoid position opposes to bad* **partial objects**—*introjected and projected, toxic and excremental, oral and anal*—*is not a good object, even it if were partial. What is opposed is rather an organism without parts, a* **body without organs,** *with neither mouth nor anus, having given up all introjection or projection, and being complete, at this price.* [LS 216, 188]

b. In Deleuze's reading of Lacan, the *paradoxical element* that is always 'missing' because it instigates a **disjunctive synthesis** between two **series**; in other words, it is always both lacking *and* in *excess* (because it is both perpetually moving and a mobile, empty space), as for example, in Edgar Allen Poe's 'purloined letter' where the letter instigates displacements and disguises between one series of the King's ignorance, the wife's relief, and the minister's intervention, and another series of the intervention by the police, the efforts to hide the letter, and its ultimate theft.

> *We must say that the* **paradoxical entity** *is never where we look for it, and conversely that we never find it where it is. As Lacan says, it fails to observe its place (elle manque à sa place).[...] We will not say, therefore, of the two series it animates, that the one is originary and the other derived [...].* [LS 48, 41]

c. (Special Type): *virtual object, object* = x: In distinction from the psychoanalytic view that reduces the object of **desire** to the phallus (or lack thereof, in accordance with the principle of castration), Deleuze's term for a **virtual** object which is 'symbolic' only in relation to the real **series** in which it is disguised and displaced (in other words; forms of **repetition** which are made symbolic when they are no longer limited to the generic **difference** of **habit**, but are instead lived as and expressive of difference in itself).

> Repetition *is constituted not from one present to another, but between the two coexistent* series *that these presents form in function of the* virtual object *(object = x). It is because this* object *constantly circulates, always displaced in relation to itself, that it determines transformations of terms and modifications of imaginary relations within the two real series in which it appears [...]. The displacement of the* virtual object *is not, therefore, one disguise among others, but the principle from which, in reality, repetition follows in the form of disguised repetition.* [DR 129, 105]

d. In Deleuze's reading of **Proust**, the object which resonates between real **series** but is confined to the domain of the **virtual** (that is, not **actual** or constituted in an order that can be lived in an experience of a certain **duration** or an order of expectation/possibilities). [P, DR]

> *Exactly what* **Proust** *said of states of* **resonance** *must be said of the* virtual: *'Real without being actual, ideal without being abstract'; and symbolic without being fictional. Indeed, the* virtual *must be defined as strictly a* part *of the real* object—*as though the* object *had one* part *of itself in the virtual into which it plunged as though into an objective dimension.* [DR 260, 208–9]

3. In D&G's analysis of capitalism, organs or working machinic parts that engender **disjunctive syntheses** of the **unconscious** which do not relate organs to an organism, parts to a unifying whole, objects to subjects (e.g. a breast to the mother), but instead act as one side of a **desiring-machine** which directs flows and constructs or fills a **body without organs**.

> partial objects *are only apparently derived from global persons; they are really produced by being drawn from a flow [...]* [AO 46]

> partial objects *are the direct powers of the* body without organs, *and the body without organs, the raw material of the* partial objects. *The body without organs is the* matter *that always fills space to given degrees of* intensity, *and the* partial objects *are these degrees, these intensive parts that produce the real in space* [AO 325–6]

- E. B. Y.

Passive synthesis

The notion of *synthesis* refers to an operation of the psyche and also in some cases of the viscera, which allows Deleuze to explore both the manner in which **unconscious** (and conscious) processes work, as well as the function of **repetition** in **serial** format, as an alternative to the 'labor' of the **Hegelian** dialectic (and apart from **Kantian** models of recognition or **active syntheses**). The term first appears in *The Logic of Sense* and *Difference and Repetition* with reference to various types of syntheses, and gets picked up again in *Anti-Oedipus* to refer to the **desiring** process.

1. In Deleuze's explanation of the **unconscious**, three syntheses which, working together against the **active synthesis** of recognition and representation, account for the real experience of time and operations of the psyche.

> It is these three **syntheses** *which must be understood as constitutive of the* **unconscious***. [...] The first* synthesis *expresses the foundation of time upon the basis of a living present [...]. The second* **synthesis** *expresses the manner in which time is grounded in a pure past[...]. The third* **synthesis***, however, refers to the absence of ground into which we are precipitated by the ground itself [...].* [DR 140, 114].

a. (Special Combination): *first passive synthesis*: The synthesis of the mind that **contracts** present instances with past instances to produce **habits**. [DR]

b. (Special Combination): *second passive synthesis*: The (erotic) synthesis of **differences** within the mind that engenders the **pure past,** disengaged from any present.

> *Whereas the* **passive synthesis** *of* **habit** *constitutes the living present in time and makes the past and the future two asymmetrical elements of that present, the* **passive synthesis** *of memory constitutes the pure past in time, and makes the former and the present present [...] two asymmetrical elements of this past as such.* [DR 103, 81]

c. (Special Combination): *third passive synthesis*: A (desexualized) synthesis of time which corresponds to the interminable and incessant force of the **Outside** (of a death that is not possible to die); **eternal return**.

> *death cannot be reduced to negation, neither to the negative of opposition nor to the negative of limitation.[...] Thanatos stands for a [passive]* synthesis *of time quite unlike that of Eros;[...] the libido loses all mnemic content and Time loses its circular shape in order to assume a merciless and straight form [...].* [DR 139, 113]

2. In D&G's explanation of **desiring-machines**, three syntheses of the **unconscious** (*Connective, Disjunctive,* and *Conjunctive*) which resist the subordination of **desire** to 1) a global and specific use of **partial objects**, 2) an exclusive and restrictive use of disjunction, or 3) a personal use of consumption.

> **Desire** *is the set of* **passive syntheses** *that engineer* **partial objects, flows,** *and bodies, and that function as units of production. The real is the end product, the result of the* **passive syntheses** *of desire as autoproduction of the* **unconscious**. [AO 28, 26]

a. *Connective synthesis*: the connection of organs/parts (**partial objects**) to other organs/parts without being specific to or localized within subjects, but to general productions (**flows of matter**, energy, etc.). [AO]

b. *Disjunctive synthesis*: the repulsion or rejection of production, and an inscription of **partial objects** onto a **body without organs** which both includes them within and separates them from connective, productive processes. [AO]

c. *Conjunctive synthesis*: the **nomadic** constitution of a provisional **subjectivity** which is the consummation of the parts that continue to be produced and repelled through the process of desiring production.

> *The molecular* **Unconscious** *[...] knows nothing of castration, because* **partial objects** *lack nothing and form free* **multiplicities** *as such; [...] because the [passive]* syntheses *constitute local and non-specific* connections, inclusive disjunctions, nomadic conjunctions *[...].* [AO 325, 295]

- E. B. Y.

Percept

1.a. In D&G's analysis of art, that which is imperceptible but nevertheless appeals to vision; that which separates itself from the **perception** of an object or the recollection of a memory. Perception in its objective state insofar as it is preserved and rendered as a work of art.

> Percepts [...]are independent of a state of those who experience them. The percept is the landscape before man, in the absence of man. [WP 164]

b. The proper entity, along with the **affect**, that engenders blocs of **sensation** and populates the **plane of composition** with aesthetic figures.

> The composite Sensation, made up of percepts and affects, deterritorializes the system of opinion [WP 196]

c. An aesthetic feature (of painting, music, literature, etc.) which renders **force(s)** (whether physical, temporal, etc.) or **affects** perceptible, sonorous, or figurative, in distinction from the **intensity** of the **affect** which is engendered by the relations between such forces.

> the percept [...] make[s] perceptible the imperceptible forces that populate the world, affect us, and make us become [WP 182]

2. A vision typical of religious and poetic 'mystics'; a subjective mirage or phantasm that expresses something outside of objective comprehension.

> The finest writers have singular conditions of perception that allow them to draw on or shape aesthetic percepts like veritable visions [...]. It is by virtue of a subjective disposition that Proust finds his percepts in a current of air passing under a door, and is left cold by the beauties others bring to his attention. In Melville, there is a private ocean [...where] Moby-Dick swims [...]. [ECC 116]

- E. B. Y.

Perception

1. A structure of **possibility** (though it bears no resemblance to its realization) which is implicates the subject and is **expressed** by **the Other**.

> *[...] the* Other *is initially a structure of the* perceptual *field, without which the entire field could not function as it does.* [LS 346, 307]

2.a. (Special Combination): *Perception-image*: In Deleuze's sensory-motor schema of the **movement-image**, that which is subtracted subjectively from a diffuse, objective, and totalizing variation, where things are indistinguishable images, thereby creating a gap or distance between space and action; in Deleuze's explanation of cinematic **signs**, the condition for movement ('**zeroness**') and the classification of images.

> Perceptions *of things are incomplete and prejudiced, partial, subjective prehensions [...]. And it is the first avatar of the* **movement-image:** *when it is related to a centre of indetermination, it becomes* perception image. [...] Perceiving *things here what they are, I grasp the 'virtual action' that they have on me, and the 'possible action' that I have on them [...]. It is thus the same phenomenon of the gap which is expressed in terms of time in my action and in terms of space in my* perception. [C1 66–7, 64–5]

> *The* perception-image *will therefore be like a degree zero in the deduction which is carried out as a function of the* **movement-image:** *there will be a* '**zeroness**' *before Peirce's firstness.* [C2 30, 32]

b. (Special Combination): *Diffuse perception* (also, *solid* or *fixed* perception): Cinematic perception that subtracts nothing from the image based on subjective need or interest, but retains an objective, albeit non-localized center within a complete image; in Deleuze's cinematic schema, the *dicisign*.

> *The thing itself must [...] be presented in itself as a complete, immediate,* diffuse **perception**. *The thing is [...] subject to their action and reacts to them on all its facets and in all its parts.* [C1 66, 63]

c. (Special Combination): *Liquid Perception*: The state in which the center of perception, created by the distance between an action and its possibility, flows by virtue of displacement; in Deleuze's cinematic schema, the *reume*.

> The more the privileged centre is itself put into movement, the more it will tend towards an acentered system where the images vary in relation to one another [...]. the camera consciousness [...] was **actualized** in a flowing **perception** and thus arrived at a material determination [...]. [C1 79–82, 74–6]

d. (Special Combination): *Gaseous Perception*: A perception that does not measure the distance between things and actions, such that the interval between the two cannot be anticipated. Rather, perception is of all possibilities or of the **virtual**; in Deleuze's cinematic schema, the *Gramme*.

> If the cinema goes beyond **perception**, it is in the sense that it reaches to the genetic element of all possible **perception**. [C1 85, 83]

- E. B. Y.

Perception-image

cross-reference: **Perception** 2.a.

Périclès et Verdi. La philosophie de François Châtelet (1988)

Deleuze had known François Châtelet when they were both completing their studies at the Sorbonne. Châtelet later directed the Department of Philosophy at l'Université de Vincennes–Paris VIII when Deleuze joined the faculty in 1969. This public homage to the philosopher is drawn from a Roundtable that took place three years after his death in 1985. Deleuze creates a portrait of Châtelet's philosophy from two composite sources: Pericles, the Athenian general who lived five centuries before the birth of Christ, and Verdi, the Italian opera composer who lived centuries afterward. Both figures address the 'crisis of reason' from different aspects:

Pericles represents the passivity of reason before an approaching disaster (i.e. the death of the Gods) and the temptation of the philosopher to embody the false pathos of the beautiful soul; Verdi represents the active decision to 'affirm something over nothing,' which embodies the image of reason in music itself as a force of affirmation. Thus, Deleuze writes, the philosophy of Châtelet must be regarded as a philosophy of decision, or of 'the singularity of the decision' to affirm something rather than nothing, a philosophy that serves as a contemporary antidote to nihilism and despair.
- G. L.

Phylum

(also, *machinic phylum*)

D&G understand evolution to be much more than a matter of mutation that occurs through reproduction's lines of filiation. They are especially interested in mutant, a-sexual, non-reproductive, and viral vectors of evolutionary mutation, as for example with the co-evolution of the wasp and the orchid. They apply a similar logic to the development of tools and technologies, positing a machinic phylogenesis. Just as there is an animal **phylum**, so are there phyla of machines or of art. They understand all of these phyla to be non-linear, constantly mutating, and imbricated within social and subjective formations. In Guattari's late work, they are one of the **four functors**.

1. The machines and machinic **assemblages** of the mecanosphere which belong to an evolutionary phylum analogous to the animal phylum in the biosphere.

> *We may speak of a* **machinic phylum**, *or technological lineage, wherever we find a constellation of singularities, prolongable by certain operations, which converge, and make the operations converge, upon one or several assignable traits of expression.* [TP 448, 406]

> *The* **phylogenetic** *evolution of machinism is expressed, at a primary level, by the fact that machines appear across 'generations,' one suppressing the other as it becomes obsolete.* [CM 40]

2. A non-linear evolutionary continuum of machinism that composes and is composed by **assemblages**.

> *The* **assemblages** *cut the* **phylum** *up into distinct, differentiated lineages, at the same time as the* **machinic phylum** *cuts across them all, taking leave of one to pick up again in another, or making them coexist.* [TP 449, 406]

3. Materiality as conceptualized by D&G; **matter** in movement and carrying particular qualities (as opposed to matter or materiality in general).

> *We always get back to this definition: the* **machinic phylum** *is materiality, natural or artificial, and both simultaneously; it is* **matter** *in movement, in* flux, *in variation, matter as a conveyor of* **singularities** *and traits of expression.* [TP 451, 409]

> *Unformed matter, the* **phylum**, *is not dead, brute, homogeneous matter, but a matter-movement bearing* **singularities** *or* **haecceities**, *qualities, and even operations (itinerant technological lineages).* [TP 563 512]

4. A domain of the discursive side of Guattari's **four-functor** schema; includes technical and scientific knowledge, schemas, blueprints; technology understood as socially formed.

> *By means of* [schizoanalytic] subjectivity, *without entirely ceasing to be a 'thinking reed,' man is currently adjacent to a reed 'that thinks for him,' to a* **machinic phylum** *that leads him well beyond his previous possibilities.* [SS 209]

- J. W.

Plane of composition

While D&G treat The Plane of Composition as a synonym for **The Plane of Immanence** in *A Thousand Plateaus*, it is useful to examine the distinctiveness they attribute to it in *What is Philosophy?*, especially in terms of the role of **chaos** and the separate operations of art and philosophy; as 'composition is the sole definition of art', what is actually composed by means of material (**affects, percepts,** and blocs of sensation) are themselves immaterial (just as art cannot be reduced to technique, **sensation** is both 'realized in the material', but 'the material passes into' it [WP 193]). In distinction from **milieus** and **territorial assemblages,** composition thus lays out a deterritorialized plane from chaos to the cosmos (or the future), through which it 'preserves' affects and percepts.

1. The medium in which (**chaotic**) matter and materials are arranged; the plane of art; in distinction from the plane of reference (science) and the **plane of immanence** or consistency (philosophy).

> *Art and philosophy crosscut the* **chaos** *and confront it, but it is not the same sectional* **plane** *[...].* [WP 66]

> *Art is not* **chaos** *but a* **composition** *of chaos that yields the vision or* **sensation** *[...].* [WP 204]

2. (Special Combination): *Aesthetic plane of composition*: The **expression** of a compound of **sensations** (**affects** and **percepts**) that does not exist outside of its material but nevertheless cannot be reduced to a (scientific) technical use of material (a 'technical plane of composition').

> *[...] technical composition [...] is not to be confused with* **aesthetic composition,** *which is the work of* **sensation.** [WP 141]

> **matter** *becomes* **expressive** *[...when] the compound of* **sensations** *is realized in the material [...] on a specifically* **aesthetic plane of composition.** [WP 196]

- E. B. Y.

Plane of consistency

cross-reference: **Plane of Immanence**

Plane of immanence

The 'Plane of Immanence' should be distinguished from '**Immanence**' proper: immanence, for Deleuze, refers to the ontological status of **difference**, while the *plane* (or 'plan', as the French term also connotes) of immanence refers to the absolute **milieu** upon which **concepts** are developed, as well as a *movement* that encompasses all blocs of space-time (in distinction from **chaos**, which as an ultimate disconnection of directional **forces**, has infinite *speed*). The second sense of movement is developed by Deleuze to explain the **movement-image**, in terms of equating **matter** with light.

1. In D&G's definition of philosophy, the unlimited **milieu** which enables connections and linkages of **concepts**; rather than functioning as a representation or image of thought that could be referenced (which would legitimate thoughts or place them within a structural system), the domain that enables thoughts to connect and vary, which is not itself 'thinkable'; an infinite movement that cannot be thought, in distinction from the infinite speed of the **intensive** concept that has subjective self-referents; the **Outside**.

> *Every* plane of immanence *is a One-All: it is [...] distributive [...].* [WP 50]

> *the problem of thought is infinite speed. But this speed requires a* milieu *that moves infinitely in itself–the* plane [of immanence], *the void, the horizon. [...] [T]he* plane [of immanence] *is the formless, unlimited absolute, neither surface nor volume but always fractal.* [WP 36]

> *The* plane of immanence *is [...] that which must be thought and that which cannot be thought.* [WP 59]

2. In D&G's discussion of **unconscious desire**, in distinction from the plane of organization where movement is always perceptible and symbolic, that region where movement is imperceptible and non-symbolic.

> *the* plane of consistency or immanence *[...] is necessarily perceived in its own right in the course of its construction: [...]* desire *directly invests the field of* perception. [TP 313, 284]

3. In Deleuze's discussion of the **movement-image**, the absolute state of **matter** or light and a series of blocs of space-time (or mobile sections) that is, diffused, conditioned, reflected,

concealed, rigidified, and brought to consciousness by the vagaries of the movement-image (**affection-images, perception-images, action-images**, etc.).

> *This infinite set of all images constitutes a kind of* **plane of Immanence** *[...]: not something hidden behind the image, but on the contrary the absolute identity of the image and movement [...] it is a mobile section, [...] a bloc of space-time [...].* [C1 61, 58–9]
>
> *images are formed in the universe (*action-images, affection-images, perception-images*). But [...] For the moment we only have movements, which are called images in order to distinguish them from everything that they have not yet become. [...] the* **plane of immanence** *is entirely made up of Light.* [C1 62, 60]

– E. B. Y.

Plato

Deleuze claims that, unlike **Aristotle**, Plato is not interested in making categorical divisions, but in distinguishing between authentic and inauthentic beings, between the 'true' and 'false': 'selection'. He notes, though, that this method is somewhat ironic since nothing in the material world can ever fit the true model of the idea—they can only be more or less authentic. Despite this, his imperative, inspired by **Nietzsche**, to 'overturn' or 'reverse' Platonism, as he insists, 'should conserve many Platonic characteristics', which are 1) that selection and distinction can be considered a primary task of philosophy, and 2) that ideas which enable selections are not transcendental *per se*, but are a 'part of objects themselves, allowing them to be grasped as **signs**' (DR 76, 63). So, Deleuze's reversal of Platonism involves the insistence that ideas are not abstract, static, other-worldly models of things, but structures that enable 'questioning' and 'problematizing'. In this sense, the status of appearances in the material world are elevated: they are precisely that which allow or enable questioning to take place. In other words, things in the world do not 'resemble' models or ideas, they (apparently) resemble one another to the extent that they express a **difference** that is hidden within their dynamic relationships. It is perhaps here, where, as Deleuze states, 'the Heraclitan world still growls in Platonism' (DR 71,

59): if **becoming** or 'change' (which is unforeseeable) is the only 'truth' of the world, then systems which are *selected* would be those which affirm that things in the 'material' world—appearances, etc., are expressions of difference and **becoming**, even and especially insofar as they 'resemble' each other and resemble themselves. This is the 'test' of **eternal return** as Deleuze describes it in **Nietzsche**. - E. B. Y.

Post-media era

Technological evolution can both enhance and diminish processes of **subjectification** which are machinic and inextricably linked to the rise of the network society in the information age. Guattari believed that despite the work of *IWC* in infantilizing mass media, producing passivity, encouraging cynicism and abdication of responsibility, reductionistically bound to equivalence, a new participatory media held great potential. Writing in the early 1990s, Guattari envisaged entry into an era understood as post-mass in the sense that interactivity would provide the tools for resingularization. The rise of *minoritarian* user groups with new modes of organization and the capacities to form alliances among themselves and with traditional organizations, inspired Guattari to tentatively theorize the internet as a site of **desire** driven by dissensus yet composing a collective **diagram** of commonalities. Given the saturation of the videotext service Minitel in France, internet use in France in 1990 remained very low, hypertext was brand new, and the World Wide Web would not emerge until the following year, followed by the later browsers that defined the Web experience, right up to the social media of our day. Guattari's observations were tentative because he did not live to see the promising new modalities of subjectification in action.

>1.a. An era in which the quality of interactions between users and creators that shows potential to reinvent communication, redemocratize consumption and enrich processes of **subjectification**.
>
>>*A way out of the present mass* **media** *era and entry into what I call a* **post-media** *era could be envisaged from a coming perspective,*

given four series of factors: 1) foreseeable technological development; 2) the necessary redefining of relations between producers and creators; 3) the establishment of new social practices and their influence on the development of the **media**; *4) the development of news.* [Guattari, 2002, 18]

b. An era in which three directions were envisaged: the first would involve new public and private forms of cooperative research into media production; the second would place limits on intellectual property as more and more user communities got involved in info-technology system design; thirdly, national media ethics commissions and public re-education programs would be founded with the power to curb corporate and state abuses of broadcast news media especially in light of the first Gulf War's circulation of a dominant mass mediatic homogenesis of subjectification.

*The junction of the audiovisual screen, the telematic screen and the computer screen could lead to a real activation of a collective sensibility and intelligence. The current equation (***media***=passivity) will perhaps disappear more quickly than one would think.* [GR 26]

c. Minoritarian **becomings** that link media upheavals to planetary problematics.

The **post-mediatic** *revolution to come will have to be guided to an unprecedented degree by those minority groups which are still the only ones to have realized the mortal risk for humanity of questions such as: the nuclear arms race; world famine; irreversible ecological degradation; mass-***mediatic** *pollution of collective subjectivities.* [SC 61]

2. An extensive use of Minitel services by the free radio movement in France to constitute groups of supporters resulting in cross-platform minoritarian resistance.

[...] the totality of technical and human means available must permit the establishment of a veritable feedback system between the auditors and the broadcast team: whether through direct intervention by phone, though opening 'studio doors', through interviews or programs based on listener-mades cassettes, etc. [...] We realize here that radio constitutes but one central element of a whole range of communication means [...]. [SS 74–5]

- G. G.

Prigogine, Ilya

cross-reference: **Stengers, Isabelle and Ilya Prigogine**

Proposition

1. The determination of truth, possibility, **value**, and belief according to a logic of **denotation, signification**, and **manifestation** which envelops **sense** indirectly between those relationships (but does not contain sense in any particular determination, as sense is a 'fourth dimension').

> **sense**, *or that which is expressed by the* **proposition**, *would be irreducible to individual states of affairs, particular images, personal beliefs, and universal or general concepts [...]. In truth, the attempt to make this fourth dimension evident is a little like* **Carroll***'s Snark hunt. Perhaps the dimension is the hunt itself, and sense is the Snark.* [LS 23, 19]

- E. B. Y.

Proust, Marcel

Proust's *In Search of Lost Time* is famous for its portrayal of **involuntary memory**, such as the 'episode of the madeleine', where the resemblance between the qualities of the madeleine that Marcel perceives brings back memories and sensations of his time in Combray. What interests Deleuze, however, is not the resemblances that produce reminiscence, but the manner in which the fragment of the past becomes the telescope through which to perceive the pure past. That is, if the taste of the madeleine *envelops* all the differences of Combray in general, then it is an experience of the past in a *new* way that was never lived, a **virtual** 'reality' that is not present but produces signs of art: to *develop* these enveloped signs is the function of the artist. If Proust is a '**symptomatolgist**' like **Sacher-Masoch** or **Kafka**, it is because his work portrays 'a symptomatology of different worlds' where the experience of time in its 'pure' state involves an eternal and *interminable* return of the signs of reminiscence; from Deleuze's perspective, this would perhaps explain why *In Search of Lost Time* is one of the longest novels in history. From here, Deleuze distinguishes between the different types of **signs** of the 'Search': worldly, amorous, sensual, and aesthetic—and the experiences of cruelty, jealousy, joy and idealism which, respectively, correspond to them.

Deleuze also comments on the portrayal of sexuality in Proust's work. On the one hand, there is the necessary deception in the concealed signs of the beloved of the opposite sex, since the two worlds never fully communicate, and on the other hand, jealously gives way to guilt in the experience of a 'hermaphroditism' and homosexuality which is *indifferent*, where the signs are revealed through 'Sodom and Gomorrah' (for men and women, respectively). For this second type of sexuality, Deleuze emphasizes Proust's 'vegetable metaphor', where each sex contains in itself both organs but is essentially sterile. And yet, even 'the hermaphrodite requires a third party (the insect) so that the female part may be fertilized or the male part may fertilize' (P 136); thus there is a third type of 'transexulaity' where each sex realizes that it contains in itself (genetically or embryologically), an undeveloped aspect of the opposite sex 'with which it cannot communicate' (P 135). In this sense, the very distinctiveness of each sex is no longer empirical or **actual**, but is **virtual** or immemorial (each gender becomes a **partial object**) and they seek (sometimes in the 'opposite' sex, sometimes in the 'same') what is masculine in a woman and what is feminine in a man in order to include or 'fertilize' that part of itself that it has no access to. Deleuze will note in *Difference and Repetition* that such virtual or partial objects that enable a 'contiguity' between two hermaphroditic sexes, much like the signs of reminiscence, are 'shreds of pure past' (DR 126, 101) that can never be really experienced in the present (but are only the source of the 'persistent question' of life and death); when the Proustian theme is taken up again in *Anti-Oedipus* to characterize syntheses of **desiring-machines** which are 'molecular', the emphasis is that they do not relate organs or parts to 'molar' subjects but are involved in a 'non-human sexuality' that constructs **bodies without organs**. - E. B. Y.

Proust and Signs

Marcel Proust et les signes (1964)

Deleuze's work on **Proust** was originally published in 1964 and revised and expanded in 1972. The original text, like Deleuze's work on **Carroll** and **Sacher-Masoch** (as well as his work with Guattari on **Kafka**), provides an original complementary philosophy which resonates much more with Deleuze's work than it does with the conventional interpretations of those writers. In this case, Deleuze focuses on the classification of **signs**, perhaps foregrounding an interest that will be developed further in the *Cinema* books in terms of the connection of signs to **action** (movement), memory, and the **virtual** (time). Many concepts introduced in the expansions to the text in 1972, such as **partial objects** and the **body without organs**, resonate with those from the Capitalism and Schizophrenia project, on which he was working concurrently. - E. B. Y.

Qualisign

cross-reference: **Affect**ion-Image (**any space whatever**)

Reason

Deleuze's usage of this term varies depending on which philosopher or thinker he is channeling; in **Hume** and **Spinoza**, reason takes on an affirmative role, while in his reading of **Nietzsche** and de Sade, it has negative connotations.

1.a. In Deleuze's reading of **Hume**, the ability of the mind to comprehend causes and effects, and form (eternal) relations between disparate terms or ideas; the **faculty** which understands and facilitates morals and passions without simply subduing them (but itself lacks **morality** and is dispassionate).

> Reason *has indeed a double role. It helps us to know causes and effects, and it tells us also whether or not 'we chose means*

> *insufficient for the design'd end'; but even so, an end has to be projected [by* **morality***].* [ES 126]

> *Undoubtedly,* **reason** *influences practice [...]. But we cannot say that* **reason** *produces an action, that passion contradicts it, or even that* **reason** *thwarts a passion.* [ES 33]

b. An operation of the mind, based on **habit** and the **imagination**, that makes inferences (the relations of causes and effects) or deals with certainty (on the relations of quantities, qualities, and contrarieties).

> *under the influence of association,* **imagination** *becomes* **reason** *and the fancy finds constancy.* [ES 123]

> *we must distinguish between two kinds of* **reason***: the* **reason** *that proceeds on the basis of certainty (intuition and demonstration) and the* **reason** *that proceeds in terms of probabilities (experimental* **reason***, understanding).* [ES 65]

2. In Deleuze's reading of **Spinoza**, the perception of: the natural order and connection of things, causality, and how things exist in common (common notions); an adequate idea of the relation between bodies, and the elimination of sad passions (which result from an inadequate idea of the body) in favor of joyful **affects**. [SEP, SPP]

> **Reason** *is defined in two ways, which show that man is not born rational but also how he becomes rational.* **Reason** *is: 1. an effort to select and organize good encounters [...] 2. the perception and comprehension [...] from which one deduces other relations (*reasoning*) and on the basis of which one experiences new feelings, active ones this time (feelings that are born of* **reason***).* [SPP 55]

3. In Deleuze's reading of the Marquis de Sade, the justification or vehicle for negation, destruction, denigration, exploitation, and universal crime which, through such demonstration, exposes the hypocrisies of institutions.

> *in the work of Sade [...] the demonstrative function is based on universal negativity as an active process, and on universal negation as an Idea of pure* **reason** [CC 35]

4. In Deleuze's reading of **Nietzsche** and critique of **Kant**, a

reactive **morality** and will to nothingness which prevents a genetical critique and affirmation of **life**.

> **reason** *appears and persuades us to continue being docile because it says to us: it is you who are giving the orders.* [N 86, 92–3]

> *Knowledge is thought itself, but thought subject to* **reason** *[...] But does not critique, understood as critique of knowledge itself, express new* **forces** *capable of giving thought another sense?* [N 94, 100–1]

- E. B. Y.

Recollection-image

1.a. In Deleuze's reading of **Bergson,** the condition of **perception** where the present image is in a continual state of resemblance with images that are recalled (rather than images in the present evoking or instigating a memory); the condition of the **contraction** of the present with the past.

> *The appeal to* recollection *is this jump by which I place myself in the* **virtual,** *in the past, in a particular region of the past, at a particular level of* **contraction.** *[...]* recollection-images *[...] are* **actualized** *or embodied [...]. We do not move from the present to the past, from* **perception** *to* **recollection,** *but from the past to the present, from* **recollection** *to perception.* [B 63]

b. In Deleuze's cinematic schema, a type of **time-image**, such as a flashback or dream, where the past is prolonged, or lived, in the present; images brought about by a break with the sensory-motor schema of the movement image (opsigns and sonsigns), and which intimate the **crystal image.** [C2]

> *We have seen that* **subjectivity** *already emerged in the* **movement-image;** *it appears as soon as there is a gap between a received and an executed movement [...]. Now, on the contrary, the* **recollection-image** *[...] makes full use of the gap, it assumes it [...]. Subjectivity, then, takes on a new sense, which is no longer motor or material, but temporal and spiritual: that which 'is added' to* **matter,** *not what distends it* [C2 45, 47]

- E. B. Y.

Redundancy

In information theory, redundancy refers to the degree of efficiency of message transmission. Human language includes a great deal of redundancy, as compared, for example, to the low redundancy of computer algorithms. From the mid-1950s, when he began attending Lacan's weekly seminars, Guattari became fascinated with semiotics, especially with its non-linguistic aspects such as biological or chemical signals and mathematical or musical notation. He identified different types of redundancy for different types of codes, symbols, and signs. Guattari associates the high degree of redundancy found in language with its capacity for exercising social constraint, as in Lacan's theory of the symbolic order. He therefore views linguistic (or semiological) redundancy as a social phenomenon. The various types of redundancy are presented in detail in the 1977 French edition of *The Molecular Revolution* and in *The Machinic Unconscious*. A modified and streamlined version is featured in *A Thousand Plateaus*, especially in the chapters on order words and regimes of signs.

1.a. In information theory, the **repetition** of information which enables interlocutors to reconstruct a message even if parts of it are garbled.

> Redundancy *furnishes a guarantee against errors in transmission, since it permits the receptor to reconstruct the message even if some of its elements are lacking on the basis of is a priori knowledge of the structure of the language.* [Moles, 1968, 54]

b. The portion of a message that does not contribute any information.

> *The dominant position that information theory occupied at the core of linguistics at that time led to the adoption of a definition of language as merely a means of transmitting messages, the remainder being simply noise and* **redundancy**. [MU 23]

c. The constraints imposed by the characteristics of a particular language.

> *The fact that the* **redundancy** *of English is 50 per cent means that*

half of what we write in English is determined by the structure of the language and half is freely chosen. [Moles, 1968, 45]

2. Adapting information theory to his general semiotics, in an early chapter of **The Machinic Unconscious**, Guattari defines two types of redundancy—of **resonance** and of interaction, the first associated with signification and the other with real existence.

> abstract machines *'charge'* themselves with **redundancies** of **resonance** *(signification)* or **redundancies** *of interaction ('real' existence).* [MU 47]

3.a. Later in **The Machinic Unconscious**, Guattari identifies 17 different types of redundancy which come to the forefront in different **assemblages**. The three basic redundancy types are intensive (or machinic), semiotic, and semiological. In addition, there are seven types of semiological redundancy, which in turn give rise to seven types of consciential redundancy.

> *Within each particular* **assemblage,** *the accent will be placed upon such and such type of* **redundancy** *[...]* [MU 209]

b. (Special Combination): *intensive or machinic redundancy*: The redundancy peculiar to one-way messages conveyed by non-linguistic encoding, as in biology, chemistry, or physics.

> *Intensive* **redundancies** *advance by way of intrinsic encoding, without involving specific* **strata** *of* **expression;** *thus they themselves remain the prisoners of encoding stratification.* [MR 130]

c. (Special Combination): *semiotic redundancy*: The redundancy of two-way messages conveyed by non-linguistic semiotic encoding, especially as concerns components of passage like faciality or the **refrain**.

> *There is no longer a basic transmitting* **assemblage,** *no longer an irreversible direction for the trajectory of the* **redundancies** *of the messenger entities which we shall call here:* semiotic **redundancies.** [MU 203]

d. (Special Combination): *semiological redundancy*: Both language and subjectivation emerge when **semiotic redundancies** (c.) are differentiated into the semiological poles of expression and content; Guattari arranges these seven types onto a triangle, and first describes the triangle's three points, then its three sides, then the center [MU 205].

ii. (Special Combinations): I. *redundancies of morphemes of the referent,* II. *a-signifying redundancies,* III. *iconic redundancies*: Correspond to the points of the semiological triangle (respectively, referent, symbol, thought or reference).

iii. (Special Combinations): IV. *redundancies of designation,* V. *redundancies of representation,* VI. *redundancies of signification*: Located on the sides of the semiological triangle, since designation expresses the relation between symbol and referent, representation that between thought and referent, and signification that between thought and symbol.

iv. (Special Combination): VII. *subjective redundancy*: Located in the center of the triangle; established from the redundancies of designation, representation, and signification; illustrates Guattari's contention that the semiological regime of language **striates** and captures subjectivity, subjugating it to the whims of the tyrannical signifier.

> *subjective* **redundancies** *[5d] take support from* **redundancies** *of* **signification,** *representation,* **denotation** *[5c] and these last on those of the* **sign-machines,** *the* **referent,** *and the* **iconic** *and conceptual world [5b].* [MU 211]

e. (Special Combination): *consciential redundancies*: Guattari defines seven consciential redundancies which emerge when a deterritorializing consciential **resonance** invades the seven **semiological redundancies** (d. i–iv); further constraining subjectivity to the point of madness, the seven consciential redundancies are: hysterical, interpretive, anxious, paranoid, obsessional, phobic, schizoid.

> **consciential redundancies** *have a function of determining* **subjectivity** *at the point where it is least discernible, at the point where it escapes all reference, all relations of the figure-ground, subject-object type, etc.* [MU 211]

4.a. Streamlining Guattari's 17-part typology of redundancy, in *A Thousand Plateaus* D&G define two types, *frequency* and *resonance*, which they associate with significance and **subjectivity**, respectively.

> Redundancy *has two forms,* frequency *and* resonance; *the first concerns the significance of information, the second concerns the* subjectivity *of communication.* [TP 88, 79]

b. (Special Combination): *redundancy of frequency*: In information theory, the frequency with which certain signs, phonemes, letters, or groups of letters appear in a given language.

> *Thus we call approximation to the order of 0 the succession of letters or phonemes belonging to the language and chosen at random. The approximation to the order of 1 is constituted by random choice taking into account the average* frequency *of units.* [Martinet, 1969, 331]

c. (Special Combination): *signifying redundancy*: For D&G, frequency expresses a relative **deterritorialization**; the type of **redundancy** characteristic of the signifying **regime of signs**, in which signs refer only to other signs.

> *In the signifying regime,* **redundancy** *is a phenomenon of objective* **frequency** *involving signs or elements of signs (the phonemes, letters, and groups of letters in a language) [...]* [ATP 132]

d. (Special Combination): *redundancy of resonance*: D&G's term for what Martinet describes as second-order redundancy; that which operates through the repetition of information through grammatical forms like personal pronouns or proper names; D&G associate this greater order of redundancy with subjectivity, rather than merely with signification.

> *The approximation to the second order takes into account transitional probabilities, which is to say probability according to the preceding unit [...].* **Redundancy** *is at its greatest with second-order approximation.* [Martinet, 1969, 331]

> *That is why subjective* **redundancy** *[of resonance, 5d, 7cii] seems both the graft itself onto signifying* **redundancy** *[of frequency] and to derive from it, as second-degree redundancy.* [TP 147, 133]

e. (Special Combination): *subjective resonance* or *subjective redundancy*: This type of redundancy pulls **subjectivity** into a **black hole** of absolute deterritorialization. (Guattari located this black hole at the center of his semiological and consciential triangles of redundancy; see definition 2 above). This type of redundancy characterizes the post-signifying **regime of signs**, in which a sign detaches itself and takes off on a line of flight.

> *In the post-signifying regime [...] the* **redundancy** *is one of* subjective **resonance** *involving above all shifters, personal pronouns and proper names... [There is] a* **black hole** *attracting consciousness and passion and in which they resonate.* [TP 147, 133]

> **redundancies of resonance**... *tend to be emptied of their substance; their own movement leads them to lose all support from stratifications,* flows *and* codes. [MU 211]

5. In D&G's theory of the **order-word**, the repetitive relation between the statement and the act.

> *The order-word itself is the* **redundancy** *of the act and the statement. Newspapers, news, proceed by* **redundancy,** *in that they tell us what we 'must' think, retain, respect, etc.* [TP 87, 79]

- J. W.

Refrain

Inspired by the study of bird songs in animal **ethology**, in *The Machinic Unconscious* Guattari borrows from music the notion of the refrain or ritornello in order to describe repeated images, gestures, rituals, or sounds that enable both human and animal social **assemblages** to hold together their heterogeneous components. In *A Thousand Plateaus*, examples of refrains which hold together assemblages include bird songs which organize mating rituals or territorial defense, a child comforting itself by whistling in the dark, or military marching songs.

1.a. Markers of human or animal **territories**, as observed in **ethology** or ethnography.

> *In a general sense, we call a* **refrain** *any aggregate of matters of*

expression that draws a **territory** *and develops into territorial motifs and landscapes (there are optical, gestural, motor, etc.,* **refrains***).* [TP 356, 323]

b. An element capable of holding **territory** or **assemblage** together.

Even in a territorial **assemblage**, *it may be the most* **deterritorialized** *component, the deterritorializing vector, in other words, the* **refrain***, that assures the consistency of the* **territory**. [TP 361, 327]

2. In response to **deterritorialization**, the **refrain** facilitates the creation of psychic entities which enable modern subjectivity to function outside of archaic **assemblages** like tribes or clans.

The **deterritorialization** *of his* Umwelt *has led man to invent* **diagrammatic** *operators such as* **faciality** *and* **refrains** *enabling him to produce new machinic territorialities.* [MU 120]

Instead of being assembled on the basis of **territorialized** *systems, such as the tribe, the ethnic group, the corporation, and the province, the subjectification of these* **refrains** *is internalized and individuated on the machinic territories which constitute egos, roles, persons, loves, feelings of 'belonging to.'* [MU 110]

3.a. Guattari uses the idea of the **refrain** to show that animals creatively acquire learned behaviors and that humans still rely on so-called innate ethological rhythms.

the study of **refrains** *deserves special attention because it seems, in fact, that their entry into animal and human* **assemblages** *systematically thwarts the rigid oppositions between the acquired and the innate, between a rigorous biological determinism and a freedom of invention.* [MU 116]

b. A catalyst for creativity or change.

A **territorial** *or territorialized component may set about budding, producing: this is the case for the* **refrain***, so much so that we should perhaps call all cases of this kind* **refrains***.* [TP 359, 325]

- J. W.

Repetition

Repetition, on the one hand, combines central issues in Deleuze's readings of **Hume** (regarding the tendency towards religious belief), **Bergson** (regarding **habit**), **Freud** (regarding the **unconscious**), Sacher-Masoch (regarding idealism), and **Nietzsche** (regarding **eternal return**). On the other hand, it testifies to his own contribution to the history of philosophy, where he locates it as the **paradox** of **difference** (whether this difference is biological, aesthetic, sociological, technological, etc.). Repetition will be distinguished from difference in that the former concerns displacement and disguise *of* the latter, where difference incessantly diverges and decenters within the systems that disguise it. While Deleuze's interest in these senses of repetition resonate throughout his work with Guattari (the syntheses of **desiring-machines**, the **milieu** within the **assemblage**, and in the distinctions between variation, variety, and variable with regard to **Chaos**), its strict usage can be found in his explanation of **passive synthesis** and **eternal return**.

1.a. In **Freud**, the function of the system of drives that re-live traumatic events based on the impact of a memory.

> *According to psychological knowledge, the memory of an experience (that is, its continuing operative power) depends on a factor which is called the magnitude of the impression and on the frequency with which the same impression is repeated.* [Freud, 1966, p. 300]

b. In Deleuze's reading of **Freud** and **Sacher-Masoch**, the *condition* of the pleasure principle which also exists independently of that principle; an originary **force** which precedes the compulsion to re-live traumatic events or discharge bound excitation, which can itself be sexualized such that it either becomes the vehicle of an apathetic, sadistic, demonstration, or a suspended, masochistic idealization.

> **Repetition** *characterized the binding process inasmuch as it is* repetition *of the very moment of excitation, the moment of the emergence of life;* repetition *is what holds together the instant; it constitutes simultaneity. But inseparable from this form of the* repetition *we must conceive of another which in its turn* repeats

> *what was before the instant—[...] Beyond Eros we encounter Thanatos; [...] beyond the* repetition *that links, the* repetition *that erases and 'destroys.'* [CC 114]
>
> Repetition *does occur in* masochism, *but it is totally different from sadistic* repetition: *in Sade it is a function of acceleration and condensation and in Masoch it is characterized by the 'frozen' quality and the suspense.* [CC 34]

c. In Deleuze's explanation of automata and brute nature, the mechanism of fixated drives where the thing or impulse is primary to its displacement and disguise.

> *The concepts of fixation and regression, along with trauma and the primal scene, express this first element. As a consequence,* repetition *would in principle conform to the model of a material, bare and brute* repetition, *understood as the* repetition *of the same: the idea of an 'automatism' in this context expresses the modality of a fixated drive, or rather, of* repetition *conditioned by fixation or regression.* [DR 128, 103]

d. In Deleuze's explanation of spiritual nature, a mode of binding or **passive synthesis** which is not systematically resolvable in the form of pleasure (in distinction from **Freud**); the contractile, underlying feature of **habit** before **contractions** are contemplated to generalize **differences** between repetitions in the form of expectation or need; that which is a feature of the viscera in distinction from (and in conjunction with) the mnemonic, **differentiating** feature of the mind. [CC, DR, DI]

> *we must beware of confusing the activity of reproduction with the passion for* repetition *which underlies it. The* repetition *of an excitation has as its true object the elevation of the* passive synthesis *to a power which implies the pleasure principle along with its future and past applications.* Repetition *in* habit *or the passive synthesis of binding is thus 'beyond' the[pleasure] principle.* [DR 121, 98]
>
> Repetition *is [...] a kind of* difference; *only, it's a difference always outside itself [...]. Indeed we saw that difference, in its very origin and in the act of this origin, was a* contraction. *[...]. The mind, in its origin, is only the contraction of identical elements, and by virtue of this, it is memory. [...] By contracting itself, the element of* repetition *coexists with itself—one might say, multiplies itself and maintains itself. [...] The identical elements of material* repetition

blend together [...]; this **contraction** presents both something new, i.e. difference, and degrees which are the degrees of this difference itself. [DI 47]

2.a. In **Hume**, an operation of the mind which reasons based on **habit** and experience, and also forms fictitious beliefs based on the **imagination**.

> [...] suppose that [...the] multitude of views or glimpses of an object proceeds not from experience, but from a voluntary act of the **imagination** [...]. For though custom and education produce belief by such a **repetition**, as is not derived from experience, yet this requires a long tract of time, along with a very frequent and undesigned **repetition**. In general we may pronounce, that a person who would voluntarily **repeat** any idea in his mind, though supported by one past experience, would be no more inclined to believe the existence of its object, than if he had contented himself with one survey of it. [Hume, 2003, 101; modified]

b. In Deleuze's reading of **Hume**, that which ultimately serves as the basis for experience, in distinction from **habit**, which initially forms expectation or probabilities based on links made in the **imagination** from that basis in experience.

> Experience causes us to observe particular conjunctions. Its essence is the **repetition** of similar cases.[...] Repetition becomes a progression, or even a production, when we no longer see it in relation to the objects **repeated**, because, if we do, it changes, discovers and produces nothing. It becomes a production as soon as we see it from the point of view of the mind which contemplates it, for it produces a new impression in it. [ES 68]

3.a. In Deleuze's discussion of faith in **Hume**, that which cannot serve as an image of the world because it is both determined only by experience and is absolutely singular; the basis of which leads to transcending experience (false beliefs) and transcending the world (illegitimate uses of causality and religion).

> there are no physical objects or objects of **repetition** except in the world. The world as such is essentially the Unique. It is a fiction of the **imagination**—never an object of the understanding. [ES 75]

> [There are] two fictitious uses of the principle of causality [based on **repetition**]. The first was defined by **repetitions** which do not

proceed from experience; the second, by a particular object—the world—which cannot be repeated, *and which is not, properly speaking, an object.* [ES 78]

Habit *is a principle which cannot invoke experience without [...] invoking fictitious* repetitions. [ES 71]

b. In Deleuze's reading of **Kierkegaard**, that which, on the one hand, opposes laws of nature (engendering novelty), but, on the other hand, must be continuous (**eternally recurring**) rather than momentary to reach its full power.

The **Nietzschean** repetition *has nothing to do with the* **Kierkegaardian** repetition; *or, more generally,* repetition *in the* eternal return *has nothing to do with the Christian* repetition. *[...]. There is a* difference *in nature between what returns 'once and for all' and what returns for each and every time, or for an infinite number of times.* [LS 340, 300–1]

4.a. In **Bergson**, on the one hand, the mechanism of **habit** which is automatic, and on the other hand, that which the spontaneous memory takes as its singular object.

how can we overlook the radical **difference** *between that which must be built up by* repetition *and that which is essentially incapable of being* repeated*? Spontaneous recollection is perfect from the outset; time can add nothing to its image without disfiguring it; it retains in memory its place and date. On the contrary, a learnt recollection passes out of time in the measure that the lesson is better known; it becomes more and more impersonal, more and more foreign to our past life.* Repetition, *therefore, in no sense effects the conversion of the first into the last; its office is merely to utilize more and more the movements by which the first was continued, in order to organize them together and, by setting up a mechanism, to create a bodily habit.* [Bergson, 1913, 95]

b. In Deleuze's reading of **Bergson, matter** which proceeds by real succession on a physical level, in distinction from **memory**, which proceeds by virtual coexistence on a psychic level.

with coexistence, repetition *must be re-introduced into* duration—*a 'psychic'* repetition *of a completely different type than the 'physical'* repetition *of matter; a* repetition *of 'planes' rather than of elements on a single plane; virtual instead of actual* repetition. *The whole of our past is played, restarts,* **repeats** *itself at the same time, on all the levels that it sketches out* [B 60–1]

5.a. In Deleuze's explanation of **eternal return**, the displacement and disguise of **difference**; the simultaneous presence, whether in space or in time, of a **virtual** object that is displaced and disguised within two or more instances.

> **Repetition** *is constituted not from one present to another, but between the two coexistent* **series** *that these presents form in function of the* **virtual object** *(object = x). [...]* **Repetition** *is constituted only with and through the disguises which affect the terms and relations of the real series [...].* [DR 129, 105]

b. A permeable or otherwise fluid form whose content or meaning is dynamic; a form which does not replicate or represent objects or ideas but expresses **difference** by virtue of likeness.

> **Repetition** *is the formless being of all* **differences** *[...]. The ultimate element of* **repetition** *is the disparate, which stands opposed to the identity of representation.* [DR 69, 57]

- E. B. Y.

Resonance

In information theory, resonance is a non-linguistic mode of communication that allows different kinds of orders to enter into a relation. The concept was introduced by Deleuze in *The Logic of Sense*, and taken up by Guattari in the 1977 French version of *Molecular Revolution* and in *The Machinic Unconscious*.

1.a. Term Deleuze borrows from Gilbert Simondon, who defines it as a kind of communication between two orders.

> *Internal* **resonance** *is the most primitive mode of communication between realities of different orders.* [Simondon, 1964, 31 n. 11]

b. For Deleuze, the **mode** of relation between two disjunctive series.

> *At least at the beginning, the phantasm is nothing else but the*

internal resonance *of two independent sexual series.* [LS 262, 228–9]

2.a. Term Guattari adapts from both Deleuze and **René Thom**; for the latter, the mode of production of linguistic meaning, described as an encounter between two dynamical systems, the utterance and the brain, that interact similarly to two tuning forks which, when brought close together, begin to vibrate at the same rate.

> *all interaction rests, in the last analysis, upon a phenomenon of* resonance [Thom, 1983, 171]

b. (Special Combination): *Redundancy of resonance*: Signification; see **redundancy** (definitions 2 and 3 c i-ii).

c. (Special Combination): *Node of resonance*: A centering of various semiological elements which produces a **black hole** capturing and emitting semiotic particles.

> *The* **black hole** *effect is produced by the node of* resonance *that emerges when a point of recentering is constituted between semiological* **redundancies**. [MU 210]

3.a. The ability of apparatuses of capture to align and center the semiotic and Oedipal triangles in order to impose homogenizing structure and **stratification,** such as the individualized subject.

> *a circular white screen divides the effects of* resonance *between the semiological triangle, the ego, and the object.* [MU 76]

b. (Special Combination): *universal resonator*: Capitalism's ability to unify, hierarchize, and homogenize various modes of subjectivation.

> *All the systems of re-enclosure and arborescence combine and enter into* resonance *in order to block the potential rhizomatic 'pressures' of a-signifying semiotic components.* [MU 80]

- J. W.

Reterritorialization

cross-reference: Territory; Territorialization

Reume

cross-reference: Liquid Perception

Rhizome

The term 'rhizome' first appears in Deleuze and Guattari's text on **Kafka**, where they draw on his story 'The Burrow' to suggest that, like the underground labyrinth in that story, his work lacks the usual linear narrative structure and can be 'entered' into at any point to map out connections with other points. Such a rhizome, they suggest, also accounts for the content of his stories, which involve *processes*—whether unending bureaucratic or juridical processes, or those involving **becoming-animal**. What matters in those cases are the **intensive** variations and unlimited 'lines of flight'.

The real implications of the concept, however, are developed utilizing the language of botany to introduce the reader to *A Thousand Plateaus* (and in fact to discuss the status of 'books') before listing six 'principle' characteristics of the rhizome: 1) connection (vs. order or model), 2) heterogeneity of **coding**, where semiotic chains connect to other **assemblages**, 3) **multiplicity** in determination, magnitude, or dimension (vs. unity in subject or object), 4) a-signifying ruptures of **segmentation, stratification**, and **territory**, 5) cartographic production (vs. *tracing*), and 6) 'decalcomania', in that any tracing (as with a decal that is transferred onto another medium) would in fact 'be put back on the map' because apparent reproduction gives way to asymmetry or **difference**. With this as a starting point, the concept is elaborated throughout their text.

It is important to note that in new-media theory, D&G are sometimes treated as prophets of the internet; such theorists often point out that the internet functions like the rhizome because of its connective and non-hierarchical nature (see, for example, the work of Stuart Moulthrop and George Landow). A closer look at features of the rhizome, however, arguably precludes such a straightforward parallel (Deleuze in fact mentions that 'Our current inspiration doesn't come from computers but from the microbiology of the brain: the brain's organized like a rhizome, more like grass than a tree' [NG 149]). For example, to be subjected to the 'choice' of a hypertext perhaps does not *map* out a path or **becoming**, but arguably makes a *tracing* between points of a binary and symbolic system. A misapplication of the term to technology in fact often coincides with a similar misreading of Deleuze's use of the **virtual** (i.e. virtual reality). While the concepts certainly can be fruitfully applied to types of technological novelty, it is also useful to consult Deleuze's concept of the **haptic** as well as D&G's portrayal of the **abstract machine**, **coding**, and **desiring-machines** to more directly discern their views on technology.

1.a. In **Kafka's** short story 'The Burrow' (according to D&G), the burrow characterized by an underground, labyrinth-like structure that was created haphazardly and contains many impasses and offshoots.

> *The* **burrow** *is not a mere hole for taking refuge in. When I stand [...] surrounded by my piled-up stores, surveying the ten passages which begin there, raised and sunken passages, vertical and rounded passages, wide and narrow passages, as the general plan dictates, and all alike still and empty, ready by their various routes to conduct me to all the other rooms, which are also still and empty [...].* [Kafka 1946, 483]

b. In D&G's reading of **Kafka**, a term to characterize his *œuvre* which presents many interpretive impasses and does not present a linear narrative with a distinct guiding thread.

> *[Kafka's] work is a* **rhizome**, *a burrow [...] We will enter, then, by any point whatsoever; none matters more than another[...]. We will be trying only to discover [...] what the map of the* **rhizome** *is and how the map is modified if one enters by another point.* [K 3]

> *some animals are* [**rhizomatic**], *in their pack form. Rats are* **rhizomes**. *Burrows are too, in all of their functions of shelter, supply, movement, evasion, and breakout.* [TP 6]

2.a. In D&G's discussion of **desire,** a model where components or points are arranged in the same manner that plants with a rhizomatic structure such as grass grow, in distinction from plants with an *arborescent* structure such as trees: a tree has a 'center' or a 'root' from which elements branch off, while grasses do not have roots but decentered stems or buds which spread sideways along a surface; in D&G's critique of **Freudian subjectivity,** a determination of space and time which does not *trace* a pre-established route or genealogy, but draws a *map* that has no pre-established trajectory; also, the manner in which the **unconscious** is constructed experimentally rather than reproduced from some archetype. [K, TP, NG, D]

> [...] *unlike trees or their roots, the* **rhizome** *connects any point to any other point, and its traits are not necessarily linked to traits of the same nature [...].* [TP 23, 21]

> *The* **rhizome** *is altogether different, a map and not a tracing.[...] What distinguishes the map from the tracing is that it is entirely oriented toward an experimentation in contact with the real.* [TP 13, 12]

> *the issue is never to reduce the* **unconscious** *or to interpret it or to make it signify according to a tree model. The issue is to produce the unconscious, and with it new statements, different* **desires**: *the* **rhizome** *is precisely this production of the unconscious.* [TP 19, 18]

b. A mapping of language which can be distinguished from **Chomsky's** tree diagram, where linguistics is not a dichotomous self-referential system independent of its referents, but a heterogeneous system that has aesthetic, scientific, social and political import which complements its semiotic import.

> *The linguistic tree on the* **Chomsky** *model still begins at a point S and proceeds by dichotomy. On the contrary, not every trait in a* **rhizome** *is necessarily linked to a linguistic feature: semiotic chains of every nature are connected to very diverse modes of* **coding** *(biological, political, economic, etc.)* [TP 7, 7]

> *Our criticism of these linguistic models is [...] that they do not reach the* **abstract machine** *[...]. A* **rhizome** *ceaselessly establishes connections between semiotic chains, organizations of power, and circumstances relative to the arts, sciences, and social struggles.* [TP 8, 7]

3.a. In D&G's discussion of **becoming**, a series of intersections and lines that lack cohesion, center, retention (memory), expectation, or signification which are thus practically impossible to locate and/or destroy (in distinction from a structure composed of points); the map of a **becoming** (i.e. **becoming-animal**) or **line of flight** which involves the deformation of **forms of content** and **forms of expression**, and a network of **intensities**, movements, and **sensations**. [TP, K, D]

> To become animal is to participate in movement, [...] vibrations, thresholds in a deserted matter: animals [...] are distinguished only by this or that threshold, this or that vibration, by the particular underground tunnel in the rhizome or the burrow. [K 13]

> There are lines which do not amount to the path of a point, which break free from structure—lines of flight, becomings, without future or past, without memory, which resist the binary machine—**woman-becoming** which is neither man nor woman, **animal-becoming** which is neither beast nor man. [...]. The rhizome is all this [...] producing the line and not the point. [D 26]

b. A *horizontally* distributive or transformative process without a beginning or end, in distinction from that which is organized *vertically*, rooted to a single spot; mathematically, that which does not distinguish between the one and the **multiple** because it operates by subtraction from any given starting point rather than by addition.

> The rhizome is reducible neither to the One nor the multiple. [...] It has neither beginning nor end, but always a middle (milieu) from which it grows and which it overspills. It constitutes linear **multiplicities** with n dimensions [...] from which the One is always subtracted (n-1). [TP 23, 21]

> Processes are becomings, and aren't to be judged by some final result but by the way they proceed and their power to continue [...]. That's why we contrasted rhizomes with trees—trees, or rather arborescent processes, being temporary limits that block rhizomes and their transformations [...]. [NG 147]

- E. B. Y.

Rhythm

While we normally think of 'Rhythm' in terms of recurrence, succession, or patterns, D&G draw on the work of the French composer Olivier Messiaen to insist that rhythm has nothing to do with cadence or measurable time; rather, it is the very arrangement of instants which *elude* measure. Although rhythm occurs in a **chaotic** space-time, it is not simply **chaotic**, because it takes place in-between **milieus**, that is, in between instants or components that *are* periodically repeating (this overturns ancient theories which would assert that rhythm reflects cycles of the cosmos). Rhythms, they argue, can in fact be found whenever there are two milieus or environments (defined by their cadence) that are communicating with or even passing into one another (and therefore diverging from that cadence). Living things thus have rhythm when they are moving in-between environments or improvising, but also when they are **becoming** and are themselves being constituted anew. Rhythm, in this sense, is a musicological term, but also a feature of nature that is found in all environments and living things (and later, along with milieus, becomes a feature of **territorialization**).

1. In the work of Olivier **Messiaen**, a conception of musical time where **durations** involve continual inequality and added value, which are exemplified by birdsongs.

    Suppose that there were a single beat in all the universe. One beat; with eternity before it and eternity after it. A before and an after. That is the birth of time. Imagine then, almost immediately, a second beat. Since any beat is prolonged by the silence which follows it, the second beat will be longer than the first. Another number, another duration. That is the birth of **Rhythm**. [quoted in Johnson, 1975, 32]

2. In D&G's theory of musical time, and *in distinction from* metered time, metered music, or measurable **expressiveness** (whether terrestrial, human, aesthetic, or cosmic), which proceeds by *periodic* **repetition** (a feature of **milieus**), a type of time or expressiveness that is a-metrical or non-pulsed (indicative of the communication between milieus), and therefore resistant to measured time, predictability, or reproducibility.

rhythm *is not meter or cadence, even irregular meter or cadence [...]. Meter, whether regular or not, assumes a* coded *form whose unit of measure may vary, but in a non-communicating* milieu, *whereas* rhythm *is the Unequal or the Incommensurable that is always undergoing* transcoding. *Meter is dogmatic, but* rhythm *is critical; it ties together critical moments [...] Action occurs in a milieu, whereas* rhythm *is located between two milieus* [TP 346, 313]

A milieu *does in fact exist by virtue of a periodic* repetition, *but one whose only effect is to produce a* difference *by which the milieu passes into another milieu. It is the difference that is* rhythmic, *not the repetition, which nevertheless produces it* [TP 346, 314]

we should distinguish cadence-repetition and rhythm-*repetition in every case, the first being only the outward appearance or the abstract effect of the second* [DR 24, 21]

3.a. In D&G's theory of **territorialization,** a phenomenon that is exploited to make **milieus** dimensional and expressive of a relation of the territory to 'directional' **forces** of **chaos.**

Territorialization is an act of rhythm *that has become expressive, or of* milieu *components that have become qualitative. The marking of a* territory *is dimensional, but it is not a meter, it is a* rhythm *[...] inscribed on a different plane than that of its actions.* [TP 348, 315]

b. (Special Combination): *rhythmic character*: A rhythm **expressive** of, and whose expansion and contraction are contingent upon, critical distance in a relation to other **milieus** and rhythms; for example, of intra-(and extra) species relations and inter-sexual relations.

Two animals of the same sex and species confront each other: the rhythm *of the first one 'expands' when it approaches its* territory *or the center of its territory; the* rhythm *of the second contracts when it moves away from its territory.* [TP 353, 320]

4. In Deleuze's theory of painting, the capacity in an artistic or **expressive** medium to make visual or auditory **sensations** not only vibrate, but resonate and communicate.

Rhythm *appears as music when it invests the auditory level, and as painting when it invests the visual level. [...] [T]he relation between* sensation *and* rhythm *[...] places in each sensation the levels and domains through which it passes.* [FB 42]

- E. B. Y.

Sacher-Masoch, Leopold Von

While the clinical term 'masochism', popularized by Krafft-Ebing in 1886, is derived from Leopold Von Sacher-Masoch's name, Deleuze gave careful consideration to the German author's *literature*, in order to explore concepts of **desire**, **imagination**, humor, and the law, and to argue that Masochism was not simply the opposite complement of Sadism, as **Freud** would contend (see entry on *Coldness and Cruelty*), but is a fundamental human disposition with profound religious and philosophical implications.

The masochistic themes that Deleuze examines resonate with major concepts from his other works. For example, he links the role of **repetition** in Sacher-Masoch's predisposition to a state which is irresolvable in the form of pleasure (see definition 1.b.); sensuality is itself 'suspended' in favor or a supersensual ideal (a cold, severe woman), with which a reconciliation is awaited indefinitely, while pain is, in the meantime, expected incessantly. Repetition, here, is a repetition where the sensual and physical world is 'repeated' by being frozen and reflected into a supersensual abyss: in a passage which perhaps indirectly prefigures Deleuze's later work on **smooth space** with Guattari, he links this with an 'ice age' (the dawn of Christianity), where 'the steppe buries the Greek world of sensuality and rejects at the same time the modern world of sadism' (CC 54), and thus 'transforms **desire**' by making sensuality the object of thought rather than an empirical reality; it is 'the generative principle of a new order' and is responsible for the creation of modern culture that expresses an 'immobile and reflective quality' and an 'arrested movement'. While the steppe here is a dry, arid land, it is also an indifferent space or non-place that crystallizes the reality of a repetition of reflection, which is incarnated in the 'icy' and 'cold' female masochistic accomplice. Perhaps unlike the '**nomad**' that *inhabits* smooth space, the masochist *idealizes* it in suspended, imaginary forms.

Deleuze also picks up on Sacher-Masoch's re-writing of a myth that conflates the figures of Cain and Christ; in both cases 'likeness to the father is abolished' through a 'loyalty to the maternal rule' (CC 96). Thus when Sacher-Masoch's female characters torture their male counterparts, asking them 'have I made a man of you?', Deleuze claims that this 'consists in obliterating [the father's] role and likeness in order to generate the new man. The tortures are in effect directed at the father, or at his likeness in the son' (CC 99). Deleuze's thesis regarding the abolishment of likeness is perhaps indicative of his general approach to **difference**; the father generates likeness by repeating himself in the son, but that likeness is abolished by including the feminine ideal (as a parodied masculine and generative power).

It is worth noting that in a letter to **Foucault** from 1977 ('Desire and Pleasure'), Deleuze draws on his work on Sacher-Masoch in order to markedly distinguish his approach to **desire** from Foucault's approach to pleasure. As he states,

> I cannot give any positive **value** to pleasure, because pleasure seems to me to interrupt the immanent process of **desire** [...] I tell myself that it is no accident if Michel attaches a certain importance to Sade, and myself on the contrary to Masoch. It's not enough to say that I am masochistic, and Michel sadistic. That would be good, but it's not true. What interests me in Masoch is not the pain, but the idea that pleasure comes to interrupt the positivity of desire and the constitution of its field of **immanence** [...]. [Deleuze 1997]

This is perhaps a reference to his distinction between, on the one hand, the demonstrative 'language of imperatives and descriptions' in Sadism, which takes pleasure in what **Foucault** might call a transgression of the law and of institutions (utilizing the knowledge of what is 'seen' and 'said'), and, on the other hand, the continuous, albeit perverse, role of **desire** in **masochism** which is only *interrupted* by pain, but has no actual expectation of sensual pleasure (it only 'desires' the supersensual ideal). The problem of masochism, in fact, remerges in *A Thousand Plateaus* as an 'empty' rather than 'full' **Body without Organs**: 'the masochist has made himself a BwO under such conditions that the BwO can no longer be populated by anything but intensities of pain, *pain waves*. It is false to say that the masochist is looking for pain but just as false to say that he is looking for pleasure in a particularly suspensive or roundabout way. The masochist is looking for a type of BwO that only pain can fill' (TP 168, 152). - E. B. Y.

Sartre, Jean-Paul

Deleuze read Sartre enthusiastically during his last year of high school (when *Being and Nothingness* was published), and speaks fondly of how his work was refreshing in light of the Nazi occupation. Some of his first published essays in fact deal with a Sartrean concept of **the Other** (which will later be transformed into a **Leibnizian** conception); in a 1964 essay (written after Sartre refused the Nobel Prize), Deleuze wrote, 'Sartre allows us to await some vague future moment, a return, when thought will form again and make its totalities anew, like a power that is at once collective and private. This is why Sartre remains my teacher' (DI 79). Despite this, he did not devote explicit, substantial inquiries into Sartre's work; his references are usually passing and often point out how Sartre's views are in conflict with his own; in *Difference and Repetition*, for example, he notes that Sartre's 'holes' of non-being, which resort to a concept of negativity, can be contrasted with a more **Heidegger**ian concept of the **folding** of being. - E. B. Y.

Guattari admired Sartre's ideas in *Being and Nothingness* from an early age and never repudiated his influence and importance; Sartre ranked among the giants of European philosophy and art. Guattari adapted a number of important concepts from Sartre's dialectical sociology and considered it better to be wrong and stay with Sartre despite his errors and the restrictiveness of his political vision (while still a member of the French Communist Party young Guattari was a Trotskyite) because his mistakes were richer than the philosophical alternatives. Guattari modeled his non-absolute distinction between subject group and subjugated group on Sartre's distinction between a group in fusion and serial being. The latter was a repetitive and empty mode of existence in which members are turned towards an exterior object without uniting in a common project; the former has liquidated its seriality and come together in a common purpose which it interiorizes and refines through a shared praxis. Guattari's little-known unpublished 'theatrical dialogues' the writing of which stretched from the late 1970s to the early 1990s, were undoubtedly inspired by Sartre's dramatic successes, but express an absurdist sensibility and commitment to issues of mental ecology rather than to situations where actions define characters. Guattari thought of Sartre as a verb that should be conjugated in the present tense. - G. G.

Schizoanalysis

This ontological pragmatics analyzes the auto-modelization capacities of subjectification in search of **singularities** that can be unfolded and constellated with other specific existential components. The schizoanalyst creates non-representational maps of processes of singularization that are not amenable to capture in psychogenetic stages, personological constructs, or in terms of universal complexes. The semiotic means at play are much more diverse than language alone. Although Guattari did not write 'case studies', he produced abundant diagrams, in *Cartographies Schizoanalytiques*, of his metamodelization of **the machinic unconscious**. His collective work with psychotics at La Borde entailed a highly diverse set of psychiatric, schizo- and psycho-analytic practices, and encouraged patients to offer analytic insights, among many other tests of hypotheses. Today few analysts work with schizoanalytic cartographies. The characterization of schizoanalysis in *Anti-Oedipus* was based on the theorization of schizophrenia as a process with revolutionary potential in the sense that it reserved the most important place for understanding how desire produced the real. Guattari emphasized how to work with the machines of an expanded **unconscious** in clinical conditions, as well as in private consultations, in this way shifting the emphasis onto pragmatic issues.

1.a. A clinical model that replaces the **Freud**ian and Lacanian **unconscious** with the **four functors** schema: **Territory** (existential subjectifications), Universe (incorporeal alterifications), **Flux** (material and energetic transformations), and **Phylum** (evolution of machines), mapping transformations between (and beyond) these domains.

b. A clinical model that refers to psychosis rather than **neurosis** as its preferred model of **subjectification**.

While psychoanalysis conceptualizes psychosis through its vision of **neurosis**, *schizoanalysis approaches all modalities of* **subjectivation** *in light of the mode of being in the world of psychosis.* [CM 63]

c. (Special Type): *Metamodeling*: The grafting of auto-modelizations onto other models by responding to **events** with potential for giving patients the opportunity to reorganize their field of references and work with other materials of expression, like social work, with the cartographic production of new **subjectifications** drawing from the history of best analytic practices.

At base, **schizoanalysis** *only poses one question: 'how does one model oneself?' You are psychotic and you construct idiosyncratic references; you are attached as with a ball and chain to a familial-oedipal territory; you stick to the collective apparatus [...] one day, instead of going to the office, you stay in bed and turn yourself into a beetle [...] Everything is possible! Nothing is mechanical, structural, but nothing is guaranteed [...]* **Schizoanalysis** *[...] is not an alternative modelization. It is a* **metamodelization**. *It tries to understand how it is that your got where you are? 'What is your model to you?' It does not work?—Then, I don't know, one tries to work together. One must see if one can make a graft of other models.* [GR 132–3]

d. A radical post-psychoanalysis where the analyst attempts to discern the emergence of something that might get a patient moving again, by scouting out opportune potentialities among nuclei of **autopoiesis**, and activating cross-componential hatchings of **subjectification** by means of found (extracted) or placed (created) elements, enriching (onto-logic) rather than reducing (logic of sets) them.

Schizoanalytic *cartography consists in the ability to discern those components lacking in consistency or existence [by introducing someone to something previously unknown to them, like cooking].* [CM 71]

... it's sometimes necessary to jump at the opportunity, to approve, to run the risk of being wrong, to give it a go, to say, 'yes, perhaps this experience is important'. Respond to the **event** *as the potential bearer of new constellations of Universes of reference.* [CM 18]

e. The topical confinement of the Real in the Lacanian system by means of the signifier that is rejected for semiosis flush with the real, where signs act directly on things.

> The construction of a **schizoanalytic rhizome** *will not aim at the description of a state of fact, the return to equilibrium of intersubjective relations, or the exploration of the mysteries of an* **unconscious** *lurking in the obscure recesses of memory. On the contrary, it will be completely oriented toward an experimentation in touch with the real.* [MU 171]
>
> *You pass from a thing to sign without ever 'forming' anything 'semiotically'. You leave the imperialism of the signifier-signified behind.* [AOP 212]

2. Open, non-representational maps which are drawn to transform lives, in two different but indissociable types: generative (interpret and illuminate) and transformative (modify and create).

> *When a* **schizoanalytic assemblage** *will take as its object a preexisting* **assemblage** *or will set out to create new ones, we will be able to attach its functionality to the generative pragmatics or the transformational pragmatics... .* [MU 185]

3. Guattari's critical use of trends in phenomenological psychiatry to investigate the intensive **rhythms** of singularization across psychosis, autism, melancholia, and epilepsy.

> *The schizo fracture is the royal road of access to the emergent fractality of the* **Unconscious**. *What could be called the schizo reduction goes beyond all the eidetic reductions of phenomenology—it leads to an encounter with the a-signifying* **refrains** *which give back to the narrative, which recast in artifice, existential narrativity and alterity, albeit delirious ones.* [CM 64]

- G. G.

Schizoanalytic Cartographies

Cartographies Schizoanalytiques (1989)

This strange book forms a sort of theoretical trilogy with *The Three Ecologies* and *Chaosmosis* insofar as all three works share the same theoretical foundation based on Guattari's **four functors**. His most densely theoretical work, *Schizoanalytic Cartographies* is filled with strange diagrams which look vaguely scientific but which are best described as belonging to what Guattari will call the **aesthetic paradigm** in *Chaosmosis*, which he published three years later. The theme of **cartography** had already been introduced in *A Thousand Plateaus* with the distinction made between maps and tracings. In this later, solo-authored work, Guattari continues the quest for theoretical frameworks less reductionist than those of the **structuralists**. He claims that he is mapping the psyche, technology, semiotics, and universal history, although most of his drawings are not directly correlated to any specific object or process. In mostly abstract terms he reformulates the semiotic categories (signifying, a-signifying, discursive, non-discursive, etc.) introduced in *The Machinic Unconscious*. A key chapter based on a conference paper reworks **Freud**'s energetic model of the psyche using complexity theory as illustrated in a series of diagrams. The paper was presented at an interdisciplinary colloquium devoted to the work of **Ilya Prigogine**, and it reportedly mystified the scientists and social scientists in attendance. In addition to borrowing from various versions of energetics, the book's diagrams (there are more than seventy-five) borrow from complexity theory, chemistry, cybernetics, information theory, open systems theory, and Lacanian mathemes. His reaction to what he describes as the computerization (*informatisation* in French) of the world is mixed, but he offers hope by calling for a **post-media era** in which transversal, **rhizomatic** processes would displace the hegemony of capitalist- and state-controlled mass media. The technical main portion of the book is followed by seven essays on topics as diverse as the **refrain**, dreams, literature, theatre, architecture, photography, and painting. - J. W.

Segmentation

1.a. In D&G's socio-historical analysis, a feature of physical structures or **strata**, that are regulated by a territorial or transcendental power in order to capture **desire**, whether in a supple, molecular or fluid manner (as in primitive societies) or in a rigid, centralized and molar manner (as in modern societies). [AO, TP]

> *Primitive* **segmentarity** *is characterized by a polyvocal* **code** *based on lineages and their varying situations and relations, and an itinerant* **territoriality** *based on local, overlapping divisions. Codes and* **territories***, clan lineages and tribal* **territorialities***, form a fabric of relatively supple* **segmentarity***.* [TP 231, 209]

> *There is no opposition between the central and the* **segmentary***. The modern political system [...] implies a constellation of juxtaposed, imbricated, ordered subsystems [...] modern life has not done away with* **segmentarity** *but has on the contrary made it exceptionally rigid.* [TP 231, 210]

b. A feature of physical structures composed either by a **territorial assemblage** to regulate **desire** or by **an abstract machine** to liberate desire along a **line of flight** (portrayed acutely by Kafka). [K, TP]

> *The* **segments** *are simultaneously powers and* **territories**—*they capture* **desire** *by* **territorializing** *it, fixing it in place, [...] But we must declare as well that an* **assemblage** *[...] extends over or penetrates an unlimited field of* **immanence** *that makes the* **segments** *melt and that liberates* **desire** *[...].* [K 86]

2.a. (Special Combination): *faraway and contiguous* segments: In D&G's reading of **Kafka's** novels, the formation of political and social institutions or structures of **desire** that are organized by a 'length' that connects the disconnected, endowing them with an *indeterminate* distance.

> *the offices are very far from each other because of the length of the hallway that separates them (they aren't very* **close***), but they are* **contiguous** *because of the back doors that connect them along the same line (they aren't very distant). [...] length [...] brings into contiguity the most separated* **segments***.* [K 77]

b. (Special Combination): *distant and close* segments: The formation of political and social institutions or structures of **desire** that are understood to be at a simultaneous and determinable distance from one another in order to regulated desire.

> *the transcendental law, the infinite tower, is infinitely* **distant** *from each block; and, at the same time, it is* **always** *very close and never*

ceases to send its messages to each block, bringing one near the other when it moves away from the other [K 77]

- E. B. Y.

Sensation

Philosophy usually treats 'sensation' in terms of the **subjectivity** of 'sense-data': things in the world appear to us differently than they really are. However, beginning in his early work on **Hume**, Deleuze insisted on the irreconcilability of such sensation with psychology; sensation may inform how the subject is constituted, but it is not 'given' to us subjectively. Rather, if the given is 'the **flux** of the sensible, a collection of impressions and images, or a set of **perceptions**' (ES 87), 'the *being of* the sensible' involves 'not a sensible being', that is, 'not the given *but that by which the given is given*', which is 'insensible', imperceptible, and 'problematic' (DR 176, 140 emphasis added). This is why he insists that 'problems must be considered not as "givens" (data)' but as an 'encounters' (of a **transcendental empiricism**) which force each **faculty** to perceive the relations between sensations rather than perceiving them as data or representations of those sensations.

As an encounter, sensation acts on the nervous system, and not on the 'brain' of the subject: beginning with **Bergson**, Deleuze links sensation to the **contraction** of matter and of cases within the **imagination** (it is thus 'psycho-organic'), and in his work on **Bacon**, he shows how the aesthetics of sensation complicates and destabilizes figurative 'givens', rendering painting dynamic. With Guattari, he in fact emphasizes the *objectivity* of 'blocs of sensation' along with **percepts** and **affects** (further divorcing the theory of sensation from psychology), in distinction from the *subjectivity* of **concepts**.

1. In Deleuze's reading of **Bergson**, the vibration of **matter**, **contracted** by the senses, which results in perceived qualities (or '**contraction**-memory').

> *What, in fact, is a* **sensation***? It is the operation of contracting trillions of vibrations onto a receptive* **surface***. Quality emerges from this, quality that is nothing other than* **contracted** *quantity.*

[...] sensation *is extensive insofar as what it* contracts *is precisely the extended, the expanded (detendu).* [B 74]

2. In D&G's explanation of experience (whether in an aesthetic, empirical, terrestrial, or cosmic **milieu**), and in Deleuze's explanation of art, a stimulus of either the human nervous system, organic and non-organic **matter**, or the **body without organs**, which results from **forces**; this involves, on the one hand, the instantaneous **contraction** of vibrations (by a particular sense organ), which are, on the other hand, **differenciated**, contemplated, and preserved (or resonating) as a qualitative impression; consequently, they are composed and made to communicate with other sensations at various levels, movements, areas, or temporal domains (such that the lived experience of any one sensation exceeds the bounds of simple organic activity).

> **Sensation** *is excitation itself,[...] insofar as it is preserved or preserves its vibrations [...].*sensation *is formed by contracting that which composes it [...].* [WP 211]

> *It is a characteristic of* sensation *to pass through different levels owing to the action of* forces. *But two* sensations, *each having their own level or zone, can also confront each other and make their respective levels communicate.[...] the different levels through which this* sensation *passes already necessarily constitute couplings of* sensation. *Vibration already produces resonance.* [FB 47, 64]

3.a. In Deleuze's explanation of the paintings of Francis **Bacon**, that which emerges through the figurative givens and from the catastrophe or **chaos** of the **diagram** by means of **intensity** (falling towards **chaos**), and, by virtue of deformation, transforms into **rhythm** and into a **Figure** by virtue of passage throughout levels of **difference** (without falling completely into chaos).

> *When* **Bacon** *speaks of* sensation, *he says [...] that the form related to the* sensation *(the* **Figure***) is the opposite of the form related to an object that it is supposed to represent (figuration).* [FB 36]

> *The active is the fall, but it is not necessarily a descent in space, in extension. It is the descent as the passage of* sensation, *as the* **difference** *in level contained in the* sensation.*[...] The fall is what is most alive in the* sensation: *[...]. The* **intensive** *fall can thus coincide with a spatial descent, but also with a rise.* [FB 80]

> *In order for the rupture with figurative resemblance to avoid perpetuating the catastrophe, in order for it to succeed in producing a more profound resemblance, the planes, starting with the* **diagram***, must maintain their junction [...]. It is through such a system that geometry becomes sensible, and* **sensations** *become clear and durable: one has 'realized' the* **sensation** [FB, 118]

b. In Deleuze's and D&G's explanation of Art (and embodiment), a feature that resists being determined by ready-mades, clichés, and opinions in favor of a violent, non-representational and indeterminate organization of and relation to the body; that which, along with **percepts** and **affects**, compose a work of art.

> *The violence of* **sensation** *is opposed to the violence of the represented (the sensational, the cliché). The former is inseparable from its direct action on the nervous system, the levels through which it passes [...].* [FB 39]

> *Art undoes the triple organization of perceptions, affections, and opinions in order to substitute a monument composed of* **percepts***,* **affects***, and blocs of* **sensations***[...].* [WP 176]

- E. B. Y.

Sense

If we were to ever have the stupid self-confidence to say 'this means that', we would not be grappling with the irreducibly uncertain and intangible nature of sense, and it is this ambiguity that Deleuze explores. In other words, determining sense, or meaning, is not straightforward, especially when avoiding the logical pitfall of having to explain the meaning of a meaning of something, and thus ascertaining sense outside of the categories of representation.

Deleuze frames the discovery of sense largely in terms its correlative aspects, which we usually mistake for actual sense, such as Good Sense and Common Sense, as well as what we usually mistake for the absence of sense—Non-Sense or absurdity. In his view, sense does not explain what was or anticipate what will be, nor does it reveal what was concealed, or concern truths and beliefs. Rather, it expresses **events**: something that paradoxically *both* has already happened and is about to happen; a way of thinking the past and future within the present. In short, sense explains what *is*. Non-sense is not the opposite of sense but that which 'announces its own sense'; it seems absurd or impossible because sense always subsists within the logic of the **proposition** (and when taken for itself, it has no traction or foundation, so appears absurd).

In his study of **Nietzsche**, Deleuze outlines the issue of sense around the **multiplicity** of **forces**, where the relations of force that engender phenomena indicate precisely that a thing has multiple senses or interpretations. If 'there are no facts, only interpretations', as Nietzsche famously claims, then there are no phenomena that simply exist: they must always be considered in terms of what they are **becoming**.

1. In Deleuze's Philosophy of Language, the fourth dimension of the proposition (**denotation, manifestation,** and **signification** being the other three), which has an integral relation with signification and **non-sense**, expressing the relationship between the proposition and that which falls outside of the **proposition** (states of affairs, things), or the **event**; a neutral **surface** effect which inheres in propositions and is indicative of **depth**.

> Let us consider the complex status of sense or of that which is expressed. On one hand, it does not exist outside the **proposition** which **expresses** it; what is expressed does not exist outside its expression. This is why we cannot say that sense exists, but rather that it inheres or subsists. On the other hand, it does not merge at all with the proposition, for it has an objective (objectité) which is quite distinct. [LS 24, 21]

> sense and nonsense have a specific relation which cannot copy that of the true and false [...]. This is indeed the most general problem of the logic of sense: what would be the purpose of rising from the domain of truth to the domain of sense, if it were only to find between sense and nonsense a relation analogous to that of the true and the false? [LS 79, 68]

> sense is presented both as that which happens to bodies and that which insists in propositions [...] as the expressed which subsists in propositions and as the **event** which occurs in states of bodies. [LS 149, 125]

2.a (Special Combination): *Good Sense*: The habitual anticipation or expectation of certain outcomes based on a distributive logic of causality and probability (a linear model of time).

> Good sense *is based upon [...]* habit. *[...]. Testifying to a living present (and to the fatigue of that present), it goes from past to future as though from particular to general.* [DR 284, 225]

> good sense *is said of one direction only: [...] it determines this direction to go from the most to the least differentiated, from the singular to the regular, and from the remarkable to the ordinary* [LS 88, 76]

b. (Special Combination): *Common Sense*: The fixation of a permanent identity of the Self (all actions are united or carried out by 'me') and the World (all objects and surroundings are familiar), which situates the past, present, and future under the umbrella of recognition and a harmonious accord of the **faculties**.

> Common sense *identifies and recognizes, no less than* good sense *foresees. Subjectively,* common sense *subsumes under itself the various* faculties *of the soul, or the differentiated organs of the body, and brings them to bear upon a unity which is capable of saying 'I.' [...]. Objectively,* common sense *subsumes under itself the given diversity and relates it to the unity of a particular form of object or an individualized form of a world.* [LS 89, 78]

> common sense *always implies a collaboration of the* faculties *upon a form of the Same or a model of recognition [...].* [DR 136–7, 173]

3. (Special Combination): *Non-Sense*: A paradoxical element which counters the doxa of good sense and of common sense, by disposing itself, firstly, from the least to most differentiated and secondly, by dissolving the identical and unified; that which, along with **signification** – which establishes the conditions of truth or falsity by virtue of implicit connections between universal concepts – contributes to the production of sense. [LS, DR]

> *The* paradox *therefore is the simultaneous reversal of* good sense *and* common sense: *on one hand, it appears in the guise of the two simultaneous* senses *or directions of the becoming-mad and the unforeseeable; on the other hand, it appears as the* nonsense *of the lost identity and the unrecognizable. [...] precisely because* nonsense *has an internal and original relation to* sense, *this*

paradoxical element bestows **sense** *upon the terms of each series* [LS 90, 78]

4. In Deleuze's reading of **Nietzsche**, the essence of something insofar as it is divorced from *conceivable* truths or images of thought, and, rather, is *interpreted* through a given **sign** in terms of the relation of **forces** (historical, political, natural, etc.) that produces it (in other words, a determination by virtue of quality without reducing relations of force to quantity).

We will never find the **sense** *of something (of a human, a biological or even a physical phenomenon) if we do not know the* **force** *which appropriates the thing, which exploits it, which takes possession of it or is expressed in it. [...]* **Sense** *is therefore a complex notion; there is always a plurality of* **senses***, a constellation, a complex of successions but also of coexistences which make interpretation an art.* [N 3, 3–4]

A new image of thought means primarily that truth is not the element of thought. The element of thought is **sense** *and* **value**. [N 98, 104]

- E. B. Y.

Series

This term is not a synonym for **repetition**, but is indicative of a *structure* of repetitions and of **differences**. In terms of **structuralism**, Deleuze notes that one series may serve as the 'signifier' and the other as the 'signified'; however, seriality allows for a 'paradoxical entity' or **partial object** to ensure their relative displacement, their communication, and the reversal of signifier-signified roles in determining **sense** (he cites examples from Lacan and **Klossowski** on this point). His work on **multiplicities** also influences this **concept**, where he distinguishes between series which may appear to differ only in degree, but ultimately differ in nature. With Guattari, the term is attributed to the 'syntheses' that are involved in **desiring-machines**, and in **Kafka's** work, series are an example of the 'proliferation' of doubles and triangles which, through their communication, are expressive of **desire**. The term is also used in his analysis of the **movement-image** (def. 3a) and **time-image** (def. 3).

1.a. In Deleuze's analysis of systems, temporal or spatial, qualitative or quantitative, successions (of **events**, things, **propositions**, words, **expressions**, etc.) whose terms *appear* homogenous (because they may differ in degree or type but do not seem to differ in nature), despite that each is actually heterogeneous because they are always implicated and/or developed by one other series (or more) with which they are in perpetual, relative displacement (that is, the terms of the series differ in nature because of their relation their counterpart and incessant lack of correspondence). [LS, DR]

> the serial *form is necessarily realized in the simultaneity of at least two* series. *Every unique* series, *whose homogeneous terms are distinguished only according to type or degree, necessarily subsumes under it two heterogeneous* series, *each one of which is constituted by terms of the same type or degree, although these terms differ in nature from those of the other* series [...]. [LS 44, 36]

> When we extend the serial *method[...] homogeneity is only apparent: it is always the case that one* series *has the role of the signifier, and the other the role of the signified, even if these roles are interchanged as we change points of view.* [LS 46, 38]

b. The condition for the development of **differenciation.**

> *Under what other conditions does* difference *develop this in-itself as a '*differenciator*', and gather the different outside of any possible representation? The first characteristic seems to us to be organization in* series. [DR 143, 117]

2. In Deleuze's explanation of **passive synthesis**, and in D&G's explanation of **desiring-machines**, that which is (ap)prehended through *connective syntheses*, and, on the one hand, when isolated from *disjunctive* and *conjunctive* syntheses, global and specific (binary), or, on the other hand, when not isolated from them, partial and non-specific.

> *connective synthesis (if .., then)* [...] *bears upon the construction of a single* series. [LS 199, 174]

> *The productive synthesis, the production of production, is inherently connective in nature: 'and ...' 'and then ...'* [...]. *[B]ecause the first machine is in turn connected to another whose flow it interrupts*

or partially drains off, the binary series *is linear in every direction.* [AO 5, 5]

3. In D&G's reading of **Kafka**, the result of doubles that no longer defer onto each other (thereby paralyzing or blocking **desire**) or refer to a third term (as with a family triangle), and instead indicate the process of liberating desire.

doubles continue to play a large role in each of these series *of the general function, but they do so as points of departure [...].* [K 85]

these proliferating series *[...] work to unblock a situation that had closed elsewhere in an impasse.* [K 53]

- E. B. Y.

Sign

Whether considered in the colloquial sense, where signs involve indications, gestures, marks, or symptoms that would point or connect us to some action, consequence, or other possibility (i.e. smoke is a sign of fire), or in the Saussurean sense of a relation between signified and signifier that is arbitrary (green means go, red means stop), it is generally viewed that signs involve a relation between two domains: one which is given in some form or language, and one which is not. These conceptions, however, do not account for complexities involving time (how do signs change and indicate change?), love (what are the signs of loving and being loved?), and even oppression (how do signs manipulate our actions or desires?). Deleuze thus complicates the understanding of signs by showing that signs maintain a variable relation with the past and future or implicate us in other possible worlds (of various types), and with Guattari, he shows how signs indicate '**de/territorialization**' where they are not a simple relation between signifier and signified (which would be negative or deductive) but a differential relation based on a shifting (often **redundant**, but sometimes liberating) interactions between **forms of content** and **forms of expression**. Finally, in his work on cinema, he both adopts and deviates from Charles Peirce's semiotics to classify images.

1. In Deleuze's reading of **Proust**, that which, whether in the world or in the mind, demands interpretation or explication (engendering thought), and, implicates or envelops **differences** as possible worlds or **virtual** fragments; accordingly, signs may be distinguished as 1) *worldly*, which involve an effacement of thought by virtue of a substitution for action, 2) *amorous*, which **express** possible but inaccessible worlds of the beloved (where time is 'lost' and the Self is dissolved through the lack of correspondence between the present and future), 3) *sensual*, in which the past appears through **reminiscence** (where time is regained and the Self is rediscovered through the identity of the past and present), or 4) *aesthetic*, which transforms the first three types by internalizing and complicating their differences (and separating them from their material explication in the beloved or in a **sensation** in favor of a spiritual explication of timeless differences).

> *Love's time is a lost time because the* **sign** *develops only to the degree that the self corresponding to its meaning disappears. The sensuous* **signs** *offer us a new structure of time: time rediscovered at the heart of lost time itself, an image of eternity. This is because the sensuous* **signs** *(unlike the* **signs** *of love) have the power either to awaken by desire and* **imagination** *or to reawaken by involuntary memory the Self that corresponds to their meaning. Lastly, the* **signs** *of art define time regained: an absolute primordial time, a veritable eternity that unites* **sign** *and meaning.* [P 87]

> *What forces us to think is the* **sign**. *The* **sign** *is the object of an encounter, but it is precisely the contingency of the encounter that guarantees the necessity of what it leads us to think [...]. To think is always to interpret—to explicate, to develop, to decipher, to translate a* **sign**. [P 97]

> *Problems and their symbolic fields stand in a relationship with* **signs**. *It is the* **signs** *which 'cause problems' and are developed in a symbolic field.* [DR 204, 164]

2. In Deleuze's reading of the **Stoics**, phenomena, problems, or **paradoxes** which, on the one hand, occupy and refer to the present in time by providing the material to be **contracted** through the contemplations of **passive synthesis** (which form **habits**), and, on the other hand, are retained from the past or projected onto the future in the **imagination** in order to

artificially form principles based on generic differences that are contemplated through **active synthesis**. [LS, DR]

> **Signs** *as we have defined them—as* **habitudes** *or* **contractions** *referring to one another—always belong to the present. One of the great strengths of* **Stoicism** *lies in having shown that every* **sign** *is a* **sign** *of the present [...]. [W]e find here [...] the distinction between natural and artificial: natural* **signs** *are* **signs** *founded upon* **passive synthesis**; *they are signs of the present, referring to the present in which they signify. Artificial* **signs**, *by contrast, are those which refer to the past or the future as distinct dimensions of the present [...]. Artificial* **signs** *imply* **active syntheses** *[...].* [DR 99, 77]

3. In D&G's explanation of power, an index, symbol, or icon of **territorialization, deterritorialization**, or **reterritorialization** (respectively), which become 'regimes' when expressions are formalized (see **form of expression**) which do not designate but maintain a general, reciprocal presupposition with a **form of content.**

> **Signs** *are not* **signs** *of a thing; they are* **signs** *of* **deterritorialization** *and* **reterritorialization**, *they mark a certain threshold crossed in the course of these movements, and it is for this reason that the word should be retained (as we have seen, this applies even to animal* '**signs**'). [TP 75, 67–8]

> *the* **form of expression** *is reducible not to words but to a set of statements arising in the social field considered as a* **stratum** *(that is what a regime of* **signs** *is).* [TP 74, 66]

4. In Deleuze's analysis of cinema, a term for the classification of images which, as influenced by Peirce, is non-linguistic (i.e. does not utilize a Saussurean signifier-signified schema), but unlike Peirce, emphasizes the **perception-image** as the *first* sign through which qualities (affections), tensions (actions), or inferences (relations) are deduced.

> *We [...] take the term* '**sign**' *in a completely different way from Peirce: it is a particular image that refers to a type of image, whether from the point of view of its bipolar composition, or from the point of view of its genesis.* [C2 31, 32]

- E. B. Y.

Simulacrum

1. In Deleuze's critique of **Plato**, the manner in which 'artificial' reproductions are expressed not as stale copies, but as **expressions** of a belief in the future or a **chaotic** change in nature.

> The **simulacrum** [...] *harbors a positive power which denies the original and the copy, the model and the reproduction.* [...] *In the reversal of* **Platonism**, *resemblance is said of internalized* **difference**, *and identity of the Different as primary power.* [LS 300, 262]

- E. B. Y.

Singularity

Borrowed from mathematics and physics, but also used by Deleuze as a synonym for the medieval term **haecceity**. D&G champion singularity, criticizing philosophers and social scientists for seeking universals. **Structuralism** delineates universal paradigms, patterns, and forms. Traditional philosophy studies abstract universals. Schizoanalysis instead focuses on events, mutations, and potentialities which produce—and are produced by—singularities. The term appears in works by both Deleuze and Guattari from *Difference and Repetition* onward.

1.a. A term that Deleuze adapts from differential calculus; the outermost points of a dynamic system plotted onto a graph.

> *Is this not the same as in the theory of differential equations, where the existence and the distribution of* '*singularities*' *are of another nature than the* '*individual*' *forms of the integral curves in their neighborhood?* [DI 87]

b. The points on a surface or curve which delineate a space.

> *Corresponding to the determination of differential relations are* **singularities**, *distributions of* **singular** *points which characterize curves or figures (a triangle, for example, has three* **singular** *points)* [...]. *Every structure presents the following two aspects: a system of differential relations*[...] *and a system of* **singularities** *corresponding to these relations and tracing the space of the structure.* [DI 176–7]

c. According to mathematician **René Thom**'s catastrophe theory, which Guattari cites at length in *The Machinic Unconscious*, the threshold at which a dynamic system dissolves or is destroyed—catastrophe—corresponds to a limited number of stable **singularities** mapped onto topological space.

> *it is possible to show that separating surfaces present only a small number of stable* **singularities** *[...]. I have drawn up a complete list of these* **singularities***, which are the 'elementary catastrophes'[...]* [Thom, 1983, p. 18]

2. Neither general laws nor abstract universals.

> *There is no abstract universal beyond the individual or beyond the particular and the general: it is* **singularity** *itself which is 'pre-individual.'* [DR 223, 176]

3. Deleuze's term for the particularities which exist prior to individuation, as defined by Simondon.

> *That is the real definition of the individual: concentration, accumulation, coincidence of a certain number of converging pre-individual* **singularities** *(it being said that* **singular** *points can coincide in a same point...)* [FLB 63]

4. For Deleuze, an **event**.

> [**Singularities**] *are not generalities but* **events***, or droplets of an event.* [FLB 64]

5. a. For Guattari, the point or moment at which a social system can mutate, as in a **molecular revolution**.

> *The dynamics of* **singularities** *always result from a small miracle, encounters that may trigger transformations that are no longer singular, since they can upset the entire planet. Certain events, the lamest as well as the most extraordinary, statistically must occur.* [SS 86–7]

b. Of or related to potentiality, as in revolutionary potentiality.

> *Indeed the metastable, defined as pre-individual being, is perfectly well endowed with* **singularities** *that correspond to the existence and the distribution of potentials.* [DI 87]

> As object 'a,' the **partial object** is detotalized and **deterritorialized**; it has permanently distanced itself from any individuated corporeity; and it is now in a position to tip in the direction of real **singularities** and open up to the molecular machinisms of every kind that shape history. [Guattari in DI 222]

c. A kind of catalyst, such as those found in poetry or art, for producing new social and subjective formations which escape the forces of capitalist standardization.

> Analysis is[...] the invention of new catalytic nuclei capable of bifurcating existence. A **singularity**, a rupture of sense, a cut, fragmentation, the detachment of a semiotic content—for example, in a Dadaist or surrealist manner—can originate mutant nuclei of subjectivation. [CM 18]

6.a. In Guattari's late work, that which precedes, exceeds, and escapes the structures, social norms, and pre-established meanings of standard subjectivation, resulting in liberation from the standards and norms of global information-age capitalism.

> What is more than ever at stake is the right to **singularity**, to freedom of individual and collective creation away from technocratic conformism, post-modernist arrogance and the leveling of **subjectivity** in the wake of new technologies. [SS 203]

b. (Special Combination): *Process of* **singularization**: Self-determination and self-regulation, especially of minority **groups**; or, authenticity, in distinction from Sartre's **seriality** (individuals living in close proximity without forming a group or community).

> The Palestinian or Irish problems, the national claims of the Basques, Poles or Afghanis actually express the need for human collectivities to reappropriate their own lives, their own destinies through what I call a **process of singularization**. [SS 78]

> And, more precisely, what must characterize [the apparatuses of subjectivation] so that they abandon seriality—in **Sartre**'s sense— and enter into **processes of singularization** which restore to existence what we might call its auto-essentialization. [CM 20]

- J. W.

Smooth space

Deserts, plateaus, steppes, and oceans are some of the breathtaking yet desolate images that may come to mind when thinking of 'smooth spaces'. Such landscapes come with a rich history of visionary **percepts** in religious and literary works (such as those of Melville, or T. E. Lawrence). In his early work, Deleuze will make reference to the harsh and indifferent nature of such spaces as an ideal of **masochism**. And yet, it is ultimately not the *tangible* characteristics of such space that will instigate the development of the concept with Guattari, but the intangible characteristics—their *absolute* or separated nature. When travelling in such a space, it is almost impossible to conceptualize or measure distance *as such* because there is nothing to mediate one locale to the next; in terms of time, it's difficult to tell how *fast* you're going, in what direction, or how far you've travelled. However, unlike the sacred yet homogenous space of religion, D&G claim that smooth space does not 'appear in a particular place', but is, paradoxically, a 'nonlimited locality [...] in an infinite succession of local operations' (TP 422, 383). For all intent and purpose, '**nomads**' who inhabit such spaces are immobile because their movement cannot be represented; they don't move as much as they cling to this space and even *construct* it. Furthermore, such space cannot be conceptualized as a whole, or as a reified object, but only experienced step-by-step, even and especially within 'striated' space (space that *does* contain points, distances, contours, architecture, etc.), as an accumulation of **differences** that only actually appear via the indifference of invisible, absolute space. For this reason they can say that 'the sea is a smooth space fundamentally open to striation, and the city is the force of striation that reimparts smooth space, [...] outside but also inside itself' (TP 531, 481).

> 1.a. On the one hand, a feature of geological space where there are little to no geographic referent points; on the other hand, a technological, mathematical, maritime, physical, and aesthetic model which permits understandings of spatial relationships that concern the nonmetrical division of time; the **haptic** function of the eye, and the primacy of directionality and **multiplicity**.
>
> *there is no line separating earth and sky; there is no intermediate distance, no perspective or contour; visibility is limited; and yet there*

> is an extraordinarily fine topology that relies not on points or objects but rather on **haecceities**, on sets of relations (winds, undulations of snow or sand, the song of the sand or the creaking of ice, the tactile qualities of both). It is a tactile space, or rather 'haptic,' a sonorous much more than a visual space. The variability, the polyvocality of directions, is an essential feature of **smooth spaces** of the **rhizome** type, and it alters their **cartography**. The **nomad**, nomad space, is localized and not delimited. [TP 421–2, 382]
>
> Now not only the sea, desert, steppe, and air are the sites of a contest between the **smooth** and the **striated**, but the earth itself, depending on whether there is cultivation in **nomos**-space or agriculture in city-space. [TP 531, 481]

b. The directional determination of a **line of flight**, in distinction from dimensional, **territorialized milieus** (with **redundant** or marked out directions).

> we shall call **striated** or *metric* any aggregate with a whole number of dimensions, and for which it is possible to assign constant directions. [...] what defines **smooth space**, then, is that it does not have a dimension higher than that which moves through it or is inscribed in it; in this sense it is a flat **multiplicity**, for example, a line that fills a plane without ceasing to be a line [...]. [TP 537, 488]

2.a. D&G's geographical, political, and historical concept of **multiplicity**.

> Not only is that which peoples a **smooth** space a multiplicity that changes in nature when it divides—such as tribes in the desert: constantly modified distances, packs that are always undergoing metamorphosis—but **smooth** space itself, desert, steppe, sea, or ice, is a multiplicity of this type, nonmetric, acentered, directional, etc. [TP 534, 484]

b. The manner in which space *itself* is distributed, multiplied, and occupied instead of being measured, **striated**, divided, and partitioned in order to distribute something (i.e. a **territory**, a code) within it; a geometry of movability and **multiplicity** (**nomadic distribution**) in distinction from a geometry of variables within immovable units or striations.

> The independence of the number in relation to space is a result not of abstraction but of the concrete nature of **smooth space**, which

is *occupied without itself being counted. The number is no longer a means of counting or measuring but of moving: it is the number itself that moves through* **smooth** *space.* [...] *The number becomes a principle whenever it occupies a* **smooth** *space, and is deployed within it as subject, instead of measuring a* **striated** *space. The number is the mobile occupant, the movable (meuble) in* **smooth** *space, as opposed to the geometry of the immovable (immeuble) in* **striated** *space.* [TP 430, 389]

- E. B. Y.

Soft Subversions: Texts and Interviews 1977–1985

In 2009, Semiotext(e) published a new, expanded edition of *Soft Subversions*, which first appeared as a slim volume in 1996. Like the older version, the revised edition includes translations of chapters from **Révolution moléculaire, Les Années d'hiver,** and **Cartographies schizoanalytiques,** as well as talks, interviews, and journalistic pieces. Most selections were written as occasional essays and therefore bear little resemblance to Guattari's more dense theoretical writing. Topics covered include Guattari's own critical practice, radical Italian politics, adolescence, technology, psychoanalysis, and globalization (which he called '**integrated world capitalism**'). Some of these texts originally appeared in the 1995 edition of **Chaosophy.** There are a few new essays, but the main change is the chronological rearrangement of the original tables of contents and the addition of a substantial new introduction. - J. W.

Soixante-cinq Rêves de Franz Kafka

Guattari greatly admired Franz **Kafka**'s writings for their comic moments and political insights into bureaucracy and perversion. He also collected Kafka's dreams, primarily from his letters, but also from stories and novels. This posthumously published collection of short pieces contains an essay of dream interpretation;

two catalogue essays from the 1984 exhibition *Le siècle de Kafka* at Centre Pompidou in Paris staged on the centenary of Kafka's birth; and an outline for an unrealized film made for television 'by' Kafka, not 'about' him. Instead of accepting that every dream has an unplumbable spot connected with the unknown, Guattari finds points of **singularity** in Kafka's dreams where interpretation gets moving and processes of subjectification are unleashed: certain gestures; things like teeth; animals such as dogs; dancers, servants, prostitutes; diabolical women; women with bad skin; young blind girls. The semiotic means that feature in the dreams are diverse. The points lack static symbolic indexes and require a technique of interpretation that acknowledges the maximal effects of the least incident, phagocytation (the blurring of dreams in Kafka's letters and literary texts), and maturation of the literary process itself. In 'Project for a Film By Kafka', Guattari wanted to make a film for television that would attract funding as a 'cultural series'. Despite Guattari's mistrust of television, it was in this instance a choice medium for forging a potential public and connecting it with independent **affects** from Kafka, precipitating becomings-Kafka. The film would build highly abstract and lyrical sequences around molecular elements such as bowed heads; heads bursting through windows, doorways, even ceilings; and the wall that is at the heart of the project operates as a machine that both breaks up and connects movements of characters. It is a screen, a molecularized face, bearing geological strata, vegetal becomings (moss) and receptacle for men's urine. - G. G.

Sonsign

cross-reference: **Time-Image** (break with the sensory-motor schema)

Spinoza, Baruch de

In his interview with Claire Parnet, in the context of a discussion about culture, Deleuze insists that he has no reservoir of knowledge or deposit of unpublished writings which would inform a conventionally 'cultured' or intellectual disposition. Everything he knows and learns (whether 'high' or low culture, philosophy or film), he does so only temporarily, and forgets everything afterwards, with the exception of Spinoza. While this is a passing comment, and Deleuze surely has a handful of other philosophers and writers who he internalized in his own way after completing temporary projects, the comment testifies to the importance of Spinoza to him intellectually and personally (that Spinoza came up during a conversation about how Deleuze identifies himself—whether 'cultured' or not, whether 'intellectual' or not, only amplifies this).

There is no doubt that Deleuze draws immense inspiration from Spinoza. Deleuze in fact closes his *tour de force* in **Difference and Repetition** with a meditation on a relation between **Univocity** in the Spinozist sense and **Eternal Return** in the **Nietzsche**an sense: when he writes that there is 'A single and same voice for the whole thousand-voiced multiple, a single and same Ocean for all the drops, a single clamour of Being for all beings: on condition that each being, each drop and each voice has reached the state of excess' (DR 378, 304). This is also perhaps what critics of his work have taken him to task on: readers of Deleuze criticism no doubt recognize the phrase 'clamour of Being' as the title of a work by Alan Badiou, who claims that Deleuze maintains a monistic philosophy; other critics of Deleuze's ontology along these lines include Todd May and Peter Hallward. - E. B. Y.

Spinoza: Expressionism in Philosophy

Spinoza et le problème de l'expression (1968)

Rationalism, the brand of philosophy that **Spinoza** is usually associated with, is usually understood in terms of the ability to grasp eternal truths that are not prone to the errors of experience or sensation. However, the reader familiar with Spinoza will note that Deleuze characterizes Spinoza's 'rationalism' in a peculiar way: in his view, Spinoza's excessive and conspicuous use of logic is in fact a disguise, a 'mask', for a vision of living, of God, and of ideas which ultimately defy logic, abstraction, and representation, and are grounded in the experience of pleasure and pain. In other words, while he does treat Spinoza in comparison with **Descartes** and Hobbes, he does not view Spinoza's geometrical method as a science; if his work resembled Newton's, for example, it certainly did not have the same purpose (it could even be considered parodic).

What makes Deleuze's approach to **Spinoza** unique? According to Spinoza's overturning of the Cartesian mind-body dualism, where our **attributes** manifest the same substance (see entry on **Descartes** for a discussion of parallelism as well as numerical and real distinction), our 'essence' is determined by eternal truths even if we necessarily only conceive of those truths by means of experience. Consider a passing comment that Deleuze makes in one of his seminars: 'every affection is affection of essence. Thus the passions belong to essence no less than the actions; the inadequate ideas [belong] to essence no less than the adequate ideas. And nevertheless there was necessarily a difference. The passions and the inadequate ideas must not belong to essence in the same way that the actions and the adequate ideas belong to it' (webdeleuze 24/03/1981). What this means is that as human beings (or '**modal**' essences), we enter into the world only with 'inadequate ideas', and yet these inadequate ideas, based on imaginary causes **affects**, are entirely the basis for adequate ideas, which are also based on non-imaginary, actual causes of affects (adequate ideas are not imaginary because they involve the real 'order and connection' of things). The difference is that, in the first case those affects are just the *effect* of external **forces** (bodies, **modes**, etc.) on our own body (which we passively receive), while in the second case, those affects are caused by our own comprehension of the external relations that cause affects to be produced (thus he puts forward the notion that they are the 'cause of themselves'). Thus the Spinozist, 'ethical', 'rational', human being is not a passive person who steps back and intellectualizes or 'rationalizes' the way things happen in a manner that they are powerless to change. Rather, they are an active person who exercises logical comprehension in order to change, will, or manipulate external circumstances so that affects between their body and external modes are agreeable (that is, they are not destructive or paralytic).

The **paradox** of Spinoza's work, in this sense, is that understanding a cause does not mean transcending the power of the **imagination** which generated the inadequate idea to begin with; in other words, adequate ideas and the 'good life' involve an ontological viewpoint of the relationships between **modes**, not an epistemological one.

In *Expressionism in Philosophy*, Deleuze insists that epistemology concerns the 'parallel' relationships between the mind and body (that is, understanding that one does not cause the other, but that there is always a corresponding thought or idea for every extension or body). He shows that we cannot always know *why* certain bodies affect each other in a certain way (although there is always a physics of quantity concerning essence), but we can know that they *do*, and that particular relations will express a certain essence or degree of power. When Deleuze states, 'it is the same Being that is present in the God who complicates all things according to his own essence, and in the things that explicate him according to their own essence or **mode**' (SEP 176), he is highlighting the ontological or *intensive* relationship between thought and extension: on the one hand, God (infinite substance) complicates or comprehends the relationship between infinite quality (**attributes**) and finite quantity (modal essences), and on the other hand, the attributes are explicated in existing modes which in turn implicate the qualities that they extend (expressing degrees of power or **intensity**). Adequate ideas concern the **univocity** of being as it is expressed (ontology), not categories of an equivocal being (epistemology). This circuitous logic is perhaps the greatest challenge of reading *Expressionism in Philosophy*. - E. B. Y.

Spinoza: Practical Philosophy

Spinoza. Textes choisis (1970): Spinoza. Philosophie pratique (1981)

Closely following the same format employed earlier in **Nietzsche: Sa vie, son œuvre, avec un exposé de sa philosophie**, one year after the appearance of **Spinoza and the Problem of Expression**, Deleuze publishes this popular edition which covers Spinoza's biography, excerpts from the correspondence with Blyenburgh on the problem of evil, and contains an index of the principle terms from the *Ethics*, and two concluding essays on the unfinished *Political Treatise* and on 'Spinoza and Us.' In the last essay, on the contemporary meaning of Spinoza in philosophy, Deleuze comments on the fact that Spinoza's has been received mostly by poets and artists, rather than by philosophers who have either avoided his philosophy, or ignored it altogether. Deleuze accounts for this fact by the problem that the 'plan of **immanence**' proposed in the *Ethics* poses for most philosophers, while non-philosophers (artists and poets especially) are often 'inspired' by this plan and adopt it pragmatically as an aspect of their own artistic composition. It is in this comment that Deleuze and Guattari return later to make the claim that Spinoza represents 'the Christ of Philosophers' by the manner in which he causes philosophy and non-philosophy to become united in a single being. - G. L.

Stengers, Isabelle and Ilya Prigogine

Belgian philosopher Isabelle Stengers and Nobel-prize-winning Russian-born Belgian chemist Ilya Prigogine collaborated on popular books explaining **chaos** theory and far-from-equilibrium thermodynamics to non-specialists. Guattari met them through his friend and colleague **Mony Elkaïm**. Stengers was a reader and admirer of Deleuze and Guattari's work, and taught their texts in her own philosophy seminars. Prigogine was interested in the philosophical aspects of complexity theory, and his work was read by many social scientists. Guattari's use of terms like **singularity**, bifurcation, and strange attractors owes a great deal to his reading of Prigogine and Stengers. The ontology underpinning his final works borrows from their explanations of how order emerges out of chaos. His ecological thinking is informed by their theories of open systems, and his conception of history by the idea of the irreversibility of processes in complex systems. - J. W.

Stern, Daniel

In *The Interpersonal World of the Infant*, Daniel Stern brings together psychoanalysis and developmental psychology in order to forge a new theory of child development. His empirically-supported description of infant's emerging sense of self differs significantly from **Freud's** Oedipal narrative or Lacan's account of the subject-splitting mirror stage. In *Chaosmosis* Guattari explains that Stern finds no evidence of Freud's stages or Lacan's tyrannical signifier, but that he instead observes the formation of levels of subjectivation which are largely pre-verbal and which remain in place throughout adulthood (CM 6). He argues that the emergent self, already present at birth, develops trans-subjectively through the infant's corporeal perceptions of its environment. Guattari incorporates this view of infant development into his own account of **heterogenesis**, using Stern to support his own argument the infant self emerges not within a Mommy-Daddy-me structure, but through a web of what Guattari calls **existential Territories** and incorporeal **Universes** of reference (see **four functors**) (CM 65–9). - J. W.

Stoics, the

While Stoicism is known for suppressing emotion and for their hypothetical and inferential logic (which can be distinguished from **Aristotle**'s categorical and deductive logic), Deleuze's interest lies in the manner in which Stoic propositions (such as 'if it is day, it is light') do not denote cause and effect with reference to the present, but are meant to infer what has taken place or will take place from effects only. Furthermore, the terms within their propositions are not contradictory because they do not demonstrate existence, and are instead meant to have singular conclusions. In other words, a simple proposition such as 'It is day' or 'it is light' may 'correspond' to a state of affairs or to that which is the case (*hyparchien*); that is, it may denote a 'fact', but does not demonstrate or prove anything about that which actually exists. This logic extends to disjunctions ('either') which interest Deleuze because they can coexist independently of their verification in a denoted state of affairs. Everything takes place on what Deleuze calls the **'surface'**, which he uses to read Alice's adventures in *The Logic of Sense*. Through this lens, the stereotype about Stoics being emotionless has more to do with their insistence upon the separation of effects from causes, and less to do with a neglect of a theory of 'bodies'; their theory of bodies and **'depth'** acknowledges their cannibalistic, terrifying, and inter-penetrating character and is arguably more profound than most ancient theories. As Deleuze states, 'The Stoics' strength lay in making a line of separation pass—no longer between the sensible and the intelligible, or between the soul and the body, but where no one had seen it before—between physical depth and metaphysical surface. Between things and **events**.' (D 63). - E. B. Y.

Strata

(*stratum*—*singular form*; *stratification*)

One of their most explicitly 'geological' concepts (in accordance with the conceptual organization of *A Thousand Plateaus*), 'strata' is Deleuze and Guattari's alternative to structure. While **structuralism** emphases interrelations that are often dehistoricized, the concept of strata allows for an understanding of *layers* both in terms of space and time (the temporal aspect is especially emphasized by Deleuze in his work on **Foucault**; though this term should be distinguished from unstratified '**planes**' which imply infinite movements); the formations of such strata are always 'double' because they have a **form of content** and **form of expression**. This alternative to structuralism creates the conditions for much more complexity in terms of conceptualizing relations of **coding** ('induction' and 'transduction') and the formation of **matter**, whether it is physical/chemical, organic, and technological, and whether conceived on a molecular or molar level.

1.a. In D&G's complementary analysis of the development of social, organic, machinic, and geological systems, the **redundant** and layered result of both **coding** and **territorialization: forms of content** and **forms of expression** on a horizontal, coded, or historical axis (*parastrata*), and, substances on a vertical, hierarchical, or layered axis of **territorialization** (*epistrata*).

> **Strata** *are* **Layers, Belts.** *They consist of giving form to* **matters,** *of imprisoning* **intensities** *or locking singularities into systems of resonance and* **redundancy** *[...]* **Strata** *are acts of capture [...]they proceed simultaneously by* **code** *and by* **territoriality.** [TP 45, 40]
>
> *Each stratum serves as the substratum for another* **stratum** [TP 81, 72]

Forms relate to **codes** *and processes of* **coding** *and decoding in the* **parastrata***; substances, being formed* **matters***, relate to* **territorialities** *and movements of deterritorialization and reterritorialization on the* **epistrata***.* [TP 59, 53]

b. A formation of content and expression (or 'double articulation'), either 1) on an order of magnitude, going from molecular content to molar expression (by virtue of **resonance** and amplification), 2) linearly, where molecular and molar are united by sequences (as with DNA or **transcodings**), such that expression is not dependent on content, or 3) synthetically, by virtue of the process of translation (as with language).

What varies from **stratum** *to* **stratum** *is the nature of the real distinction between content and* **expression***, the nature of the substances as formed* **matters***, and the nature of the relative movements.* [TP 80, 72]

c. A unity of composition (which has multiple centers in the epistrata and fragments in the parastrata) of materials and elements, in which the **plane of consistency** (that is, the *unstratified*—this also includes the **BwO** and **diagram**) is enclosed or encased.

Materials [of a stratum] are not the same as the unformed **matter** *of the* **plane of consistency***; they are already* **stratified***, and come from 'substrata.'* [TP 55, 49]

We should not forget that the **strata** *rigidify and are organized on the* **plane of consistency** *[...].* [TP 371, 337]

The **plane of consistency** *is always* **immanent** *to the* **strata** *[...].* [TP 63, 57]

2. In Deleuze's reading of **Foucault**, forms of knowledge, whose visibilities (contents) and statements (expressions) communicate by virtue of the non-stratified element of power and which constitute an inside of the past and present (forms of **subjectivity**) that is coextensive with an **outside** of the future (new subjectivities).

Knowledge concerns formed **matters** *(substances) and formalized functions, divided up* **segment** *by segment according to the two great formal conditions of seeing and speaking, light and language: it is*

> *therefore* stratified [...]. *Power, on the other hand, is* **diagrammatic**: *it mobilizes non-*stratified *matter and functions, and unfolds with a very flexible segmentarity.* [F 61, 73]

> *the* **strata** *are the affair of archaeology, precisely because* [...] *There is an archaeology of the present.* [...] *On the limit of the* **strata**, *the* [...] *inside condenses the past (a long period of time) in ways that* [...] *confront it with a future that comes from* **outside**, *exchange it and re-create it. To think means to be embedded in the present-time stratum that serves as a limit.* [F 98, 119]

- E. B. Y.

Striated space

1. Space designed for a sedentary lifestyle, where movement concerns the relationship between points or nodes which are imported onto it from a higher plane or another dimension; the dimensional movement of **territorialized milieus**, in distinction from directional movement within **lines of flight** or **smooth space**.

> *Homogeneous space is in no way a* **smooth space**; *on the contrary, it is the form of* **striated space**. [...] *It is striated by the fall of bodies, the verticals of gravity, the distribution of matter into parallel layers, the lamellar and laminar movement of* **flows**. *These parallel verticals have formed an independent dimension capable of spreading everywhere* [...]. [TP 408, 370]

> *What is both limited and limiting is* **striated space**, *the relative global: it is limited in its parts, which are assigned constant directions, are oriented in relation to one another, divisible by boundaries, and can interlink; what is limiting (limes or wall, and no longer boundary) is this aggregate in relation to the* **smooth spaces** *it 'contains,' whose growth it slows or prevents* [...]. [TP 422, 382]

- E. B. Y.

Structuralism

The school of thought known as structuralism has many strands. The most common variants mentioned by Guattari are Saussurean and Chomskyan, and the Barthes-**Hjelmslev** variations of linguistics, as well as Lacanian psychoanalysis. Structures are typically composed of relations between entities in a topological space; features are distributed with some regularity; structure displays **surface** and **depth**, and its terms are defined by binary value-giving axes and the presupposition of differential and oppositional relations. By regaining and going beyond **Hjelmslevian** glossematics in a radical way, and by introducing a machinic element into structure, Guattari diversified the semiotic register and delinguistified structure.

1.a. In Guattari's renouncement of the realist ontological assumption of underlying structure (that the **unconscious** was structured like a language), pure positivities with multiple and multiplex relata, enveloping syntagmatic trees in proliferating **rhizomes**, erecting a detotalizing machine characterized by breakdowns, disequilibria, and **autopoiesis**.

> *What specifies human language is precisely that it never refers back to itself, that always remains open to all other modes of semiotization. [...]Its* 'structure' *results from the petrification of a sort of grab-all through which the elements come from borrowings, amalgamations, agglutinations, misunderstandings—a kind of sly humour governing its generalizations.* [MU 27]

b. A version of **Hjelmslev's** glossematics as a theory of **flows** beyond the effects of the signifier.

> *[glossematics is]...the only linguistics adapted to the nature of both the capitalist and the schizophrenic flows [...].* [AO 264, 243]

c. A rejection of the alleged scientificity of structuralism, and the centrality of the signifier as a fetish that overcodes all of expression, in favor of a pragmatics and a hybrid semiotics that concerns materiality, power, and the social field.

> *In the heyday of* **structuralism** *the subject was methodically excluded from its own multiple and heterogenous material of* **expression***. It is time to re-examine machinic productions of images, signs of artificial intelligence, etc., as new materials of* **subjectivity***.* [CM 133]

d. An introduction of elements of alterity and disequilibrium by the machine, with ontological implications of an irreducible heterogeneity and **virtuality**.

Subjectivity does not only produce itself through the psychogenetic stages of psychoanalysis or the 'mathemes' of the **Unconscious**, *but also in the large-scale social machines of language and the mass media—which cannot be described as human. A certain balance still needs to be struck between* **structuralist** *discoveries—which are certainly not unimportant—and their pragmatic application, so as not to flounder in the social abandon of post-modernism.* [CM 9–10]

- G. G.

Subjectivity

This term is explored separately by Deleuze and Guattari (though the 'subject' is bound up with their **collective assemblage of enunciation**—see def. 5); while Deleuze explored the subject in relation to **Hume** and **Foucault** (see def. 1 and 2), the Guattarian subject is neither an individual nor a person. This subjectless subject is non-homogeneous, mutable, hence not essentialist, and assembled from heterogeneous components, beyond and before the human and language. In this respect it is auto-organizing, largely self-referential, but influenced and modified by dominant traits of a historical period. Guattari prefers to consider processes of subjectification rather than classical subjects. There are two periods in his thought: a focus on characterizing the components of self-referentiality and how they intersect, and the external **territorialities** or alterities, that is, from the late 1970s to the early 1990s.

1. In Deleuze's reading of **Hume**, the inventive state of the human mind which is constituted within and transcends any given set of circumstances and experience; the qualification of mind insofar as it is both constituted by passion and **sensation** (as reflected in the **imagination**) and by **reason** which forms associations based on experience.

   subjectivity *is essentially practical. Its definitive unity [...] will be revealed in the relations between motive and action, means and end. [...] The fact that there is no theoretical* subjectivity *[...]becomes the fundamental claim of empiricism.* [ES 104]

the impressions of sensation only form the mind, giving it merely an origin, whereas the impressions of reflection constitute the subject *in the mind, diversely qualifying the mind as* subject [ES 97]

2. In Deleuze's reading of **Foucault**, that which is unfolded by the relation between power and knowledge, and, in his critique of Foucault, that which is **folded** by **force** to resist subjectification or dependence upon **diagrams** (of power) and **forms of content/expression**.

Foucault's fundamental idea is that of a dimension of subjectivity *derived from power and knowledge without being dependent on them.* [F 83, 101]

3.a. In Guattari's work, dense crossing points of a machinic nucleus which are stabilized by various consistencies (molar and molecular), semiotic matters of enunciation, components of passage, extractions and reconnections to points on the mechanosphere, and openings to the cosmos.

The subject *and the machine are inseparable from one another.* [MU 159]

b. A productively self-positing process (auto-modelization) that is performed relationally in terms of points of reference like the body and the social **group**, but also shaped by alterities and the transit of autonomous **affects** and social constructions that impose limitations such as models of identity, and semiotic redundancies that define competence.

... the provisional definition of subjectivity *I would like to propose ... would be: 'The ensemble of conditions which render possible the emergence of individual and/or collective instances as self-referential existential* **Territories***, adjacent, or in a delimiting relation, to an alterity that is itself* subjective*'.* [CM 8–9]

c. Human existence that is produced and punctuated by points of **singularity** and transformed by exploring the potential consistencies they bear; it may be exploited by capitalism as a raw material for affective labor, yet as an emergent phenomenon, it constantly escapes capture and may be differently recovered, and is in the process of inventing its autonomy.

> The machinic production of **subjectivity** *can work for the better or for the worse.* [GR 194]

d. Human existence influenced by **affects** that stick to it and by **refrains** that count it out, both helping to build a **territory** in which it may existentially instantiate itself, and from which it may take flight.

4. A type of **Ecosophy** that contributes new incarnations inspired by artistic production.

> *One creates new modalities of* **subjectivity** *in the same way that an artist creates new forms from the palette.* [CM 7]

5. (Special Type): **Collective Assemblage:** That which is irreducible to a single common denominator, hence polyphonous, and indescribable in fixed genetic stages; production that is collective (and machinic) and self-posits through enunciative assemblages.

> *The collective* **assemblage** *is at once subject, object and expression. The individual is no longer the* **universal** *guarantor of dominant significations.* [RM 10/18 43]

- E. B. Y. and G. G.

Superpositions. Richard III par Carmelo Bene, suivi de *Un manifeste de moins* par Gilles Deleuze (1979)

The Italian playwright and director Carmelo Bene was a principal renovator of Italian post-war theater through the period of the late-1950s. This small work represents the French edition of Bene's experimental adaptation of Shakespeare's Richard III, one in which the central action is reduced to the figures of Richard and the female characters in Shakespeare's original drama, and the historical basis of the tragic representation of the Monarchy is 'amputated' in favor of the personage of Richard himself. In the afterword, which takes the form of a manifesto on the principles of a minor theatre, Deleuze argues that by subtracting the State personages of power from the drama, Bene's version renders a purer portrait of Richard's power as an expression of a '**war machine**,' including the true nature of his deformities and suicidal characteristics, than any tragic representation of Royal or State power. It is by this method of subtraction (methode par moins) that the perverse face of power is attains reality and force. Thus, Deleuze writes, it represents neither a critique of Shakespeare, nor a metatheatrical play, nor even a new version of the play, but rather a 'theater-experimentation' that displays more love of Shakespeare than all of his commentators. - G. L.

Surface

1. The incorporeal domain of effects which evade presence (**Chronos**) and are instead always oriented toward the past and future (**Aion**).

> It is not that surface has less nonsense than does depth. But it is not the same nonsense. Surface nonsense is like the 'Radiance' of pure events [that...] let an incorporeal rise to the surface like a mist over the earth, a pure 'expressed' from the depths: not the sword, but the flash of the sword, a flash without a sword like the smile without a cat. [ECC 22]

> if the surface evades the present, it is with all the power of an 'instant,' which distinguishes its occurrence from any assignable present subject to division and redivision. Nothing ascends to the surface without changing its nature. [LS 189, 165]

- E. B. Y.

Symptomatology

1. In distinction from *etiology* (the science of causes of disease) and therapy (the treatment of diseases), the discovery of the arrangement of **signs** and symptoms of diseases; a *clinical, literary, and* artistic methodology employed by writers who 'diagnose' new patterns of illness through an exploration of their cultural and social contexts.

> *Whereas etiology and therapeutics are integral parts of medicine,* **symptomology** *appeals to a kind of neutral point, a limit that is premedical or sub-medical, belonging as much to art as to medicine: it's all about drawing a 'portrait.' The work of art exhibits symptoms, as do the body or the soul, albeit in a very different way. In this sense, the artist or writer can be a great* **symptomatolgist,** *just like the best doctor [...]* [ECC 22]

> *Another question we should ask is whether* **Masoch** *does not present a* **symptomatology** *that is more refined than Sade's in that it enables us to discriminate between disturbances which were previously regarded as identical.* [CC 16]

- E. B. Y.

Synsign

cross-reference: **Action-Image** (actualization—milieu)

Territory; Territorialization

(also, *deterritorialization, reterritorialization*)

For Deleuze and Guattari, the human being is located at the border between the animal and the machine, between the earth and the cosmos. While there are, no doubt, innate, visceral and biological functions—such as aggressiveness, sexuality, gregariousness, etc.—which establish our interactions within our environment, it is usually presumed by ethologists that 'territorial' behaviour is an extension of such 'instincts'. D&G suggest, however, that it is the other way around: 'territorialization' seizes these functions and reorganizes them so that they work relative to, and for the purpose of, the 'territory'. For example, we aren't territorial because we're 'innately' aggressive, we're aggressive because we're territorial; in this case, however, the function of aggression would change—it does not occur relative to other functions (sexuality, etc.), but only relative to the 'territory'. But what is the territory?

D&G explain that the earth and cosmos are composed of both 'mechanical' phenomena (that is, stable **forces** or **milieus**) and of 'machinic' phenomena that express the **rhythmic** relation between such stable milieus. 'Territorialization' does not necessarily emerge from some *interior*, repressed or neurotic drive (as **Freud** might have it), but is a seizure and **assemblage** of these *exterior* forces. The animal or human being acts (individually or in **groups**) on these phenomena in order to establish itself in its environment, to create a border between inside and outside. While territorialization can function in a 'transcendental' fashion for assemblages of oppression, this establishment has no function analogous to the functions that it appropriates; therefore, they conclude that when taken for itself, its actual function is *expressiveness*. This locates territorialization as the origin of art and music: nature and the interactions of living things, following Von Uexkull's insights, is a symphony. It is not 'an impulse triggering an action', but the *style* of motifs, counterpoints, and **refrains**.

The novelty of territorial expressiveness often comes from its 'opening' onto other **assemblages,** or onto the 'cosmos'; that is, when expressiveness no longer functions strictly for the territory but expresses a **becoming**—a loss or change of function—it is *de*territorialized (this is especially liberating—socially and politically—when territories have an oppressive function—as with aspects of modern capitalism). Enter the **abstract machine**: no longer are phenomena within the **milieu** a function of the territory but of 'assemblages of another type, the molecular, the cosmic [or a new, unforeseen territorial assemblage]'; this notion that the territory is inseparable from its deterritorialization highlights the **Nietzschean** tenet that **becoming** is the **force** of being.

1. The result of a tendency of living beings to utilize both the predictability and functionality of **milieu** components in order to ensure a critical distance from other living things or

chaotic forces which would dissipate that environment, and the **rhythmic** markings (animal and human posters, placards, gestures, mannerisms, songs, and dances) which result from this process and transform or manipulate milieus so that they are *no longer* functional but *qualitative* and *expressive* (i.e. that 'function' to express the territory).

> A **territory** *borrows from all the* **milieus**; *it bites into them, seizes them bodily (although it remains vulnerable to intrusions). It is built from aspects or portions of milieus.* [TP 347, 314]

> Territorialization *is an act of* rhythm *that has become* expressive, *or of* milieu *components that have become qualitative.* [TP 348, 315]

> *a* **territory** *has two notable effects: a reorganization of functions and a regrouping of* **forces**. *[...] when functional activities are* territorialized *they necessarily change pace (the creation of new functions such as building a dwelling, or the transformation of old functions, as when aggressiveness changes nature and becomes intraspecific). [...]These functions are organized or created only because they are* territorialized, *and not the other way around.* [TP 353–4, 320–1]

2.a. In terms of art, the **expression** of the romantic artist who isolates and digresses within the groundless depths of the singular force of the earth, exploring the relation between **form** and **matter**.

> *the romantic artist experiences the* **territory**; *but he or she experiences it as necessarily lost, and experiences him- or herself as an exile, a voyager, as* deterritorialized, *driven back into the* milieus *[...].* [TP 374, 339]

b. (Special Type): **deterritorialized** expression: The material of the modern artist who abandons the relation to the earth (interior **milieu**) in favor of capturing a relation to cosmic forces (exterior milieu), exploring the relation between *material* and **force**.

> *If there is a modern age, it is, of course, the age of the cosmic. [...] The earth is now at its most* deterritorialized: *not only a point in a galaxy, but one galaxy among others. [...] It is only after* matter *has been sufficiently* deterritorialized *that it itself emerges as molecular [material] and brings forth pure forces attributable only to the Cosmos.* [TP 377 and 382, 345 and 347]

3.a. (Special Combination): *Territorial Assemblage*: The vertical side of the **assemblage** and the territorializing movement that creates **assemblages**; the other side of **strata** that works in solidarity with **coded milieus** on a horizontal axis.

> *the* **assemblage** *is fundamentally* **territorial***. But how could it not already be in the process of passing into something else, into other assemblages?* [TP 356, 323]

> *on a vertical axis, the* **assemblage** *has both* **territorial** *sides, or* **reterritorialized** *sides, which stabilize it, and cutting edges of* **deterritorialization***, which carry it away.* [TP 98, 88]

> *Just as* **milieus** *swing between a stratum state and a movement of destratification,* **assemblages** *swing between a* **territorial** *closure that tends to restratify them and a* **deterritorializing** *movement that on the contrary connects them with the Cosmos.* [TP 371, 337]

b. (Special Type and Combination): *Deterritorialized Assemblage, Deterritorialization:* The manner in which the assembled, milieu components of a territory lose their transcendent, territorial function (by virtue of an **abstract machine**) to communicate or meld with other assemblages outside of it (or the cosmos).

> *Whenever a* **territorial assemblage** *is taken up by a movement that deterritorializes it [...] we say that a machine is released. [...] a machine is like a set of cutting edges that insert themselves into the* **assemblage** *undergoing* **deterritorialization***, and draw variations and mutations of it.* [TP 367, 333]

c. (Special Combination): *Relative deterritorialization:* Movements on or within **strata** which induce or precede reterritorialization (as when religious figures are projected *on* the **plane of immanence**) or absolute deterritorialization (as when **concepts** directly mark out the plane of immanence); also, a feature of capitalism which deterritorializes subjects and objects through value and reterritorializes them on the State. [AO, TP, WP]

> *the* **territory** *is constantly traversed by movements of* **deterritorialization** *that are relative and may even occur in place, by which one passes from the intra-***assemblage** *to inter-assemblages, without, however, leaving the* **territory** *[...].* [TP 360, 326]

When relative deterritorialization *is itself horizontal, or* immanent, *it combines with the* absolute deterritorialization *of the* plane of immanence *[...].* [WP 90]

city-towns [...] pushed deterritorialization *so far that immanent modern States had to [...] recapture and invest them so as to carry out necessary* reterritorializations *[...].* [WP 98]

d. (Special Combination): *Absolute deterritorialization*: Movements of destratification on the **plane of consistency** (or a 're'-territorialization *on* the plane), which emerge from relative deterritorializations (and result in reterritorializations on the plane through the inevitable new **concepts**, conceptual personae, people, or earth which populate it); an a-signifying semiotic which, due to its subjectivity, cannot be incorporated into a semiotic system.

This **absolute deterritorialization** *becomes relative only after* **stratification** *occurs on that plane or body* [TP 63, 56]

absolute deterritorialization *can only be thought according to [...] relationships with relative* deterritorializations *that are not only cosmic but geographical, historical, and psychosocial.* [WP 88]

Absolute deterritorialization *does not take place without* reterritorialization. [WP 101]

The most essential distinction between the signifying regime and the subjective regime and their respective **redundancies** *is the movement of* deterritorialization *they effectuate. Since the signifying* **sign** *refers only to other signs [...], the corresponding semiotic enjoys a high level of* deterritorialization; *but it is a* deterritorialization *that is still relative, expressed as* frequency. *[...] the subjective regime proceeds entirely differently: precisely because the sign breaks its relation of significance with other* signs, *it attains an* **absolute deterritorialization** *expressed in the* **black hole** *of consciousness and passion.* [TP 147, 133]

4.a (Special Combination): *Primitive Territorial Machine*: In D&G's analysis of economic and social history, that which marks or inscribes populations with memory for technical machines; the local, social encoding of **desire** that precedes geographic territorialization.

The **territorial** *machine is [...] the first form of socius, the machine* *of primitive inscription, the 'megamachine' that covers a social field.* [AO 155, 141]

The primitive **territorial** *machine codes* **flows**, *invests organs, and marks bodies.* [AO 158, 144]

the savage, primitive socius was indeed the only **territorial** *machine [...which] consists in the following: the declension of alliance and filiation—declining the lineages on the body of the earth, before there is a State.* [AO 160, 146]

b. The function of the *Despotic Machine* or the State which overcodes the alliances and filiations of the primitive territorial machine (deterritorializing their indirect, local connections and reterritorilializing them through a direct affiliation with the Sovereign).

the residence or **territoriality** *of the State inaugurates the great movement of* **deterritorialization** *that subordinates all the primitive filiations to the despotic machine [...].* [AO 215, 197]

c. In capitalist societies, a process of seizure upon **decoded** flows (of capital, labor) that marks them with artificial drives or imperatives to produce and **desire**; or, conversely, a process that *deterritorializes* flows, resulting in surplus value that is in turn reterritorialized.

Capitalism institutes or restores all sorts of residual and artificial, imaginary, or symbolic **territorialities**, *thereby attempting, as best it can, to recede, to rechannel persons who have been defined in terms of abstract quantities [...]. The more the capitalist machine* **deterritorializes**, *decoding and axiomatizing flows in order to extract surplus value from them, the more its ancillary apparatuses, such as government bureaucracies and the forces of law and order, do their utmost to* **reterritorialize**, *absorbing in the process a larger and larger share of surplus value.* [AO 37, 35]

5.a. *Territorialization*: In Deleuze and Guattari's reading of **Kafka**, the manner in which **desire** is paralyzed or represented by blocks and **segments** of power structures, engendering and reinforcing relations of servitude and mastery, as well as paranoia.

each block-segment was a concretization of power, of desire, of territoriality *or* reterritorialization, *regulated by the abstraction of a transcendental law.* [K 86]

b. *Deterritorialization*: the point at which a movement of escape or the **line of flight** for **desire** is reached; the exile and continual traversal through social and political machines that engenders schizophrenia rather than paranoia. [AO, K, TP]

> *an* assemblage *has points of* deterritorialization; *[...] it always has a* line of escape *by which it [...]liberates* desire *from all its concretizations and abstractions[...]*. [K 86]

- E. B. Y.

Thom, René

French mathematician René Thom is best known for his groundbreaking catastrophe theory, which he developed in 1968. In the early 1970s he published two widely-read books for non-specialists, in which he applies his complex topographical models of mathematical **singularities**—which he calls catastrophes—to many different domains and disciplines, including linguistics, hence Guattari's interest in his work. Thom describes meaning as a catastrophe, a bifurcation or sudden change in the state of a system, theorizing that information is transferred between dynamic systems (such as two brains) through **resonance**. New information creates a mathematical catastrophe in the receiving system, which reaches equilibrium only after the initial state of excitement dissipates as a result of understanding. Guattari might have been seduced by this seemingly machinic alternative to the signifier-signified model of language, were it not for Thom's strict adherence to mathematics, which for Guattari remains too abstract to intervene in the biological realm. Accordingly, Guattari defines his notion of the **abstract machine** against the mathematical abstraction of Thom's theories (MU 9–13). However, he remained fascinated by the temporal inversions involved in Thom's notion of retroactive smoothing (SC 161). - J. W

The Three Ecologies

Ecosophy is Guattari's critical transdisciplinary approach to the three ecological levels: macroscopic environmental challenges like global warming; intermediary social issues like homelessness and poverty; and molecular mental ecology or processes of subjectification under cognitive capitalism. The eco-logic concerns how the three levels are knit together **transversally**, and the implications for mental ecology are focused on. Eco-praxes scout out promising vectors for singularizing subjectifications and try to nurture them, along the way enlisting the work of artists to assist in the process. Guattari favored the diverse works and media of David Wojnarowicz, George Condo, Sarenco, and Shin Takamatsu. Eco-praxis has an ethico-aesthetic dimension in the forging of new value systems that may be communicated to audiences affectively, precipitating a transference of **singularities** and assumption of eco-responsibility. When Guattari refers to ecology he means macro-machinic ecology: the evolving phylum of telecommunications, synthetics, drugs, biogenetics, urban sprawl, in which the biosphere and mecanosphere are mutually imbricated, and which the processes of subjectification must negotiate. On the phylum molecular mutations bubble up and new developments emerge like mobile media (cell phones) whose subjugating and liberatory potentialities eco-praxis must grapple with: technological advances within machinic evolution are constantly challenging how subjective cartographies are going to be sketched. This book deeply analyses the **territories** of existential incarnation in Guattari's ontology and enlists art to provide a means for heterogeneous diversification in the creation of new universes of reference. - G. G.

A Thousand Plateaus

Mille plateaux. Capitalisme et schizophrénie 2, avec Félix Guattari (1980)

After the controversy that surrounded the publication of **Anti-Oedipus**, much of which forms the basis of the interviews and conversations that are later collected in the first two sections of *Negotiations*, in 1980 Deleuze and Guattari publish the second full volume of the Capitalism and Schizophrenia project. The work is markedly different from first volume, and employs a spatial logic of multiple sections (or plateaus) as the method of organization, as already announced in the introduction to *The Rhizome* published in 1976. The various plateaus form an **assemblage** belonging to a 'geo-philosophy,' a term that Deleuze and Guattari return to explicate later on in *What is Philosophy?* Each plateau is designated by a date and a corresponding topic (*topos*), modeled on the sudden or emergent events that occur on an evolutionary or geological scale of duration, which can signal anything from a transformation of phyla to entire planetary shifts. The concept of 'desiring-machine,' which was introduced in the first volume, is abandoned in favor of the concept of *agencement* (assemblage), which signals the departure from the structuralist domain of psychoanalysis for a heterodox and dizzying array of knowledges (general linguistics, cartography, physics, molecular biology, noology, statistics, theory of numbers, musicology, and computer sciences). The diversity of the knowledges employed follow the principle announced in *The Rhizome* that any assemblage can be connected to any other assemblage by using whatever is immediately to hand, replacing the authority of the book with a notion of a plateau as a flat surface of inscription upon which everything is potentially connected, including territories, peoples, and races. Returning to the argument concerning 'Universal History' of the first volume, Deleuze and Guattari prefer the geological model, along with its opposing tendencies of '**territorialization**' and 'deterritorialization,' over the teleological and Hegelian version of History in order to 'liberate' the force of contingency and the power of the 'milieu' against the notion of Structure and what they call 'the cult of Necessity.' Following the principle of the **Nomadology**, 'a territory' is a basic pattern that is both physical and mental, like the double aspect of a landscape, and becomes the privileged point of their analysis since it is also from within the **milieu** of a territory that variation is introduced into any assemblage (linguistic, cultural, political, biological, etc.) in a manner that they identify by a musical notion of **rhythm** (*ritornello*). Similar to the conclusion of *Anti-Oedipus*, as well as several of Deleuze's works on philosophers such as **Nietzsche** and **Spinoza**, *A Thousand Plateaus* ends with a glossary of major concepts, or 'concrete rules and abstract machines,' as a further emphasis to the pragmatic nature of their thought and a vivid demonstration of the first mandate of their philosophy: always experiment! - G. L.

Time-image

The time-image, also the subtitle of Deleuze's second volume on **cinema**, is a taxonomic concept which includes many sub-varieties (opsigns, sonsigns, hyalosigns, etc). In this case, while he initially draws on **Bergson**'s conception of time (which corresponds to the second **passive synthesis** of time), that leads him to **Blanchot**'s conception of **the Outside** where there is no longer a 'whole' (even an 'open' one) that is created through linear narrative; rather, images (and sounds) are related to express and engender the thought of **difference** (forcing a more active participation on the part of the viewer), which corresponds loosely to the third **passive synthesis** of time. That is, when memory and recognition 'fail', and images feel organized as in a dream (but nevertheless real), they are 'lived' or experienced according to logic that is unique to them. It is important to note that 'noosigns' described in def. 4.b. differ from the noosigns of the **movement-image** (3.b.) in that they do not form a sequence but a **series**.

1. Images characteristic of modern, that is, post WWII cinema, which originate in **recollection-images** (where the past is re-lived in the present), that give way to crystal images (where the past and present, imaginary and real, become interchangeable), and finally take the form of images which form novel connections between past and present that do not depend on a linear relationship or a reality/whole to unite them.

> *The modern* image *initiates the reign of 'incommensurables' or irrational cuts: [...]* images *are no longer linked by rational cuts, but are relinked on to irrational cuts. [...]*. [C2 266, 277]

> *There are [...]* time-images, *that is, duration*-images, *change*-images, *relation*-images, *volume*-images *which are beyond movement [...].* [C1 12, 11]

2.a. Images which are intimated (but not actually expressed) by the *opsigns* and *sonsigns* which break with the sensory-motor schema of the **action image** (that is, the **movement-image**) by dissociating the links made between perception and affection (*opsigns* by way of the visual, *sonsigns* by way of sound), exceeding our sensory-motor capacities; images which resist the clichés that are formed through the **good sense** and **common sense** of the **movement image**, inducing **recollection-images**.

> The **image** had to free itself from sensory-motor links; it had to stop being action-**image** in order to become a pure optical, sound (and tactile) **image**. But the latter was not enough: it had to [...] escape from a world of clichés [...and] open up to [...] the **time-image**, of the readable **image** and the thinking **image**. It is in this way that opsigns and sonsigns refer back to 'chronosigns', 'lectosigns' and 'noosigns'. [C2 22, 23]

> In everyday banality, the action-**image** and even the movement-**image** tend to disappear in favor of pure optical situations, but these reveal connections of a new type, which are no longer sensory-motor and which bring the emancipated senses into direct relation with **time** and thought [...]. [C2 17, 17]

b. (Special Type): direct time image, *crystal image* (hyalosign): An image (intimating the time-image) where the **virtual** is not lived in the present, as in a **recollection-image**, but where it forms a circuit between the real and imaginary; the manner in which the past and the present oscillate between or spill into each other (rather than the past being lived in the present, as in flashbacks and dreams).

> By raising themselves to the indiscernibility of the real and the **imaginary**, the signs of the **crystal** go beyond all psychology of the recollection or dream, and all physics of **action**. What we see in the **crystal** is no longer the empirical progression of **time** as succession of presents, nor its indirect representation as interval or as whole; it is its **direct** presentation, its constitutive dividing in two into a present which is passing and a past which is preserved [...]. [C2 262, 274]

3. A direct, subjective relationship with time rather than movement, such that the past is experienced in terms of sheets or layers that are renewed or lived anew by virtue of the present; the manner in which a **series** of images does not form a linear narration or causal relation of events, but places into

question the truth of previous imagery by virtue of new imagery (**chronosign**), either through relations of coexistence (*aspect*), simultaneity (*accent*), or **seriality** (*genesign*).

> *It is the possibility of treating the world or life, or simply a life or an episode, as one single* **event** *which provides the basis for the implication of presents. [...]We find ourselves here in a direct* **time-image** *of a different kind from the previous one: no longer the coexistence of sheets of past, but the simultaneity of peaks of present. We therefore have two kinds of* **chronosigns:** *the first are* **aspects** *(regions, layers), the second* **accents** *(peaks of view [pointes de vue]).* [C2 97, 100]

> *This is a third* **time-image**, *[which...] concerns the* **series** *of* **time**, *which brings together the before and the after in a becoming, instead of separating them; its* **paradox** *is to introduce an enduring interval in the moment itself.* [C2 150, 155]

4.a. The manner in which images confront the **Outside** as an exterior that is simultaneously interior to our perceptions, affections, and sensory-motor reactions, rather than interiorizing the Outside as an open whole within a linear model of time, forcing the viewer to think, view, and hear relationships or **differences** that are unthinkable or unrepresentable; the manner in which the whole, or the world, no longer serves as the basis for the association or linkage of images.

> *Between two actions, between two affections, between two perceptions, between two visual* **images***, between two sound* **images***, between the sound and the visual: make the indiscernible, that is the frontier, visible (Six fois deux). The whole undergoes a mutation, because it has ceased to be the One-Being, in order to become the constitutive 'and' of things, the constitutive between-two of* **images***. The whole thus merges with that* **Blanchot** *calls the force of 'dispersal of the* **Outside***', or 'the vertigo of spacing': that void which is no longer a motor-part of the* **image***, and which the* **image** *would cross in order to continue, but is the radical calling into question of the* **image** *[...].* [C2 174, 180]

b. The manner in which *images* are united or associated by virtue of that which cannot be subsumed by the representational demands of linear storytelling or of resemblance to common experience (in the sensory-motor schema), and instead express a new relationship that is impossible or inexpressible without cinematic techniques which therefore must be *thought* (the *noosign*); also, the manner in which images *and sounds* are united or associated by virtue of that which cannot be subsumed by the representational demands of linear storytelling or of resemblance to common experience, such that speech-acts are dissociated from **action images** and thus must be *read* (the *lectosign*).

> The direct **time-image** *effectively has as* **noosigns** *the irrational cut between non-linked (but always relinked) images, and the absolute contact between non-totalizable, asymmetrical outside and inside.* [C2 266, 278]

> The visual image *will thus never show what the sound* image *utters. [...] There will none the less be a relation between the two, a junction or a contact. [...] So each one [...] discovers the common limit which connects them to each other in the incommensurable relation of an irrational cut [...]. These new signs are* **lectosigns**, *which show the final aspect of the direct* time-image *[...].* [C2 268, 279]

> 'Lectosign' *refers to [...] the* image *when it is captured intrinsically, independent of its relationship with a supposedly external object.* [C2 275, 284]

- E. B. Y.

Tournier, Michel

Tournier is a novelist and was close friend of Deleuze's especially during his late high school and college years; he influenced Deleuze's **Leibnizian** conception of **the Other** which reemerges throughout his entire career (from his first publication in 1945 to his major philosophical works in 1968–9, and again in *What is Philosophy?* in 1991). - E. B. Y.

Transcendental empiricism

(also '*Superior Empiricism*')

1.a. In Deleuze's conflation of philosophies of empiricism (**Hume**) and transcendentalism (**Kant**), the conditions of an encounter that generates ideas; that is, the conditions of real experience which are expressed when reality is understood in terms of the **Nietzschean** criterion of art (**simulacrum**), in distinction from its representations by the **faculties**, conditions of possible experience, or an abstract difference which unties the faculties (as in Kantian philosophy).

> *The work of art leaves the domain of representation in order to become 'experience',* Transcendental Empiricism *or science of the sensible.* [...] Empiricism *truly becomes* transcendental, *and aesthetics an apodictic discipline, only when we apprehend directly in the sensible that which can only be sensed, the very being of the sensible:* difference, *potential difference and difference in* intensity *as the reason behind qualitative diversity.* [DR 68, 56–7]

b. In Deleuze's critique of **Kant**, rather than transcendental **faculties** legislating themselves in an accord with other **faculties**, the manner in which each empirical faculty transcends or exceeds its limits to produce a discord or **difference** between faculties.

> *The* transcendental *form of a* faculty *is indistinguishable from its disjointed,* superior *or* transcendent *exercise.* Transcendent *in no way means that the faculty addresses itself to objects outside the world but, on the contrary, that it grasps that in the world which concerns it exclusively and brings it into the world.* [DR 180, 143]

c. In Deleuze's reading of **Nietzsche**, the genetical principle of the will to power which selects and affirms active **force** to **eternally return**, despite being contingent upon any given relation of forces.

> *If* [...] *the will to power is a good principle, if it reconciles* empiricism *with principles, if it constitutes a* Superior Empiricism, *this is because it is an essentially plastic principle that is no wider*

than what it conditions, that changes itself with the conditioned and determines itself in each case along with what it determines. [N 46, 50]

- E. B. Y.

Transcoding

(see also **code**)

1. In D&G's cosmology, the manner in which living things within **milieus** communicate with other milieus or with **chaos** by virtue of **territorialization** and **deterritorialization**.

> **Transcoding** *or transduction is the manner in which one* **milieu** *serves as the basis for another, or conversely is established atop another* **milieu**, *dissipates in it or is constituted in it.* [TP 345, 313]

- E. B. Y.

Transmutation

1. In Deleuze's reading of **Nietzsche**, the transformation of negation into affirmation through completed nihilism; the separation of the will to nothingness from incomplete nihilism and its connection instead to the will to power.

> *In and through the* **eternal return** *negation as a quality of the will to power* **transmutes** *itself into affirmation, it becomes an affirmation of negation itself [...].* [N 66, 71]

- E. B. Y.

Transversality

This important concept emerged as a key element in Guattari's conceptual vocabulary in the early 1960s. He applied it at the Clinique de la Borde, developing a number of tools for its application, including the grid, a table of rotating work schedules (times and tasks) that involved medical, non-medical staff and patients. The grid was not a static timeable for role redefinition, but evolved alongside resistances to it and with emerging collective projects and artificial 'family' groupings called Base Therapeutic Units. Importantly, the grid did not represent the institution, but was a dynamic means for its creation. The grid changed over time, displaying periods of centralization and decentralization, and was modified to maximize its therapeutic effects in response to changing conditions in the clinic from which were extracted whatever displayed the greatest transversal potential.

1.a. A type of interactive therapy where the quality and amount of communication between different levels of an institution are maximized, ensuring multidirectional **flows** and enriching encounters, demystifying the doctor-patient relation.

> **Transversality** *is a dimension that strives to overcome two impasses: pure verticality, and a simple horizontality. It tends to be realized when communication is maximized between different levels and above all in different directions [...] it is possible to modify the different* **unconscious** *coefficients of transversality at different levels of an institution.* [PT 80]

b. In the environment at La Borde, subject-**groups** which could better accept openness without letting it become a threat to the negotiation of otherness, as well as a loss of security precipitating decay into a subjugated group; likewise, the capacity for subjugated groups to pass through the walls of silent retreats and find their voice at certain moments.

> *The modification [of the structure of blindness] must occur at the level of a structural redefinition of the role of each person and a reorientation of the whole.* [PT 80]

c. Therapy which requires the modification of introjects such as alienating fantasies of a leader's power, or the realization that a **group** is not a revolutionary subject of history, so that the super-ego can admit new ideals and demands.

> *About ten years ago I introduced the notion of* **transversality** *to express the capacity of an institution to remodel the ways of access it offers the super-ego so that certain symptoms and inhibitions*

are removed. Modification of the local *coefficient of* **transversality** implies the existence of an erotic focal point, a group eros, and a take-over—if only partial—of local politics by a subject-group. [CY 215]

- G. G.

Unconscious

Utilizing his work on the three **passive syntheses**, Deleuze critiques **Freud** to argue that while the unconscious involves mechanisms of the mind that function below or beyond the level of awareness, that does not mean that they have content or *being* that would negate what we are conscious of; the unconscious, as he states, 'lives off the (non)-being of problems and questions, rather than the non-being of the negative' which would affect only the **active syntheses** of the mind (DR 140, 114). Deleuze thus replaces Freud's concept of 'binding' with the **Bergson**ian concept of **contraction**, the Freudian concept of the libido (or Eros) with the **Proust**ian concept of **reminiscence**, and his concept of death with both **Blanchot**'s concept of the 'other death' (which has no relation to the ego) and the **Nietzsch**ean concept of active forgetting (it is important to note that 'active' here does not carry the pejorative sense that it carries with '**active synthesis**').

As a domesticated species, we are separated from what **Freud**, in his 'Project for Scientific Psychology', calls the 'exigencies of life'; in contrast to this, Deleuze emphasizes that the acts of the unconscious are not 'speculative', 'conflictual', or teleological, as they operate in a different domain than that of 'satisfaction' and resolution. This formulation echoes in his work with Guattari, where the syntheses of **desire** are characterized as being without representative content; this can be contrasted to Freud's version of the unconscious that becomes like a theater production which always involves something behind the scenes which hides what we see and experience consciously (in this sense, we would never discover the force of the unconscious, but find in it only what we expect to).

1. **Freud**'s system of the mind (later referred to as the 'Id') responsible for the drives and instincts that are repressed, hidden and/or regulated by the conscious mind (ego), which in itself

contains no formal structure (i.e. no 'negation'), awareness of time, or mortality.

> *Properly speaking, the* **unconscious** *is the real psychic; its inner nature is just as unknown to us as the reality of the external world, and it is just as imperfectly reported to us through the data of consciousness as is the external world through the indications of our sensory organs.* [Freud, 2012, 119–20]
>
> *Everything that is repressed must remain* **unconscious** *[...]* [Freud, 1957, 'The Unconscious']
>
> *There are in this system no negation, no doubt, no degrees of certainty [...]. Negation is a substitute, at a higher level, for repression. In the [*unconscious*] there are only contents, cathected with greater or lesser strength.* [ibid]
>
> *The processes of the system [*unconscious*] are timeless; i.e. they are not ordered temporally, are not altered by the passage of time; they have no reference to time at all.* [ibid]

2.a. In Deleuze's reading and critique of **Freud**, the problematizing and questioning **force** of the mind (of which we cannot grasp or represent to ourselves) that instigates thought, memory and **sensation** (but contains no content in itself), whose **desire** and power comes from the three **passive syntheses** of **contraction**, immemorial memory, and **eternal return** (before they are apprehended, recognized, and/or reflected in **active synthesis**).

> *The phenomena of the* **unconscious** *cannot be understood in the overly simple form of opposition or conflict. [...] It is true that the* **unconscious desires**, *and only desires. However, it appears neither as a power of negation nor as an element of an opposition, but rather as a questioning, problematizing and searching force which operates in a different domain than that of desire and satisfaction.* [DR 131, 106]
>
> **Freud** *supposes the* **unconscious** *to be ignorant of three important things: Death, Time and No. Yet it is a question only of time, death and no in the* **unconscious**. *[...]It is these three syntheses which must be understood as constitutive of the* **unconscious**. [DR 140, 114]

b. In D&G's critique of **Freud**, the connective, conjunctive, and **disjunctive syntheses** which correspond to actual, productive processes of **desire**, containing no representative content or resolvable (cathectable) energy.

> *Nothing is lacking, nothing can be defined as a lack; nor are the disjunctions in the* **unconscious** *ever exclusive, but rather the object of a properly inclusive use [...].* [AO 67–8, 60]

> *the* **unconscious** *itself is no more structural than personal, it does not symbolize any more than it imagines or represents; it engineers, it is machinic. Neither imaginary nor symbolic, it is the Real in itself, the 'impossible real' and its production.* [AO 60, 53]

c. **The Plane of Immanence.** (def. 2) [TP]

3.a. (Special Combination): *reactive unconscious*: In Deleuze's reading of Nietzsche (in comparison with Freud), an inactivity of the mind that 'feels' (*senti*) or reacts to memories or 'imprints' that leads to a *ressentful* morality which influences and even dominates behavior by preventing the ability to forget.

> *The reactive* **unconscious** *is defined by mnemonic traces, by lasting imprints. It is a digestive, vegetative and ruminative system [...].*

b. (Special Combination): *superior unconscious:* In Deleuze's reading of **Nietzsche** (via **Freud**), a positive power of forgetting (or a 'super-consciousness') that 'acts' reactions by preventing fixated memories from influencing 1) the fluidity and adaptability of consciousness, 2) active **force**, and 3) the repetition of **eternal return**.

> *It is no doubt more difficult to characterize these active* **forces** *for, by nature, they escape consciousness, 'The great activity is* **unconscious**' *(VP II 227).* [N 38, 41]

> *A specific active force must be given the job of supporting consciousness and renewing its freshness, fluidity and mobile, agile chemistry at every moment. This active* **super-conscious** *faculty is the faculty of forgetting.* [N 106, 113]

> *It is in* **repetition** *and by repetition that Forgetting becomes a positive power while the* **unconscious** *becomes a positive and superior* **unconscious** *(for example, forgetting as a force is an integral part of the lived experience of* **eternal return***).* [DR 9, 8]

– E. B. Y.

Universes

One of Guattari's **four functors**. In an **assemblage**, the domain of shared **affect, values,** and culturally specific references. Also used in *What is Philosophy?* to designate the affective, perceptual domain which is produced on art's plane of composition.

1.a. According to Guattari's **four-functor** schema, the shared aspects of subjectivity, whose existence depends on their incorporation into **existential Territories**.

> *An incorporeal* **universe** *is not supported by coordinates embedded in the world, but by ordinates, by an intensive ordination coupled for better or worse to these* **existential Territories**. [CM 28]

b. The existential domain of alterity.

> *The* **ethology** *of a child's pre-verbal phases reveals a psychical world where family characters [...] disclose [...] multiple, dislocated and entangled,* **existential Territories** *and incorporeal* **Universes**. *The maternal, paternal, fraternal* **Universes**—*territories of the self—agglomerate into a kind of phenomenon of an* **autopoietic** *snowball which renders the development of the sense of self and the sense of the other totally interdependent.* [CM 65]

c. (Special Combination): *Universes of value or reference:* The **schizoanalytic** counterpart to universal principles or truths, universes of reference belong to specific moments and territories; a constellation of values or references characteristic of a particular age or social **assemblage**.

> *Nevertheless, these constellations of* **Universes of value** *do not constitute Universals.* [CM 55]

> *For example, the incorporeal* **Universes** *of classical Antiquity [...] underwent a radical reshaping with the trinitary revolution of Christianity [...]* [CM 61–62]

> *in a sense all systems of* **modeling** *are equally valid, all are acceptable, but [...] they have no other aim than to participate in the cartography of* **existential Territories**, *implicating* **Universes** *that are sensible, cognitive, affective, aesthetic, etc.—and in strictly limited spaces and time periods.* [SC 12]

2. In *What is Philosophy?*, the sensorial, **affective** domain of possibility which is opened up by art; also, the qualitative domain specific to a particular art, whose relations to other aesthetic universes are determined by **lines of flight**.

- J. W.

Univocity

In a sense, 'univocity' is a provocation, rather than a speculative **proposition**, because it challenges us to think in terms of essence or power rather than formal qualities. There are two formulas that Deleuze uses to distinguish philosophies of equivocity, that is, being which has 'many voices' (a view defended especially in the middle ages) and univocity, that is, being which has 'one voice' (championed by Duns Scotus): on the one hand, 'being is said in several senses of that of which it is said', and on the other hand, 'being is said absolutely in one and the same sense of everything of which it is said' (webdeleuze 14/01/1974). In the first case, God's power or God's grace is said in an analogical, but different sense, than Man's power or grace, while in the second case, they are said in the same sense. This is where the provocation arises, and in the middle ages, the idea was considered heresy (even today, Deleuze is himself criticized by the philosopher Alan Badiou for an apparent irreconcilability of **multiplicity** with univocity). However, Deleuze insists on the univocity only to point out that beings cannot be distinguished categorically, as in **Aristotle**; as he states in his reading of **Spinoza**, such a 'formal' distinction is not 'real' (see entry on **Descartes**).

Real distinction, for Deleuze, involves the manner in which each being realizes a degree of *power*: how does one thing actualize 'everything', but *differently*, with a different emphasis, such that it combines with other things uniquely (in **Spinozist** terms, how do **modes** with an 'infinity of parts' express the same infinite substance such that they are more or less capable of being **affected** positively)? In other words, how does the **multiplicity** of things, which **express** the potentiality of the same thing (or all express the substance that encompasses everything), actually express *differences*? How can we ask what makes the same different, rather than asking what makes supposedly different things similar? This provocation brings ontology immediately to a pragmatic domain of consequences or effects (in fact, Deleuze also points out the univocal aspect of 'effects' and **events**): we begin making distinctions by presuming that things are the same, *in order* to determine what actual, effective differences they express in terms of their *action* and power (rather than the other way around, which would presume they are different based on transcendent categories, reaching difference only as a foregone conclusion).

1. In Deleuze's reading of **Duns Scotus**, the theory that God's existence is not a different type of existence than things in the world; rather, there is only one being, which is **differentiated** formally. The difference between matter, man, and God is only a difference of degree, not a difference in being.

> *In the greatest book of pure ontology, the* Opus Oxoniense, *being is understood as* **univocal**, *but* **univocal** *being is understood as neutral, neuter, indifferent to the distinction between the finite and the infinite, the singular and the universal, the created and the uncreated.* [DR 49, 39]

2. In Deleuze's reading of **Spinoza**, a feature of **attributes** (thought, extension) which **express** the same substance in parallel; the object of adequate ideas insofar as they comprehend, in a limited capacity (through the infinite immediate mode), this parallelism in its modifications and in the plurality of beings; this is in distinction from inadequate ideas which result from a belief in eminence or equivocity. [SEP, SPP]

> *The* **univocity** *of the* **attributes** *is the only means of radically distinguishing the essence and existence of substance from the essence and existence of the* **modes**, *while preserving the absolute unity of Being. Eminence, and along with it, equivocity and analogy are doubly wrong in claiming to see something in common between God and created beings where there is nothing in common [...].* [SPP 63–4]

3. The ontological status of being, where things cannot be distinguished by virtue of analogy (where one form of being is 'like' or 'unlike' another), or hierarchy (where one form of being is 'higher' or 'lower' than another), but only in terms of **differences**

of **intensity** or power, and thus are existentially united by an unlimited power of Being.

> *if I say being is* **univocal**, *it's said in the same sense of everything of which it's said, then what could the* **differences** *between [beings] be? They can no longer be differences of category, they can no longer be differences of form, they can no longer be differences of genus and species [...]. The only difference conceivable at this very moment, from the point of view of a* **univocal** *being, is obviously difference solely as degrees of power [puissance].* [webdeleuze 14/01/1974]

> *From Duns Scotus to* **Spinoza,** *the* **univocal** *position has always rested upon two fundamental theses. According to one, [...] forms involve no division within being [...]. According to the other, that of which being is said is repartitioned according to essentially mobile individuating* **differences.** *[...]* **Univocity** *signifies that being itself is* **univocal***, while that of which it is said is equivocal: precisely the opposite of analogy.* [DR 303, 377]

4. An absolute **disjunctive synthesis** of all actual **events** and attributable **senses** by virtue of the same neutral, sterile, metaphysical **surface** upon which they depend (**Aion**).

> *The* **univocity** *of Being does not mean that there is one and the same Being; on the contrary, beings are* **multiple** *and* **different***, they are always produced by a* **disjunctive synthesis** *[...].* [LS 205, 179]

- E. B. Y.

Value

1. In **Nietzsche**'s work, on the one hand, the dogmatic image of both religion and science, which are, on the other hand, the object of critique and revaluation; a distinction whereby anything abstract (truth, **morality**, knowledge etc.) can be critiqued by virtue of **life**.

> *[...] it would seem laughable to us today if man were to insist on inventing* **values** *that were supposed to surpass the* **value** *of the real world.* [Nietzsche, (The Gay Science # 346), 2001, 204]

> *Whenever we speak of* **values***, we speak under the inspiration—from the perspective—of* **life***: life itself forces us to establish* **values***; life*

itself evaluates through us when we posit **values**. [Nietzsche, 1998, 24]

2.a. In Deleuze's reading of **Nietzsche,** the essence of something insofar as it is divorced from *believable* truths or **images of thought**, and, rather, undergoes a critique based on its reactive (affirmative only of being) or active (affirmative of **becoming**) qualities.

> *Genealogy signifies the differential element of* **values** *from which their* **value** *itself derives [...]. The differential element is both a critique of the* **value** *of* **values** *and the positive element of a creation.* [N 2, 2]

> **Nietzsche**'s *distinction between the creation of new* **values** *and the recognition of established* **values** *should not be understood in a historically relative manner [...]. The new [...] remains forever new, just as the established was always established from the outset.* [DR 172, 136]

b. (Special Combination): *Higher Value*: In a pejorative sense, a symptom of reactive morality which judges and transcends life in favor of the supersensible (and is thus 'higher').

> **Values** *superior to* **life** *are inseparable from their effect: the depreciation of life, the negation of this world. [...]Thus [...] nihilism signifies the* **value** *of nil taken on by life, the fiction of higher* **values** *which give it this* **value** *and the will to nothingness which is expressed in these higher* **values**. [N 139, 147]

- E. B. Y.

Varela, Francisco and Humberto Maturana

In *Chaosmosis*, Guattari cites Chilean biologists Humberto Maturana and Francisco Varela in his lengthy discussion of 'machinic heterogenesis.' During the 1970s, the biologists defined living beings as a type of machine. However, they insisted on the difference between biological machines and man-made machines. Guattari appropriates their term **autopoiesis** and, despite their insistence that this idea applies only to biological machines, applies it to social and technological machines. In his late work,

Guattari redefines the machine using **Prigogine** and **Stengers**'s work on self-organizing open systems, as well as **Heidegger**'s essay on technology. Unlike Maturana and Varela, Guattari does not conceptualize technological machines as discreet entities, but rather as components of heterogeneous machinic **assemblages** that also include human beings. He compares this larger machinic assemblage to the biological machines described by Maturana and Varela. Much of the rest of the biologists' work (especially in *The Tree of Knowledge* and *The Embodied Mind*) is in keeping with Deleuze and Guattari's philosophy. - J. W.

Vector

cross-reference: **Action-Image** (fragmentation of space)

Virtual

While we normally associate the virtual with a 'reality' engendered by computers, 'virtual reality' would be a tautology in Deleuze's terms: the virtual is not another plane of reality that exists above or beyond this reality; rather, the virtual both *composes* reality and, in itself, contains *all possible* realities. This **'differentiated'** virtuality cannot be perceived or felt because in order for those realities to be conflated (or 'co-implicated'), they cannot all occur simultaneously in regular time or space. Thus the virtual is 'real', but that which we do perceive and feel from it is '**actual**'.

After studying **Bergson**'s notion of the pure past, **Proust**'s immemorial memory, and **Nietzsche**'s **eternal return**, Deleuze insists that the **actualization** of the virtual is not the 'realization' of possibilities; there is not, in other words, some omniscient creator, à la **Leibniz**, that would realize the best possible world. Nor does the actual world somehow 'resemble' a more perfect 'virtual' world (à la **Plato**). Rather, if the past is infinite, all possibilities have essentially already occurred: the question is whether they can be 'thought', and whether they will be 'actualized'; it is in this sense that virtual **concepts** retain the infinite and inclusive whole of possibility (which distinguishes them from scientific variables).

Deleuze utilizes the notion of the virtual in the *Cinema* books, where it initially situates itself between the **affections** and **recollections** we experience (when watching film) and ultimately forms a circuit where we associate images and **affects** independently of chronological time and memory (since the virtual is limited by neither).

1.a. A term that Henri **Bergson** uses to describe the past in general, distinct from the presence of **duration** and **succession**.

> *Whenever we are trying to recover a recollection [and...] we become conscious of an act sui generis by which we detach ourselves from the present in order to replace ourselves, first in the past in general [...] our recollection still remains* virtual *[...]. Little by little it comes into view like a condensing cloud; from the* virtual *state it passes into the* actual *[...] it remains attached to the past by its deepest roots, and if, when once realized, it did not retain something of its original* virtuality *[...] we should never know it for a memory.* [Bergson 1913, 171]

b. The basis for a link that Deleuze makes between **Bergson**'s spontaneous **memory** and **Proust**'s involuntary memory, where the past and present coexist because the memory of the past is not particular. [P, B, DR]

> *There is a resemblance between* **Bergson**'s *conception and* **Proust**'s *[...] That we do not proceed from an actual present to the past, that we do not recombine the past with various presents, but that we place ourselves, directly, in the past itself. [...] this being of the past in itself is what Bergson called the* virtual. *Similarly Proust, when he speaks of states induced by the signs of memory: 'Real without being actual, Ideal without being abstract'.* [P 58]

2.a. In Deleuze's explanation of thinking, the real, differential (un**differenciated**), unactualized state which grounds ideas; in D&G's explanation of philosophy, a state that contains all possibilities (and therefore cannot be 'realized') by virtue of the philosophical **concept** or idea which expresses **differentiated** variations (in contexts that are historical, aesthetic, scientific, political, etc.) by retaining some features of **chaos** (infinite speed) but occupying a relative position with regard to its survey or problem.

> *The only danger [....] is that the* **virtual** *could be confused with the possible. The possible is opposed to the real; the process undergone by the possible is therefore a 'realization'. By contrast, the* **virtual** *is not opposed to the real; it possesses a full reality by itself. The process it undergoes is that of* **actualization.** *[...] The* **virtual** *[...] is the characteristic state of Ideas: it is on the basis of its reality that existence is produced, in accordance with a time and a space* **immanent** *in the Idea.* [DR 263, 211]

> *[P]hilosophy wants to know how to retain infinite speeds while gaining consistency, by giving the* **virtual** *a consistency specific to it.* [WP 118]

b. In D&G's explanation of **chaos**, a reality which contains all possibilities, but in a formless manner which cannot be thought because the appearance or shape of that reality is simultaneously its disappearance (possessing an infinite speed). [WP, FLB, D]

> *[***Chaos***] is a void that is not a nothingness but a* **virtual** *[...].* [WP 118]

3.a. In Deleuze's analysis of cinema, a subjective, **affection image** that *occupies* the gap between stimulus and response.

> *[T]he* **virtual** *is subjective: it was initially the* **affect***, that which we experience in time* [C2 80, 83]

b. That which actualizes a **recollection image** in accordance with the demands of objective **perception** and chronological time; the origin of a recollection image that *fills* the gap between stimulus and response.

> *[T]he* **recollection image** *is not* **virtual***, it actualizes a* **virtuality** *(which* **Bergson** *calls 'pure recollection') on its own account. This is why the* **recollection image** *does not deliver the past to us, but only represents the former present that the past 'was'.* [C2 52, 54]

c. That which, through forming a circuit with an **actual** image, engenders the **crystal image**; a *pure* recollection that does not form a relative, organic circuit between the present and past but a subjective, simultaneous, non-chronological circuit.

> *The* **virtual** *image in the pure state is defined, not in accordance with a new present in relation to which it would be (relatively) past,*

but in accordance with the **actual** *present of which it is the past, absolutely and simultaneously [...] as a pure* **virtuality***, it does not have to be* **actualized***, since it is strictly correlative with the actual image with which it forms the smallest circuit [...].* [C2 77, 79]

- E. B. Y.

Virtual object

cross-reference: Partial Object

Vitalism

cross-reference: Life

War machine

We all know that a military mind-set is considered fundamentally different than a 'civilian' mind-set: those with violent dispositions or even military discipline often *desire* war, as if there were no other *raison d'être*. The conflict arises when the government needs the military in order to maintain peace and order, but the military, at the same time, longs for violence and war. D&G provide a unique twist to this conflict, suggesting that what we might call a military mind-set is actually a ***nomadic*** mind-set that was already opposed to the 'sedentary' or 'civilized' mind-set necessary to function in a State (in their terms, the nomad has encountered **'striated' space,** or been essentially forced to 'slow down', but at the expense of becoming violent). In other words, according to this theory, the entire military apparatus is conceived according to a 'nomad science' where space and movement are treated absolutely rather than relatively.

1.a. In D&G's theoretical understanding of **nomadism**, the disposition defined by a numerical organization and **subjectivity** within **smooth space** which maintains a **milieu** exterior to the State apparatus and along a **line of flight** (distinct from sedentary transport), whose speed and action require a continual functional conversion between work and war, or between tools and weapons; the condition for the formation of machinic **assemblages**, such as those which combine man, animal, and/ or weapon (e.g. the 'man-horse assemblage' of the knight, or the 'trans-historical assemblage' of the ambulant worker who utilizes technology [TP 403]).

> *the* **war machine**, *with infinitely lower 'quantities,' has as its object not war but the drawing of a creative* **line of flight**, *the composition of a* **smooth space** *and of the movement of people in that space. At this other pole, the machine does indeed encounter war, but as its supplementary or synthetic object, now directed against the State [...].* [TP 456, 422]

> *it is more frequent for a worker, industrial or agricultural, to reinvent a* **war machine**. *[...] men of war [...] know the uselessness of violence but [...] are adjacent to a* **war machine** *to be recreated, one of active, revolutionary counterattacks.* [TP 444–5, 402–3]

b. In D&G's historical understanding of **nomadism**, a defensive disposition and indefinitely prolongable inclination to violence (in distinction from State or fascist domination); a form of raising and breeding consistent with the capacity to endure and maintain **nomadism** (in distinction from sedentary raising and breeding).

> *Rather than operating by blow-by-blow violence, or constituting a violence 'once and for all,' the* **war machine**, *with breeding and training, institutes an entire economy of violence, in other words, a way of making violence durable, even unlimited.* [TP 437, 396]

c. As a **sign**, the **form of expression** whose **form of content** is metallurgy insofar as it functions to simultaneously create tools and weapons.

> *In short, what metal and metallurgy bring to light is a life proper to* matter, *a vital state of* matter *as such, a material* vitalism *[...] Not everything is metal, but metal is everywhere. Metal is the conductor of all matter. The* machinic phylum *is metallurgical. [...] The nomad* **war machine** *is the* **form of expression**, *of which itinerant metallurgy is the correlative* **form of content**. [TP 454, 411]

2.a. In D&G's explanation of fascism, the primary object of capture of the State apparatus which is, on the one hand, irreducible to it, and, on the other hand, necessary for its goals of capture, **segmentation**, and **territorialization**.

> *One of the fundamental problems of the State is to appropriate this* **war machine** *that is foreign to it and make it a piece in its apparatus, in the form of a stable military institution [...].* [TP 253, 230]

b. The use of a nomad science, which involves a conception of **smooth space**, absolute speed, the solidarity of lineages, and people in numbers, by the State for the purposes of war.

> *The hydraulic model of nomad science and the* **war machine** *[...] consists in being distributed by turbulence across a* **smooth space** *[...], instead of being held by space in a local movement from one specified point to another.* [TP 401, 363]

> *State apparatuses appropriate the* **war machine***, notably by arranging a* **striated space** *[...]. It can happen that speed is abstracted as the property of a projectile, a bullet or artillery shell, which condemns the weapon itself, and the soldier, to immobility.* [TP 438, 397]

- E. B. Y.

What is Philosophy?

Qu'est-ce que la philosophie ?, avec Félix Guattari (1991)

This dense and introspective work by D&G was published over ten years after the final volume of their Capitalism and Schizophrenia project (*A Thousand Plateaus*), and in it, the stakes of what it means to think itself are similar to those in Deleuze's ***Difference and Repetition***, though they are recast: here, the question is framed specifically in terms of the disciplinary status *of* philosophy, and even the personae of the philosopher. Furthermore, much of the terminology from D&G's previous works is employed productively to define philosophy, such as the **plane of immanence** (here, unlike in *A Thousand Plateaus*, in distinction from the **plane of composition**), the **territory**, the **milieu**, and the **diagram** (as well as terms from Deleuze's sole authored works, such as **intensity** and the **virtual**). Since Deleuze, in his early work, emphasized that the thought of **difference** is threatened by representation, in this case, the past, present, and future of philosophy is likewise threatened by types of social and political organization which would eclipse the creative act of thinking by relegating it to the imperatives of science, religion, and capitalism. In this sense, the text can be seen as a re-exploration of some concerns from their earlier work, but instead of framing the problem of capitalism in terms of the status of **desire**, they are inquiring into the disciplinarity of philosophy in relation to art (and literature), as well as science. This is perhaps an essential gesture in an era when the relevance of philosophy, especially with respect to the sciences, is often questioned (especially in formal education).

D&G trace philosophy's origins to the Greek city-state, and consider its survival throughout the Christian middle ages to capitalist modernity, in distinction from the East, which they argue does not displace its external limits or re-create conditions for **planes of immanence**. In contrast to the East, they argue that the constantly expansive nature of Western capitalism creates conditions for philosophy similar to those in Greece. In this case, they utilize a refrain which appeared in their definition of **minor literature** regarding the scarcity of talent necessary to forge new communities, as well as their claim about the modern artist (in distinction from the classical and romantic artist) from the 'Refrain' chapter in *A Thousand Plateaus* where the 'people' and the 'earth' (that is, the **milieus** and **rhythms**), are both 'carried off' or **deterritorialized** by the cosmos, to suggest that Philosophy likewise is 'reterritorialized' on the concept not within the democratic state or within consumerist enterprises, but within a society or community that does not yet exist (and therefore *resists* all current forms of dominant opinion and political organization). Despite the favorable conditions that capitalism creates for philosophy, however, it always is threatened both by demands of marketing, communication, exhibition, and promotion, as well as the propositional and referential demands of modern science (especially the Human Sciences, echoing a Foucauldian concern). With regard to the latter case, D&G make a great effort to positively distinguish science from philosophy.

With these considerations in mind, **chaos** attains a crucial role in relation to all three disciplines. In fact, understanding that each discipline creates its own 'plane' (one of *reference* for science, *composition* for art, and *immanence* for philosophy) shows that this is not simply a formal or categorical question, but perhaps a **modal** distinction where each 'discipline' involves a different relationship between the brain and the 'planes' that it encounters. In other words, each discipline has its own objects and domains within which they view those objects (science has 'functives', philosophy has concepts, and art has 'blocs of sensation', affects, and percepts); they are in fact, different dispositions towards 'reality' (or, in **Nietzschean** terms, chaos). If chaos is an infinitely fast and unthinkably complex play of **repetition**, then the scientific brain focuses on variables, the artistic brain focuses on varieties, and the philosophical brain focuses on variations. - E. B. Y.

Whitehead, Alfred North

Deleuze makes reference to Whitehead's philosophy primarily when discussing the **event** in *The Fold*, with regard to the **concept** of 'prehension', as well as in his lectures on **Leibniz** which provide a more thorough engagement with the philosopher. Rather than resort to a Leibnizian model of (ap)perception that involves perceptions of the remarkable within the ordinary, Whitehead drops the prefix ap- from 'apprehend' to insist that we 'prehend' events without being cognitive of this fact, and this is what makes us individuals. Whitehead himself notes that individuals are not **monads** nor independent worlds, but **modes** that are interconnected by the same substance (see Whitehead, 2001, pp. 86–7). Deleuze picks up on this to insist that all monads 'prehend' a **series** of elements outside of them through the **unconscious** power of contraction (see **habit** and **repetition**); this is how **events** make the individual, but also how the individual is part of an objective world of singularities which it traverses or connects. - E. B. Y.

Zeroness

cross-reference: **perception** (def. 2)

BIBLIOGRAPHY

Artaud, Antonin. 'To Have Done with the Judgment of God' in *Selected Writings*. Edited by Susan Sontag. University of California Press: Berkeley, CA. 1976.

Bergson, Henri. *Creative Evolution*. Translated by Arthur Mitchell. Henry Holt and Company: New York. 1911.

—*Matter and Memory*. Translated by Nancy Margaret Paul and W. Scott Palmer. George Lalen & Co.: London. 1913.

—*Time and Free Will: An Essay on the Immediate Data of Consciousness*. Translated by F. L. Pogson. Macmillan Company: New York. 1913.

Blanchot, Maurice. *The Infinite Conversation*. Translated Susan Hanson. University of Minnesota Press: Minneapolis. 1993.

Deleuze, Gilles. *Le bergsonisme*. Presses universitaires de France: Paris. 1991.

[*Bergsonism*. Translated by Hugh Tomlinson and Barbara Habberjam. Zone Books: New York. 1990.]

—Cours Vincennes – 26/03/1973 (Anti Oedipe et Mille Plateaux) Translated by Daniel W. Smith. (http://www.webdeleuze.com/php/texte.php?cle=167&groupe=Anti%20Oedipe%20et%20Mille%20Plateaux&langue=2)

—Cours Vincennes – 14/01/1974 (Anti Oedipe et Mille Plateaux). Translated by Timothy S. Murphy (http://www.webdeleuze.com/php/texte.php?cle=176&groupe=Anti%20Oedipe%20et%20Mille%20Plateaux&langue=2)

—Cours Vincennes – 21/03/1978 (Kant). Translated by Melissa McMahon. (http://www.webdeleuze.com/php/texte.php?cle=67&groupe=Kant&langue=2)

—Cours Vincennes – 12/12/1980 (Spinoza). (http://www.webdeleuze.com/php/texte.php?cle=23&groupe=Spinoza&langue=2)

—Cours Vincennes – 24/03/1981 (Spinoza). Translated by Timothy S. Murphy. (http://www.webdeleuze.com/php/texte.php?cle=114&groupe=Spinoza&langue=2)

—*Critique et clinique*. Éditions de Minuit: Paris. 1993.

—'Désir et plaisir'. *Magazine littéraire* 325. October 1994. pp. 59–65.
['Desire & Pleasure'. Translated by Melissa McMahon. 1997. (http://www.artdes.monash.edu.au/globe/delfou.html)]
—*Deux régimes de fous: textes et entretiens, 1975–1995*. éd. préparée par David Lapoujade. Éditions de Minuit: Paris. 2003.
[*Two Regimes of Madness: Texts and Interviews 1975–1995*. Translated by A. Hodges and M. Taormina. Semiotext(e): Los Angeles. 2006.]
—*Différence et répétition*. Presses universitaires de France. Paris. 1989.
[*Difference and Repetition*. Translated by Paul Patton. Columbia University Press: New York. 1994.]
[*Difference and Repetition*. Translated by Paul Patton. Continuum International Publishing Group: New York & London. 2004.]
—*Empirisme et subjectivité*. Presses universitaires de France: Paris. 1988.
[*Empiricism and Subjectivity*. Translated by Constantin V. Boundas. Columbia University Press: New York. 2001.]
—*Foucault*. Éditions de Minuit: Paris. 1986.
[*Foucault*. Translated by Seán Hand. University of Minnesota Press. Minneapolis. 1988.]
[*Foucault*. Translated by Seán Hand. Continuum International Publishing Group. New York & London. 2006.]
—*Francis Bacon: logique de la sensation* Éd. de la Différence: Paris. 1996.
[*Francis Bacon: The Logic of Sensation*. Continuum International Publishing Group: New York & London. 2003.]
—*L'île déserte et autres textes: textes et entretiens, 1953–1974*. éd. préparée par David Lapoujade. Éditions de Minuit: Paris. 2002.
[*Desert Islands and Other Texts (1953–1974)*. Translated by M. Taormina. New York: Semiotext(e), 2002.]
—*L'image-mouvement*. Éditions de Minuit: Paris. 1983.
[*Cinema 1: The Movement Image*. Continuum International Publishing Group: New York & London. 2005.]
[*Cinema 1: The Movement Image*. University of Minnesota Press. Minneapolis. 1986.]
—*L'image-temps*. Éditions de Minuit: Paris. 1985.
[*Cinema 2: The Time Image*. Continuum International Publishing Group: New York & London. 2005.]
[*Cinema 2: The Time Image*. University of Minnesota Press. Minneapolis. 1989.]
—*Logique du sens*. Éditions de Minuit: Paris. 1989.
[*The Logic of Sense* Translated by Mark Lester. Columbia University Press: New York. 1990.]
[*The Logic of Sense* Translated by Mark Lester. Continuum International Publishing Group: New York & London. 2004.]

—*Nietzsche et la philosophie* Presses universitaires de France: Paris. 1988.
[*Nietzsche and Philosophy*. Continuum International Publishing Group: New York & London. 2006.]
[*Nietzsche and Philosophy*. Columbia University Press. New York. 1983.]
—*Nietzsche*. Presses universitaires de France: Paris. 1995.
—« *Périclès* » *et Verdi la philosophie de François Châtelet*. Éditions de Minuit: Paris. 1988.
—*La philosophie critique de Kant: doctrine des facultés*. Presses universitaires de France: Paris. 1991.
[*Kant's Critical Philosophy: The Doctrine of the Faculties*. University of Minnesota Press. Minneapolis. 2003.]
—*Le pli: Leibniz et le baroque*. Éditions de Minuit: Paris. 1988.
[*The Fold: Leibniz and the Baroque*. Translated by Tom Conley. University of Minnesota Press: Minneapolis. 1993.]
—*Pourparlers: 1972–1990*. Éditions de Minuit: Paris. 1990.
[*Negotiations*. Translated by Martin Joughin. Columbia University Press: New York. 1990.]
—*Présentation de Sacher-Masoch: le froid et le cruel*. Éditions de Minuit: Paris. 2007.
[*Coldness and Cruelty*. Translated by Jean McNeil. Zone Books. New York. 1981.]
—*Proust et les signes*. Presses universitaires de France: Paris. 1993.
[*Proust and Signs: The Complete Text*. Translated by Richard Howard. University of Minnesota Press. Minneapolis. 2000.]
—*Spinoza : philosophie pratique* Nouv. édn. rev. et augm. Éditions de Minuit: Paris. 2003.
[*Spinoza: Practical Philosophy*. Translated by Robert Hurley. City Lights Books: San Francisco. 1988.]
—*Spinoza et le problème de l'expression*. Éditions de Minuit: Paris. 1985.
[*Expressionism in Philosophy: Spinoza*. Translated by Martin Joughin. Zone Books: New York. 1992.]
Deleuze, Gilles and Claire Parnet. *Dialogues*. Flammarion: Paris. 1977.
[*Dialogues II*. Translated by Hugh Tomlinson and Barbara Habberjam. Columbia University Press: New York. 2007.]
Deleuze, Gilles and Félix Guattari. *L'anti-Œdipe*. Éditions de Minuit: Paris. 1973.
[*Anti-Oedipus: Capitalism and Schizophrenia*. Translated by Robert Hurley, Mark Seem, and Helen R. Lane. University of Minnesota Press: Minneapolis, MN. 1983.]

[*Anti-Oedipus: Capitalism and Schizophrenia*. Translated by Robert Hurley, Mark Seem, and Helen R. Lane. Continuum International Publishing Group: New York and London. 2004.]
—*Kafka : pour une littérature mineure*. Éditions de Minuit: Paris. 1975.
[*Kafka: Toward a Minor Literature*. Translated by Dana Polan. University of Minnesota Press: Minneapolis, MN. 1986.]
—*Mille plateaux*. Éditions de Minuit: Paris. 1989.
[*A Thousand Plateaus: Capitalism and Schizophrenia*. Translated by Brian Massumi. Continuum International Publishing Group: New York & London. 2004.]
[*A Thousand Plateaus: Capitalism and Schizophrenia* Translated by Brian Massumi. University of Minnesota Press: Minneapolis and London. 1987.]
—*Qu'est-ce que la philosophie?* Éditions de Minuit: Paris. 1991.
[*What is Philosophy?* Columbia University Press: New York. 1994.]
Derrida, Jacques. *Margins of Philosophy*. Translated by Alan Bass. The University of Chicago Press: Chicago. 1987.
—*Speech and Phenomena* Translated by David B. Allison. Northwestern University Press. 1973.
—*Positions*. Translated by Alan Bass. The University of Chicago Press: Chicago. 1981.
Descartes, René. *The Philosophical Works of Descartes, Vol II*. Translated by Elizabeth S. Saldane and G. R. T. Ross. Dover Publications: USA. 1934.
Foucault, Michel. *Discipline and Punish: The Birth of the Prison*. Translated by Alan Sheridan. Vintage Books: New York. 1995.
—*Power/Knowledge: Selected Interviews and Other Writings 1972–1977*. Edited by Colin Gordon. Harvester Press: Brighton. 1980.
—*This is not a Pipe*. Translated by James Harkness. The University of California Press: Berkeley and Los Angeles. 1983.
—'The Subject and Power' *Critical Inquiry*, Vol 8 No 4. Summer 1982. pp. 777–95.
Freud, Sigmund. *Dream Psychology; Psychoanalysis for Beginners*. Translated by M. D. Eder., The James A. McCann company: New York. 1921.
—*Dream Psychology*. Translated by M. D. Eder. CreateSpace Independent Publishing Platform: USA. 2012.
—'Project for a Scientific Psychology' in *Complete Psychological Works: Volume One*. Translated by James Strachey. The Hogarth Press: London. 1966.
—*The standard edition of the complete psychological works of Sigmund Freud. / Volume XIV, 1914–1916, On the history of the psychoanalytic movement, Papers on metapsychology and Other works*.

Translated by James Strachey, Anna Freud, Alix Strachey and Alan Tyson. Hogarth Press: London. 1957.
—*Totem and Taboo*. Translated by James Strachey. Routledge: London. 2003.
Genosko, Gary. *The Party without Bosses: Lessons on Anti-Capitalism from Félix Guattari and Luís Inácio 'Lula' da Silva*. Arbeiter Ring, Semaphore Series: Winnipeg. 2003.
Guattari, Félix. *The Anti-Oedipus Papers*. Translated by Kélina Gotman. Semiotext(e): New York. 2006.
—'Capital as the Integral of Power Formations' Translated by C. Wolfe and S. Cohen, in *Soft Subversions*. Semiotext(e): New York. 1996. pp. 202–24.
—*Chaosmosis: An Ethico-Aesthetic Paradigm*. Translated by Paul Bains and Julian Pefanis. Indiana University Press: Bloomington. 1995.
—*Chaosophy: Texts and Interviews 1972–1977*. Edited by Sylvère Lotringer. Semiotext(e). New York, NY. 1995.
—*Chaosophy: Texts and Interviews 1972–1977*. Translated by David L. Sweet, Jarred Becker, and Taylor Adkins. Semiotext(e): New York, NY. 2008.
—*The Guattari Reader*. Edited by Gary Genosko. Blackwell Publishers: Oxford and Cambridge, MA. 1996.
—*The Machinic Unconscious: essays in schizoanalysis*. Translated by Taylor Adkins. Semiotext(e): Cambridge, MA. 2011.
—*Molecular revolution in Brazil*. Translated by Karel Clapshow and Brian Holmes. Semiotext(e): Cambridge, MA and London. 2008.
—*La philosophie est essentielle à l'existence humaine*. Éditions de l'aube: Paris. 2001.
—'Plutôt avoir tort avec lui,' *Libération* (samedi/dimanche 23–24 juin 1990).
—*Psychanalyse et transversalité*. Maspero: Paris. 1972.
—*La révolution moléculaire*. Union générale d'éditions 10/18: Paris. 1980.
[*Molecular revolution: psychiatry and politics*. Translated by Rosemary Sheed. Penguin: New York. 1984.]
—*Soft subversions*. Translated by Chet Wiener and Emily Wittman. MIT Press: Cambridge, MA. 2009.
—*The Three Ecologies*. Translated by Ian Pindar and Paul Sutton. Athlone Press: New Brunswick, NJ. 2000.
—'Toward an Ethics of the Media,' *Polygraph* 14. Translated by Janell Watson. 2002. pp. 17–22.
Guattari, Félix and Antonio Negri. *Les nouveaux espaces de liberté*. Dominique Bedou: Paris. 1985.

Heidegger, Martin. *The End of Philosophy*. Translated by Joan Stambaugh. The University of Chicago Press: Chicago. 1973.

Hjelmslev, Louis. *Prolegomena to a Theory of Language*. Translated by Francis J. Whitefield. The University of Wisconsin Press: London. 1961.

Hume, David. *A Treatise of Human Nature*. Dover publications: Mineola, NY. 2003.

Johnson, Robert Sherlaw. *Messaien*. University of California Press: Berkely and Los Angeles, CA. 1975.

Kafka, Franz. *Collected Stories*. Edited by Gabriel Josipovici. Translations by Willa and Edwin Muir. Alfred A. Knopf: New York. 1946.

Kant, Immanuel. *The Critique of Judgement*. Translated by John Miller Dow Meiklejohn. MobileReference. 2010.

—*The Critique of Judgement* (2nd edn revised). Translated by J. H. Bernard. Macmillan: London. 1914.

—*Kant's Critique of Practical Reason and Other Works on the Theory of Ethics*. Translated by Thomas Kingsmill Abbott. Longmans, Green & Co.: London. 1889.

Klein, Melanie. *The Psychoanalysis of Children*. Translated by Alix Strachey. Grove Press: New York. etext.

Lacan, Jacques. *Écrits*. Translated by Bruce Fink. W. W. Norton & Company: New York and London. 2006.

—*The Four Fundamental Concepts of Psychoanalysis*. Translated by Alan Sheridan. W. W. Norton & Company: New York and London. 1981.

—*The Seminar of Jacques Lacan: Book II The Ego in Freud's Theory and in the Technique of Psychoanalysis 1954–1955*. Translated by Sylvana Tomaselli. W. W. Norton & Company: New York and London. 1991.

Leibniz, Gottfried Wilhelm. *Leibniz: The monadology and other philosophical writings*. Translated by Robert Latta. Clarendon Press: Oxford. 1898.

Martinet, André. "Redundancy" in *La Linguistique: Guide alphabétique*. Denoe: Paris. 1969.

Merleau-Ponty, Maurice. *Phenomenology of Perception*. Translated by Colin Smith. Routledge; Taylor and Francis: New York and London. 2005.

Moles, Abraham. *Information Theory and Esthetic Perception*. Translated by Joel E. Cohen. University of Illinois Press: Urbana, Chicago and London. 1968.

Murphy, Timothy S. *Deleuze and Guattari: Critical Assessments of Leading Philosophers*, Vol. 2, edited by Gary Genosko. Routledge: London. 2001.

Negri, Antonio. "Notes de prison et projet Ulysse," *Chimères* 39. 2000. pp. 113–25.
Nietzsche, Friedrich. *The Gay Science*. Translated by Josefine Nauckhoff. Cambridge University Press: Cambridge. 2001.
—*Nietzsche's Werke; Vol XVI: Der Wille zur Macht*. A. Kröner: Leipzig. 1922.
—*Philosophy in the Tragic Age of the Greeks*. Translated by Marianne Cowan. Gateway; Regenery Publishing: Washington, DC. 1998.
—*Thus Spoke Zarathustra: A Book for All and None*. Translated by Adrian Del Caro. Cambridge University Press: Cambridge. 2006.
—*Twilight of the Idols*. Translated by Duncan Large. Oxford University Press: Oxford. 1998.
—*The Will to Power*. Translated by Walter Kaufmann and R. J. Hollingdale. Vintage Books: New York. 1968.
Patton, Paul and John Protein (editors). *Between Deleuze and Derrida*. Continuum Books: London. 2003.
Sartre, Jean Paul. *Being And Nothingness: an essay in Phenomenological Ontology*. Translated by Hazel Barnes. Citadel Press: New York. 2001.
—*Critique of Dialectical Reason: Theory of Practical Ensembles*. Translated by Alan Sheridan-Smith. New Left Books: London. 1976.
Simondon, Gilbert. *L'individu et sa genèse physico-biologique (l'individuation à la lumière des notions de forme et d'information)* Presses universitaires de France: Paris. 1964.
Spinoza, Benedictus de. *The Ethics*. Translated by G. H. R. Parkinson. Oxford University Press: New York. 2000.
—*Theological-Political Treatise*. Translated by Michael Silverthorne and Jonathan Israel. Cambridge University Press: Cambridge. 2007.
Thom, René. *Mathematical Models of Morphogenesis*. Translated by W. M. Brookes and D. Rand. Halsted Press: New York. 1983.
Toynbee, Arnold. *A Study of History, Vol. 1: Abridgement of Volumes I–V*. Oxford University Press: Oxford and New York. 1946.
Varela, Francisco J. *Principles of Biological Autonomy*. North Holland: New York. 1979.
Whitehead, Alfred North. *Science and the Modern World*. Cambridge University Press: Cambridge. 2011.

INDEX

How to use this index: terms in the index that are entries in the dictionary are followed by page references in **bold**: these pages refer to the entry for the term itself (note that some terms, especially terms from the *Cinema* books, do not have their own entry but are defined in other entries; those page references are still bolded). All other pages given refer to important entries in which the term appears; if the term appears in a "Key Terms" entry, parentheses follow the page reference that indicate which definition number the term can be found (however, if it can be found in the introduction to the definition, no number is given; if it can be found in the introduction *and* one or more definitions, 'intro' and definition numbers are listed).

a-signifying semiotics, and the diagram 87
   and deterritorialization 310 (3d)
   and Hjelmslev 158
   in *The Machinic Unconscious* 187
   and minor cinema 195 (1c)
   and the rhizome 262
   and *Schizoanalytic Cartographies* 274
abstract machine **17–19**
   and assemblage 35–6 (1b, 1c, 3b, 3c)
   and Chomsky 64
   and deterritorialization 309 (3b)
   and diagram 89 (3)
   and matter 190 (3a)
action-image **19–21**
   and affect (5b)

   and movement-image 208 (2)
   and plane of immanence 241–2 (3)
   and time-images 315–16 (2a)
active synthesis **21–2**
   and passive synthesis 223 (1)
   and signs 284–5 (2)
actual, actualization **22**
   and counter-actualization 75–6
   and differenciation 94 (1)
   and differentiation 95–6
   and life 180 (1b)
   and the virtual 330–3
aesthetics 11–14
   and aesthetic paradigms 23
   and affect 25–6 (3b, 3c)
   and figures 124–5 (1, 2)
   and the plane of composition 240 (2)
   and signs 284 (1)
   see also art

aesthetic paradigm 23
  in *Schizoanalytic Cartographies* 274
affect 23–7
  and action-images 20 (2a)
  and aesthetic figures 125 (2)
  and any-space-whatevers 29
  and Artaud 33
  and becoming-animal 43 (1a)
  and becoming-intense 45
  and ethics 112–13 (1a, 1c)
  and force 135–6 (3a, 3b)
  and imagination 160 (2b)
  and intensity 168 (3a)
  and mode 199 (1)
  and Spinoza 294
  and universes 325–6
affection-image 26 (5a)
Aion 28
  and Chronos 64
  and events 116 (1)
  and the surface 305
  and univocity 328 (4)
analogy, and aristotle 32
  and difference 91 (1)
  and univocity 327–8 (3)
Les Années d'hiver 28–9
Anti-Oedipus 29–31
any space whatever 29
  and affection images 27 (5c)
arborescence, and Chomsky 64
  and resonance 261 (3b)
  and rhizomes 264 (2a)
architecture, and gothic expression 182 (2d)
  and Kafka 275–6 (2a, 2b)
  and smooth space 289
  and strata 298
Aristotle 32–3
  and difference 91–2 (1b)
  and Hegel 155
art, and philosophy 13
  and aesthetic paradigm 23 (3)

and chaos 60–1 (intro, 4a)
and code 68 (3)
and contraction 74–5 (4)
and diagrams 89 (4)
and ecosophy 100–1 (1a, 1b)
and ethology 115 (1c)
and figures 124–5 (intro, 2, 3)
in *Francis Bacon: The Logic of Sensation* 145–6
and the haptic 153–4 (1a, 1b)
and heterogenesis 157 (2c)
and life 182 (2d)
and matter of expression 121 (3)
and minor cinema 195 (1a, 1b)
and molecular revolution 201 (2c)
and percepts 235 (1a)
and the plane of composition 239–40 (intro, 1)
and Proust 245
and rhythm 267–8 (4)
and sensation 277 (2)
and signs 284 (1)
and singularities 288 (5c)
and subjectivity 304 (4)
and symptomology 306
and territory 307–8 (intro, 2a, 2b)
in *The Three Ecologies* 313
and transcendental empiricism 319 (1a)
and universes 325–6 (intro, 2)
in *What is Philosophy?* 335–7
see also aesthetics
Artaud, Antonin 33
  and the body without organs 52–3 (1a, 1b, 1c)
  and depth 77 (1a)
  in *The Logic of Sense* 187
assemblage 34–7
  and black holes 50 (2)
  and collective assemblages of enunciation 70–1

and desire 83 (4b)
and deterritorialization 309 (3b)
and diagram 89 (3)
and existential territory 118 (3)
and flows 127 (5b)
and form of content 137–8 (2a)
and form of expression 129 (2a)
and group 150 (5)
in *Kafka: Toward a Minor Literature* 171
and phylum 238 (1)
and the refrain 255 (1b)
and substance 190 (3a)
and territory 309 (3a)
in *A Thousand Plateaus* 314
and universes 325
and the war machine 333–4 (1a)
attribute **37–8**
and Descartes/Spinoza 78
and expression 119 (1a, 1b)
and the fold 131 (4a)
and immanence 162 (2)
and mode 198–200
in *Spinoza: Expressionism in Philosophy* 295
autopoiesis **38–9**
and Francisco Varela and Humberto Maturana 329

Bateson, Gregory **39–40**
and Mony Elkaïm 102
becoming **40–2**
and chaos 60 (1a)
and deterritorialization 307
and eternal return 106–7 (1a, 1b)
and ethics 114 (2a)
and the Other 226 (3b)
and Plato 243
and the rhizome 265 (3a)
and value 329 (2a)
becoming-animal **43–4**
and Freud 147
and Kafka 170
and line of flight 185 (2a)
and multiplicities 213 (4)
becoming-imperceptible **44–5**
becoming-intense **45**
becoming-woman **45–6**
Bergson, Henri **46–7**
in *Bergsonism* 47–8
in *Cinema* Vol I & II 65–6
and contraction 73 (1)
and duration 98–9
and *Élan Vital* 180 (1a)
and habit 152 (2a, 2b)
and intensity 166–7 (intro, 1a, 1b)
and the movement-image 208 (2a)
and the recollection-image 249 (1a)
and repetition 259 (4a, 4b)
and Riemann/multiplicity 210 (1a, 1b)
and sensation 276–7 (1)
and the virtual 331 (1a)
Bergsonism **47–8**
and differenc/tiation 95
Bichat, Marie François Xavier
and life 181 (2b)
binomial **20 (2a)**
black hole **49–51**
and assemblages 35–6 (2)
and Node of resonance 261 (2c)
and subjective resonance 254 (4e)
Blanchot, Maurice **50–1**
and the fold 130–1 (3b)
and force 133–4
and form of expression 140–1 (3b)

and Heidegger 156
and life 180–2 (intro, 2b)
and the Outside 227–8 (1, 2a, 2b)
and time-images 315, 317 (4a)
and the unconscious 322
blocks, and segmentation 169 (5), 311–12 (5a)
body
 and affect 24–5 (1, 2a)
 and existential territory 117 (1b)
 and force 134 (1b)
 and intensity 168 (3b)
 and Klossowski 175–6
 and mind-dualism 78, 294–5
 and monad 204 (2b)
 and Nietzsche/Spinoza 218–19
 and sensation/art 278 (3b)
 without organs 51–2
body without organs; BwO **51–6**
 and Artaud 33
 and desiring-machines 86 (2)
 and disjunctive synthesis 234 (2b)
 and existential territory 117
 and intensity 168 (3c)
 and life 182 (3)
 and masochism 269–70
 and Melanie Klein 231 (2a)
 and morality 207 (4)
 and sensation 277 (2)
Boulez, in *The Fold* 133

Cahiers de Royaumont: Nietzsche 56–7
capitalism/capital, and the body without organs 54 (2a)
 and code 67–8 (2a, 2b)
 and globalization 164–6
 and the history of philosophy 336
 and Kafka 179

and life 182 (3)
and Marx 189
and molecular revolution 202
and partial objects 232 (3)
and relative deterritorialization 309 (3c)
and subjectivity 63, 303–4 (2c)
and the universal resonator 261 (3b)
Carroll, Lewis **57–8**
 and Artaud 33
 and becoming 42 (3)
 and depth 77 (1a)
 in *The Logic of Sense* 185–6
cartography **58–9**
 and matter 190 (b)
 in *Schizoanalytic Cartographies* 273–4
chaos **59–62**
 and complication 13
 and concepts 72 (1a), 169 (6)
 and contraction 74–5 (4)
 and diagram/painting 89 (4)
 and diagram/sensation 90 (5)
 and differenciation 95 (1b)
 and events 116–17 (2)
 and Isabelle Stengers and Ilya Prigogine 296
 and matters of expression 121 (3)
 and haptic vision 145
 and heterogenesis 157 (intro, 1)
 and milieus 194 (1b)
 and the plane of composition 239–40 (intro, 1)
 and rhythm 267 (3a)
 and sensation (3a)
 and transcoding 320 (1)
 and the virtual 331–2 (2a, 2b)
 in *What is Philosophy?* 336–7
chaosmos, and chaos/rhythm 61 (3)
 and art 61 (4a)

Chaosmosis: An Ethico-Aesthetic Paradigm **62–3**
Chaosophy: Texts and Interviews **63–4**
Chomsky, Noam **64**
   and language/rhizomes 264 (2b)
   and metamodelization 191
Chronos **64**
   and Aion 28 (1a)
   and depth 77 (1b)
   and events (intro, 1)
chronosign **316–17 (3)**
Cinema (Vol I & II) **65–6**
circuit, and crystal images 316 (2b)
   and the virtual 331–3 (intro, 3c)
code **67–8**
   and ethology 115
   and milieus 194 (1a)
   and redundancy 141
   and strata 298–9 (1a)
Coldness and Cruelty **68–70**
collective assemblage of enunciation **70–2**
   and Descartes 79
   and group 148
   and multiplicities 213–14 (3)
   in *On the Line* 223
   and subjectivity 304 (5)
common sense **280 (2b)**
   and the faculties 122–4 (intro, 1, 2a, 3)
   and morality 207 (3b)
complication, and chaos 59–61 (intro, 2)
   and Spinoza's God 295
concept **72**
   and affect 25–6 (3b)
   and chaos 62 (5a)
   and the faculties 122–3 (1, 2a)
   and immanence 162
   and intensity 166–9 (intro, 6)
   and plane of immanence 241 (intro, 1)
conceptual personae, and concepts 72
   and reterritorialization 310 (3d)
contraction **73–5**
   and Bergson 46
   in *Bergsonism* 47–8
   and duration 98–9 (intro, 1c)
   and habit 152 (2b, 3)
   and light 153 (1a)
   and presence 7–8
   and recollection-images 249 (1a)
   and repetition 257 (1d)
   and sensation 276–7 (intro, 1, 2)
   and the unconscious 232 (2a)
   and virtual multiplicity 211–12 (2a)
counter-actualization **75–6**
   in Blanchot 50
crowned anarchy
   see nomadism
crystal image **316 (2b)**
   and recollection-images 249 (1b)
   and the virtual 332–3 (3b)

dark precursor **135 (2a)**
   and the fold 131 (4b)
   and intensity 168–9 (4)
death, in Blanchot 50
   and the body without organs 55 (3a)
   and desiring-machines 85–6 (1b)
   and eternal return 107 (3a)
   and Proust 246
   and the third passive synthesis 233–4 (1c)
   and the unconscious 232–3 (intro, 2a)

denotation 77
   and desire 84 (5)
   and the proposition 245
depth 77
   and Artaud 33
   and the body without organs 51–3 (intro, 1b)
   and partial objects 231 (2a)
   and sense 279 (1)
   and the Stoics 297–8
Derrida 2, 4–8
   and difference 93
Descartes, René **78–9**
Desert Islands & Two Regimes of Madness 79–80
desire **80–4**; 11
   and abstract machines, in *Anti-Oedipus* 30
   and assemblages 34–6 (1a, 2, 3c)
   and becoming-animal 44 (2)
   and the body without organs 52–5 (intro, 1c, 2a, 2b, 3a)
   and collective assemblages 71 (2b)
   and desiring-machines 85–7
   and flows 126 (4a)
   and Foucault 141
   and immanence 163 (4)
   and Kafka 169–70
   and Kant 173
   and lines of flight 183–6 (intro, 1a, 1b, 1c, 2a)
   and manifestation 188;
   and masochism 268–70
   and microfascism 193 (2)
   and nomadism 22 (3c)
   and the Other 225–6 (2a, 2b)
   and partial objects 239–32 (intro, 2c)
   and plane of immanence 241 (2)
   and rhizome 264 (2a)
   and segmentation 274–6
   and series 283 (3)
   and territory 310–12 (4a, 4d, 5a, 5b)
   and the unconscious 322–4 (intro, 2a, 2b)
desiring-machines **85–7**
   and code 67 (1b)
   and disjunctive synthesis 96 (1a)
   and molecular revolution 201 (2a)
   and passive synthesis 234 (2)
   and series 281–3 (intro, 2)
determination, and chaos 59–60
   and Descartes 79
   and diagram 90 (5)
   and differentiation 95–6 (intro, 1)
   and Kant 172
deterritorialization **307–12 (intro, 2b, 3b, 3c, 3d, 5b)**
   and the abstract machine 19 (3b)
   and assemblage 35–6 (3a, 3b, 3c, 4)
   and collective assemblages of enunciation 70–1 (intro, 2a)
   and desire 84 (4c)
   and desiring-machines 86 (2)
   and ethology 114–15 (1a)
   and form of content 138 (2c)
   and form of expression 140 (2c)
   in *Kafka: Toward a Minor Literature* 171
   and redundancy 253–5 (4c, 4e)
   and the refrain 255 (2)
   and signs 285 (3)
   and transcoding 320
diagram **87–90**
   and abstract machine 18 (3a)
   and figure 124–5 (1, 3)

and force 136 (3b)
in *Francis Bacon: The Logic of Sensation* 145
and matter 190 (3b)
and molecular revolution 201–2 (2c)
and power 9–10
and sensation 277–8 (3a)
Dialogues I & II 90
dicisign **236 (2b)**
difference **91–2**
and Aristotle 32–3
and the body without organs 54 (2a)
and chaos 61–2 (2, 5a)
and concepts 72
and contraction 73 (intro, 1)
and Descartes 79
in *Difference and Repetition* 93–4
and differenciation 94–5 (1a)
and differentiation 95–6 (intro, 1)
and duration 98–9 (1b)
and eternal return 107–9 (3a, 3b)
and the fold 128–30 (intro, 2)
and force 135 (2a)
and Hegel 154–6
and Heidegger 156
and intensity 167–9 (2b, 4)
and Leibniz 177–9
and multiplicity 210–12 (1b, 2a, 2b)
and Nietzsche 217–18
and nomadic distribution 220
and the outside 227 (1)
and repetition 256–60 (intro, 1d, 5a, 5b)
and sensation 277 (3a)
and thought 1–15
and the time-image 317 (4a)
and transcendental empiricism (1a, 1b)

and univocity 326–8 (intro, 1, 3)
Difference and Repetition **93–4**
differenciation **94–5**
and duration 98–9 (1b)
and life 180 (1b)
and series 282 (1b)
differentiation **95–6**
digital, and code 68 (3)
and the haptic 153–4 (1b)
disjunctive synthesis **96–7**
and Klossowski 176
and overcoding 67 (2a)
and partial object 231 (2b)
and passive synthesis 234 (2b)
and univocity 238 (4)
displacement and disguise 2–7
and difference 92 (1c)
in *Difference and Repetition* 79
and eternal return 108–9 (3b)
and immanence 163 (3a)
and partial objects 231–2 (2b, 2c)
and repetition 256–7 (intro, 1c)
and series 281–2 (intro, 1)
dividual **26–7 (5b)**
double articulation, and form of content 138 (2b)
and form of expression 140 (2b)
in *Foucault* and *A Thousand Plateaus* 141
and strata 299 (1b)
Duns Scotus, and haecceity 153
and univocity 327 (intro, 1)
duration **98–100**
and affect 24–5 (2a)
and becoming-imperceptible 44–5
and Bergson 46–7
and contraction 73 (1)
and existing mode 200 (3b)
and life 180 (1b)

INDEX

and movement-images 208 (2a)
and rhythm 266 (1)

ecology, and Bateson 40
 in *The Three Ecologies* 313
ecosophy **100–2**
 and Bateson 40
 in *Chaosmosis* 62–3
 and subjectivity 304 (4)
Elkaïm, Mony **102–3**
 in *Chaosmosis* 63
 in *Chaosophy* 63
Empiricism and Subjectivity **103–4**
enunciation, *see collective assemblage of enunciation*
equivocity, and univocity 326–7 (intro, 2)
Essays Critical and Clinical 104
eternal return **105–10**
 and becoming 41 (2a)
 in Blanchot 50
 in *Cahiers de Royaumont: Nietzsche* 57
 and chaos 60 (1b)
 and ethics 111–14 (intro, 2a)
 and force 135 (2b)
 and Nietzsche 217–18
 and repetition 256, 260 (5a)
 and the unconscious 324 (3b)
ethics **111–14**
ethology **114–15**
 and ethics 113 (1c)
 and the refrain 254–5 (1a)
event **116–17**
 and aesthetic figures 125 (2)
 and Aion 28 (1a)
 and becoming 42 (3)
 and counter-actualization 75–6 (intro, 1a, 1b)
 and disjunctive synthesis 97 (2)
 and expression 120 (2a)
 and haecceity 153 (1)
 in *The Logic of Sense* 186

and sense 278–9 (intro, 1)
and singularity 287 (4)
existential territory **117–18**
explication/implication, and chaos 13
 and attribute 37–8 (2)
 and chaos 60–1 (intro, 2)
 and expression 119–20 (1b, 2c)
 and the fold 128, 131 (4a)
 and Leibniz 178
 and the Other 226 (2b)
 and signs 284 (1)
 in *Spinoza: Expressionism in Philosophy* 295
expression **118–21**
 and immanence 162–3 (2)
 and simulacrum 286
 and de/territorialization 308 (2a, 2b)

faciality, and black holes 49 (2)
 and redundancy 251 (3c)
faculty **122–4**
 and common sense 280 (2b)
 and desire 81 (1a, 1b)
 and Kant 172–3
 and paradox 229 (1b)
 and transcendental empiricism 319 (1a, 1b)
fascism and desire 83 (4b)
 and microfascism 192–3
 and the war machine 334–5 (1b, 2)
figure **124–5**; 13
 and the percept 235 (1b)
 and sensation 277 (3a)
flows **125–7**
 and the body without organs 54–6 (2a, 3b)
 and partial objects 232 (3)
 and transversality 321 (1a)
flux *see flows*
 and desiring-machines 87 (4)

and diagram 88 (1)
and four functors 143
fold **128–32**
  and force 136 (5)
  and Heidegger 156
  and the other 225 (1c)
  and the outside 228 (2b)
The Fold: Leibniz and the Baroque **132–3**
force **133–7**
  and affect 25 (2b)
  and chaos 60 (1)
  and the diagram (87–9 (intro, 2c, 4)
  and eternal return 106–7 (1a, 2a, 2b)
  and the fold 130–1 (3b)
  and intensity 166–9 (intro, 3b, 4)
  and life 179–82 (intro, 2a, 2b, 3)
  and monad 204 (2b)
  and sensation 277 (2)
  and sense 279, 281 (4)
  and territory 307–8 (intro, 1, 2a, 2b)
  and transcendental empiricism 319–20 (1c)
form of content **137–9**
  and abstract machine 19 (3b)
  and assemblage 36 (4)
  and collective assemblage of enunciation 70–1 (2a)
  and diagram 88 (2b)
  and Foucault 141
  and major literature 188 (2)
  and matter 190 (3b)
  and signs 285 (3)
  and the war machine 334 (1c)
form of expression **139–41**
  and abstract machine 19 (3b)
  and assemblage 36 (4)
  and collective assemblage of enunciation 70–1 (2a)
  and diagram 88 (2b)
  and figures 125 (3)
  and Foucault 141
  and major literature 188 (2)
  and matter 190 (3b)
  and signs 285 (3)
  and the war machine 334 (1c)
Foucault, Michel **141**; 2, 5–6, 9–10
  and assemblage 37 (5)
  and diagram 87–8 (2a, 2b)
  and the fold 128–31 (intro, 2, 3b)
  and force 136 (3b)
  in *Foucault* 142–3
  and masochism 269–70
  in *Negotiations* 213–14
  in *Un Nouvel Archiviste* 223
  in the Outside 228 (2b)
  and strata 299 (2)
  and subjectivity 303 (2)
four functors **143–4**
  in *Chaosmosis* 62–3
  and schizoanalysis 271 (1a)
Francis Bacon: The Logic of Sensation **145–6**
French theory 2–11
Freud, Sigmund **146–7**
  in *Coldness and Cruelty* 69
  and desire 82 (2a, 2b)
  and neurosis 216 (1b)
  in *Nietzsche and Philosophy* 219
  and repetition 256–7 (1a, 1b)
  and the unconscious 322–3 (1, 2a)
functive, *see four functors*
  and science 337

genesign **316–17** (3)
good sense **280** (2a)
gramme **237** (2d)
group **148–50**

and cartography 59 (3)
and collective assemblage of enunciation 70 (1)
and transversality 321 (1b)
The Guattari Reader 150

habit **150–2**
　in *Bergsonism* 48
　and contraction 73–4 (intro, 3a, 3b)
　in *Empiricism and Subjectivity* 103–4
　and good sense 280 (2a)
　and Hume 158–9
　and imagination 160–1 (1a, 2a)
　as passive synthesis 233 (1-a)
　and reason 248 (1b)
　and repetition 257–9 (1d, 2a, 2b, 3a)
haecceity **153**
　and life 182 (2c)
　and singularity 286
haptic **153–4**
　in *Francis Bacon: The Logic of Sensation*, 145
　and smooth space 289–90 (1a)
harmony, in *The Fold: Leibniz and the Baroque* 132
　and Descartes 79
　and the faculties 122
Hegel, Georg Wilhelm Friedrich **154–6**; 15nn. 2, 5
　and difference 91–2 (1b)
　and Leibniz 178
　in *Nietzsche and Philosophy* 219
Heidegger, Martin **156**
　in *Chaosmosis* 63
　and the fold 129–30 (1a, 2)
Heraclitus, and becoming 41 (1)
heterogenesis **156–7**
　and Stern 297
Hjelmslev, Louis **158**
　and form of content 137–8 (intro, 1, 2a)
　and form of expression 139 (1, 2a)
　and matter 190 (1, 2)
　and structuralism 300–1 (intro, 1b)
Hobbes, Thomas, and ethics 111
Hume, David **158–9**
　and contraction 74 (2)
　in *Empiricism and Subjectivity* 103–4
　and habit 150–1 (intro, 1a, 1b)
　and imagination 159–61 (1a, 2a)
　and morality 204–6 (intro, 1a, 1b, 1c)
　and reason 247–8 (1a)
　and repetition 258–9 (2a, 2b, 3a)
　and subjectivity 203–3 (1)
humor, and masochism 83 (3c), 186
　and Carroll 186
　and Kafka 168
　and Kierkegaard 175
Husserl, Edmund, and Kant 172
hyalosign **316 (2b)**

icon **27 (5d)**
image of thought, and Aristotle 32
　and Kant in *Difference and Repetition* 172–3
　and sense 281 (4)
imagination **159–61**
　and contraction 73–4 (intro, 2)
　and habit 151 (1b)
　and reason 248 (1b)
　and repetition 258 (2a, 2b)
　in *Spinoza: Expressionism in Philosophy* 294–5
immanence **162–3**
　and expression 118
　and life 182 (2c)

implication/explication, *see* *explication/implication*
impression 20 (**2b**)
inadequate & adequate ideas, and affect 24 (1)
 and Descartes 78
 and reason 248 (2)
 in *Spinoza: Expressionism in Philosophy* 294–5
 and univocity 327 (2)
incompossibility, and disjunctive synthesis 97 (2)
 and Leibniz 178–9
index of equivocity **21** (**3b**)
index of lack **20** (**3a**)
Instincts and Institutions **164**
integrated world capitalism **164–6**
 in *Soft Subversions* 291
intensity **166–9**
 and affect 25–6 (3b)
 and becoming-intense 45
 in *Bergsonism* 47–8
 and the body without organs 54–6 (2a, 3b)
 and the haptic 154 (1c)
 and life 179–80, 182 (3)
 and sensation 277 (3a)
 and univocity 327–8 (3)
irony, and sadism 69
 and Klossowski 186
 and Kierkegaard 110 (4b), 175
 and Plato, 242

Kafka, Franz **169–70**
 and the abstract machine 17–8 (intro, 1)
 and assemblage 36 (3c)
 and becoming-animal 44 (2)
 and collective assemblages of enunciation 70–1 (intro, 2a)
 and desire 84 (4c)
 and immanence 163 (4)
 and intensity 169 (5)
 in *Kafka: Toward a Minor Literature* 170–2
 and line of flight 183–5 (intro, 2a)
 and minor literature 197
 and the rhizome 262–3 (intro, 1a, 1b)
 and segmentation 275–6 (1b, 2a, 2b)
 and series 283 (3)
 in *Soixante-cinq Rêves de Franz Kafka* 291–2
 and de/territorialization 311–12 (5a, 5b)
Kafka: Toward a Minor Literature **170–2**
Kant **172–3**
 and active synthesis 21
 and Descartes 79
 and desire 81 (1a, 1b, 1c)
 and the faculties 122–4
 and intensity 167 (2a)
 in *Kant's Critical Philosophy* 173–4
 and reason 248–9 (4)
 and transcendental empiricism 319 (1b)
Kant's Critical Philosophy **173–4**
Kierkegaard, Søren Aabye **175**
 and eternal return 110 (4b)
 and repetition 259 (3b)
Klossowski, Pierre **175–6**
 and perversion 69
 in *The Logic of Sense* 186

Lacan, Jacques, and Freud **146**
 in *The Anti-Oedipus Papers* 31
 and desire 82 (2b)
 and desiring-machines 85 (intro, 1a)
 and Jean Oury 227
 in *The Machinic Unconscious* 187

and partial objects 229–31
    (intro, 1b, 2b)
and redundancy 250
and Saussure/Hjelmslev 158
and schizoanalysis 271 (1a),
    271 (1e)
and structuralism 301
Laroche, Emmanuel, and
    nomadism 220–1 (intro, 1)
Lawrence, D.H. **176**
lectosign **317–8 (4b)**
Leibniz, Gottfried Wilhelm **177–9**
    and difference 8, 15n. 5, 91–2
    (1b)
    and events 116–17 (2)
    and expression 119–20 (intro,
    2b)
    and the fold, 128, 130 (3a)
    in *The Fold: Leibniz and the
    Baroque* 132–3
    and monads 203–4
    and morality 207 (5)
    and the Other 11, 16n. 8,
    224–5 (intro, 1c)
    and the Outside 228 (2b)
    and Whitehead, 337
Lenin, Vladimir Ilyich **179**
life **179–82**
    and autopoiesis 38 (1)
    and the body without organs
    51–2, 55 (3a)
    and desiring-machines 85–6 (1b)
    and machinic ecology 101 (2a)
    and Nietzsche 217
    and value 328–9 (1, 2a)
line of flight **183–5**
    and assemblage 36 (3c)
    and deterritorialization 312
    (5b)
    and form of expression 36 (4)
    and segmentation 275 (1b)
    and smooth space 290 (1b)
The Logic of Sense **185–7**

machinic phylum, *see phylum*
*The Machinic Unconscious: Essays
    in Schizoanalysis* **187**
major literature **188**
manifestation **188**
Marx, Karl **189**
    in *Anti-Oedipus* 30
masochism, and an empty BwO
    56 (3b)
    in *Coldness and Cruelty* 68–70
    and repetition 256–7 (1b)
    and Sacher-Masoch 268–70
    and smooth space 289
matter **189–90**
    in *Bergsonism* 47–8
    and contraction 73 (1)
    and the diagram 88–9 (2b, 2c)
    and duration 98–9 (intro, 1b,
    1c)
    and flows 126 (2a)
    and form of content 137–8 (2a)
    and form of expression 139–40
    (2a)
    and Hjelmslev 158
    and life 180–1 (1c)
    and milieus 194 (2)
    and the monad 204 (2b)
    and phylum 239 (2)
    and plane of composition 240
    (1)
    and the plane of immanence
    241–2 (intro, 3)
    and repetition 259 (4b)
    and sensation 276–7 (intro, 1, 2)
Maturana, Humberto, *see Varela,
    Francisco and Humberto
    Maturana*
meaning, *see sense*
mechanosphere, and assemblage
    36 (3b)
    and subjectivity 303 (3a)
Melville, Herman, and percepts
    235 (2)

and smooth space 289
Messiaen, Olivier, and rhythm 266 (intro, 1)
metamodelization, **191–2**
   and cartography 59 (2)
   and the four functors 143 (2)
microfascism **192–3**
   see also fascism
micropolitics, and line of flight 184 (1a)
   and microfascism 193 (2a)
milieu **193–4**
   and action-images 20 (2a)
   and assemblages 36 (3a, 3b)
   and chaos 60–1 (intro, 3, 4)
   and code 67 (1a)
   and life 180–1 (1c)
   and matters of expression 121 (3)
   and minor literature 197–8 (1b)
   and plane of immanence 241 (1)
   and rhythm 266–7 (intro, 2, 3a, 3b)
   and territory 307–9 (intro, 1, 2a, 2b, 3a, 3b)
   in *A Thousand Plateaus* 314
   and transcoding 320
minor cinema **195–6**
minor literature **196–8**
   and collective assemblage of enunciation 70–1 (2a)
   in *Kafka: Toward a Minor Literature* 171
   in *What is Philosophy?* 336
mode **198–200**
   and affect 24–5 (2a)
   and attribute 37–8 (1, 2)
   and duration 100 (3)
   in *Spinoza: Expressionism in Philosophy* 294–5
   and univocity 326–7 (intro, 2)
   and Whitehead 337

molar
molecular revolution **200–2**
   and singularity 287 (5a)
Molecular Revolution **202**
Molecular Revolution in Brazil **202–3**
monad **203–4**
   and Leibniz 177–9
   and morality 207 (5)
   and the other 225 (1c)
morality **204–7**
   and ethics 111, 114 (2b)
   and reason 247–9 (1a, 4)
   and the unconscious 324, 3a
   and value 329 (2b)
movement-image **207–9**
   and action-images 20 (1)
   and affection images 26 (5a)
   and any-space-whatevers 29
   and Bergson 48
   in *Cinema (Vol I & II)* 65–6
   and perception-images 236 (2b)
   and the plane of immanence 241–2 (3)
multiplicity **210–13**
   and becoming-animal 42 (1a)
   and collective assemblage of enunciation 71 (2b)
   and differentiation 96 (1)
   and duration 98–9 (1b)
   and monad 204 (2a)
   and nomadism 222 (3b)
   and smooth space 289–91 (1a, 1b, 2a 2b)
   and univocity 326–7
music, and Aion 28 (1b)
   and chaos 61 (3)
   in *The Fold: Leibniz and the Baroque* 133
   and force 136 (4)
   and forms of expression 140 (2c)
   in *Périclès et Verdi* 238

and redundancy 250
and the refrain 254
and rhythm 266–8 (intro, 1, 2, 4)
and territory 307
in *A Thousand Plateaus* 313–15

Negotiations 213–14
Negri, Antonio 215
   in *Desert Islands & Two Regimes of Madness* 80
   in *Negotiations* 214
neurosis 215–17
   and Freud 147
   and schizoanalysis 272 (1b)
Nietzsche, Friedrich 217–18
   and becoming 40–2 (intro, 1, 2a, 2b)
   in *Cahiers de Royaumont: Nietzsche* 56–7
   and chaos 60 (1b)
   and Derrida/Foucault 4–5
   and eternal return 105–7 (intro, 1, 2a, 2b)
   and ethics 111–12, 114 (2a, 2b)
   and force 133–4 (intro, 1a, 1b)
   and Freud 146–7
   and Heidegger 156
   and Kant 173
   and life 181 (2a)
   and morality 206–7 (3a)
   in *Nietzsche and Philosophy* 218–19
   and *Nietzsche...*, 219–20
   and reason 248–9 (4)
   and sense 281 (4)
   and transcendental empiricism 319–20 (1c)
   and transmutation 320
   and the unconscious 324 (3a, 3b)
   and value 329 (2a)
Nietzsche and Philosophy 218–19

Nietzsche. Sa vie, son œuvre, avec un exposé de sa philosophie 219–20
nomadism 220–2
   and affect 26 (4)
   and conjunctive synthesis 234 (2c)
   and the haptic 154 (1c)
   and masochism 268
   and smooth space 289–91 (intro, 1a, 2b)
   in *A Thousand Plateaus* 314
   and the war machine 333–5 (intro, 1a, 1b, 1c, 2b)
Un nouvel archiviste. Michel Foucault 223

Oedipus complex, in *Anti-Oedipus* 30
   and Freud 147
   and neurosis 215–16 (intro, 1b, 1c)
   and partial objects 230 (1a)
On the Line 223
order-word, and redundancy 254 (5)
Other, the 224–6
   and Descartes 79
   and desire 82–3 (2b, 3a, 3b)
   and expression 120 (2c)
   and the fold 128
   and partial objects 230–1 (1b)
   and perception 236 (1)
   and Sartre 270
   and Tournier 318
Oury, Jean 227
Outside, the 227–8
   and Blanchot 50–1
   and the diagram 89 (2c)
   and eternal return 107–8 (3a)
   and the fold 130–1 (3b)
   and force 133–4, 136 (3b)
   and monads 204 (2b)

and passive synthesis 223–4 (1c)
and the plane of immanence 241 (1)
and time-images 317 (4a)

paradox 228–9
and the aesthetic/unthinkable 12
and Carroll 58
and contradiction 10
and disjunctive synthesis 97 (1b)
and non-sense 280–1 (3)
and paradoxical (partial) object 231 (2b)
and signs 284–5 (2)
and thinking 7, 8
partial object (also paradoxical object) 229–32; 7
and the body without organs 55
and desire 60–1 (intro, 4a)
and desiring-machines 85–6 (1b, 2)
and Proust 246
as virtual object 260 (5a)
passive synthesis 233–4
and active synthesis 21–2
and the body without organs 54 (2b)
and contraction 74 (3a, 3b)
and eternal return 107–8 (3a), 218
and habit 150
and imagination 161 (3)
and life 180–1 (1c)
and repetition 257 (1d)
and series 282–3 (2)
and signs 284–5 (2)
and the time-image 315
Peirce, Charles, and the diagram 88 (1)

in *Molecular Revolution* 202
and the perception-image (2a)
and signs 285 (4)
percept 235
and aesthetic figures 125 (2)
and affect 25–6 (3a, 3b)
and chaos 61 (4a)
and the milieu 194 (1a)
and the plane of composition 239–40 (intro, 2)
and sensation 278 (3b)
and smooth space 289
perception 236–7
and action-images 20 (1)
and affection-images 26 (5a)
and any-space-whatevers 29
and becoming-imperceptible 44–5
and cinema I & II 66
and monads 204 (2a, 2b)
and movement-images 209 (2b)
and the Other 225 (1b)
and the percept 235 (1a)
and time-images 315–16 (2a)
and the virtual 332 (3b)
perception-image 236–7 (2a, 2b, 2c, 2d)
and the movement-image 208 (1)
and signs 285 (4)
Périclès et Verdi. La philosophie de François Châtelet 237
phantasm, and percepts 235 (2)
and resonance 260 (1b)
philosophy 13
and chaos 62 (5a)
and concepts 72 (1a)
in *Difference and Repetition* 93
and the plane of immanence 241 (1)
and the virtual 331–2 (2a)
in *What is Philosophy?* 335–7
phylum 238–9

and four functors 142–3 (intro, 2, 3)
and machinic ecology 101 (2a)
and microfascism 192 (1a)
and molecular revolution 201 (2b)
plane of composition **239–40**
 and aesthetic figures 125 (3)
 and affects 26 (3c)
 and chaos 61 (4a)
 and percepts 235 (1b)
plane of consistency, *see plane of immanence*
plane of immanence **239–42**
 and Blanchot 51
 and concepts 72 (intro, 1a)
 and desire 83–4 (4b)
 and diagram 90 (5)
 and ethics 113 (1c)
 and immanence 163 (3b)
 and intensity 169 (6)
 and the Outside 227–8 (2a)
 and relative deterritorialization 309 (3c)
 and the unconscious 324 (2c)
 in *What is Philosophy?* 335
Plato, **242–3**
 and difference 91 (1b)
 and eternal return 109 (4a)
 and the simulacrum 286
portmanteau words, and disjunctive synthesis 97 (1b)
post-media era **243–4**
 in *Les Années d'hiver* 29
power, and Foucault 5–6, 9–10
 and affect 24–5 (2a)
 and Blanchot 51
 in *Expressionism in Philosophy* 294–5
 and de Sade 69
 and the diagram 88 (2a)
 and ethics 111–13 (1a, 1b, 1c, 1d)

and force 133, 135–6 (3a, 3b)
and imagination 161 (3)
and irony 186
and life/resistance 181 (2a)
and modes 199 (1)
in *Nietzsche and Philosophy* 218–19
and strata 299–300 (2)
and subjectivity 303 (2)
and territorialization 311–12 (5a)
and univocity 326–8 (intro, 3)
Prigogine, Ilya, *see Stengers, Isabelle and Ilya Prigogine*
in *Schizoanalytic Cartographies* 274
proposition **245**
 and Carroll 57–8
 and denotation 77
 in *The Logic of Sense* 186
 and manifestation 188
 and paradox 228–9 (1a)
 and sense 279 (intro, 1a)
 and the Stoics 297
Proust, Marcel **245–6**; 16n. 7
 and desire 84 (6)
 and the Other 226 (2b)
 and partial objects 232 (2d)
 in *Proust and Signs* 247
 and signs 284 (1)
Proust and Signs **247**
psychoanalysis, in *Anti-Oedipus* 30–1
 in *Chaosmosis* 62–3
 in *Coldness and Cruelty* 69
 and desire 81–3 (1c, 2a, 2b, 4a)
 and Freud 146–7
 and groups 148–9 (intro, 2)
 and Lacan 187
 in *Molecular Revolution in Brazil* 202–3
 and neurosis 215–16 (intro, 1b)
 and Oury 227

and partial objects 229–31
(intro, 1a, 1b)
and Stern 296–7
psychosis, and neurosis 216 (1a, 1b, 1c)
and schizoanalysis 272 (1b)
Pure Immanence, Essays on a Life, see *Nietzsche. Sa vie, son œuvre, avec un exposé de sa philosophie*
and immanence 16
and life 182 (2c)
pure past, and active synthesis 21–2 (1a)
and eternal return 107 (3a)
and partial objects 230
and passive synthesis 233 (1b)
and Proust 245–6

qualisign **27** (5c)

reason **247–9**; 24–5 (2a)
in *Coldness and Cruelty* 69
and ethics 112–13 (1a, 1c)
and the faculties 123–4 (2b, 3)
in *The Fold* 132-2
and Hume 159
and imagination 162 (2a, 2b)
and Kant 173
and morality 205–6 (1a, 1b, 1c)
in *Périclès et Verdi* 237–8
and subjectivity 302–3 (1)
recollection-image **249**
and 315–16 (1, 2a, 2b)
redundancy **250–4**
and resonance 261 (2b)
refrain **254–5**
and black holes 50 (4)
and semiotic redundancy 251 (3c)
subjectivity 304 (3d)
religion, and eternal return 106–7 (2a)

and figures 125 (3)
and imagination 160 (1a)
and morality 206 (1b)
and value 328 (1)
reminiscence, and Proust 245–6
and signs 284 (1)
repetition **256–60**
and becoming 41–2 (2a)
and chaos 59–61 (chaos, 1b, 2)
in *Coldness and Cruelty* 69
and contraction 73 (intro, 1, 3a)
and Derrida 4–5
and Descartes 79
and difference 91 (1a)
in *Difference and Repetition* 93–4
and duration 99 (1c)
and eternal return 107–10 (3a, 3b, 4b)
and force 114 (2a)
and Freud 146
and habit 151–2 (1b, 2a)
and Hegel 155–6
and Hume 158–9
and Kierkegaard 175
and Klossowski 175–6
and milieus 193
and partial objects 231–2 (2c)
and redundancy 250 (1a), 253 (4d)
and rhythm 266–7 (2)
and Sacher-Masoch 268
and series 281
and thought 6–8, 10
and the unconscious 324 (3b)
resistance, and Foucault/power 9–10
and force 133–4, 136 (3b)
and integrated world capitalism 164–5
and life 179–81 (intro, 2)
resonance **260–1**

and black holes 49 (2)
and concepts 72 (1a)
and partial objects 230, 232 (2d)
and redundancy 251 (2)
and strata 299 (1b)
and Thom 312
reterritorialization, *see territory*
reume **236–7 (2c)**
rhizome **262–5**
  and cartography 58–9 (1b)
  and Chomsky 64
  in *Kafka: Toward a Minor Literature* 171; 201 (2b)
  and multiplicity 212–13 (3)
  in *On the Line* 223
  in structuralism 301 (1a)
  in *A Thousand Plateaus* 314
rhythm **266–8**
  and Aion 28 (1b)
  and chaos 60–1 (intro, 3)
  in *Francis Bacon: The Logic of Sensation* 145–6
  and milieus 193
  and schizoanalysis 273 (3)
  and sensation 277–8 (3a)
  and territory 207–8 (intro, 1)
  in *A Thousand Plateaus* 314

Sacher-Masoch, Leopold Von **268–70**
  in *Coldness and Cruelty* 68–70
  and Kafka 169
  and Klossowski 175
  and repetition 256–7 (1b)
Sade, Marquis de (and sadism), in *Coldness and Cruelty* 68–9
  and Foucault 269
  and Klossowski 175
  and reason 248
Sartre, Jean-Paul **270–1**
  and groups 148–9 (intro, 1)
  and the Other 224–5 (intro, 1a, 1c)

and singularity 288 (6b)
Saussure, Ferdinand de, and forms of content 137
  and Hjelmslev 158
  and signs 283, 285 (4)
schizoanalysis **271–3**
  in *Anti-Oedipus* 30–1
  and cartography 58 (intro, 1)
  and *Chaosmosis* 62
  and four functors 143
  and metamodelization 191 (1b)
  and molecular revolution 200–2 (intro, 2c)
  and neurosis 215–17 (intro, 1a, 2)
Schizoanalytic Cartographies **273–4**
science, and chaos 60, 62 (6)
  in *Chaosmosis* 62, and ethology, 115 (1b)
  and figures 125 (3)
  and fluxes 126
  and Freud 146
  and metamodelization 191
  and multiplicity 210
  and plane of reference 240 (1)
  and nomadism 335 (2b)
  and science 134 (1)
  in *What is Philosophy?* 335–7
segmentation **274–6**
  and flows 127 (4b)
  and lines of flight 183–4 (intro, 1a, 1b, 1c)
  and the rhizome 262
  and the war machine 335 (2a)
sensation **276–8**; 7–13
  and affects 26 (3c)
  and contraction 74–5 (4)
  and the diagram 89–90 (4–5)
  and differenciation 84–5 (1a)
  and figures 124–5 (intro, 1, 2, 3)
  and force 136 (4)

in *Francis Bacon: The Logic of Sensation* 145–6
and Hume 158–9
and imagination 161 (3)
and intensity 167–8 (1a, 3c)
and percepts 235 (1b)
and the plane of composition 239–40 (intro, 1, 2)
and rhythm 267–8 (4)
and subjectivity 302–3 (1)
in *What is Philosophy?* 337
sense **278–81**
and disjunctive synthesis 97 (1b)
and eternal return 107 (2b)
and expression 120 (2a)
in *The Logic of Sense* 185–6
and paradox 228–9 (1a)
series **281–3**
and chaos 61 (2)
and difference 92 (1c)
and differenciation 95 (1b)
and disjunctive synthesis 96–7 (1a, 1b, 2)
and the dynamics of repetition 8–11
and events 116–17 (2)
and force 135 (2a)
and immanence 163 (3a)
and intensity 168–9 (4, 5)
and Leibniz 178–9
in *The Logic of Sense* 185–6
and monad 204 (2a)
and movement-images 209 (3a)
and partial objects 230–2 (intro, 2b, 2c)
and resonance, 260–1 (1b)
and time-images 316–17 (3)
sign **283–5**
and assemblages 36–7 (4)
in *Cinema (Vol I & II)* 66
and collective assemblages of enunciation 71 (2b)
and forms of content 137 (intro, 1)
and forms of expression 139 (1)
and Hjelmslev 158
and matter 190 (1)
and minor cinema 195–6 (intro, 1c)
and the Other 120–1 (2c)
and Proust 245–6
in *Proust and Signs* 247
signification 281 (3)
and the proposition 245
and redundancy 252 (3d, 4 a-e)
and schizoanalysis 273 (1e)
simulacrum **286**
and difference 92 (1b)
and eternal return (4a, 4b)
and force 135 (2a)
singularity **286–8**
and subjectivity 303–4 (3c)
smooth space **289–91**
and the haptic 154 (1c)
and multiplicity 211 (1c)
and nomadism 220–2 (intro, 2b, 3a, 3b)
and Sacher-Masoch 268
Soft Subversions: Texts and Interviews **291**
Soixante-cinq Rêves de Franz Kafka **291–2**
sonsign **315–16 (2a)**
Spinoza, Baruch de **292–3**
and affect 24–6 (intro, 1, 2a)
and attribute 37–8 (1,2)
and the body without organs 51–2
and Descartes 78
and duration 100 (3)
and ethics 111–13 (intro, 1a, 1b, 1c, 1d)
and expression 118–20 (intro, 1a, 1b)
and the fold 128, 131 (4a)

and Hume 159
and imagination 160–1 (1b, 2b)
and immanence 162–3 (intro, 1, 2)
and intensity 168 (3a)
and modes 198–200
and morality 206 (2)
and Nietzsche 218–19
and reason 248 (2)
in *Spinoza: Expressionism in Philosophy* 293–4
in *Spinoza: Practical Philosophy* 295–6
and univocity 326–7 (intro, 2)
Spinoza: Expressionism in Philosophy 293–5
Spinoza: Practical Philosophy 295–6
state of affairs, and counter-actualization 75–6 (intro, 1a)
and denotation 77
and depth 77
and desire 84 (5)
and manifestation 188
and multiplicity 212 (2c)
and the Stoics 297–8
Stengers, Isabelle and Ilya Prigogine **296**
Stern, Daniel **296–7**
Stoics, the **297–8**
and signs 284–5 (2)
strata, **298–300**
and abstract machines 18–19 (3a)
and chaos 62 (b)
and milieus 194 (2)
and the Outside 228 (2b)
and segmentation 274–5 (1a)
and territory 309–10 (3a, 3c)
striated space **300**
and nomadism 220–1 (1)
structuralism **301–2**

and Hjelmslev 158
and singularity 286
and strata 298
subjectivity **302–4**
and aesthetic paradigms 23 (2)
and autopoiesis 39 (4)
and black hole 49–50 (intro, 2, 3)
and the body without organs 53 (1c)
and cartography 59 (3)
in *Chaosmosis* 63
and ecosophy 100–1 (intro, 1a)
in *Empiricism and Subjectivity* 103–4
and existential territory 118 (2)
and Foucault 299–300 (2)
and heterogenesis 157 (2c)
and metamodelization 191 (2a)
and the movement-image 208 (2a)
and Negri 216–17 (2)
and nomadism 222 (3b, 3c)
and redundancy 251–3 (3d-iv, 3e, 4a)
and Sartre 224 (1a)
and sensation 276
and universes 325 (1a)
substance, and attribute 37–8 (**1, 2**)
and the body without organs 52
and Descartes 78
and expression 119 (1a)
and the fold 131 (4a)
and forms of content 137–9 (2a, 2b, 3)
and forms of expression 139–40 (2a, 2b, 3a)
and Hjelmslev 158
and immanence 162–3 (1, 2)
and matter **190**, 3a
and milieu 194 (2)

and mode **198–9** (intro 2)
in *Spinoza: Expressionism in Philosophy* 294–5
and strata 298
and univocity 326–7 (intro, 2)
and Whitehead 337
Superpositions **304–5**
surface **305**
and Artaud 33
and the body without organs 51–2
and events 116 (1)
in *The Logic of Sense* 186
and sense 279 (1)
and the Stoics 297–8
and surface 77
and univocity 328 (4)
symptomatology **306**
in *Essays Critical and Clinical* 104
in *Instincts and Institutions* 164
and Proust 245
synsign **20** (**2a**)

territory; territorialization **306–12**
and assemblages 36–7 (4)
and code 67 (1a, 1b)
and lines of flight 184–5 (1a, 1b, 1c)
and matter of expression 121 (3)
and milieus 194 (1a, 1b)
and minor literature 197–8 (1a, 1c)
and nomadism 221–2 (3a)
and the refrain 254–5
and rhythm 267 (3a)
and segmentation 274–5 (1a, 1b)
and signs 285 (3)
and strata 298–9 (1a)
and striated space 300 (1)
and transcoding 320
and the war machine 335 (2a)
theology, and immanence 162

in *The Fold: Leibniz and the Baroque* 132–3
Thom, René **312**
and resonance 261 (2a)
and singularities 287 (1c)
thought **4–13**
and Descartes 78
and difference 91 (1)
and Kant 173
and noosigns/time-images 317–18 (4b)
and signs 284 (1)
and the unconscious 323 (2a)
and the virtual 331–2 (2a, 2b)
and the Outside 227–8
and the plane of immanence 241 (1)
A Thousand Plateaus **313–15**
The Three Ecologies **313**
time, as constituted 7–8
and becoming 41–2 (2a, b, 3)
and Bergson 46–7
and duration 98–100 (1b, 2)
and incessance/the Outside 227 (1)
and movement-images 207–9 (intro, 1, 2b)
and passive synthesis 223–4 (1, 1a, 1b, 1c)
and rhythm 266–7 (intro, 1, 2)
and the time-image 315–18
time-image **313–18**
and Blanchot 51
in *Cinema (Vol I & II)* 65–6
and the recollection-image 249 (1b)
Tournier, Michel **318**
and desire 82–3 (3b)
and the Other 224–5 (intro, 1b, 1c)
Toynbee, Arnold
and nomadism 220–1 (intro, 2a, 2b)

transcendental empiricism **319–20**
   and the faculties 123 (3)
   and Kant 172
   and sensation 276
transcoding **320**
   and coding 67 (1a)
   and rhythm 266–7 (2)
   and strata 299 (1b)
transmutation **320**
transversality **320–2**
   and groups 148–9 (intro, 2)

Uexküll, Jakob von, and territory 307
unconscious **322–4**
   in *Anti-Oedipus* 29–31
   and desire 80, 82 (2a)
   and Freud 146–7
   and molecular revolution 201 (2a)
   and Nietzsche 219
   and partial objects 323 (3)
   and passive synthesis 233–4 (intro, 1, 2, 2c)
   in the plane of immanence 241 (2)
   and rhizomes 264 (2a)
   and schizoanalysis 271–3 (intro, 1a)
universes **325–6**
   and cartography 59 (4)
   and existential territory 118 (2)
univocity **326–7**
   and modes 199 (intro, 2)
   and Spinoza 293
   in *Spinoza: Expressionism in Philosophy* 295

value **328–9**
   and Nietzsche 217–18
Varela, Francisco and Humberto Maturana **329–30**
vector 21 (4)

virtual **330–3**
   and the actual 22 (1)
   and any-space-whatevers 29
   and the body without organs 52
   and chaos 61–2 (4b)
   and concepts 72 (1b)
   and counter-actualization 76–7 (1a)
   and differenciation 94 (1a)
   and differentiation 96 (1)
   and duration 98–9 (1b)
   and gaseous perception 237 (2d)
   and life 180–1 (1c)
   and multiplicity 211–12 (2a)
   and partial objects 231–2 (2c, 2d)
   and Proust 246–7
   and the recollection-image 249 (1a)
   and repetition 259–60 (4b, 5a)
   and signs 284 (1)
   and technology 263
   and the time-image 316 (2b)
virtual object, *see partial object*
vitalism, *see life*

war machine **333–4**
   and affects 26 (4)
   and nomadism 222 (3b)
What is Philosophy? **336–7**
white wall, and black holes 50 (3)
Whitehead, Alfred North **337**
   and events 117 (2)
   in *The Fold: Leibniz and the Baroque* 132–3
will to power, and affect 25 (2b)
   and force 135–6 (3a)
   and transcendental empiricism 319–20 (1c)
   and transmutation 320

zeroness **236** (2a)